Praise for A REVOLUTIONARY

"This book is a welcome addition to the compo. ___ ___...
of Walter Rodney and deals with the cover up of his assassination in the
most authentic way since the Commission of Inquiry report of 2016."
—Donald Rodney

"Seeing, listening to or reading Walter Rodney, before and after his un-
fortunate death, something always puzzled and stayed with me—the *how*
of Walter Rodney. How did this relatively young brother from a small
Caribbean nation gain such a vast world view? How was he able to grasp
the conditions of the Pan-African world so firmly and translate those conditions through his socialist worldview? How was Rodney able to move
so fluidly, accepted and loved as kin, through communities across the
whole Pan-African world? How did he become the number one target of
a Guyanese government desperately plotting to end his life? And of late,
my big one, how does Walter Rodney still endure timelessly in the immediate consciousness of so many Pan-African activists and thinkers today?
Without fail Leo Zeilig's enduring *A Revolutionary for Our Time* answered
these and so many other "how's" beyond my considerations."
—Paul Coates, Black Classic Press

"Through exacting research, exacting presentation, and careful analysis,
Leo Zeilig offers a remarkable contribution to radical thought and practice worthy of Walter Rodney's legacy."
—Olúfe.mi O. Táíwò, assistant professor of philosophy at Georgetown University and author of *Reconsidering Reparations* and *Elite Capture*

"Leo Zeilig takes readers through the choices that Walter Rodney made.
Choices both small and large, but all taking Rodney to the heights of
scholarship, organization, family, comradeship. Zeilig offers a compelling
narrative and an incisive analysis of Rodney's ferocious commitments to
revolutionary change. This is a fascinating and vital study of Rodney's life."
—Diane C. Fujino, author of *Heartbeat of Struggle:
The Revolutionary Life of Yuri Kochiyama*

"The Black Lives Matter movement's embrace of radical and Pan-Africanist ideas has introduced Walter Rodney to a new generation of activists. *A Revolutionary for Our Time* is an urgently-needed contribution, one that situates the importance of Rodney's Marxism, his life and work, in working-class and antiracist struggle. It is a must-read account of a revolutionary who understood that nothing short of socialism could bring liberation."

—**Lee Wengraf**, author, *Extracting Profit: Imperialism, Neoliberalism, and the New Scramble for Africa*

"This is a splendid narrative of Walter Rodney's legendary life and work across three continents. Leo Zeilig's singular achievement is to have brilliantly located Rodney, the Black Power Marxist, at the intersection of the politics of radical nationalism and visionary socialism that suffused the Pan-African world in the '60s and '70s. An unforgettable read."

—**Issa Shivji**, emeritus professor, University of Dar es Salaam

"*A Revolutionary for Our Time* is both timely and necessary. Through Walter Rodney's ideas and actions, it engages the weighty issues of the current moment. More than a biography of a remarkable individual, we get the optics of a family committed to radical, worldwide transformation and the crosscurrent of people who embraced them as well as the local-global networks of power they dared to challenge."

—**Kwasi Konadu**, John D. and Catherine T. MacArthur Endowed Chair, Colgate University

"The book connects Rodney's thinking to his lived experiences across the world and the decades in which he lived. At a time when context is particularly essential, Zeilig's book provides an essential narrative that situates Rodney not only in the history of revolutionary thought, but also at our contemporary moment, arguing that Rodney's ideas make him a revolutionary not only for his but for our time."

—**Erin MacLeod**, Vanier College

A Revolutionary for Our Time

The Walter Rodney Story

Leo Zeilig

Haymarket Books
Chicago, Illinois

Published in 2022 by
Haymarket Books
P.O. Box 180165
Chicago, IL 60618
773-583-7884
www.haymarketbooks.org
info@haymarketbooks.org

ISBN: 978-1-64259-581-9

Distributed to the trade in the US through Consortium Book Sales and
Distribution (www.cbsd.com) and internationally through Ingram Publisher Services International (www.ingramcontent.com).

This book was published with the generous support of Lannan Foundation and Wallace Action Fund.

Special discounts are available for bulk purchases by organizations and
institutions. Please email info@haymarketbooks.org for more information.

Cover photograph from the Walter Rodney Papers, Atlanta University
Center Robert W. Woodruff Library Archives. Cover design by Rachel
Cohen.

Printed in Canada by union labor.

Library of Congress Cataloging-in-Publication data is available.

10 9 8 7 6 5 4 3 2 1

For Tunde Zack–Williams, Janet Bujra, and Peter Lawrence

Contents

Preface

At the end of May 2020, I stared, sickened, at the footage of George Floyd being slowly choked to death by Minneapolis police. I marched in the first demonstrations in my hometown of London with thousands of protestors, most of whom were under the age of twenty-five. At the end of the month, we gathered near the US embassy in the capital's southern borough of Battersea. Once again, there were several thousand of us, many with homemade placards in hand. The mood was angry, and we were not going anywhere. Police had formed a human barricade, leaving no way for us to reach the embassy. In front of me, about twenty meters from where I stood with hundreds of other mask-wearing demonstrators, there was a wall about two meters high. A young man, about fifteen, scrambled up the wall, helped by his friends. When he was finally standing, he turned matter-of-factly to the crowd sprawled below him. At first his words, shouted into the microphone of a small handheld megaphone, were difficult to hear due to the static and crackle of the machine; he repeated, "We shouldn't wait here, wasting our time. We need to march to Downing Street and confront the prime minister." There was a cheer, and the boy proceeded to clamber down, falling into waiting hands and arms. He and a convoy of his friends proceeded to the front of the protest, toward the road that would lead us out of the impasse. Following his instructions, the entire protest then marched to Westminster and Downing Street—the center of the UK government.

It was exhilarating to be led by a fifteen-year-old, who told us clearly what we needed to do. I thought of Walter Rodney and imagined the pleasure he would have felt witnessing the same scene; a pleasure no doubt tempered by frustration that, decades later, we were still fighting the same fight. However, more than anything else, the extraordinary Black Lives Matter movement would have thrilled and excited him. It would also have told him where he needed to be: where he always was, at the site of burgeoning rebellion. The Black Lives Matter movement has rippled across the globe, and its demand for justice and answers to decades-long violence and racism has resonated on every continent.

Interviewed a few weeks before his murder in 1980, Rodney explained to the journalist Margaret Arkhurst that in Africa he was known as a historian, in Jamaica as a political figure, and in Guyana as a historian and politician. But Rodney did not link politics to personal power, nor did he see himself as a politician. Representing the most radical elements of the Working People's Alliance in Guyana, Rodney sought an empowerment of the poor and working class for themselves, by their own hand, and in their own name. He knew there could be no change that was lasting or desirable that did not come through the action and mobilizations of the poor themselves.

As we gathered on that unseasonably warm day in May 2020, it would have delighted Rodney to see the crowd of protestors being led by a working-class teenager. Perhaps he would have seen himself in that child. And whatever the fate of the movement, he would have known its success depended on deepening popular involvement, until the global system of endless accumulation itself was challenged and overthrown.

In a grainy film recording of a lecture that Rodney gave while he was living in the United States, he spoke of a "crisis in the periphery," in reference to Africa and the Caribbean. He was a man of average height with a slim build; that day, he wore a leather jacket and sported a large afro. He was confident and spoke without notes, but there was not a shred of arrogance. On this occasion, he explained to the audience that a missing suitcase, which had his notes and books, had caused some delays. As Rodney began his lecture, he rarely dropped his eyes from the audience.

The talk was characteristic of Rodney's approach: first, he unraveled the topic historically, providing a full panorama of the question; only then would he reveal the contemporary predicament and the political and popular challenges it posed. Fifty minutes into the lecture, Rodney turned his attention to the revelations that Egypt's president, Anwar el-Sadat, had recently been in France and Austria negotiating the export of their nuclear waste to Egypt. Rodney explained:

> We know, those of us who are familiar with the pattern of life in this society, that capitalism in its drive for profit maximization has been totally oblivious of the effects on the environment. We know that capitalism has been killing the environment in the process of expanding capital. But the alienation which this has produced in the capitalist countries has at least sparked off the ecological movements, and now there is some resistance to the wanton development. . . . In this country, in Germany

and Austria and France, etc., people are saying we refuse to have you planting nuclear waste in the soil when you know that you have no control over it for the next 2,000 years. When you know that this is the most vicious form of pollution . . . and here is a foremost African head of state advancing spurious arguments that there is more space in Egypt and the sub-strata is more stable and he is contemplating doing some deal, so Egypt becomes the nuclear garbage heap of Europe.[1]

Rodney paid particular attention to the role of the environment and ecology in his 1972 masterwork, *How Europe Underdeveloped Africa*—showing how many African societies, prior to the arrival of Europeans, had demonstrated a keen awareness of what he describes as the "total ecology" of society. This was, in his words, the "soils, climate, animals, plants and their multiple interrelationships."[2] When the colonialist invaded, catastrophe followed—for human beings *and* the environment. A form of agriculture that had sustained complex societies and cultures for centuries was based on a keen understanding of soil potential, yet, in Rodney's words, "when the colonialists started upsetting the thin topsoil, the result was disastrous."[3] Indeed, Rodney had a keen and historical sense of the complex interrelationship between human society, production, and the environment. For him, this "total ecology" was vital to sustaining human life and protecting nature. Predating the era of the climate emergency, Rodney's work remains remarkably prescient on this dimension.

Completing the present study amid the global horror of the COVID-19 pandemic—a direct consequence of capitalism's destruction of the planet—has been a chastening experience. There can be few more lonely and dubious activities than sitting endlessly at the computer while people suffer and die. The pandemic has been driven by an economic system programmed to accumulate ceaselessly, no matter the consequences: after all, capitalism regards the natural environment as a product that can be bought and sold, and the increasing proliferation of viruses is intimately connected to food production and the profit margins of international businesses. As Rob Wallace, author of *Big Farms Make Big Flu*, has stated, "Anyone who aims to understand why viruses are becoming more dangerous must investigate the industrial model of agriculture and, more specifically, livestock production." Once-"contained," viruses are now trickling into livestock and human populations. Africa's political economy has spearheaded these developments, so, in Wallace's words, "Ebola, Zika, the coronaviruses, yellow fever again, a variety of avian influenzas, and African swine fever in hogs are among the many pathogens making their way out of the most remote hinterlands into peri-urban loops, regional capitals, and ultimately onto the global travel network."[4]

A world system that generates deadly viruses as a result of the climate emergency would be immediately recognizable to Rodney. Canadian activist and writer Naomi Klein wrote in 2019 that the economic system of "limitless consumption and ecological depletion" is at the heart of the climate crisis. Yet this is a story that begins, she argues, "with people stolen from Africa and lands stolen from indigenous peoples, two practices of brutal expropriation that were so dizzyingly profitable that they generated the excess capital and power to launch the age of fossil fuel-led industrial revolution and with it the beginning of human-driven climate change."[5] It was the roots and branches of this system that Rodney sought to understand and transform in Guyana, and the world.

Rodney was a Marxist for our time; a man who spent his life on political education, aware that it was only through careful and painstaking study that capitalism could be known and ultimately overthrown. Armed with this knowledge, he threw himself into efforts to change the world in Tanzania, Jamaica, and then, most remarkably, in his home of Guyana after 1974. He was a principal figure in an extraordinary period: moving through the Caribbean, Africa, and North America, he achieved a daring and exciting synthesis of Black Power and Marxism. Today, the global uprising of the Black Lives Matter movement that exploded across the world in the summer of 2020 has challenged the deep roots of vicious oppression and exploitation, and it calls for us to return to Rodney's work and life for insights and answers.

A world in which the monuments to the US Confederacy, UK slave owners, and settler colonialism are crashing down at the hands of protestors would be familiar to Rodney. Yet it was the system behind these statues, and crimes, that was his ultimate target. Indeed, Rodney not only analyzed the historical roots of slavery and colonialism but also saw how capitalism had mutated and developed in the modern world.

In Africa, Europe, the United States, and beyond, there can be no final reckoning with these legacies without a challenge to the global financial institutions and governments that remain in place. The profits of today's rich still drip with the blood and sweat of slavery and colonialism. In Rodney's practice, he attempted to show that a new kind of society could be built, but only if it was based on a sharp understanding of the past.

Rodney's Legacy

In recent years, there has been a flurry of brilliant books on Rodney. At the time of his murder in 1980, he was at the height of his powers as a revolutionary and thinker. He was also in the midst of drafting more than one book. One of these volumes, *The Russian Revolution: A View from the Third World*, was assembled only recently from copious notes Rodney had made in the early 1970s.[6] The Russian Revolution was a central event in the twentieth century and, Rodney argued, in human history. Yet the Russian working class had been almost entirely wiped out in a civil war that the young Soviet state ostensibly won. In its place, there emerged a powerful bureaucracy centered around the Bolsheviks, which increasingly substituted itself for any notion of popular power. Survival of the state began to dominate all decision making, and the very notion of socialism came to be defined not as the self-emancipation of the poor but as a state project of a communist party. Rodney's work demonstrates the breadth and depth of his reading; in his approach to research, every primary source had to be read, and he refused a hand-me-down approach to scholarship. As a consequence, Rodney's posthumous volume on the Russian Revolution spans Soviet historiography, a variety of political traditions and perspectives, and a full account of the revolution itself.

One Marxist whom Rodney read with interest was Tony Cliff. Cliff believed that what had developed in the late 1920s in the Soviet Union was actually "state capitalism." A small minority of the communist bureaucracy, he argued, had become a new "ruling class" who saw "catching up" with the capitalist countries as the Soviet Union's primary goal. Every decision was subservient to this aim, and every life was ultimately expendable in its pursuit. In Cliff's view, international allies, friendly states, and support for anti-colonial struggles flowed from this central preoccupation.[7]

The principal export from the Soviet Union was not the revolutionary liberation of the early years of the Russian Revolution but its ugly—and frequently grotesque—opposite. State development, protection of industry and agriculture, and "socialism in one country" became the most important components for building a socialist society. Though there was enormous variety—and complexity—in this model, with divergent "paths" offered by Bulgaria, Yugoslavia, Moscow, or Peking, the project was essentially the same: state-led socialist development. There was no role for the independent self-activity of the working class—a central component of Marxism and liberation, and in the 1970s, Rodney's lodestar.

Cliff added an additional level of analysis: in place of the working class's central role in anti-colonial revolutions or anti-capitalist uprisings in the Third World, another class takes its place. In the French and Belgian colonial world, this class was specifically defined as the *évolué* (literally, the "evolved") as a class chosen by the late colonial administration to take up specific, minor responsibilities in the state. Many of those who went on to lead the independence struggle came from this social category—in one way or another. Cliff saw this intelligentsia in the global South leading the revolution, with a distinct project and ambition. For those attracted by socialism, or what went by the name of socialism, it was to the model championed by the Soviet Union that they turned. For instance, Kwame Nkrumah and, to a lesser extent, Julius Kambarage Nyerere—the leaders of Ghana and Tanzania, respectively—both admired the "autonomous" development in the Soviet Union, a country that seemed to have propelled itself from feudalism to socialism in two or three decades. This in spite of the fact that neither considered themselves followers of the Soviet Union—in fact, Nyerere was quite anti-Soviet.

The model for this new class was state development, led by an enlightened intelligentsia delivering emancipatory projects from above and directed by the state. The urban and rural working poor was entirely irrelevant to this model, a class that was expected to know its place—which was frequently inside state-sponsored trade union federations, where their interests were subservient to national development. Development had to be incubated in the national state, free of cross-border influence, and built up in the isolation of the nation-state. This analysis offers us the clearest explanation of how change in the colonial and early post-colonial world actually occurred, and the role of the petty-bourgeois intelligentsia in this transformation. Rodney analyzed the behavior of this class in detail, and, in the 1970s, he became one of the most brilliant proponents of self-emancipation, elevating the activism of the working class and poor to the heart of any serious project of revolution.

A number of prior studies on Rodney inform the present volume. A group of colleagues, including Jesse Benjamin, worked with his daughter, Asha Rodney, in the development of the new editions of Rodney's writings that have been republished by Verso.[8] There have also been invaluable recent studies, including Amzat Boukari-Yabara's book, a detailed and passionate account of Rodney's life and work. Other works abound, including Rupert Lewis's vital 1998 biography, which brings to life Rodney's world, with his wife, Patricia, as a central part of the story. Karim Hirji's brilliant analysis of Rodney's classic *How Europe Underdeveloped Africa* is another important volume and a passionate restatement of the book's relevance—from someone who knew Walter as a friend, comrade, and teacher. A recent short biography by Chinedu Chukwudinma covers the major contours of Rodney's life in remarkable concision, providing a brief but incisive account of Rodney's life and activism. These sources are too numerous to list—though each has been invaluable.[9]

This book is not intended as an academic contribution to the study of Rodney—as Patricia Rodney noted in 2019, too numerous are academics who want to advance careers on the basis of her husband's writings.[10] My intention, rather, has been to write a detailed book on Rodney's entire life, with a focus on his revolutionary activism and work. The book is written in the context of the Black Lives Matter movement; responding to that movement's desire for theory, history, and practice, it is hoped that a full account of Rodney's life will help to elucidate our struggles to forge a new society.

The book does not do everything, say all, or provide encyclopedic knowledge of Rodney's life and writings. For this, there are better places to turn. Instead, it attempts to put Rodney in his context, in Guyana, Jamaica, and Tanzania—in the incredible, heady days of the late 1960s and early 1970s. I have depended on a range of sources and used—extensively—the archive of Rodney's papers at the Atlanta University Center's Robert W. Woodruff Library. What I hope emerges is a rich picture of Rodney and his world; nevertheless, it remains a partial and incomplete one.

Writing the Book

To shake off lingering feelings of misery in the morning, I take a morning run or a cycle ride—normally no more than twenty minutes, as I am a lifetime asthmatic. I live by a small, pebbled beach in Kent, England, in an old fishing town called Whitstable. Increasingly, this town attracts day trippers from London, with many of the small late Victorian terrace houses bought up as second homes, while the full-time residents of the town are forced out by rising prices.

I often cycle up Borstal Hill, the steep road that leads out of town; it is an exhausting climb, but this is what I need in the morning. Under leaden skies, I pant up the hill until I reach the cycle lane that runs along a main road to the coastal towns of Herne Bay and Margate. I pass a junk and antique yard with a mass of scattered goods on the roadside—fluttering on a tall pole is the Union Jack (the national flag of the United Kingdom). Along the route back, the grassy edges of the road are carpeted with litter, disposable coffee cups, and food wrappers, thrown out by passing drivers and covered in the spring and summer by vegetation. With the onset of winter, the sea of rubbish is exposed as life is pared back and the trees and plants are laid bare. A "campaign" launched by the tabloids a few years ago called for a nationwide cleanup; however, "Clean for the Queen" was more or less entirely ignored (an indication of the place of the royal family in the country's heart). Recently, the Tory government has spoken about the glories of empire, and Prime Minister Boris Johnson, whose government has presided over the largely avoidable deaths of thousands during the COVID-19 pandemic, has spoken about the need to end "a bout of self-recrimination and wetness" about British history.

With this comment, the prime minister was referring to the decision of the British Broadcasting Corporation (BBC) to play only the music, not the lyrics, of the jingoistic, imperialist songs "Land of Hope and Glory" and "Rule Britannia," which are featured every year on the closing night of an eight-week summer festival of classical music known as "The Proms." Indeed, the British ruling class continues to use patriotism to build popular support, even if it is no longer used to shore up a real empire, as it was in the nineteenth century and the first half of the last century. Nationalist ideology is essential to persuade us to pay taxes, fight in wars, and a lot more. As I cycle in the morning through a sea of half-buried rubbish and flags fluttering over pavement junk, I ponder how today's politicians continue to employ nationalist slogans, to speak of the "glories of empire" to scapegoat asylum seekers, and to label refugees attempting to cross the English Channel—only miles from where I exercise—as an "invasion." The racism of slavery and empire lives on.

However, "global Britain"—as it is called in some quarters—is an exhausted, second-rate power, an international rubbish dump of neoliberal politics and bigotry. The noise of the traffic as I cycle on the uneven path is loud; I slow down to let pedestrians pass, then make a sharp left turn onto an unpaved road that leads me back to town. Recently, even apparently left-wing politicians have spoken about how British patriotism can be wielded for "progressive" purposes: the history of slavery, death, and colonialism can somehow be repurposed! The island that profited richly from empire, slavery, and colonial occupation—in Rodney's Guyana, for example—faces an environmental emergency, provoked by centuries of capitalist globalization, with staggering, even comical, blindness.

To change this history, Rodney told us, we must do certain things. We must read and understand the history that has been silenced by academic and establishment historians—a key task. Indeed, much of Rodney's life was spent "explaining," teaching from the bottom up—literally, whether from an oil drum in Kingston's Trench Town, to students at the University of Dar es Salaam, or to workers and the poor across Guyana in the 1970s. Wherever he went, he talked, lectured, and taught. If there is ever a single purpose in any life, this was it for Rodney: education. In his books and speeches, he educated, to the highest and most exacting standards. But he did not do this purely for the sake of enlightenment; Rodney was a teacher who sought revolutionary change that he knew could only come from informed and grounded practice. Walter Rodney was a revolutionary socialist who understood, as he wrote in 1972, that the only great people "among the unfree and the oppressed are those who struggle to destroy the oppressor." This is what he taught.

Acknowledgments

Shortly before Walter Rodney published his groundbreaking 1972 book, *How Europe Underdeveloped Africa*, he received a note from his publisher expressing a certain nervousness. The publisher felt unequal to the task of judging the academic merits of Rodney's manuscript and wanted to send it for peer review. Rodney's response was swift and fierce: "The main request, which you made, is that the manuscript should be passed on to an African historian, because you felt yourself unequal to the task of judging its worth as 'serious history.' It is an ideological challenge . . . to pass it on to a serious bourgeois historian would be a sheer waste of time."

The book, he explained, was aimed at secondary school students and working people; it was this audience, Rodney argued, who would "judge whether it makes sense in the light of present conditions in Africa." I share his contempt for "serious bourgeois" academics, who stake everything on peer review, publication, and career progression.

In a famous statement in his 1972 book—which came out without academic review—Rodney argued that unlike most acknowledgments (which indicate "responsibility for all mistakes in the text" is the author's own), he implicated his readers and comrades in the final manuscript in what, he states, is always a collective endeavor.

In this spirit, I would like to incriminate a large number of friends and comrades who have helped me with this book: Peter Dwyer, Lee Wengraf, Chinedu Chukwudinma, Ian Birchall, Issa Shivji, Hannah Cross, Marjorie Mblinyi, Colin Stoneman, Jörg Wiegratz, Clare Smedley, Yao Graham, Reginald Cline-Cole, Hakim Adi, Peter Lawrence, Marika Sherwood, Elisa Greco, Gabrielle Lynch, Jesse Benjamin, Janet Bujra, Ray Bush, and Anne Braithwaite.

Further incrimination is owed to Ruby Abercrombie for her careful work and assistance on a late version of the manuscript. Colin Barker, who died as this book was being written, remains a continual presence and inspiration hovering over my shoulder. Yen Ly endured my anxiety, and occasional jubilation, over the long, slow gestation of this book. In the final stages of revision, Sam Smith stepped in and deepened the color, clarity, and purpose of the book. Their own profound sympathy with Rodney's work, and revolutionary project, informed their careful and expert copyedit.

The book was assisted enormously by a small grant from the *Review of African Political Economy*—which for a number of years has been my workplace, intellectual base, and political home. For fieldwork, I received funds from the Lipman and Miliband Trust, which supported a trip to Tanzania in 2018.

This book would not have been possible without the extraordinary work and commitment of the Rodney family—especially Walter's wife, Patricia, and their children, Asha, Shaka, and Kanini. Their decades-long work in promoting and defending the legacy of Walter Rodney, fighting for justice while confronting the unending grief at their father and husband's assassination, is nothing short of remarkable.

Patricia's patience with me—with the innumerable mistakes in earlier drafts, and in her close, meticulous reading of countless versions of the manuscript—has immeasurably improved the book and provided me with something I could not get elsewhere: an intimate sense of Walter as a loving father and husband who managed something that few of us ever achieve in life: a full and equal partnership with the people closest to us.

As parents and activists, Patricia and Walter refused the tempting and dangerous division of life between home and politics; the children were involved in the couple's working lives and in Walter's political organizing and teaching, and they were never hidden away from a world that the couple wanted to see transformed.

Through Patricia, I also experienced Walter's remarkable work discipline, attention to detail, and forensic focus on the task at hand; each draft was carefully read and speedily returned to me with corrections and suggestions for further reading and deeper, more critical inquiry. Donald Rodney, Walter's brother, also read closely a draft of the book, and suggested sources and corrected details that only he could. His fight for justice, for his brother, the family and himself, has been an inspiration.

The astonishing archive, the Walter Rodney Papers, donated by the Rodney family to the Robert W. Woodruff Library of the Atlanta University Center, is an indispensable resource for students, activists, and researchers. The relentless and necessary pursuit of justice for Walter Rodney and the family, and the dedication to his legacy—the battle of memory over forgetting undertaken by Patricia, Asha, Shaka, Kanini, and Walter's brother Donald—is nothing short of astonishing and inspiring. The Walter Rodney Foundation, which the family established, is an invaluable resource in this battle.

Tiffany Atwater Lee and Stacy S. Jones, staff at the archive in the Atlanta University Center, were expert and patient with my requests (in person and over email).

For the enthusiasm, patience, and comradeship of Haymarket—especially Anthony Arnove (for his wise counsel), Rachel Cohen, and Nisha Bolsey—in coaxing the book to completion, and for remaining steadfast and long suffering amid innumerable delays and excuses, I owe great thanks.

I dedicate the book to my comrades Tunde Zack-Williams, Janet Bujra, and Peter Lawrence for imparting something of the spirit of Tanzania in its hopeful heyday. Janet and Peter spent years in the country with Walter and Patricia, and have sustained their radicalism and politics through the years—perhaps because of what they lived through and experienced there.

Finally, I hope this book is a useful resource for activists, students, and workers who want to plunge into the life and work of one of last century's greatest revolutionaries and historians—not to read history for its own sake, but as a tool to strengthen our movements and struggles in order to revolutionize the world today.

CHAPTER 1

Beginnings

Born on March 23, 1942, to a working-class family in Georgetown, Guyana, Walter Anthony Rodney was the second of six children. Walter's father, Edward Percival, was a tailor who worked largely for himself.[1] However, when work was scarce, Edward would accept lower-paying work for a weekly wage at a small outlet in Georgetown. Walter's mother, Pauline, worked from home as a seamstress.

In the 1940s, Guyanese society was divided between "Indian" and "African," and Black and white. As Walter would later recall, "One interrelated with Indian families and with Indians at school," but there was little day-to-day contact with other groups. It was commonplace, among his African peers and neighbors, to accord an idealized status to those in the Indian community: "You see those Indian students. They go to school and they go back home, and they help their parents. So, you must help your parents. . . . He's studying hard. So, one must study."[2] Though this division was not always strict or hostile, it would later become so. These racial fault lines had deep roots in Guyana's colonial past—a long history for which we must account before we can begin to understand the trajectory of Rodney's life and political development.

Politics and Economics in Rodney's Guyana

Since its very germination, Guyana had been structured to the demands of capitalism. Its primary exports were unprocessed raw materials ranging from sugar and rice to gold and bauxite. Sprawling sugar plantations—an instrument that would become a key area of study for Rodney—had long been a feature of Guyana's export-oriented economy. In contrast, bauxite—a rock with a high aluminum content—has been mined (and exported) for a little more than a hundred years in the country.

Established as a slave economy in the seventeenth century by the Dutch, the country saw successive occupations, including on the part of the French and eventually the British. There were numerous slave rebellions in the nineteenth century, the most famous of which took place in 1823, when the colony was known by its British name, Demerara-Essequibo (later to be renamed British Guiana). Though it was eventually crushed, the rebellion saw thousands of slaves throw off their chains. It also made an indelible mark on the history of the territory by forcing an acceleration in the pace of abolition. When this was finally and formally accomplished fifteen years later, in 1838, thousands of former slaves left their plantations, giving rise to an Afro-Guyanese peasant class. The appearance of this new working class served to undermine the planters' political power and the colony's economic activity—which remained, principally, the export of sugar from large plantations.

Following the abolition of slavery, labor shortages forced the British authorities to source workers from other colonial possessions; eventually, this led them to bring thousands of indentured workers to Guyana from India. Known as "East Indians"—many coming from eastern Uttar Pradesh, and a minority from the Tamil- and Telugu-speaking regions in southern India—these laborers were transported to the Caribbean to work, ostensibly, for a finite number of years, where they were tied to planters. After their period of "service," they were formally permitted to return to India with money saved from their work in the sugar fields. This was, however, a rare occurrence. Poverty and famine in British-occupied India drove the continuing trade in indentured labor—a form of unfree labor that bore many similarities to the recently abolished slavery. Indeed, unfree labor was a central pillar of the sugar plantations' profitability.

The Caribbean activist and economist Clive Thomas—a close friend of Rodney—describes the fundamental role of the Caribbean in the new global economy: "I don't think that we can easily forget that . . . the Caribbean was the cradle of capitalism. We . . . forged . . . through the plantation, and through slavery, through all of those experiences, the prototypical institutions."[3] In their nascency, these relations and means of production were, Thomas argues, "cutting edge" transformations. Brutal and terrible though the plantation system was, it represented the birth of a new system—built from the blood and bones of an entire people.

Due to the shifting political economy of late-nineteenth-century British Guiana, sugar production gradually became less profitable—even though sugar exports continued to dominate production and exports until the 1880s. Plummeting cane sugar prices subsequently fueled a move to timber production, the cultivation of rice, and the mining of precious metals and gems. However, despite the best efforts of the scions of British Guiana's founding capitalist class, the exploitation of gold and diamond deposits in the colony remained a minor revenue stream.

The political and economic landscape was dominated for generations by the London-based Booker Group of companies. By the late nineteenth century, its owners controlled most of the cane sugar plantations in the colony; by 1950, they held all but three. Leading the expansion and diversification of the economy in the twentieth century, the Booker Group increasingly invested in rum, medicines, printing, marketing, and timber. Indeed, their monopolies and profits were so secure under the British colony that the country became known by the nickname "Booker's Guyana." In sum, the company emblematized the modern-day efforts of an entrenched capitalist class to promote and profit from indentured labor.

However, it was bauxite that became a larger and more important export in the twentieth century—part of the country's primary product diversification. The need for bauxite, the raw material for producing aluminum, meant the country was the object of near-obsessive interest of northern countries, which increasingly depended on the metal for their development. During the US and European economic boom following the Second World War, the metal was used in armaments, airplane construction, and a host of other industries, such as cans, foils, kitchen utensils, window frames, and beer barrels. Among Guyana's bauxite customers, the United States was the most powerful of all, producing almost half of the world's aluminum.[4]

US engagement escalated considerably during this era, and it would remain a powerful influence throughout the twentieth century. Now the foremost and undisputed power in the Americas, the United States adopted an aggressive approach toward Guyana and its rich supply of bauxite. Without doubt, the postwar stance of the US State Department was inflected by a fear of communist influence; however, there were also other, more pressing economic motivations. Uruguayan historian Eduardo Galeano, in his 1972 classic, *Open Veins of Latin America*, emphasized the political impact of US intervention and the country's dependence on Guyana's bauxite:

> Minerals had much to do with the fall of Cheddi Jagan's socialist government, which at the end of 1964 had again won a majority of votes in what was then British Guiana. . . . The CIA played a decisive role

in Jagan's defeat. Arnold Zander, leader of the strike that served as a provocation and pretext to deny electoral victory to Jagan, afterward admitted publicly that his union had dollars rained upon it. . . . The new regime—very Western and very Christian—guaranteed the Aluminum Company of America (Alcoa) against any danger to its interests in Guyana: it could continue tranquilly removing the bauxite and selling it to itself at the same price as in 1938, although the price of aluminum had since soared. . . . The danger was indeed past.[5]

US involvement in the extraction and export of bauxite in Guyana dates to the beginning of the twentieth century. In 1913, only a few years after the ore's discovery on the banks of the Demerara River, Alcoa president Arthur Vining Davis turned his attention the Guyanese reserves. Given the scarcity of bauxite in the United States, Alcoa was determined to capture as much of the ore as possible. Initially duping the British into thinking it was purchasing land for citrus plantations, by 1916 Alcoa had obtained access to the majority of the rich deposits along the Demerara.

The same forces that had propelled Guyana and its Caribbean neighbors into the maelstrom of global capitalism in the seventeenth century, with the birth of the plantation system and slavery, now exposed the region once more to the iron laws of economic and imperial control—tying it to the production of raw materials for export. Ultimately, Walter Rodney would come to understand these historical shackles as the primary challenge facing the Guyanese people and would dedicate his life to confronting them.

A Georgetown Childhood

Walter's father, Edward, had traveled for work in the 1930s to Curaçao—a Dutch-held Caribbean island, off the coast of Venezuela—before joining the nationalist movement in Guyana led by union activist Cheddi Jagan. When Walter was eleven years old, his father encouraged him to participate in the 1953 election campaign, leafleting and canvassing for the People's Progressive Party (PPP). In fact, following the PPP's victory in 1953, Walter Rodney would be among the first batch of bright children from working-class homes to be selected for a new scholarship program initiated by the party.

Rodney's schoolmate Rupert Roopnaraine, who would later become a Guyanese politician, recalls, "You could not be at Queen's [College] at the time and not know of his skills at debating, his activities on the sports field, and his academics."[6] The Georgetown secondary school was, at the time, exceptionally hierarchical, informally divided between the "cart-horses" and the "thoroughbreds," terms used by students. Walter was one of the school's talents.

Founded in January 1950, the PPP was a merger of the British Guiana Labour Party, led by Forbes Burnham, and the Political Affairs Committee, led by Jagan. From its beginnings, the party was a remarkable formation, the first mass organization in the country, with an impressive multiethnic base and the support of workers and intellectuals. After the election in 1953, Jagan became chief minister. However, his reforms, regarded by some as too radical, provoked the fury of the British, who worried about the possibility that a revolution might be provoked.

Walter's parents would sometimes host branch meetings at their home, and the party's activists were often coming and going. His father gave his son political tasks to carry out: "I was given the sort of humdrum task to distribute party manifestos," he recalls, "which one doesn't necessarily understand, but you come up against certain things." Thus, at the age of eleven, Walter was already learning about popular politics, canvasing, leaflet distribution, and class: "[Without] knowing anything about class, I knew that there were certain kinds of Guyanese into whose yard we did not . . . carry a PPP manifesto. You could tell from the kind of house or the shade or complexion of the lady reclining, sipping her tea, or whatever she may be doing."[7] This instinctual class feeling meant that he quickly understood the city—that is, he read its dynamics of wealth and politics. As such, he avoided houses with long drives but knocked confidently on those doors where you could "go right up" to the people.

In this way, as a young boy, the struggle made sense to Walter. He felt it—as children can—in his gut. There was not a gender divide in political activity inside his home. "My mother," he records, "would walk far distances from our house to go to political meetings, perhaps carrying a little bench in hand so that ultimately she could sit down, since these meetings lasted for hours."[8]

Walter not only studied; he excelled also at sport. It was not enough to be academically excellent; one had to be whole, or complete, and that meant shining in a range of activities. He loved cricket and knew all about it; he could talk about its history and field and bowl impressively. He was also an athlete at school, a high jumper. As Roopnaraine remembers,

> In those days, we didn't see any great conflict in excelling academically and excelling at sports or going to parties. We lived quite fully . . . Walter led an extremely full life at school. He was an absolutely outstanding academic. He was a debater of rare quality. He was a sport person. He partied with the best of them. He was quite a dancer.[9]

Rodney, however, was critical of the place and its teachings. "There was training in what was called debating, which was to talk about nothing provided you said nothing as cleverly as possible and as entertaining as possible. Then you got full marks. If you said anything too substantial, your marks would come down."[10] Saying clever things as long as they meant nothing, a skill that was handed down to the secondary schools across British colonies. This form of public discussion—one that contemporaries of Rodney often celebrate—was in fact one of a number of devices used to herd and control political discussion. Master of the form though he may have been, Rodney was nonetheless scathing about its purposes.

The desire for "completeness" of which Walter speaks—a refusal to be compartmentalized—lent itself to the development of a radical politics. All facets of life, he came to understand, were connected, and all skills were relevant to living in the world. Rodney seems to have excelled in all subjects, including science, literature, and languages. He took two languages at "O" level—French and Spanish—and continued with Spanish to "A" level: a language proficiency which would equip him for the archival work he would later pursue in Europe, as well as during public meetings of liberation movements in Dar es Salaam—for which he would sometimes provide Spanish translation.[11]

Joining the school as a teacher in October 1955, Robert "Bobby" Moore encountered Walter:

> His peers enjoyed his self-confidence, which did not come with arrogance. They bonded with his sense of humour. They were impressed by how much reading he had done and how much of it he could quote from memory. On top of all that, his teachers were clearly taken with his writing: lucid, concise, questioning, and flavoured with the Rodney wit.[12]

Walter's passion for history was stirred by Moore in 1956, when he was thirteen years old. At the time, the course syllabus focused almost entirely on the British Empire, starting with the sixteenth century and ending in the late 1940s. However, faculty and students had already caught on to the fact that changes to the history curriculum were taking place at the University in Kingston. Queen's, they insisted, had to catch up. Moore explains,

> In 1957, there was no history textbook of the West Indies suitable for those lively teenagers of the Upper Fourth forms. A very scholarly *History of the West Indies* did come out that year, but its style was much too magisterial to ignite the interests of students in their mid-teens. . . . After much reflection, I realized that the notes I made at Dr. Elsa Goveia's lectures of 1953–54 at [University of the West Indies] would be the best temporary substitute for a textbook. . . . She was a convinced West Indian, eager to witness the creation of a West Indian political entity.[13]

Such radical improvisation captured the imagination of the students, and Walter, the keenest of all, suggested that Moore allow the students to type up his notes to create a text resource that could be distributed to every student. By this route, West African history found its way into the body and soul of Queen's curriculum. As we will see, Rodney spent much of his working—and political—life involved in such initiatives (curriculum development, as it is called today) in Jamaica and Tanzania. History was the essential tool in raising political consciousness.

Walter grew up in an environment where slavery—the real history of the West Indies—was gradually, and hesitantly, becoming an urgent and legitimate scholarly topic. Other global issues were also beginning to influence students. After South Africa's formal introduction of apartheid, Moore's students raised questions. When he suggested that South Africa's apartheid amounted to a form of modern slavery, "there was an 'aha' moment across the class."[14] Seizing on the interest, Moore circulated Trevor Huddleston's critique of apartheid and slavery, *Naught for Your Comfort*. When the book was returned to him, "it was no longer a book but a series of chunks of print held together loosely by a bit of glues, but I knew that it existed in its entirety with the boys."[15] This prompted further revisions of the curriculum, so that the study of South Africa's apartheid became part of the new course on the history of slavery and "its modern equivalents."

The intellectual atmosphere at Queen's, pioneering a radical new agenda on history, meant that the school became a center of cultural and political activity for the whole city. Walter's "tremendous skill" as a debater was an important part of the school's reputation in the city. Moore explains, "[H]is probing of the issues and mastery of words . . . would draw audiences beyond the school. Teachers and senior public servants were among those who made Queen's their senior public activity during the school year."[16] For many, Walter was the attraction, and they would come simply to marvel at his control of argument and delivery. This early training—while still a teenager—equipped him for his work as a teacher and activist.

Unlike an earlier generation of militant thinkers and activists, including Frantz Fanon in Martinique, C. L. R. James in Trinidad, and others in Africa, Rodney's path to socialism did not involve a sharp break. The PPP was already sympathetic to Marxism, and it was clear that they were endeavoring to create a new anti-capitalist society. By the time Rodney left Queen's and Georgetown, he had a keen sense of the politics from below—as it appeared in popular and radical nationalist organizations, as well as in political meetings where speakers would reference socialism and speak of Karl Marx and Vladimir Lenin. There was never a barrier to surmount. Rodney explains, "That's probably why my own development has been sort of very incremental. It didn't have to take a flying leap at some point over the unknown."[17] He was not required to leapfrog over a religious or moral belief system into the uncertainties beyond—as opposed to Fanon, for example, who had been devastated by the collapse of his moral universe in the Second World War. There were shifts and turns in Rodney's early life, but not breaks and ruptures.

Strikes, Coups, and Colonialization

The emergence of these radical figures, and the PPP, came on the back of an almighty struggle of the working class in the 1940s. Interestingly, this struggle was frequently—indeed overwhelmingly—led by rank-and-file bauxite workers in the country's open-pit mines around the mining town, Linden,[18] and against the established trade union bureaucracy. In a powerful history of the period, Odida Quamina writes that from "the 1940s onwards, wildcat strikes throughout the industry have been the result of Management's autocratic rule, on the one hand, and the Union's oligarchic rule, on the other."[19] The rank-and-file movement, and worker-led groups, came together to provide leadership against the official union movement. One of these was the Man Power Citizens' Association (MPCA), founded in Georgetown in 1937, which was "brought" into the mines after it had shown itself able to speak and advocate for workers on sugar plantations.

The MPCA gathered support in opposition to the British Guiana Labour Union. The MPCA was put to the test between 1946 and 1947 with radical, escalating strikes and action across the mining region.

In April 1947, a general strike was called in the mines over demands on pay and services for mine workers. The risks of an all-out strike were great to the thousands of workers, but perhaps no greater than those of the work itself; as one worker commented: "We felt no safer on the job than on the picket lines. We went to work every morning wondering if we would last the whole day. When we survived the day, we merely extended the anxieties to the following day."[20] After the sixty-four-day general strike ended on June 16, 1947, two major mining companies agreed to implement recommendations, but they refused to reemploy the union's branch president and other executive members. The Demerara Bauxite Company (DEMBA) was then the largest of the country's two bauxite companies. Quamina explains, "Again the response of the more militant sections of the workforce was very positive: if the Company did not reinstate their leaders, they would return to the picket lines."[21] The threat of another strike was sufficient to ensure that the leaders of the mine workers were reinstated by the end of July. By 1950, the MPCA had won respect and recognition, and its branches came together to become the British Guiana Mine Workers' Union (on independence renamed the Guyana Mine Workers Union). Wildcat strikes had established union recognition and set the scene for working-class militancy against a trade union bureaucracy that would continue through the 1960s and 1970s. The strikes also gave a major boost to the emergence of the radical nationalist party, the PPP.

In 1953, the British government executed what historian and journalist Mark Curtis refers to as a "coup" in British Guiana—which, at the time, had been "permitted" limited self-government. In short, the colonial authorities overthrew the Georgetown government to which Cheddi Jagan and the PPP had been elected on a pro-poor program of redistribution and economic transformation. The British interpreted these "radical" policies as an existential threat to their rule and economic interests—especially those of the Booker Brothers who controlled much of Guyana's economy and sugar plantations, an important export crop. The colonial government in Westminster therefore sent seven hundred troops to unseat Jagan's administration, claiming that his party was "part of the international communist conspiracy" in British Guiana. New elections were deemed too risky, given the likelihood that the PPP would be reelected.

Under a British edict, the PPP government was removed by force from office, and by the time fresh elections were held in 1957, the party—which had been, for a moment, a mass multiethnic movement—had split into two blocs, which now were pitted against each other in the elections. Jagan won the election, and the die was cast; Burnham's bloc abandoned the party and founded the People's National Congress (PNC), which sought the support of the Afro-Guyanese community, with the PPP left to represent the Indo-Guyanese. Brutal interethnic violence would plague the next two decades, informing much of Rodney's political efforts to forge the unity of the Guyanese working poor.

Nervous about Jagan's left-wing politics and convinced he was a communist, the United States helped compel the United Kingdom to campaign to expel the PPP government. Civil unrest followed colonial efforts to stir up divisions between the different communities—with many killed in 1962 and 1963 as anti-PPP rioting destroyed large parts of the capital of Georgetown.

In 1963, what is often regarded as a second "coup" took place in Guyana, with blatant US and British involvement. Though in the 1964 elections the PPP won more seats, the PNC and the United Force—a conservative political party whose support base came from the country's Portuguese population—together were invited to form a government. In the dying days of British rule, Jagan was removed from office by Governor Richard Luyt.[22]

Independence came in 1966, and, in the elections two years later, the PNC, led by Burnham, won another disputed victory. The political scene was brutally scarred by ethnicity, even if Burnham announced, in 1970, a republic based on socialist values. Few believed the lies of the new apparently radical and nonaligned government.

To Kingston

Walter's passion was history. Stimulated by Moore's encouragement and teaching, he became the president of the history society at the school, as well as vice president of the debating society and editor of the school magazine, *The Lictor*. In 1960, at the age of seventeen, Rodney left Guyana for the first time to start a degree at the University of the West Indies (UWI). Like many colonial universities at the time, it was set up in 1948 as a satellite of the University of London—the apparent font of all learning and

culture. Regarded as an elite institution training students who would become civil servants, politicians, and minor intellectuals, it was envisaged
that the UWI would provide the West Indies with the cadre needed to
run ex-colonial states.

Initially, Walter thought of pursuing a career as a lawyer, and his father wanted him to be a diplomat. Finally, however, he decided to pursue
his interest in history under the tutelage of Douglas Hall, Roy Augier,
and Elsa Goveia—whose lectures he had used to prepare an improvised
book at Queen's. Though popular at university among both students and
lecturers, Walter's "spontaneity" and his radical opinions, in a conservative
environment, occasionally worked against him. Rodney's radicalism was
clearly unpopular among some students who saw his increasing interest in
the poor and marginalized in Jamaican society as a worrying sign, as seen
in his 1962 loss in an election to join the student council.[23]

Nevertheless, the university was changing, and Rodney absorbed the
new mood. As he recalled in 1975, "[T]he university had begun the nationalist pilgrimage. University faculty and students in disciplines such
as history and in other fields such as economics, politics and sociology
had made the breakthrough against a purely externally oriented kind
of syllabus."[24] This was a process that Rodney labeled the "nationalist
phenomenon"—in which the people of the Caribbean could start seeing
themselves as a nation, a collective, with the task of overturning a rotten
and racist history.

> The faculty and program at UWI were helpful in this regard. They were
> at least raising the nationalist question and by raising the nationalist
> question it ultimately pointed me, for instance, in the direction of Af-
> rica. From Caribbean history, from looking at the slave trade, one de-
> cided that one needed to understand slavery and understand the cultural
> background of Africa.[25]

These were early days, and the connection between the Caribbean and
Africa, automatic and obvious as it seems today, was still felt mainly at
the intuitive level for Rodney. However, he was moving toward a deep
and connected understanding of the people, politics, and history of the
two regions.

Rodney was not just a bookworm; he was also a young man who
wanted to live fully. Arriving in Jamaica in 1960, he saw a society and
people who were a "breed apart"—lively, dynamic, and energetic. He

siphoned the spirit of the island into his work and life, and was changed by the island. His praise was high: "[F]or staying power, for sheer energy, Jamaican people seem to have us all beat." He saw rebellion cut deeply into the people's psychology. "Jamaicans can curse more proficiently than any other Caribbean people . . . and I think this is a testimony to their combativeness."[26] He would later credit this energy and mettle for their ability to nip British racism in the bud. "Jamaicans had a way of striking back that did not brook too much playing about . . . [they] would behave in what I used to think was an amazingly bellicose and provocative manner . . . [and] would take on a whole railway station if necessary and would move forward to single out a white man, snatch him and hit him."[27] The Jamaicans had shown Rodney, as a university student, their cheeky, rebellious irreverence in the early 1960s, but he would see this again in the UK, and later in the 1960s when he returned to the island. In London, "the Jamaican brothers were out there in the street defending the whole race, as it were."[28] A people who could do this—survive and resist in a hostile land (and run the entire transport, health care, and welfare system)—were clearly "people who had almost unlimited capacity for change."[29]

Times were also changing, and it was not in Washington or London but in the countries of the global South where the new world would be made. Less than 250 miles away in Cuba, a revolution in 1959 had recently overturned the brutal US-backed puppet dictatorship led by President Fulgencio Batista. Walter watched these developments with keen interest. Declining an invitation to attend a meeting of the USSR-backed, Prague-based International Union of Students (IUS) in Moscow in June 1961, he instead undertook a tour of the Caribbean. Returning to Kingston, Walter was immediately on the radar of the Jamaican intelligence services—the Special Branch. Worried, they contacted their Guyanese counterparts to find out if they had a file on him in Georgetown.

On a trip to Cuba in January 1962, the Jamaican security apparatus, who were now keeping close tabs on Walter, wrote with exaggerated imaginings that there "is reason to believe that whilst in Cuba Rodney and his companions were visited in the Hotel by Castro himself." When the group of three students returned to Kingston, they had with them, as the intelligence service recorded, a "considerable amount of Communist literature and subversive publications of the IUS, including Che Guevara's 'Guerrilla Warfare.'" The books were seized by customs and temporarily held.[30] In a student newsletter, a defiant Rodney denounced the authorities for seizing what was a "quite innocuous" gift from the Cubans. In a tone of panic, a brief in Rodney's intelligence file complained that he was consorting with students, "most notably Colin A. Moore, a Guyanese and Communist sympathizer," to form the Students Democratic Party, "the aim of which was to spread Marxism throughout the West Indies."[31]

Interestingly, at about this time, in early 1962, Rodney—according to the intelligence files—"made his first contact with the Rastafarians." Rodney's political agitation on campus also continued, undeterred by state surveillance; as the global development scholar Michael O. West writes, "[T]he tireless agitator threw in his lot with the working people." By May, Rodney was apparently attempting "to instigate a strike of the subordinate staff of the UWI."[32]

In August 1962, Walter traveled to Leningrad to attend the annual meeting of the IUS that he had not been able to attend the previous year—flying first to Havana. Traveling over such an enormous distance to the Soviet Union—likely on board Czechoslovak State Airlines (CSA), which directly linked the island to the Soviet bloc by commercial aviation in 1961—was no mean feat, for it required refueling at multiple stops on the way, possibly in Conakry, Guinea (a newly independent West African state aligned to the Soviet Union), or in Prague. Passenger air travel was still the technological avant-garde in the early 1960s, and it was not until 1963 that there was a regular "nonstop" service from Havana to Moscow—which was still considered "dangerous" and involved refueling in Murmansk. In fact, an entire CIA file in August 1963 was dedicated to the opening of this route.

Using these opportunities to travel far from the prying eyes of Jamaican censors, he continued to read the abundance of literature on the history of revolutions and socialist politics. These expensive international trips were facilitated by success at the university; winning the "student of the year" prize in 1962, for example, had awarded Rodney the funds for his extended trip to various islands throughout the Caribbean.

Years later, Rodney would recall the impression that his visit to the Soviet Union had on him: "I was struck on arrival at the airport by the physical demeanor and the social aspect of the people in the airport. They were workers and peasants, as far as I could see, who were flying on those TU-104's to Moscow, to Leningrad, etc., as though they were using a bus."[33] There is some exaggeration in Rodney's account. By 1950, passenger air travel was only 1.4 percent of total passenger turnover, rising to almost 19 percent in 1987.[34] But the country had pioneered one of first passenger jets in 1956, and the rate of expansion was rapid. By 1968, for example, air travel was possible to thirty-five hundred cities and towns,[35] though the cost was still high and certainly out of reach for most workers and peasants.

When Rodney traveled to the Soviet Union on tours organized—or choreographed—by "friendship" organizations, he was amazed, he explained, "at the number of books they sell—in the streets, on the pavement, all over." What is more, there did not seem to be such a sharp social division in cultural activities; Rodney was surprised to see "ordinary people" going to the Bolshoi Ballet. This was not the elite activity of the ruling class. Exaggerated though these observations might now appear, Rodney was also responding to the fact that the Soviet Union had emerged from semi-feudalism only a few decades before and now seemed to be at the vanguard of highly technical and complex development.

If Rodney reacted to the sights and sounds of the Soviet Union with awe and surprise, in Cuba, a neighboring island in the Caribbean, the effect was one of inspiration. "I got some insight at an early period into the tremendous excitement of the Cuban Revolution. This was 1960, just after the victory of the revolution. One has to live with a revolution to get its full impact, but the next best thing is to get there and see a people actually attempting to grapple with real problems of development." The Soviet Union had appeared "settled" and "smooth" to the young traveler; the revolution had taken place years before. However, Cuba still moved and throbbed to the beat of the transformation that had just taken place. The Cubans, Rodney recalls, were "talking and bustling and running and jumping and really living the revolution in a way that was completely outside of anything that one could read anywhere or listen to or conceptualise in an island such as Jamaica, which is where I was still."[36]

Returning to the classroom in colonial-controlled Jamaica, Rodney confronted tutors and lecturers still steeped in the suffocating, self-obsessed tedium of academic privilege and superiority. Writing a term paper on Lenin and the Russian Revolution, Rodney observed that the founding Bolshevik was a man of "doing," or practice, and, at the same time, "intellectualizing"—"a revolutionary intellectual" as Rodney labeled him. For academia, there could be no greater insult. Rodney's tutor stated, "There is no such thing. One can be an intellectual or one can be revolutionary. You can't combine the two . . . the moment he moves into practical activity he must abandon intellectualism." To be chastised in the classroom, told or ordered onto the correct path, can work in exactly the opposite way it is intended; in this case, Rodney learned the lesson: "I felt that somehow being a revolutionary intellectual might be a goal to which one might aspire," he recalls, "for surely there was no real reason why one should remain in the academic world . . . and at the same time not be a revolutionary."[37]

Rodney was exploring a world that was beginning to emerge from centuries of slavery and colonialism. Clive Yolande Thomas, a comrade and friend, describes the period in terms of the possibilities and the sense of hope: "We felt the world was really our oyster. . . . So many people of our generation were motivated to do something toward the development of a more prosperous society, and certainly to re-establish dignity and development of the West Indian people."[38] None of these extraordinary trips alone made Rodney a Marxist, but they did constitute one of the "little levers" that pushed him further along the path.

By mid-1963, Rodney was finishing his first degree—the first step toward an academic career. The intelligence report on Rodney recorded that from December 1962 to June 1963, "he seems to have been politically inactive, probably because he was preparing for his finals." The file acknowledged Rodney's seriousness, "a diligent and intelligent student," who graduated with first-class honors. After pausing to complete his studies, he quickly returned to activism as a "sympathizer" of the Young Socialist League, a left-wing grouping within the opposition People's National Party (PNP), whose objective, according to the intelligence file, "was social revolution in Jamaica. It was non-violent."[39]

The University of Guyana was ready to secure him a post, on condition that he continue his studies and obtain a higher degree; the Institute of Social and Economic Research at UWI offered him a short-term contract as an assistant researcher. However, Rodney decided to apply for a doctorate in the UK—at Cambridge, Oxford, and Edinburgh, and, in last place, the School of Oriental and African Studies (SOAS) at the University of London. In an entry dated June 1964, his "student record"—a document noting his academic progress from school to his completed bachelor's in history at UWI—states:

> Walter Rodney entered the University College in October 1960 on an Open Scholarship. He was nominated for the Faculty of Arts Prize at the end of his first year. Awarded the BWIA prize [a "student of the year" award sponsored by the British West Indian Airways] as the outstanding second year male student in the College.

Walter's professor of history commented in the report: "Rodney is a first-class man. Intends to specialise in African History and has an excellent future before him in that field."[40]

Studying in the UK must have seemed an obvious choice for Rodney. Still, he had no illusions: he knew that the UK had been the violent center of the slave trade, and that Europe was a center of the modern world of which he was already an astute critic. Moreover, Rodney's life in Kingston had not been solely about debate and academic study. While he was at the UWI, he had also started a relationship with Patricia Henry, who lived in Guyana and, quite soon after they met, left to study nursing in the UK in 1961. They kept in touch by letter, then resumed their relationship in London in 1963. Their life together soon began.

A Young Historian in London

Walter arrived in the UK in September 1963, after a sea voyage on the *Solingen*, part of the Hamburg-America Line, which docked in Hamburg for a few days before going on to the UK. Arriving in the UK must have been exciting and disturbing—this was the country whose history of kings and queens he had been taught, where the school textbooks in Georgetown were written, and where the profits from the slave plantation of the New World had been amassed. The country had been transformed by the arrival of large numbers of Caribbean workers, recruited to work in an expanding welfare state that had emerged in the aftermath of the Second World War—which had ended only eighteen years before.

Between 1948 and 1970, almost half a million people left the West Indies to live in Britain, traveling on boat from more than twenty Caribbean islands. When Rodney arrived in the UK, there was already a considerable number of people who had recently arrived from Jamaica, Barbados, Trinidad, and Guyana. Many came to work for a short time and then return home; others had been recruited because the UK was chronically short of workers to run hospitals and an expanding transport system. Some were former soldiers from the West Indies who had fought in the Second World War.

Some figures will serve to indicate what the country—and London in particular—would have felt like to a twenty-one-year-old Guyanese student. Linda McDowell, a UK-based human geographer, writes:

> From 1948 when the *Empire Windrush* arrived until 1952, between 1,000 and 2,000 people from the Caribbean entered Britain each year, followed by a steady and rapid rise until 1957, when 42,000 migrants from the New Commonwealth, mainly from the Caribbean, entered. The numbers declined by almost a half in the two succeeding years but by 1960 had increased again to 58,000, and then in 1961 more than doubled, in anticipation of the 1962 Commonwealth Immigrants Act that would restrict opportunities for entry. By 1961, according to the national population census, the number of people living in England and Wales who were born in the Caribbean was just over 161,000: 90,000 men and just over 71,000 women.[41]

Many of these newly arrived workers were highly skilled and experienced—yet they faced immediate prejudice and were frequently consigned to menial positions: street cleaning, portering, and general laboring. McDowell, for example, reports that "[o]ver half the men from the Caribbean initially accepted jobs with a lower status than their skills and experience qualified them for."[42] As demand for skilled labor increased through the 1950s, the UK's National Health Service became more aggressive in their recruitment strategy, sending managers and politicians to various islands of the Caribbean to employ trained nurses to come to the UK, offering some training to become nurses (an opportunity that Patricia had taken up). The process of recruitment in the Caribbean was fairly systematic. Across the UK's colonial empire in 1955, sixteen had established recruitment agencies to supply candidates to travel to the UK, many of whom trained as nurses. As Marxist historian Peter Fryer wrote, in his magisterial history of Black settlement in the UK, "[W]illing black hands drove tube trains, collected bus fares, emptied hospital patients' bed-pans."[43]

Contradictions were also rampant. For instance, in 1963 the Conservative health minister, Enoch Powell (who later led a racist campaign for tighter controls on immigration), was personally involved in a campaign to employ trained doctors and nurses from the former colonies (now increasingly part of the British Commonwealth). More than eighteen thousand were recruited from India and Pakistan alone.

These were processes that involved the continued underdevelopment of the former colonies by the metropolitan power—a relationship that had been established over centuries of exploitation. Wealth, education, and expertise were systematically drained from the (ex-)colonies in recruitment drives and publicity campaigns that spoke of a new life that could be led in the UK. For thousands, however, the reality was very different.

One woman, who had come to the UK from the Caribbean in the 1950s to train as a nurse, recalled:

> We were told to clean lockers and the beds, we were made to go and clean the wheelchairs and the commodes . . . we did a lot of menial jobs. . . . When I first started coming in the country and was nursing, the older patient was not used to black people so they were very nasty. They will take their things and throw at you or call you black and whatever and things like that.[44]

Orchestrated racism whipped up by politicians and racist groups was also part of the welcome party for new arrivals.

However, it was also a time of record levels of employment. With real wages rising by more than 25 percent between 1952 and 1962, the economy drew in thousands, which meant that the most menial jobs were "left" to the skilled workers arriving from the Caribbean and elsewhere. Most of those who arrived inclined toward the big cities—especially London, but also cities and towns in the North, like Bradford.[45]

The reception of those who arrived was harsh and frequently brutal. Academic Ruth Brown writes that "[b]y 1964 virtually no Member of Parliament in the [House of] Commons would speak out openly in favour of unrestricted immigration and by the mid-to late 1960s levels of immigration from the Commonwealth were down to virtually zero as a direct result of government legislation."[46] But what had changed? The UK economy was no longer as buoyant as it had been, and new arrivals became useful scapegoats for politicians. Increasingly, restrictions on immigration, supported by Tory and Labour politicians alike, came into force.

Racist violence had been a serious threat to Black communities across the country since the late 1940s. Even by the mid-1950s, white working-class "Teddy Boys" were organizing openly against newly arrived Black families in the country. In addition, white working-class attitudes were exploited by Oswald Mosley's Union Movement—a fascist organization with a long pedigree on the Far Right of the British political scene—and other explicitly racist groups, such as the White Defence League. Violent attacks and rioting by groups of racists marked the period—including a 1958 episode in Notting Hill when approximately four hundred white people attacked a West Indian community in the area.[47]

This was Rodney's welcome—a divided and racist UK, full of prejudice and misinformation, but that offered a brilliant young scholar from Guyana opportunities to study in its most prestigious universities. The experience was simultaneously exhilarating and repellent. Walter explained in an interview his impressions of arriving in the UK in vivid detail:

> [H]ere I was within the society which had dominated our way of thinking in the British Caribbean. It's the kind of experience which has to be lived to be understood, for it's very difficult to communicate to others. Probably the only people who have succeeded in some measure in communicating what it means to be a colonial going to the metropole have been novelists, because there is an emotive quality that must be conveyed by the artist. There are a host of emotions and fears, phobias and illusions and disillusionments that come from looking at that very, very cold society; the cold buildings, the cold people, the cold food, and everything else that one had to come up against.[48]

To start with, it looked as though Rodney was heading for Oxford and Nuffield College. In the end, though, he opted for SOAS, in the center of London's Bloomsbury district—an area of the city that is wealthy and cosmopolitan, with bookshops, high-end stores, and universities.

Life in the Metropolis

When Walter arrived in London, Patricia was already living in the city and studying nursing at the Royal Northern Hospital; she lived at a facility run by the hospital on Holloway Road. The couple passed much of their time in Islington (which was not the chic, upper middle-class neighborhood that it is today) in South East London—a poor working-class borough of the city with a large African and Caribbean population. London was the only real choice for Walter—indeed, life in the pretty, green university city of Oxford would have been stifling. When Walter arrived in London in 1963, he lived with Albert (known as "Al") Parkes in the South London district of Brockley. Walter and Al had been high school friends in Guyana, so it was natural for them to share an apartment. When Walter and Patricia got married in January 1965, they moved, with Al, to an apartment in Golders Green in North London.

In London, there was life and action, and communities and faces from around the world. Walter and Patricia were welcomed by friends—along with Al Parkes, they were reunited with the Jamaicans Richard Small and Orlando Patterson, their Guyanese friend Ewart Thomas, and sev-. eral others. Rodney also immediately connected to his elder brother, Edward, or "Eddie" (whose birth name was "Lawrence"). Eddie had stowed away from Guyana at age fifteen; arriving in Liverpool as a minor, he was held at a Borstal—a youth detention center. He later joined the Royal Air Force, then settled for a time in London.

In the two years since Walter's arrival, his relationship with Patricia had blossomed, and Al served as a witness when they married on January 2, 1965. The couple's wedding was simple, with a few friends and then a meal. Somewhat unusual for the time, it was not held in a church. Walter's father approved, and Patricia did not mind—remembering, years later, that Walter did not believe you had to "go to church to do good things."[49]

Patricia provides a vivid description of their lives together in London. Walter was extremely active—politically and socially. The young couple attended debates and meetings at the already-famous West African Students' Union (WASU), which was based in Central London's Convent Garden. Formed in 1925 in London, the Union was regarded as the training ground for nationalists and for several generations had welcomed students from West Africa and, increasingly, from the Caribbean. For some, WASU provided accommodation and financial support. However, it was principally not a welfare organization but a political and campaigning union. By the time Walter and Patricia started to attend its events, the Union had already spent years denouncing colonial racism, forced labor, the expropriation of land, and the unequal relationship linking the colonial metropoles with their African and colonial dependencies.[50]

In addition to these debates and meetings, Walter was a regular at Hyde Park corner, where street speakers would discuss political issues to assembled crowds. This was not the London "tourist attraction" that it is today, nor a peculiar cockney tradition of the city, but a real forum of debate and political discussion. Rodney's skills as a debater were perfect for this weekly street scene; he spoke on African and Caribbean politics, and racism in the UK and the United States. His passionate desire to speak from below—from the soapbox on the London streets or the oil drum in the Kingston slum, rather than in lofty debate chambers, university venues, or "official" government buildings—never left him.

In 1975, Rodney described the atmosphere at these Hyde Park gatherings, and the mix of real debate and "freaks": "It was, of course, a place where a number of freak shows were also held, a place where things were said that weren't serious. But quite a number of West Indians did go there as a meeting place, as an expression that they were under pressure and they wanted to find ways of talking and dealing with their exploitation and racism."[51] This was a time, Rodney later recalled, when he was reading Marx extensively and had realized the urgency of relating to "working people." Hyde Park was one of the forums where he could do this, speaking there for the three years he was in the UK, every summer "from the time it got warm enough to speak until the time it was too cold to speak."[52]

Patricia, describing her impressions of Walter, says that what attracted her to him was

> [h]is simplicity. I think he was a very sincere person. I think he was a very attractive man. He was a very interesting person, a very intellectual person, but he did not behave in that way that most people who had higher education behaved. He wasn't arrogant, he was a very simple person who could talk about anything, could associate with any and everybody. He was always somebody who I felt very comfortable with, and I think we enjoyed a lot of the same things. He liked dancing, he liked music.[53]

Throughout their life together, they shared the domestic work. When Patricia was working night shifts at the hospital, Walter would prepare the meal when he returned from the library. Though Patricia was the mainstay of the family, there was not a strict division of labor. Walter "was a very good cook," Patricia recalled, and taught her a number of recipes. "He loved Chinese food and he is very good at Chinese food. . . . Coming from a large family I didn't have to cook and I never had to cook, so really he did a lot of that."[54]

Rodney was fully aware of how his experience, as a reasonably well-funded graduate student, was distinct from most Caribbean men and women, who were forced to scrape together a living at the bottom of an inhospitable and racist society. These "contradictions" he felt through his life—as a scholarship student, as a PhD candidate in London, and then as a university lecturer in Tanzania. Simultaneously, in his political life and activism, Walter sought constantly to break down these barriers. In

London, living with his friend Al, and then with Patricia, mixing with his friends in South East London, he was never far from the realities of life for most Black people in 1960s England.

However, he felt the differences acutely when attending university seminars, socializing with other PhD researchers and lecturers, and traveling around Europe for his research. Reflecting on this period years later, he explained:

> Here was I, as a young migrant if you like, part of a migrant community, but functioning in exactly the same way as most of my brothers and sisters who were worker-migrants. They were directly involved in production. They had to deal with discrimination where it mattered, at the job and in getting a job; and having got the job they had to deal with discrimination in housing, which as a student, if you wanted to, you could avoid. In fact, though, I was living outside the university all the time, so that I did have a touch of what it meant to go to doors in answer to an advertisement and knock and be told that it was already taken once the landlady perceived the colour of my face.[55]

Consciously surrounding himself with "real experiences" and people, not the rarefied and privileged minorities at university—even among other African and Caribbean students—Rodney immersed himself in the world of his brother Eddie, Al (who worked in London), and later in his wife's daily toil in a city hospital.

Learning from Eddie and the political migrant life his brother led, Walter absorbed, in his words, "from the mass of migrant workers."[56] He quickly became part of London's migrant "working community"; indeed, this was perhaps the most important thing for him. Walter and Patricia took in a Guyanese woman, Ms. Duncan, who became a kind of adoptive mom to the couple, along with many other young Caribbean people living in the city. She was a caregiver for children and pieceworker seamstress in London's sweating system—where workers would receive the materials to do the work in their own homes. Patricia recalls how important Ms. Duncan and Al were to the couple: "Al was a major part of our life in London. He and Mom were witnesses at our civil wedding."[57]

Toward a PhD in Bloomsbury

This cocktail of experiences—Rodney's life as a student, dedicated to his research and reading, and his permanent, conscious jostle with the real experiences of migrant life in the UK—drew him closer to Marxism as a "lived practice," as opposed to a mere component in a course on "political thought." As he remembered, "For the first time, I realized that this was not just material within a course, or a segment within a totality of bourgeois knowledge, but that it had something fundamentally different to offer." Contemporaneous developments in the world also contributed to Rodney's intellectual work, specifically the "transformational experiences" in China; he explained the Chinese Revolution as having an "important emotional appeal because it was a non-white country at a time when one's racial consciousness was very high."[58]

The experience of trying to make it in a UK university, in a hostile city, was grueling, but Rodney survived. Indeed, the prejudice came quick and fast. As he enrolled at SOAS, the question was raised of whether he was suitably qualified to start a PhD, despite his first-class honors from the UWI (then known as the University College of the West Indies, UCWI). Until 1962, it was a branch—literally a college—of the University of London, no different (theoretically) than any other college in London or elsewhere. But Rodney had come from the colonies, and to the deeply conservative staff at SOAS, UWI was merely a colonial outpost.

The process of enrolling—never mind Rodney's glowing references, academic record, and extracurricular achievements—was arduous and humiliating, even though his Student Record from the UWI clearly stated that the college was "in special relationship with the University of London, and its courses and examinations are of the same standard . . . as those of London University."[59] The issue of his enrollment had to be "debated," as he later recalled: "[O]ne had to vindicate oneself."[60] The wider significance was not lost on Rodney: "The colonial had to show that colonized people had the same capacity. . . . The moment you go there you're under that load, that you're not just you, but you are a representative of a whole people, who have been victimised, and who not only have been victimised but who are also regarded as agents of their own victimisation."[61]

SOAS, which had until recently been an openly colonial institution that was training officials in "native affairs" in Africa and the "Orient," was still overwhelmingly bourgeois—without a hint of the creeping radicalism that had started to infect the London School of Economics in the period, for example. The institution was dripping in the "defence of bourgeois ideology," as Rodney put it. He describes the Tuesday seminars as the most urbane seminar that you could think of, led by all these deans of knowledge on Africa, who had this tremendous flair for keeping everybody at a lower level. Even if one were an African or West Indian, and one wanted to talk about the questions in the seminar, they could dominate partly because of their greater expertise, and familiarity with the paper, and partly because they had been at this for a long time.[62]

Shocking though this description is, thirty years later, when I myself studied at SOAS, the seminars—held now on Friday afternoon—were similarly august events, deeply hierarchical and often unpleasant in the time-honored manner of academic discussions. Seminars were full of senior scholars, as Rodney remembered, with a well-honed flair for keeping people in their place; if you wanted to leave intact, you either said nothing or spoke in deference to the scholarly hierarchy, citing the relevant literature and "authorities." Rodney recalls how these authorities "represented the outgrowth of centuries of an intellectual tradition."[63] Well-trained, disciplined, and frequently (though narrowly) bright, these pillars of the academic establishment were both a deadweight on learning and guardians of the correct scholarship. The history department, in Rodney's time, was led by Roland Oliver and John D. Fage, conservative "Africanists" typical of the period (though Fage moved to the University of Birmingham in 1963). Thirty years later, it was Richard Fardon and Graham Furniss who played the same role as gatekeepers of the university's academic standards. It is one thing to experience the force of this world, as a white man in the 1990s, and be disgusted by it; for Rodney, three decades earlier and from the Caribbean, the impact was far more dramatic.

Yet there was no one better equipped to deal with the experience than Rodney. He could have abandoned the misery of the weekly seminars, and shrunk away into his research, but he dealt with them differently: "[M]y own response was to try and cope with it," he explained.[64] He was helped in this determination by a sympathetic supervisor, Richard Gray, who had, as Rodney recorded, "certain basic skills as well as integrity." Though he was a "liberal bourgeois historian," Gray encouraged Rodney to develop his own view, while directing his research where necessary, including toward Italy and the archives held at the Vatican, where Gray had direct experience and expertise.

On Gray's recommendation, Rodney was invited to be the keynote speaker at an event in February 1966 on African history, held at an adult-education college in Buckinghamshire called Missenden Abbey. Lecturing on the "early history of Africa," he was the only nonwhite speaker in the entire program. Following the weekend conference, he was praised in a letter from the organizer for his "first class lecture . . . this set the scene admirably for the weekend . . . and the splendid way in which you handled the discussion period."[65]

Quite soon after the two became student and supervisor, Gray sent typed letters to Walter, who was already visiting an archive in Lisbon, with brief feedback on a seminar paper his student was planning to present later that term. In the first of these, sent January 27, 1964, he writes of his student's PhD: "I had hoped that the paper would help to focus your ideas for the subject as a whole and act as an interim plan of campaign." He observes that the last time they met—only months after the PhD had begun—he was left with a "vague impression" of what the problem was that Walter was planning to deal with: "In a subject so large as the one in which you are engaged it is I think imperative to keep re-defining in greater detail your major questions, and this is all the more important in a subject such as this where the evidence is so scattered and fragmentary." He encourages his student to "jot down," once the seminar paper is done, the preliminary chapters and subheadings, "highly tentative" as they will be at this stage. He then urged Walter to target specific files in the archive in Lisbon—with details of writers and documents he could consult—then concluded his letter, "[Y]ou must be prepared to sift through a lot of irrelevant material to find your grains of gold!"[66] He opened the second letter, sent February 4, by typing "Dear Walter," and then writes—in pen—"may we drop formalities and please feel free to drop the Dr. G." Richard's letters to Walter are supportive and friendly; commenting on his student's seminar paper, which he "liked very much indeed," he encourages his student to include "ethnographic background," and, at the end of the short note, he queries Walter's "use of the word 'native'; would not 'African'; or the name of a tribe be more appropriate?"[67] All of this advice—thoughtful, and not overly "directive"—was sound research supervision.

Additional funding for the research was provided by a grant from Senate House, the administrative center of the University of London—which allocated the funds on the advice of the Central Research Funds Committee. Rodney was already well versed in the academic nightmare of applying for research funding for every trip or research expedition, not to mention extra expenses. This pattern of applications, deadlines, and submissions for funds was one that would continue, uninterrupted, for the rest of his life. The approval of the committee included £256 (a little under $7,000 today) for travel to Spain, Portugal, and Italy and "additional maintenance" and travel in these countries.[68]

There was a habit of thoroughness—playing by the rules—that Rodney learned at SOAS. He recalled:

> One had to master that because, if one didn't, it was as though one was speaking of "sour grapes." One could never challenge them unless one was up to those criteria. In a way it was good thing, too, because even if some of the extensive reading was reading of useless material which, in the end, you found out was loaded and ideologically very hostile, nevertheless, it was an intellectual exercise, a mental exercise that lent discipline.[69]

There were no shortcuts for Rodney, and he applied himself to "mastering details" in his work and encouraged, a few years later, his students to do the same. This rigor was necessary, he believed, to better take on the gatekeepers of the academic establishment, by challenging their hegemony over scholarship and learning. As Rodney understood it, one had to master the fundamental techniques of boxing—the jab, the uppercut, the cross, and the hook—in order to knock out the opponent—without this training, Rodney believed, you were simply leaving the "ring" in the hands of the enemy.

However, Rodney argued, one had to establish a clear boundary; if it was not, there was the danger—rife in academic life—that a radical student would simply be transformed by the academy into yet another establishment scholar. According to him, "The format in which you operate, the journals in which you publish, the language in which you express yourself, the people to whom you feel responsible for justifying this or that position, the books that you are called upon to review and so on, makes you a part of this bourgeois academic community."[70] Rodney saw SOAS as a training ground, on which much of his learning had to be rejected. However, this could only be accomplished on the basis of "mastering" the academic ropes in the first place: "The game is to show that, after all, if one is in a given field, you must start with so and so and come down the line and pay your deference to each one of these authorities through your intellectual work. That is ultimately self-defeating, and in fact has quite clearly defeated a number of us who have entered this field."[71] Many more, Rodney admits, have been defeated by the field, failing to knock out the opponent in the academic ring.

The main purpose of Walter's life in London was his PhD, and he dedicated himself to the research with his typical dedication and brilliance. Completed under circumstances that were far from straightforward, his research entailed intense study and archival work on the genealogy of the Portuguese slave trade in West Africa. Like many PhDs, the work and research—initially suggested to him by his supervisor, Richard Gray—meant he had to visit archives, which in this case included ones in Lisbon, Seville, and Rome. He delved into old Portuguese manuscripts, the writings of friars of the Spanish Catholic Church (who carried out mission work in Africa), and the Vatican Archives, where he examined records on the Jesuit missions to Guinea. Already proficient in Spanish, Rodney also learned to read Portuguese and Italian. Travel was not always straightforward for him, given that he was a Black man from the Caribbean traveling to dictatorships in Spain and Portugal. However, because he was proficient in the countries' languages, he was able to navigate them relatively easily. Of course, both Spain and Portugal had African colonies, and long (and brutal) histories with the continent; therefore, Black people were not uncommon in either of their capitals.

Navigating the complex labyrinth of SOAS while trying to develop his own understanding of Marxism meant that Walter had to work out numerous concepts for himself, with little formal assistance. SOAS, at the time, was entirely devoid of radical scholars, or anyone seriously engaging with Marxism. The task, therefore, of reading Marxism by himself, and then attempting to apply it to the "historical data," was "painful." Nevertheless, on July 5, 1966, a few hours after the birth of his first child, Shaka, Walter became Dr. Rodney upon the successful defense of his dissertation, "A History of the Upper Guinea Coast, 1545–1800."

Completed in less than three years, the PhD was not published as a book until 1970. The text traces the history of a part of the West African coast from modern-day Gambia to Liberia, beginning from first contact with Hispano-Portuguese sailors in the mid-fifteenth century. In 1965, Rodney described his research as covering "the coastal areas between Gambia and Cape Mount, and seek[ing] to reconstruct the society of that region, and to measure the impact of external forces acting from the interior and from the Atlantic." He continued: "Both the wide time-span and the general nature of my enquiries have led me to reflect upon the Upper Guinea Coast in the context of the whole West African littoral."[72]

Rodney challenged contemporary scholarship on account of its cautious and conservative approach, and its imposition of colonial borders and frontiers on pre-colonial societies. The work traces the complex network of coastal societies prior to European contact, challenging still-fashionable fallacies of "primitive" stateless coastal societies. In the text, Rodney also embraces the nuanced complexity of the evolving Afro-European trade, illustrating the shifts in African social formations as they were transformed, and deformed, by the slave trade. He emphasized that while the continent was fundamentally shaped by European contact, Africans were not simply passive observers of these processes.

The complexity of the book and its nuanced reading of history—a debunking of colonial and academic myths that accorded Africans agency—showed the influence of Rodney's reading of Marxism on his research. However, ten years after it was completed, he was clear that it was certainly not "a strong statement of Marxian scholarship by any means. It was just strong enough, let's say, to upset some members of the establishment who perceived the direction in which I was trying to move."[73] The book is better than that, and it remains an exciting and important study today—a remarkable achievement for a piece of work written by a twenty-four-year-old.

All chapters in it are worthy of study, but perhaps the final one "Slave Trading: 1690-1800" is the most astonishing. It powerfully debunks myths current at the time, and still popular today, including the argument that the Atlantic trade was somehow built on preexisting slavery in West Africa—this is nonsense, says Rodney. One comment—notable in its way—gives a sense of the shibboleths he was challenging in the book. Discussing traditional society, Rodney writes, "[F]ar too often there has been a ready acceptance of reports on West Africa in the eighteenth and nineteenth centuries as representing certain timeless institutions, and it is even assumed that field studies of 'indigenous' African societies in the twentieth century disclose a fundamentally unchanged pattern."[74] This attitude is totally misleading, he explains—all aspects of society, "social, political and economic" in West Africa, had become reorganized over the centuries of the Atlantic trade to secure a flow of slaves to the coast.

For the purposes of the PhD, Rodney had managed to survive the bourgeois trapeze—delivering a work of serious, radical, *and* respectable scholarship to pass his exam, but also managing to say things that were in many ways groundbreaking. Nigel Westmaas, a scholar of Rodney, explains the power of the book's contribution—which rings out loudly even today:

> [T]he analysis of the slave trade was significant for the manner in which he parted company with the method of European scholars who had tended, up to that point to examine and measure the slave trade from the vantage point of its repercussions on Europe and the Americans. In direct contrast Rodney's emphasis was clearly the impact of the slave trade on Africa especially in the West Coast and interior. He dissected the ways in which these traditional African societies were weakened in economic, social, political and cultural term.[75]

London's Marxists

In the story of Rodney's self-education as a Marxist in London, the Caribbean radical C. L. R. James played a significant role. Rodney found the political climate on the Left in the UK inhospitable, remote, and "not conducive . . . there was nothing on the English political scene as such that was helpful."[76] This is a harsh statement; the radical Left was small, but vibrant. On the anti-Stalinist Left, serious and important developments were taking a new and revolutionary direction as they attempted to chart a path between Maoism, Guevarism, and Stalinism. Yet these groups were miniscule, almost entirely white, and seemed extremely remote—even irrelevant—to Rodney's political concerns.

The tiny groups of the "Trotskyist" fringe—who were fairly unique in developing a thorough anti-Stalinist critique—offered little to this young radical from Guyana. In fact, these groups were lumped together in Rodney's mind as "old Communist party types." The official Communist Party of Great Britain (CPGB), at its peak in the 1940s, had a membership of almost sixty thousand. By the time of the 1956 crisis, after the Hungarian Revolution, it was only about half that figure; indeed, the Hungarian Revolution was a shocking wake-up call for the Left. The country was formerly communist and under Soviet influence, and the revolution, led by the militant working class and youth against the government, caused a deep and lasting period of soul-searching for the international Left. The revolution was crushed by a Soviet intervention. By the mid-1960s, it had hemorrhaged membership, though its influence continued, especially in the unions and the Labour Left.

The one or two "young Trotskyite types" Rodney did encounter appeared to him as pompous and ridiculous, particularly in their assertion that they constituted a "movement." Rodney records that "[f]rom then and until now [1975], I've always found it difficult to understand what Trotskyism is because I couldn't really get anything out of these people's positions. It tended to be inarticulate. It tended to be whimsical. It tended to be downright foolish on many questions."[77] For Rodney, the Trotskyist Left in the UK would also have seemed overwhelmingly white, Eurocentric, and focused almost exclusively on questions that did not directly address his concerns, or those of the developing world and specifically the Caribbean and African world.

Many members of the radical, anti-Stalinist Left were lukewarm on Third World issues, unlike the CPGB, which had an Africa section under the leadership of Jack Woddis (who wrote a number of studies on the continent). The Soviet Union also had strong connections with some of the liberation movements, and members in the UK were active in anti-apartheid movements and other organizations. Prominent Communist Party members like Ruth First and Joe Slovo had settled in the UK in the 1960s.

It is worth citing Rodney extensively on his experience of the Left in the UK, both inside and outside the Communist Party—one that is hauntingly familiar to many who know the radical Left then and now:

> All I knew was that I didn't want to be in some of these movements that were called Marxist—neither the Communist party, which was old and effete with an average age, it seemed to me, of about 60 or 65, with most everybody there past working age, nor the Trotskyites, who were something else again, the result of a period of sectarianism that had gone on for decades. One would come across Trotskyites factions within which I found majority and minority elements. And then I heard about factions! And one would go to conferences and you would find that there was a faction comprising two people. They had been struggling and defending the truth for 30 years, since the 1930s, and of course, if one of them died, that would leave one person to guard the whole destiny of the human race by concentrating on this particular version of what was accurate. And often, as I said, it was just foolish. From any perspective it didn't make any sense. It certainly was not about struggle against capitalism.[78]

However, remembering the period later, Rodney was careful to distinguish between "Trotskyism," as it presented itself to him the mid-1960s in the UK, and "Trotsky's role in the Russian Revolution." More on this will be said later, but Rodney had high praise of Leon Trotsky's historical involvement in the revolution, as well as his towering *History of the Russian Revolution.*

In his later writings, Rodney touches on an even more uncomfortable truth about the period and its left politics. He found the small groups remote and obscure, removed from the realities of working-class life and people. The Left appeared to him divided and sectarian, in spite of serious efforts and developments that were underway; of course, many of these would have been difficult to see from the vantage of the early and mid-1960s. Small groups like the International Socialists, formerly the Socialist Review Group, were "unorthodox Trotskyists" who had broken, under their leading figure, the Jewish Palestinian Tony Cliff, with the sectarianism of the "Trotskyite" Left that Rodney caricatures. The group developed an important part of their politics from an analysis of the anti-colonial movements and the role of class and organization in the Third World. They did not simply beat the drum of Third World revolutions, in Cuba and parts of Africa and Vietnam, but attempted to understand and unpick what they characterized as "deflected" movements, led by a petty-bourgeois elite. Yet during Rodney's relatively short sojourn in the UK in the 1960s, the group was small enough that it would have been difficult, though not impossible, to glimpse their activities. Until the mid-1960s, there were between two and three hundred members in the International Socialists, and its base was not so much students as Labour Party Young Socialists (mainly nonstudent, white-collar workers). It did, however, have a relatively high profile on account of its publication of the youth paper *Young Guard*, which had a certain impact in the Labour Party.[79] In fact, some of their class analysis and critiques of the early post-colonial experiments in socialism were remarkably similar to ones that Rodney developed himself over the next fifteen years.

When it came to the part of the Left that surrounded the *New Left Review* (*NLR*), a publication set up in the aftermath of the Hungarian Revolution by former Communist Party intellectuals, Rodney was scathing: "[F]rom my brief meetings with some of them and my readings of their materials," he recalled, "my impression was that they tended to be very facile, within a tradition of attempting to be clever—the idea was who could put forth clever formulations."[80] That such individuals were arrogant and pretentious may well be true. But the *NLR* did publish some important work on Africa that would have been relevant to Rodney's concerns—not least Tom Wengraf and Roger Murray's important article on

Algeria in 1963, or Perry Anderson's work on Portugal and its colonies. The *NLR* also had links to the so-called African Research and Publications Bureau, run by a Tanzanian exile Dennis Phombeah.

Yet, Rodney argued, in none of these groups were there any serious efforts to mobilize workers or to address the situation of migrants. Running through Rodney's criticism of the Far Left in the UK at the time is a far more unpleasant fact. In his contact with activists, the *NLR* intellectuals at the London School of Economics, or Trotskyist students, he later described his relationship with them as "upsetting." Behind the politics and declarations, he found a "latent racism," as he recorded, "sometimes coming in paternalism, sometimes coming out in hostile manifestations."[81]

This amounted, Rodney noted, to a complete lack of curiosity and respect, and an inability to *listen* to someone from the Caribbean, and from a British colony, for his insights into political developments. Instead, Rodney encountered the habit of interrupting, belittling, and "talking over" with supposedly superior formulations and cleverer perspectives. Antiracism, Rodney knew, had to do not simply with taking the correct position but also with the directness with which one-to-one relationships were conducted. Beneath the surface, Rodney detected hostility and even racism on the radical Left. Many of the radical Left in the UK at the time had grown up with a whole set of imperialist assumptions, and they did not recognize just how deeply rooted they were.

However, Walter did find a political home on the British Left that was more conducive. The extraordinary Caribbean intellectual and revolutionary C. L. R. James had returned to the UK and was living in London with his wife, the writer Selma James. James was a towering figure. A Marxist of astonishing erudition, he had been a supporter of Trotsky in the 1930s and visited him in exile in Mexico City in 1939; later, he was a champion of the Ghanaian revolution led by Kwame Nkrumah in 1957. He was widely known as an editor and activist in Trinidad and a historian of the Haitian Revolution.

One comrade and friend of James, Ajit Mookerjee Roy, wrote of James in the 1930s:

> I had rarely come across a finer political polemicist than C. L. R. James. His attacks on Stalinism were absolutely devastating. He was then thinking in terms of building an independent Trotskyist party. I joined him readily. There was no doubt in my mind that all we had to do was to start with a clean slate. We had the answer to all the problems.[82]

When Rodney met James, he was a man in his sixties but still strong, tall, athletic—he too had been a keen cricketer, and he had just published a book on the sport, *Beyond a Boundary*. James was always elegantly turned out. The effect of meeting him for the first time must have been electrifying on Walter.

Rodney had already read James's book *The Black Jacobins*, on the Haitian Revolution of 1791–1804, while in Jamaica, and its impact had been profound. "One could recognise one's self in that history. One could feel with it . . . *The Black Jacobins*, which was about black people involved in revolution, involved in making choices, involved in real movements of history, in which there were splits and some people fell by the wayside."[83] James's influence on a radicalizing Caribbean was immense, and Walter felt his presence long before they actually met. "James exercised a sort of model image for many young West Indian progressives. Again, and even before one had fully come to terms with the question of Marxist ideology, he did stand out . . . it was as simple as that."[84] Curiously, C. L. R. had a reputation as a prominent Marxist and (former) Trotskyist—a fact that was not missed on Walter.

By 1963, the Jameses were in London—though still traveling back and forth to the Caribbean. For two or three years, Walter was a dedicated member of a study group organized around the presence of the couple. Meeting regularly, the group gave him the chance to do the studying and reading that was not taught or encouraged at SOAS. As he explained, it helped him "to acquire a knowledge of Marxism, a more precise understanding of the Russian Revolution, and of historical formations."[85] Run by Richard Small and Norman Girvan, the study group was organized around C. L. R. and Selma and held in North London. The group focused specifically on West Indian students in the city. The requirements were considerable: with occasional papers prepared by members of the group, and a substantial range of readings that extended beyond Marx, to include Hegel, Heidegger, and many others. The group was fortunate to have C. L. R. as its guiding influence, but also for not having a strict political or party line to enforce. There was no encouragement to learn quotes or memorize passages—as you might do in a Bible study group or in another left-wing reading group. The aim was, rather, to be immersed in the history and method of Marxism.

Through his participation in the group, C. L. R. James gave Rodney a full historical understanding of Marxism, explaining that "it was not enough to study Lenin's *State and Revolution*. It was important to understand why it was written and what was going on in Russia at that precise point in time."[86] With James at the service of the group, this vital, indispensable context—the "historical situation"—was always at hand. After all, here was a man who had met one of the leading revolutionaries of the Russian Revolution. At a public meeting called for the fiftieth anniversary of the Russian Revolution in London in October 1967, James remarked on the Trotskyist movement in the 1930s: "At that time in the Trotskyist movement I more or less was the Third World."[87]

During their meetings, James ensured that Marxist theory—the focus of the group—was tightly threaded with history, without which he believed it would be unmoored and rootless. He would often interrupt the discussion to provide historical details to the group or to explain where a polemic had originated. As Rodney recalled, James would explain, "[T]his is what Lenin was about; this is what Trotsky was doing; he had just come from this conference or this debate, or this was his specific programmatic objective when he was writing and so on."[88]

Reflecting in 1980 on this time, James remarked on the differences between the generations that had come from the Caribbean. The foundations of analysis in the 1960s, he argued, had already been built by a former generation that included Aimé Césaire, George Padmore, W. E. B. Du Bois, and Frantz Fanon (whose work Rodney would come to admire greatly). James, too, was a representative of this group. As James wrote:

> [W]e had to fight the doctrines of the imperialist powers in order to establish some Caribbean foundation or foundations for the underdeveloped peoples. *Walter did not have to do that.* Walter grew up in an atmosphere where for the first time a generation of West Indian intellectuals was able, not only to study the revolutionary and creative works that had been created in Europe, but also to benefit from and be master of what had been done in the same tradition in direct reference to the Caribbean.[89]

These foundations were central to who Rodney could become, and how he was able to quickly access a body of political work that asserted the history and politics of the Caribbean, written by its colonial subjects. As James described:

> To be born in 1942 [Rodney's birth year] was to have behind you a whole body of work dealing in the best way with the emerging situation

in the Caribbean and the colonial world. That was Walter Rodney. He grew up in the world . . . where Nkrumah succeeded in securing independence for the Gold Coast and establishing Ghana; then a little later Nyerere did so for Tanganyika, which united with Zanzibar to become Tanzania. Walter had an upbringing and development which many of you cannot quite appreciate, because to you it is natural. To him, it was not, it was something new. That is why when he completed his studies, he was able to build on these foundations. The work that had been necessary to motivate him to study Africa and the Caribbean had been done already. That is an aspect of the importance of the personality and particular politics of Walter Rodney.[90]

There might be some exaggeration in James's formulation, though. Rodney and his classmates in Guyana were, after all, forced to fashion for themselves a course on slavery and history in the Caribbean. However, many of these foundations *were* taught in London, and James was central to that pedagogy. Rodney would soon become a pioneer in his own work, contributing in ways that James could not have predicted.

Selma James was an impressive figure. An American, she was a Marxist, feminist, and activist with many years' experience. While Selma was almost thirty years her husband's junior, she was nevertheless an intellectual force to be reckoned with, and this was abundantly apparent in the group's meetings. She was proud, forceful, opinionated, and sharp-witted, a sort of personality quite unfamiliar to Walter and the other students.

Walter explained that she would take a ridiculous position, and when she "was finished indicated why it was foolish, one had very little doubt about its foolishness. She did, along with C. L. R., exemplify the power of Marxist thought."[91] One could not go into a discussion with the Jameses ill prepared or take a position of a "leading bourgeois critic" and expect to get away with it. The group had a lasting influence on Rodney's work, as well as his own study and appreciation of Marxism—he went on to run similar study groups with students in Tanzania and Guyana.

C. L. R. James was also an influence on Walter in another respect. By the time the men met, James was a proven public intellectual; he readily addressed not only large crowds, such as at the end of a demonstration in Trafalgar Square, but also small groups of Caribbean students in the kitchens and living rooms of the capital. Even as an old man, James was ready to get his hands dirty in the daily nitty-gritty of building "cadres" among Caribbean and working-class youth.[92] Rodney noted, in the mid-1970s, that

> James has become a model of the possibilities of retaining one's intellectual and ideological integrity over a protracted period of time. In other words, I've always said to myself that I hoped that at his age, if I'm around, I will still have some credibility as a progressive, that people wouldn't look around and say, "This used to be a revolutionary." [93]

Heading South

Walter and Patricia had a plan, but, like all plans, it came with interruptions and unforeseen circumstances. The couple were on a temporary stay in the UK, while Walter completed his studies; when this was done, they would return to the Caribbean—and eventually to their home in Guyana. Nothing in the UK disabused them of this plan—the politics, climate, and life were meager in comparison. Walter was clear from the start that his commitment was to Guyana and the Caribbean, where his political heart and duty resided. He felt the pull of responsibility to a society and people who had facilitated his study, travel, and "privileges," while most of the population remained impoverished.

Initially, the couple envisaged working for a time in West Africa before returning to the Caribbean and the University of the West Indies, in Rodney's words, "to teach African history and to relate to our people on the African question." "Specifically," he notes, "I was returning to the Caribbean by way of Africa."[94] At the encouragement of his supervisor, Richard Gray, in November 1965 Walter wrote to Professor Terrance Ranger, head of history at the University of Dar es Salaam, about an appointment as lecturer in West African History. He explained that he was only seeking a temporary post at the Tanzanian university, on account of his commitments to the University of the West Indies, which meant that he needed to return to Jamaica in October 1967 to "start a programme in West African Studies."[95] In a letter dated March 14, Ranger wrote: "I am glad to be able to inform you at last that you are offered a post as lecturer in history here in Dar es Salaam . . . in this instance you will be offered an 18 month period of appointment."

Once more, Walter made a move between the University of London's affiliated "colleges," from Jamaica to London and on to Tanzania—the

University College Dar es Salaam, too, was an affiliate, through the University of East Africa. The college paid the airfares of the young family and provided accommodation on campus. They encouraged him to travel at the start of July—shortly after the formal completion of his PhD—for the start of the academic year in Dar es Salaam. In a welcoming tone, Ranger suggested the new lecturer "take advantage of your time in East Africa to attend the specialist East African lectures and seminars and to add an East African expertise to your West African." He concluded the letter, "May I again say how pleased I am that we shall be seeing you." [96]

Rodney's appointment in Tanzania was to be brief—only eighteen months—after which the family would return to the West Indies.

CHAPTER 2

Socialist Africa or African Socialism?

Walter and his small family, Patricia and Shaka, arrived in Tanzania at different times. Walter left for Dar es Salaam a week after the couple's son, Shaka, was born. As Patricia recalls, Walter had sent a telegram to his Uncle Henry stating, "Shaka and PhD received on the same day"—June 5. Patricia and their son joined him three weeks after Walter had left, traveling with Anne (Ms. Duncan's youngest daughter, aged seven). There was no time for family travel or a holiday, or even to take stock; he had been given clear instructions to begin work at the start of July, in preparation for the beginning of the academic year.

As Patricia describes her first impressions of the country, "Tanzania immediately entered my soul."[1] The country had been independent for only five years and bore all the contradictions of decolonization. A year after official "flag independence," on December 9, 1962, Tanganyika became a republic, with Julius Nyerere as president. From 1954, Nyerere had run the Tanganyika African National Union (TANU), whose principal objective was national sovereignty and independence from the British. He became prime minister in 1961, and president a year later.

Nyerere, a scholar famous for his writings on African socialism, cut an impressive profile. Less known, though, were his Kiswahili translations of *Julius Caesar* and *The Merchant of Venice* for Oxford University Press. He was an African socialist who promoted the ideology of "*Ujamaa*" ("familyhood" in Swahili) rather than Marxism-Leninism. He had studied at Makerere College in Uganda, then at Edinburgh University in the United Kingdom. A slight man with a high forehead and an ever-present stamp-sized mustache, he was always elegantly dressed, charming, and focused. Like many other new leaders of independent African countries, he presided over a nominally independent state—a contradiction in terms, to say the least. At the time, Tanganyika still depended on the British to purchase its exports of sisal, gold, coffee, cashew nuts, and cotton; the supply chains—where the exports went and how—were all tied to the former colonial state, its companies, businesses, and agents.[2]

The early years of the new state had been stormy, and at times its very existence was in peril. In 1963, a disputed election on the island of Zanzibar—off the coast of Tanzania's capital, Dar es Salaam—led to an uprising in January 1964 that overthrew the Arab dynasty, which had long claimed the island as theirs. Initially, the revolutionaries' actions were met with horror by the former colonial power, which threated to intervene. In the end, however, the island united with the mainland, and on October 29, 1964, the country, which now included Zanzibar, was renamed the United Republic of Tanzania.

Only a few years after its independence, the country faced another crisis. On January 19, 1964, a mutiny broke out among the Tanganyika Rifles soldiers—known as the Dar Mutiny—against their overwhelmingly white officers, which was crushed by British military forces who were ordered in by the president. The soldiers were clear about their demands—a substantial pay rise, the immediate dismissal of all the British officers, and assurances of no subsequent victimization of the mutineers. Similar anger was spilling over in other newly independent countries—expressing the slow pace of change, the frustrations at the continuity of colonial power on the continent, and continued massive inequality. The mutiny in July 1960 in Congo's capital, which helped to unravel the country's newly won independence, would have been present in Nyerere's mind. In the first decade of independence, new governments would call in the ex-colonial power to establish order from insurgent populations—in Senegal, Gabon, and the Congo, for example. Even in Ghana, which was led by the militant father of African independence, Kwame Nkrumah, Britain had left officials in charge of the army. By October 1964, Tanzania declared itself committed to socialist development.

In proclaiming its socialism, the new country was not particularly original—for decades, varieties of "socialism" had dominated the political scene around the world and especially among anti-colonial activists and movements. Whether these movements were Maoist—proclaiming loyalty to the Chinese Communist Party—or saw in the Soviet Union's rapid industrialization a model for Africa's own development, or even if these new governments did not align themselves explicitly to a Communist bloc, the influence of "Marxist" ideas and models was overwhelming. There were important differences, and these were frequently fought over; at the same time, some neighboring states rejected all association with socialism in the 1960s—for example, Kenya.

In the early period of independence, the ideas of "African socialism" were increasingly celebrated; they were seen as promising an authentic path to development based on the continent's supposed historical predilection to socialism or communalism. Kwame Nkrumah in Ghana, Tom Mboya in Kenya, and Julius Nyerere all presented their own versions of African socialism. Mboya, a trade unionist and leading nationalist, noted in 1963: "African socialism has an entirely different history from European socialism. . . . There is no such division into classes in Africa. . . . So there is no need in Africa to argue over ideology or define your actions in terms of doctrinaire theories."[3]

Such ideas were unsurprising, given the centuries of imperial and colonial control, in contrast to which proponents of African socialism declared the continent to have its own rich history that would determine its future development. But in the eyes of many, the ideas of African socialism, varied and nuanced as they were, quickly took the form of state ideologies that denied the blindingly obvious: that the continent was deeply and irrevocably divided by class and dominated by capitalism. Nkrumah and Nyerere, with different emphasis in the early 1960s, proclaimed a socialist and humanist pre-colonial Africa. Nyerere's socialism, Ujamaa, essentially appealed to Africa's egalitarian past as a model for future development while proclaiming a socialist system of village cooperatives and nationalization of foreign capitalist activity. Across the continent, Africa's apparent "classless" past was celebrated by states eager to control a chaotic and class-ridden present. Ujamaa would not enter widespread public discourse until 1967. Until then, Nyerere's socialism remained less well defined—and was certainly not acted on.

When Rodney arrived in Tanzania on July 12, 1966, important and varied political changes had already taken place on the continent. Algeria, which had fought a long and brutal war for independence, became independent in 1962. The French state claimed 141,000 were killed in war, while the new Algerian state referred to a million martyrs. Even though the actual figure was considerably lower than the Algerian estimate, the number of Algerians killed was nevertheless staggering. The war was bloody. Ghana's transition to independence, compared to Algeria, was relatively peaceful, with Nkrumah leading a popular mass party, the Convention People's Party. In Gabon, the first president, Léon M'ba, declared, "Gabon is independent, but between Gabon and France nothing has changed; everything goes on as before."[4] As crude as this statement was, it honestly expressed the reality of independence for much of the continent in the early 1960s.

Despite such a variety of experiences, South African activist and writer Ruth First wrote that the entire era of decolonization had been little more than "a bargaining process with cooperative African elites. . . . The former colonial government guarded its options and . . . the careerist heirs to independence preoccupied themselves with an 'Africanisation' of the administration."[5] By the end of the first decade, independence had begun to seem like a charade to a whole generation; the proclamation of the states, whether openly capitalist or socialist, appeared largely irrelevant to most people who lived there.

Thus, almost as it was born, independence was stolen. The Congo's case was illustrative—not so much as a unique case study but as an exemplar of the whole continent. Patrice Lumumba—who would become the country's first independent leader—led the anti-colonial revolution in the late 1950s, and the country, which had been brutally governed by Belgium, became independent on June 30, 1960—years before the colonial power had planned to relinquish control. No sooner was independence declared than it started to unravel. Lumumba fought efforts to undermine the new nation. Subsequently, when mineral-rich areas of the country seceded weeks after formal independence—with the encouragement, arms, and troops of the former colonial power—he organized a resistance. Deposed in September, he eventually fled the capital to rally his supporters in the East, only to be arrested by United Nations forces. They transported him back to Léopoldville and into the hands of Joseph Mobutu, who sent him to the "independent" province of Katanga to be murdered by a Belgian firing squad. Lumumba was killed on January 17, 1960—six and a half months after independence. When news finally broke, the world erupted in impotent rage. A few thinkers drew important lessons from the outcome. In a forthright analysis, the Algerian revolutionary Frantz Fanon argued that Lumumba had been mistaken to call in the UN. Fanon wrote,

> In reality the UN is the legal card used by the imperialist interests when the card of brute force has failed. . . . Africa must remember this lesson. If we need outside aid, let us call our friends. They alone can really and

totally help us achieve our objectives because, precisely, the friendship that links us is a friendship of combat.[6]

By 1964, the country was being convulsed by rebellions led by Lumumba's former supporters. One of them, Laurent Kabila—backed by Ernesto "Che" Guevara, who fought in the east of the country—was determined to end "Yankee imperialism" in Africa. Both the United States and Britain were worried—after all, Zanzibar's revolution had also just overturned its conservative rulers, and, now united with Tanganyika, the island's Afro-Shirazi Party was busy advocating for Cuban-style reforms. The fear in Washington and London was that Africa—or at least its eastern and central parts—were about to turn. With South African support, the CIA funded the fight against the rebellion in the Congo. Cuban exiles, now marooned in the United States, were hired to fly missions against rebels in Central Africa. In 1964, Belgian paratroopers were flown into Central Africa on US Air Force planes from British and then Congolese bases. Air support was provided by US Air Force B-26s, flown by Cuban exiles who had been trained by the CIA. The whole of the Congo—briefly the greatest hope on the continent for independence and freedom—was awash with mercenaries, imperialist armies, and their advisors.

Soon other developments shook the hopes of independent Africa. Ben Bella, the leader of Algeria's new state who had promised radical reforms in Algeria and socialist transformation, was overthrown in a coup by his defense minister and thrown in prison. Meanwhile, hundreds of supporters fled into exile, while others were imprisoned—many of whom were tortured and killed. While in Ghana, Nkrumah—regarded by some as the father of independence on the continent—was popular abroad but increasingly unpopular at home. He was toppled by a CIA-backed coup on February 24, 1966. Whether noted at the time by Walter or not, the uncomfortable fact was that Nkrumah's fall was lamented in demonstrations around the continent—by students in Dakar, the West African capital of Senegal, for example—but celebrated by students in Ghana. Nkrumah had lost support. The country had seen a period of mass mobilization between 1949 and 1951; subsequently, a wave of protests, strikes, and militancy had led to independence in 1957. However, Nkrumah became increasingly isolated in the political administration and centralized state he had inherited from the British. While many lamented his downfall, he had already grown unpopular—distant from what had been his mass base across the country. The edifice of Ghanaian African socialism collapsed.[7]

When Walter and Patricia arrived in Dar es Salaam in July 1966, the continent's independence had already been unmasked—the promise of transformation from the first generation of African leaders was beginning to look threadbare and problematic—assailed from within, and without. For millions in Ghana, Mali, Mauritania, and Guinea, social change was seen increasingly as a project instigated by a state machine that bore a strong resemblance to that of the previous colonial state. Yet Tanzania was different. Indeed, it promised an entirely untried project that could still break from the past.

Dar es Salaam: A New City, a New Culture

When Walter and Patricia first arrived in Dar—as the city was affectionately known by its inhabitants—what did they see? The city had a population of around 250,000, in a country of twelve million. The airport was small, with a single landing strip and a modest departure and arrival hall. When Patricia, Shaka, and Ms. Duncan's youngest daughter, Anne, arrived at the end of July they were picked up by Walter and then driven through the town to the university, which is situated on its outskirts on a series of rolling hills. Today, the city is large, with a population of over six million and choked by traffic, jam-packed with informal housing, office blocks, and factories. Then, however, much of the area was green, with abundant palm, baobab, acacia, and kigelia trees. The downtown area, comprised of the ex-colonial city and its administrative buildings, was neat and orderly. Smart policeman stood in the road directing traffic, while government workers and civil servants walked to their offices, and in the morning and afternoon, schoolchildren noisily gathered around buses.

This was the couple's first experience of the continent, which Rodney would later describe as his "return to Africa." The contrast with the city and continent he had just left was great, but the climate was familiar to the couple. The embrace of the sun was immediate, unavoidable, and satisfying; like Georgetown, Dar was humid, hot, and located near the coast. Overlooking the Indian Ocean, the city lies just south of the Equator. The couple would have been struck by the smell of the sea, the faint salty fragrance in the air, and possibly a breeze rolling inland. July is the end of the rainy season, a time that is normally cooler, with less cloud cover and sunshine throughout the day. It was a good time of the year to arrive.

At first sight, the university would have been impressive. This was not a large building in the middle of a busy city, squeezed between apartment blocks for middle-class Londoners and department stores on Tottenham Court Road. The winding road on the campus snakes up lush, green hills and past houses built specifically for academic and administrative staff. Curiously labeled "the Hill" by those who know the university, the campus is actually built on a series of "hills," with faculty offices and lecture halls perched atop them. Linking them are paths that run along the grassy, knotted valleys and groves of the campus. To Walter and Patricia, the campus—a peculiarly privileged space—would have seemed at once magnificent and familiar; after all, Walter had spent three years in Jamaica at the University of the West Indies, similarly remote from the island's poverty and worries—beautiful, verdant, and overwhelming.

Arriving in the country two years later, in June 1968, Peter Lawrence was then a doctoral research student from Leeds University, conducting his fieldwork in various parts of northeastern Tanzania, as well as in Dar. He describes the atmosphere on the campus:

> I arrived in Dar in June 1968. The weather was pleasantly temperate, especially on the Hill. The rainy season had ended, and the air was fresh. The campus was still relatively small and surrounded by bush—there were wild animals close by. Dar was known as "town" and had some posh hotels and some not so posh with bars—there was a drive-in cinema and an ordinary one—so our entertainment was either drinking or films or wandering in and out of each other's houses and apartments, and of course there was the open-air swimming pool. The night skies were stunning—no pollution then. It took around 10–15 mins to get to "town" by car compared with up to an hour now.
>
> It was both an environmental and political paradise—Giovanni Arrighi, John Saul, Lionel Cliffe, Walter Rodney, Arnold Kettle, Tamás Szentes, Ann Seidman, and others—and there were always people visiting—during my time Immanuel Wallerstein, Samir Amin, Colin Leys etc. And then there were the radical students of course—Yoweri Museveni (a radical Marxist then), Issa Shivji, Karim Hirji and the late Henry Mapolu come to mind.[8]

Arriving a couple of years before the Rodneys was Akilagpa Sawyerr from Ghana. Like Walter, he had recently graduated from the School of

Oriental and African Studies with a master's in law and was a qualified barrister; he had also been encouraged to apply for a job by a university colleague in the UK. Sawyerr describes the astonishing political atmosphere in the country:

> I was thrown into the Tanzania of the 1960s. Independence had come in 1962 [*sic*], and I got there in 1964—at the height of the political ferment in Tanzania's history. I was thrust right in the middle of the African revolution, as it were. What was striking about Tanzania at that time for a young Lecturer in Law like me was the atmosphere of openness to new ideas that prevailed under the leadership of President Julius Nyerere—an extraordinary phenomenon.
>
> The thing about the Dar es Salaam experience was that, at the time, the country was going through a process of actively exploring radical alternatives to the status quo in economy and politics, and there were, therefore, a lot of new ideas and much contestation at the University and within the national political atmosphere generally. In addition, with Dar es Salaam hosting the Liberation Committee of the Organization of African Unity, many of the African liberation movements and the freedom fighters were based there. All this, combined with Tanzania's openness to outsiders who were willing and able to contribute to the various struggles, created an incredible atmosphere which drew in progressive thinkers and scholars from all over the world. Before I went to Tanzania, I hadn't been particularly leftist or radical, but I responded to the lived experienced there. That was the beginning of the development of my progressive posture. Not only were we involved in exploring new ideas, radical thinking, but also, there was much reading of the progressive literature. Thus began my introduction to Marxism—in the Dar es Salaam years.[9]

The Hill was familiar to the Rodneys, in both its construction and social organization. The university was a uniquely rarefied space, and intentionally so; academic life was meant to be separate, even peculiar. As Lawrence indicates, large numbers of expatriates from Europe and North America were senior members of the university, comprising much of its teaching staff, researchers, and professors.

For a university in the heart of East Africa, the faces seen around campus were remarkably white. Writing in the UK's *Guardian* newspaper in 1970, the left-wing journalist Richard Gott noted that for all its

> socialist practice the Tanzanian government and the nationalised business concerns are still forced to rely on expatriates in senior posts. Increased

government spending, the complexity of operations, and the emigration of many Asians had forced the country to continue importing foreign advisers and assistants.[10]

What was true of society at large was also a dominant fact of life on campus. Colonialism had drained the country of capacity—sucked dry its resources and left it dependent. Rodney could see this stark reality on campus.

Across the continent, the university was seen as an institution that could be mobilized for development. Therefore, it was not entirely surprising when President Nyerere explained in 1966:

> I believe that the pursuit of pure learning can be a luxury in society. . . . Both in University-promoted research, and in the content of degree syllabuses, the needs of our country should be the determining factor. . . . The real problem is that of promoting, strengthening and channelling social attitudes which are conducive to the progress of our society.[11]

The university was seen as the force par excellence that could bring about the desired transformations.

In Tanzania, this relationship was relatively informal, but in the case of Nigeria, every university was under the direct control of the government. There, the federal government assumed control over regional universities in 1973, with administrative command flowing from the head of state through federal governments to the National Universities Commission, then to university councils and vice chancellors. At the university in Ghana, repeated opposition and violence arose over the question of academic freedoms. Nkrumah struck what would become a predictable pose: "If reforms do not come from within, we intend to impose them from outside, and no resort to the cry of academic freedom . . . is going to restrain us from seeing that our university is a healthy Ghanaian University devoted to Ghanaian interests."[12] There were distinct and sharp tensions between the interests of the government and students studying at the new national universities.

Turmoil and Hope in Tanzania

Largely in response to the mutiny in 1964, the ruling Tanganyika African National Union created the National Service to serve as a political and paramilitary organization for the country's youth. Its creation was, in fact, a tacit acknowledgment of the grotesque inequalities and the failure of the government to raise living standards. This would soon lead to a crisis for the Hill, starting in October 1966. It would be Rodney's first experience of Tanzania's post-colonial paradox.

Student protests erupted as soon as news reached the campus of the new, mandatory National Service requirement for graduates. It stipulated that students spend several months in National Service camps, widely regarded as repressive, after which there would be a deduction by the university bursary or conferral of a grant. A few protestors carried incendiary placards that read "Colonialism was better," which infuriated Nyerere. In one protest, led by the police, demonstrators marched to the State House, where they met with Nyerere and some of his senior cabinet ministers. The students raised what they saw as naked hypocrisy—high salaries for politicians and now enforced "youth service" for university students. Nyerere addressed the students:

> You are right when you talk about salaries. Our salaries are too high. You want me to cut them? (some applause) . . . Do you want me to start with my salary? Yes, I'll slash mine (cries of "No.") I'll slash the damned salaries in this country. Mine I slash by twenty per cent as from this hour. . . .
>
> The damned salaries! These are the salaries which build this kind of attitude in the educated people, all of them. Me and you. We belong to a class of exploiters. I belong to your class. Where I think three hundred and eighty pounds a year [the minimum wage that would be paid in the National Service] is a prison camp, is forced labour. We belong to this damned exploiting class on top. Is this what the country fought for? Is this what we worked for? In order to maintain a class of exploiters on top? . . .
>
> You are right, salaries are too high. Everybody in this country is demanding a pound of flesh. Everybody except the poor peasant. How can he demand it? He doesn't know the language. . . . *What kind of country are we building?*[13]

These protests were not limited to the campus but quickly came to dominate Tanzania's national political agenda; they ultimately resulted in the expulsion of 338 of the university's students.[14]

Essentially, the issue centered around TANU's attempt to dislodge the university's students from what they regarded as a privileged position. The Hill was thus both an achievement of the new government and an irritant. TANU's agenda of a "socialist" future saw them attempt to draw university students away from their educational advantage to participate fully in the state's efforts at social and political transformation. In turn, the period led to deep and profound soul searching within the university.

Josaphat Kanywanyi, a comrade and colleague of the Rodneys, was pursuing his master's at the University of California, Berkeley, in 1966, on secondment from the law faculty. Removed from the center of the action, he nevertheless followed events closely. As Kanywanyi explains, "There was a general attitude among radical teaching staff that 'orientation' needed to be given to the students . . . to make them a bit more patriotic." Returning to the university later that year, he found colleagues, departments, and faculties in flux. Lively debates were taking place about what needed to be taught and how each discipline required urgent reform. In law, for example, faculty members would talk about law and development, or law and class, while researchers in the political sciences would increasingly emphasize radical political economy. This shift marked the origins, within disciplines and across faculties, of what would become known as the Dar es Salaam School. A historical and socioeconomic approach to learning and teaching, its adherents stressed how education could assist Tanzania's efforts to build a socialist society.[15]

In February 1967, as a direct result of the student crisis, Nyerere's TANU formalized its intention to build Ujamaa in the Arusha Declaration. A bold and impressive statement of the country's commitment to socialism and self-reliance, the declaration centered on an idealized notion of socialism as a "way of life; and as a 'belief.'" Much like other notions of African socialism, it had at its center a definition of socialism as "egalitarian principles" and not specific relations of production—in the classical Marxist sense. Nyerere was of the opinion that socialism and democracy were deeply embedded in African history. The document also made it clear that the "previous" "capital dependent" model of the first wave of independence, from 1961 to 1967, had failed. Self-reliance was the new doctrine—distinct from direct investment and neocolonial networks, which had already proved themselves insufficient for the project of industrialization.

A large number of companies—the commanding heights—were nationalized in the aftermath of the declaration, while a leadership code was also introduced in a bid to stem accumulation of the political class. Nyerere was making good on his promises to students at the gates of State House a few months earlier. Perhaps more startling than the statement itself, however, was the response to the declaration. The UK-based scholar Patrick Norberg writes that it led to a "popular political awakening, as Nyerere's socialist policies [saw] the springing up of grassroots movements across the country."[16] The university was one example.

Rather than standing aloof from the process, university administration, faculty, and members from the party met—from March 11 to 13, 1967—to discuss the role of the University College, Dar es Salaam in a socialist Tanzania. According to Issa Shivji, who had started his degree there in 1967, a group including Walter Rodney and fellow faculty members, John Saul, Sol Picciotto, Giovanni Arrighi, Grant Kamenju, and Catherine Hoskyns, presented proposals on a new curriculum and the reform of the university administration, which was still based firmly on a Western and colonial model of higher education. They rejected any notion of standing apart from what the Nyerere and TANU had declared in the Arusha Declaration the previous month, arguing that the university should be mobilized to support the development of socialism in Tanzania. The university, they insisted, had a responsibility to throw its weight and energies behind the project of social transformation—a deep process of decolonization.

Though he had only been in the country for a few months, Rodney was at the forefront of these discussions and committed to the project announced by the state. By Christmas, his shock at the demonstrations in October and the role of students, regarded by many as defending their privileges against a progressive government, led him to request a "salary cut," in conjunction with other comrades and colleagues. Bizarre as it may seem that a faculty member would make such a request, the move reflected the intensity of the debates taking place at the university. A letter from the registrar in January reiterated Rodney's request:

> Your interest of joining the Tanzania members of staff in cutting down your salary and contributing to the Tanzania development by giving that part of the salary to the Treasury of the Government of Tanzania. I am quite sure the members of the staff of Tanzania Nationality as well as the Government Tanzania and the people will very much appreciate your generous gesture by offering this contribution.[17]

What is clear from this letter is that it was an initiative of the "Tanzania members of staff" and not the expatriates. Thus, Rodney was already clear about where and with whom he stood. Though he worked collaboratively with colleagues on political and university matters, coexistence with white expatriates was not always straightforward. For example, he would later be accused of "behaving racistically [*sic*]" for following a Black Power agenda.[18]

Rodney was a leading member of what has been described as the "Group of Nine"—expatriate radical scholars and comrades—that challenged what was seen as the university's autonomy, or isolation. They set themselves the task of reorienting the university to what was actually happening in the country. One of their main recommendations was an interdisciplinary, university-wide course on social analysis. At the conference, there was the argument that a "common course" could provide the bridge between the university and society—though there was still little clear sense about its content. Eventually, the program began, starting in July 1967 as a non-examinable "Common Course." Shivji argues that the course was heavily directed from outside the campus by the party.[19] However, set up in haste, the course was in fact a loose muddle of political, cultural, and economic topics, organized by an interfaculty committee, with classes that often resembled political rallies.

Other initiatives were also taken. In the same academic year, the Faculty of Law launched a compulsory first-year course called "Social and Economic Problems of East Africa" under Sol Picciotto. Shivji recalls—as one of the first students of the course—that it was "very well organised . . . and the nine authors of that proposal participated in teaching the course."[20] The Social and Economic course, unlike the Common Course, was popular with students and the faculty. While the Common Course only survived two years, it grew into the thorough and well-organized Development Studies, led by the left-wing academic Lionel Cliffe.

The Development Studies course was succeeded in 1971 by East African Society and Environment (EASE), team-taught by Abdalla Bujra, Gilbert Gwassa, Peter Lawrence, Marjorie Mbilinyi, and John Saul—with Gwassa handling the history part of the course. EASE was part of the contentious faculty reorganization in which Saul, Archie Mafeje, and later Lawrence were involved; as we shall see, they later burned their fingers when they failed to fully accept the position of the Tanzanian staff.

Apart from the changes that were taking place in the university's curriculum, there were exciting political shifts among the students. The flowering of radical creativity and expression that followed the declaration saw a small group of people organize the Socialist Club, which brought together Malawians, Ugandans, Ethiopians, and other students to discuss radical and socialist change—explicitly taking up Nyerere's call to debate socialism. By 1967, the group became the University Students' African Revolutionary Front (USARF)—founded, in Norberg's words, to "promote radical left-wing ideas to transform East African campuses from spaces of reaction to hotbeds of revolution."[21] Student radicals declared loudly that they were not an elite in waiting, though they acknowledged that they might be a political vanguard. The actual number of USARF militants was relatively small—approximately 100 out of a student population of 1,600.[22] Though the group was inspired and, to a large extent, galvanized by the declaration, USARF was more than a mouthpiece for the state's political projects; after all, TANU Youth League, with its branch on campus, was more than adequate to play that role. USARF embraced a broad and largely theoretical Marxist canon, in contrast to the idealism of Nyerere and the declaration. They were supportive of the Tanzanian socialist project, but at the same time they remained keenly aware of its contradictions and limitations.

Shivji records that "Walter was one of the few young faculty who was involved but purely within a relationship of equality. There was no professor and student there."[23] Compared to the university-run courses, these meetings were more radical, as they were generated by debates among the students themselves. Typical of Rodney, his natural milieu was not in bureaucratic faculty meetings, or mixing with senior colleagues in academic seminars, but grounding with students on radical politics. The texts they discussed were varied, including the history of Marxism as well as more recent political texts like Fanon's *The Wretched of the Earth*. First published in English in 1963, the book described the rise of a "petty bourgeoise" in independent Africa who would usurp independence, "only too glad to *accept the dividends* that the former colonial power hands out to it." They also studied the writings of Paul Baran, Samir Amin, and Paul Sweezy, among other Marxist classics. The group's activities extended well beyond those of more typical discussion circles. During spirited meetings, students discussed the emerging civil rights movements in the United States, the struggle against the "American war" in Vietnam, and later the global protests in 1968, and how they could respond.[24]

Dar was also a hotbed in another respect: it had become a headquarters for the Southern African liberation movements, serving as a base for groups from South Africa's anti-apartheid movement, Mozambique's struggles against the Portuguese, and the Zimbabwean movement against the white minority regime, a thousand miles further south. More will be said on this below, but this irresistible force camped out in Dar—comprised of actual movements and their organizations—quickly drew students from USARF into its orbit. Vigorous and challenging debates were underway about the experience of independence, and the new projects to radicalize it in a "second wave" of struggles, amid the unfinished revolutions still going on across the continent—particularly in Portugal's colonial possessions.

The politics and motivations of USARF were not homogenous; rather, the group reflected an admixture of the left politics of the era. Lawrence describes the group as principally anti-imperialist:

> [S]ome were pro-Chinese, and I got the sense of some being anti-Soviet. Whether they could be described as Marxist-Leninist reminds me of a brief conversation I had with a Stalinist one time who asked me if I was a Marxist-Leninist. I said, well, Marxist, yes, but Leninist, I'm not so sure. "You intellectual cunt!," he exclaimed. I obviously associated Marxism-Leninism as Stalinism, but I am not sure the USARF students did. They read Marx, they read Lenin. They called their magazine *Cheche* ("spark" in Kiswahili—the name of Lenin's celebrated Bolshevik paper, *Iskra*) and were told to change its name because of the connection to *Iskra*. So, it became *Maji Maji* because that was a Tanganyikan rebellion against colonialism.[25]

The attitude of radical staff and students toward Tanzania's Ujamaa was complex. Many believed it to be a popularist movement with no real foundations for socialist development—premised on a socialism of ideas, with a Christian or Fabian element. For example, Nyerere wrote in 1974 that "human equality before God which is the basis of all great religions of the world is also the basis of the political philosophy of socialism."[26] Socialism was thus a moral challenge and depended on individual honesty and integrity. Lacking, in the analysis of USARF, was an understanding of the Tanzanian and African political economy—its ties of economic dependence on core capitalist countries and companies. These aspects of the post-colonial situation were independent of individuals; development was not stalled by lazy and greedy capitalists but because of capitalist production (and how it had developed in a poor, underdeveloped country like Tanzania). USARF, therefore, saw their role not as party crashers but as fraternal comrades who regarded the Arusha Declaration as a start toward a break with capitalism, pushing TANU's weak and idealistic notions of socialism toward a thorough and rigorous scientific socialism.

Teaching, Politics, and Neocolonialism

Rodney was immediately thrust into teaching and university work, and he had little time to fully inhale the new world. As soon as he arrived in

July, Rodney had begun to prepare his first lectures and courses—typed instructions that were distributed to his students. They were required to answer the question: "To what extent can we reconstruct the history of 'stateless societies'? Discuss with reference to at least two communities in West Africa and one in East Africa." The readings, provided by him on the same sheet of instructions, were extensive and impressive for an undergraduate class: E. E. Evans-Pritchard on African political systems, J. D. Fage on West Africa and Ghana, and Basil Davidson on the general history of West Africa were among thirty suggested readings. Other questions included: "In what ways were the contacts between the West African coast and its hinterland influenced by the arrival of the Europeans?" and "Comment on the assertion that 'the Africans took an active, one might even say a predominant part in the (Atlantic slave) trade.'" These questions—for a course on the slave trade and West Africa—were central themes in the debates within African history at the time.[27] Rodney's students would have been thrust into them by someone who was aware of how they were not simply "academic" questions, but pressing issues on how the present was understood, and with what analytical tools.

In 1967, Rodney—on top of what was already a heavy schedule of writing, increasing engagement with campus, and debating countrywide—prepared for a new, first-year course, "History: African Outline." In his suggestions and recommendations to students, they were equally encouraged to read Frantz Fanon (as "essential theoretical reading") but also, on the "other extreme," mainstream accounts like those of Elliot Berg and Jeffrey Butler on trade unions in "tropical Africa." The term papers he assigned, prepared two weeks in advance and then written under exam conditions in the "Arts Theatre Lecture Hall," included, "The reasons why mass nationalist parties were formed and won independence in either Ghana or Nigeria or Malawi" and, even more topical, "Write on the causes of the Algerian revolutionary war of 1954–61."[28]

Even at this early stage, Rodney encouraged his students to dig deeply into the class dynamics of African nationalism: in a question on the "aims and organisations of the African National Congress," he urges his students to read "a brilliant sketch of the social background to the Congress dilemma" in Leo Kuper's *An African Bourgeoisie*—noting that "the photographs in the book are wonderful."[29]

Though shaped and inspired by this first trip to Tanzania, Rodney's experience and political perspectives were already well defined. Unlike many,

Rodney already felt himself as a product "of a neo-colonial society"—that is, one quite distinct from a colonial society. This had been the experience in Guyana, with its tentative democratic experiment in the 1950s and the suspension of the elected authority in 1953 by the British. Indeed, Rodney's vision of the neocolonial world had already been sketched out in his early adolescent activism in Georgetown. As he explained in 1975: "[A]lthough we hated the British, it was very clear from then [1953] right up until 1966 when we got independence, that the issue was no longer just Guyanese versus the British. It was one set of Guyanese against another set of Guyanese."[30] He had lived through many of these years—first as a politically aware teenager, then as a university student in Jamaica, where he faced, once more, the same experience: progressive Jamaicans with a vision for a post-colonial society and "more conservative elements."

Unlike many of his contemporaries in Tanzania, Rodney arrived ready-equipped with a clear sense of the class nature of independence, which he regarded as a vital step toward lasting socialist transformation—fought on an open class basis. As he recalls, "I would say that already my consciousness of West Indian society was not that we needed to fight the British"; this "fight," after all, was almost complete. However, it was necessary to fight not only the British but also "their indigenous lackeys." "That," he explains, "I see as an anti-neo-colonial consciousness as distinct from a purely anti-colonial consciousness."[31]

By 1967, it was clear that this "anti-neocolonial consciousness" was seeping into Rodney's lectures, reading lists, and class and campus discussions. Though inspired and infected by the atmosphere of political hope and optimism in Tanzania, he knew that a much-deeper struggle and consciousness was required. He was also a point of contact for activists and radicals from the United States and the Caribbean. By then, the civil rights movement had been raging in the Unites States for a number of years, and 1967 saw the emergence of an explosive new militancy: Black Power. In October 1967, Stokely Carmichael, then regarded as the young radical spokesperson of the Black Power movement, traveled to Tanzania as part of an international trip and speaking tour. His biographer Amandla Thomas-Johnson writes that the trip to Dar took him to the "nerve centre of Southern African liberation movements, where he spent hours in conversation with then-president Julius Nyerere."[32] His guide at the University of Dar es Salaam was Rodney. The five-month global tour, which began in August 1967, had the effect of radicalizing Carmichael even further. The impact on the twenty-six-year-old was made clear a little later; as historian Clive Thomas, then teaching in Tanzania, writes: "He glimpsed what armed struggle, coalition building, sacrifice and transnational solidarity looked like. He also witnessed the resilience of ordinary people." As Stokely himself wrote: "For me, the international struggle became tangible, a human reality, names, faces, stories, no longer an abstraction. . . . And our struggle in Mississippi or Harlem was part and parcel of this great international and historical motion. It was both humbling and inspiring. I felt recommitted, energised."

During this first sojourn in Dar, Patricia and Walter never lost sight of their family's trajectory; they were heading back to the Caribbean. Part political, part emotional, the return to the West Indies felt to the couple like a political duty. Yet they had already set down roots in their new home.

Friendships, Debates, and Parties in Dar

The Rodneys met an extraordinary group of friends in Tanzania—many of whom became lifelong comrades in the heady atmosphere of Tanzania. Marjorie Mbilinyi had come to Tanzania in autumn 1967. An activist of some experience, she had been an active participant in the civil rights movement in the United States. Therefore, Mbilinyi did not arrive in Tanzania naive to racial politics and the pernicious danger of racial arrogance. As she explains, her experience had taught her "how to be and how not to be as part of a movement."[33]

Mbilinyi explains that some of the white students who participated as "Freedom Riders"—activists who traveled to the segregated southern states in the early 1960s to challenge the nonenforcement of the US Supreme Court decision on desegregation—regarded their role as "to teach." Indeed, their participation posed important questions: "[W]hen you talk about organisers from outside the community coming in, do you come to lead? Do you come to teach? Do you come to work in solidarity?" Yet what they encountered were organized movements. Her own position quickly became clear: "We were not there to teach people but to bear witness."

Married to the Tanzanian academic and nationalist Simon Mbilinyi, she had a distinct relationship to the white community in Dar. Early into her arrival in Tanzania, Marjorie became a mother. "As mothers," she explains, "we had our own circles, and it included spouses from all the different sides [of the department and faculty debates]." She spoke to her children in fluent Kiswahili and was very much part of the Tanzanian community—even if there was "community bonding" between the different groups on campus.

Mbilinyi noted that there was an attitude that without the "white Marxist expatriate staff," the Left on campus would disappear. This betrayed, she believed, both an arrogance and a failure—a failure to have built lasting bonds and roots *with* the Tanzanians, through which a Left could flourish and grow. "You need to create people to work with, in order to generalise these ideas, and generalising to all Tanzanians as if none of them were progressive enough was not helpful."

When the young couple came to the university in autumn 1967, Mbilinyi was pregnant with their first child. They moved into a campus house next door to the Rodney family.

> It was Pat Rodney who introduced us to Mwamvua Saidi, otherwise known as Mama Shija—she was the young wife of their cook. They said, "We know you have a new baby, and we would like to introduce you to Mama Shija." They explained that she had been helping them with their children and didn't have a proper job. We hired Mwamvua and she has been a member of our family ever since. The kids [the Rodneys and the Mbilinyis] were back and forth.[34]

Widely known today as a leading Tanzanian feminist who has pioneered feminist research and activism, Mbilinyi makes a critical point: the focus on Walter often eclipsed the role played by his partner, Patricia. "That is the thing: everyone is talking Walter, Walter, Walter. Yet Pat is still a figure." She recalls the Rodney house being a base of social activity—a place of frequent parties, jointly hosted and organized by both Walter *and* Pat. Rather than incidental facts in a life of a revolutionary, ephemera in a serious study of politics and activism, these gatherings made up the central bone, muscle, and cartilage of their life.

Indeed, in Dar, parties—whether in the form of dinners, drinks, or dancing—were the lubricant of a full engagement in Tanzania's life. If the worst Marxists are entirely bookish, incapable of communicating with the world, Rodney was a party animal, and Pat also thrived on socializing. As Marjorie Mbilinyi explains, "The Mbilinyis *and* the Rodneys were both party people, and our households had this reputation." Walter was perceived as charming by just about everyone, especially women, she remembers.

Shaka, then a toddler, often attended public lectures with his parents. Mbilinyi remembers vividly how unusual this was; how easy it would have been to leave their son at home with their live-in nanny. "He was just a little kid," she recalls, "but they would come together, exposing him to these kinds of things."

Infused by the radical and highly politicized environment inside Tanzania, Rodney was inspired and challenged by what he saw. At the height of Ujamaa and the possibility of a Tanzanian path to socialist development in the late 1960s and early 1970s, President Nyerere would visit the university and debate with the students. According to Akilagpa Sawyerr (more widely known as Aki), he would appear on campus unaccompanied and could "occasionally be seen wandering around the campus by himself, stopping to talk to people."[35] Whether this story is true or more of a nostalgic myth, it reflects a prevailing attitude toward Nyerere at the time.

Mbilinyi explains how in the university's Nkrumah Hall, staff and students would be encouraged to write down questions and submit them to Nyerere to answer. On one occasion, he addressed the revolutionaries in USARF directly: "[U]se a language that my mother will understand. Do not be so far ahead," he cautioned, "that you are out of touch with the community." Mbilinyi's story illustrates the atmosphere at the time: peculiar, exhilarating. Indeed, it electrified Pat and quickly, in her words, "entered their souls."

This was a unique community: while there were sharp political differences on nearly every question, there were also clear objectives, hopes, and aspirations shared by all. Mbilinyi is clear about this: "We were all a family; we were all families together in a new society being created, with lots of debates at the university. In that sense we were all a part of it." To some extent, the parties and socializing served to break down the barriers that existed at a political level.

However, this environment was not utopian; it existed to some extent inside the rarefied atmosphere of a beautiful, well-provisioned university campus. Even for a mixed couple like Marjorie and Simon Mbilinyi, there were issues. Their daughter struggled as a mixed-race child in a Tanzanian school—not from racism but from what Marjorie describes as "parochialism." This was only resolved when Simon went to the school to give his daughter money for lunch, in front of the teachers and pupils. A Black father taking his mixed-race child to school sent a powerful message, and one that helped eliminate the "parochialism" his daughter had experienced.

There were other problems and contradictions too. Mbilinyi was clear that she could not countenance expatriate tea parties, or the events organized for the white wives of Tanzanian husbands. This would have been counterintuitive and meaningless to her, because her hopes and instincts were to forge a multiracial coalition of thinkers and organizers. Nor did she want her children to be raised in "European" schools, unable to speak with their own grandparents in Kiswahili and alienated from their Tanzanian roots. Her commitment and connection—both personal and political—to Tanzania gave Mbilinyi a deeper, perhaps more direct, connection to the Rodneys than she felt with other white staff members and comrades at the university. "We also shared a family connection," she remembers. "The person who came to work for us was the wife of their employee; there were lots of different ways that we were connected."[36]

Walter's colleague and comrade Josaphat Kanywanyi recalls him as being "very articulate, a very clear mind, for what he believed and for what he knew. He was always ready to share his views and what he knew with us, discussing ideology in social meetings and in homes." Quite unlike the stereotype of an arrogant and remote intellectual, Rodney "brought himself down . . . in order to able to have a comradely relationship with the students. He was able to relate very well with everyone as a comrade, as a friend, as a person who shared ideas and was ready to engage in discussion."[37]

Rodney was a man of great seriousness when necessary, but he also knew how to enjoy himself. "Sometimes we would meet at his house and enjoy ourselves at his expense, but we all did this. So, we socialised, he invited us, we went; we invited him, he came with his wife, with his children. Our children were playing together." The environment on campus among close comrades, colleagues, and friends, sharing a fundamental outlook, was "a family."

Like Marjorie Mbilinyi, Kanywanyi remembers Patricia's force of character: "She participated in whatever we were doing. At meetings where Rodney spoke, she was there. At public lectures we held at the university when people would travel in from the city, she would, once in a while, stand up and speak."

Even though he only met the Rodneys briefly before they departed for Jamaica, Kanywanyi was left with an impression of Walter as "distinct," with qualities that set him apart from everyone else in Dar. When Rodney "brought himself down" to speak, he explains, he was making a fundamental point about the nature of political work. It could not simply be conducted from above, in front of a class, or as a preacher in a pulpit;

it had to take place exactly where people were. Kanywanyi explains that this meant "going down to his people, living their life, eating their food, speaking their language, and taking up their cause; to be able to make their demands and refusing to see things being done to them and to do nothing."

Rodney's profound love for working people, Kanywanyi argues, is what marked him out: "Rodney was on some kind of a mission that he had to fulfil and would die for." There was something about this man that separated him from all of his comrades in Tanzania, in the Caribbean, and in North America. For Kanywanyi, it was "his commitment for the downtrodden, the marginalized, and the oppressed."

Nevertheless, Walter's ability to speak Kiswahili was limited—a frustration that he would have felt acutely as a socialist and activist. Kanywanyi recalls:

> He tried to learn Kiswahili. The language of instruction here is English, and most of the time he was with the students and the staff. Patricia learned more because she had to go to the market and buy food. But he would know how to greet, although he would have a difficulty because he would go at such a speed that the person didn't understand what he was saying. Social interaction was in the English medium, and in the village, he had to be "carried around." He never really settled into Kiswahili. The children learned the language at school, so at the family level he was the least articulate in Kiswahili.[38]

In spite of the relative brevity of the Rodneys' time in Tanzania, it was an experience that would change them forever. Reflecting on that powerful ferment, Akilagpa Sawyerr remarks:

> [I]n Dar es Salaam, the reality of experience moved everybody on. I recall people who came to join us as fairly regular middle-class liberals, but who, by the time they left had adopted a progressive stance. Everybody moved on, I moved on. The interesting thing was that the radical scholarship at the University encouraged innovation, fresh thinking among the students as well as faculty, which fed back into classroom work and what was happening all round. It was just an extraordinary experience of feeling totally involved and belonging. It also meant that the atmosphere attracted some of the most serious thinkers in the field.[39]

When Walter left the country to take up his appointment in Jamaica in early 1968, there is little to no doubt that he had also "moved on"; Tanzania was transformative to all that he would later write, think, and do.

Jamaica

At the conclusion of Walter's eighteen-month teaching assignment in Dar, Walter, Patricia, and Shaka left for the Caribbean so he could take up his new position at the University of the West Indies. Leaving the country and university must have been a wrench for the young family, who had laid down roots, made friends, established reputations, and found momentum on Tanzanian soil. It was Patricia's first visit to Jamaica.

Returning to the University of the West Indies, Mona, in Kingston, Walter threw himself into his teaching and research. However, he was also—characteristically—repelled by the stuffy and colonial atmosphere at the university. Walter and Patricia had a life set out for them, and most of this life they rejected; the couple could have lived like expatriates, in a campus house surrounding by lush, tropical vegetation. Jamaica is a dramatic and deceptive paradise—with Jurassic mountains that plunge into white-sand beaches, turquoise lagoons, and mangrove creeks and rivers. It would have taken resolve to resist the seduction—especially with such ready access to it, untrammeled by the daily struggle for survival. The couple knew this well.

Jamaican society was undergoing multiple crises, including political upheaval, popular resistance, and deep, national soul-searching. The country had become independent in 1962, yet, apart from the paraphernalia of independence—the national flag and anthem, and annual holidays—the country was remarkably unchanged. It remained a former slave society populated overwhelmingly by Black people, but where there was little consciousness of "being Black" or of the history of slavery. As one observer reported at the time, "To examine these questions could be subversive of 400 years of the colonial viewpoint and the colonial relationships on which the present society is based."[40]

Such was the complex situation into which Walter threw himself, bringing his astonishing knowledge of African history, as well as his modesty and commitment to socialism. He quickly orientated to the popular forces off campus, especially through a series of "mass" democratic talks to the island's Rastafarian community that would come to define his time in Jamaica.

The couple arrived in Kingston inspired by the extraordinary developments taking place in North America—indeed, what sentient revolutionary could not be? For years, the United States had been in the grip of a radicalizing civil rights movement. Three years before, in February 1965, the iconic African American activist Malcolm X had been murdered. Meanwhile, civil rights leader Martin Luther King Jr., previously more cautious in his rhetoric, had radicalized and now focused increasingly on social and working-class issues, accompanied by an explicit anti-capitalist agenda. King was an outspoken opponent of the American war in Vietnam, and it was in December 1967—as the Rodneys were packing for their move to Kingston—that he launched the Poor People's Campaign in Washington, DC, mobilizing mass civil disobedience to compel the government to end poverty. Before his murder in April 1968, King's radicalization had deepened with his involvement in the Memphis, Tennessee, sanitation workers' strike. Indeed, Black struggles in the United States were rapidly growing—radically mutating into a far more systematic challenge to power and capitalism. The slogan "Black Power" was already reverberating across North America and the Caribbean. A loud and declaratory demand for a full and unapologetic struggle against racism and social injustice, the movement did not limit itself to constitutional means or nonviolent protest. Rodney followed the developments of these movements avidly.

As exciting and urgent as Tanzania had been for the couple, the whole world seemed to be alive to the beat of a new generation who were not simply asking for equal rights but increasingly stating that they were, in the words of the singer Nina Simone, "young, gifted and Black." However, Walter Rodney's second stay in Jamaica, which the couple expected to last for years, would not go entirely according to plan.

CHAPTER 3

On an Oil Drum

When Patricia and Walter arrived in Kingston in 1968 with their eighteen-month-old son, Shaka, it was winter. However, this is not an entirely meaningful seasonal category in Jamaica; the climate on the island is tropical, hot all year round, with just a few degrees difference between winter and summer. That January, daytime temperatures would have risen to around 86 degrees Fahrenheit, falling to 68 degrees at night. The contrast with Dar was vast, not only in terms of the sights, but also when it came to the people, the music, the food, and the smells.

The island was already on the map for wealthy tourists and expatriates. Like other islands in the Caribbean, famous and wealthy interlopers had started to make it their second home—among them the writer Ian Fleming, writer and actor Noël Coward, and, in the 1950s, actor Errol Flynn. Soon, parts of the island, apportioned into exclusive resorts and housing estates, became redoubts of the rich and famous. Commercial flights, first from Miami then direct from New York and London, made Jamaica accessible to anyone who had the money. Even as the region became dominated by the demands for self-rule—or, in the case of Cuba, overwhelmed by rebellion—Jamaica in the 1960s saw foreign investment serve mainly to open new hotels, resorts, and restaurants. The capital, Kingston, boasted lavish hotels, intracity trams, and thriving shopping districts. Indeed, it had everything an aspirant middle-class family could have desired—though not the Rodneys.

Walter might have wielded his immense knowledge and command of African history and politics to become a university superstar. The academic world could have been at his feet—if he cared to have it. However, Walter and Patricia had other ideas. Their ambitions for society and their own family did not involve career promotions, material pleasures, or new, more comfortable housing. One of the principal scholars of Walter Rodney, Rupert Lewis, wrote in 1998:

The mid-sixties had seen him making decisions that resulted in his rejection of much of what was considered conventional West Indian middle class values—the striving for status, the distancing from one's social background, the imitation of an English accent, the marrying of an English wife, or marrying what was considered the next best, a light-skinned woman.

In fact, Walter's life is notable for exactly what he and Patricia *didn't* do. As the middle-class pressures of university life and salary attempted to pull him from his foundations, he fixed his feet firmly on the ground and resisted any possibility of being drawn further from the roots he had known as a boy and to which he owed everything.

The Rodneys also looked different. Walter wore an Afro hairstyle and a trimmed beard—looking like, as Lewis observes, an "unexaggerated" 1960s Black radical. He would wear colorful dashiki shirts, a dominant style in West Africa. Pat kept her hair cut short and wore African-patterned wraps. It was a far cry from the Western-influenced attire of suits and the hair-cuts worn formally around campus. As in Tanzania, the couple did things together—and not just on weekends and evenings. They shared activities whenever their timetables corresponded and Pat was free from her work as a nurse at the university hospital.[1]

In love with the island's astounding beauty, the couple traveled to other towns as well as the lush, rolling valleys of the island's interior. Nevertheless, Walter, Patricia recalls, cautioned against any romantic ideas: "Walter took me down to Trench Town and I met a lot of his friends. I saw the poverty; I saw the other side of Jamaica. It upset me because I saw people rummaging through dustbins. But Walter said he never wanted me to get a false image at any time of wherever we lived, or what life was really like for the majority of the people."[2]

There was no gap between Rodney's political statements and his behavior, his practice—his capacity to speak from the "oil drum" to friends and comrades in the slums and working-class communities. Smart, articulate, and well-read, he could be devastating in an academic setting, but among Kingston's poor he was humble and sincere. He was there to listen and learn as much as he was to teach and educate. The couple made a deliberate decision to live off campus; Walter despised what he regarded as the elitism of his university colleagues, whose lives revolved around seminars, lecture halls, and drinking in the Senior Common Room.

The couple lived in Trafalgar Park, a centrally located, comfortable neighborhood located only a short drive from the university and a walk to the shops. The family would have been able to look out at the Blue Mountains and breathe in the winds blowing in from the nearby coast. Importantly, they were also not far from the famous West Kingston slum—the "Dungle," after the English "dunghill"—that surrounded a garbage dump. Their home's proximity to the Dungle allowed Rodney to familiarize himself once more with the shantytown where he had spent so much time during his undergraduate studies at the university years prior.

Following the contours of Jamaica's past, the Black Power movement in the Caribbean was at once inspired by events in the civil rights movement in the neighboring United States and distinct from them. Historically, the island's communities were obsessively demarcated by color and were divided into a small class of white planters and businessmen (who could trace their descendants to plantation owners and original settlers), "mulattoes," and Black people. The color hierarchy had continued to work as sharply, and crudely, as this. On the island, pigmentation, specifically the whiteness of your skin, to a large extent determined your trajectory in life and your sense of self-worth. The relatively large number of mixed-race Jamaicans—about 6 percent of the population today—were somewhat privileged, receiving the best jobs and promotions, and regarded by the colonial authorities, right up to independence, as being more like them. This was the profound impact of slavery, which had equated skin color with status and "racial" superiority. The lighter you were, the more cultivated and intelligent.

Through the 1950s, Jamaica slowly edged toward independence from the United Kingdom, attaining greater powers of self-government and autonomy. Like other countries in Britain's Caribbean colonies, in 1958 it joined the Federation of the West Indies—an effort by the British to control political independence and maintain the influence of and connection to the UK. Jamaica left the federation and became fully independent on August 6, 1962. Since World War II, a two-party system had taken shape on the island, with the emergence of the Jamaican Labour Party (JLP) led by Alexander Bustamante and the People's National Party (PNP) under Norman Manley. Bustamante became the country's first independent prime minister.

The few years of Jamaica's independence had already been tumultuous. The so-called Henry protests in 1960 reflected regional turmoil. Buffeted by the success of the Cuban Revolution the previous year, as much of the Caribbean had been, it led to efforts by Reverend Claudius Henry to launch an attack on Jamaica—from a base in New York—to mimic the revolution that had taken place on neighboring Cuba. The "First Africa Corp." was foiled in their attempts, and Henry was tried and then imprisoned for much of the decade.

Nevertheless, until 1972, during its first decade of independence, the country experienced consistent economic growth of about 6 percent per annum and was led by successive JLP governments. This impressive macroeconomic indicator was deceptive—largely generated by private investment in bauxite, an emerging tourism sector, and, to a lesser extent, manufacturing and some agricultural growth. Geopolitically, for the first years of independence, the country remained firmly tied to its former colonial power and to the United States.

However, positive as these elements seemed for the state, Jamaican society at the bottom was still desperately poor. Independence had, if anything, brought the preexisting inequalities into sharper focus. Among Afro-Jamaicans—the overwhelming majority of the island's population of around 1.7 million—little or none of the benefits of growth had trickled down to the poor. Walter and Patricia would have seen this on their trips to Trench Town and in the shantytowns and slums in the city. Political frustration was widespread; indeed, anger at the slow pace of change was palpable to anyone who ventured into the city's poor neighborhoods or the island's poverty-stricken rural areas.

It was this sense of frustration and injustice at a decade of promises and failures—despite the "growth" of the economy—that led to the electoral victory of the PNP, led by Michael Manley, a self-declared democratic socialist. However, Manley's government would soon have to deal with the economic tsunami that was about to wash over the entire Caribbean and much of the developing world. In October 1973, members of the Organization of Arab Petroleum Exporting Countries proclaimed an embargo, which saw the price of oil rise almost 400 percent in just a year. Poor oil-importing states like Jamaica were plunged into turmoil. Despite this, Manley's government managed to bring in various reforms, including a minimum wage, land reform, women's equality, and housing and education for the poor. Manley also edged the government closer to the Communist bloc and publicly challenged the apartheid regime in South Africa. His success in carrying out these reforms, even as the country fell deeper into economic ruin and crisis, was an act of considerable virtuosity. However, as the crisis began to bite, long-standing rivalry between the two major parties, the JLP and PNP, deteriorated, so that by the mid-1970s gang-related political violence had become a major issue on the island. By 1980, Jamaica's gross national product had fallen by 25 percent from its 1972 level.

Some have associated the advent of Black Power in the Caribbean with the "Rodney riots"—the protests that took place when Rodney was expelled from the country in October 1968—but this incorrect.[3] Hakim Adi, a UK-based activist and scholar of Pan-Africanism, writes that Black Power has much deeper roots in the region: "Black Power in the Caribbean," he argues, "was often a manifestation of opposition to the emergence of neo-colonialism."[4] There was a convergence of color and class: while the majority of the population of African descent was poor and without economic power, the "metropolitan-imperialist" interests, in Rodney's words, were white and racist. These were the underlying facts—the political economy of Jamaican society that provided a ready base for Black Power.

Moreover, the organized presence of Black Power had arrived on the island before Rodney, earlier in 1967. Rodney, for his part, helped to spread the influence of these ideas into the university and poor neighborhoods of Kingston. In turn, he became one of the most celebrated exponents of Black Power across the Caribbean, adding and elaborating complex historical (and Marxist) layers to its development.

Groundations

Walter was a rarity on campus and in the intellectual life on the island: he was an activist, already known to many from his student days, but he was also an expert on African history and had just returned from the continent. Robert Hill, Rodney's friend and fellow historian, notes, "[A]nything about Africa has instant appeal to Rastafarians, so when they heard about this young brother who had lived in Africa, taught about Africa, they immediately established contact on campus with Walter."[5] Rodney spoke in public lectures at the university on Black Power, at the same time that he deepened his connection with the Rastafarian community off campus. This behavior, for the authorities, was quasi-illegal—and certainly subversive. One could say what they liked in the safety of the campus—shielded and protected to some extent—but to attempt to spread these ideas beyond the boundary wall, to the poor, was seditious, to put it mildly.

Rodney's "groundings" with the Rastafarian community were an exceptional occurrence: here was a young scholar with an international reputation speaking as an equal to a small but militant Rastafarian community. The Rastafarian religious and political movement, which had been founded on the island in the 1930s, combined various religious practices, including Protestant Christianity, mysticism, and Pan-Africanism. Influenced by the Old Testament story of Exodus, they see people of African origin across the world to be "exiles in Babylon," tested by Jah (God) in slavery and the presence of economic hardship and racial oppression—or downpression, in the Rasta lexicon. Rastas believe in their release from captivity and ultimate return to Zion, an allegorical name for Africa based on biblical sources. They see Ethiopia as the site of a hereditary power and the final and true home for all Africans. Some Rastas believe that the Ethiopian emperor, Haile Selassie I, crowned in 1930, was the Second Coming of Christ promising the redemption of all Black people. The very name of the movement originates from the emperor's original appellation, Ras Tafari. The community in Jamaica, however, is small—approximately thirty thousand. In the most recent census, in 2011, the community made up approximately 1.1 percent of the population.[6]

Rodney was aware of the complex political role of the Rastafarian community across the region, and its history. The richest account of the Rastafarian movement is Horace Campbell's *Rasta and Resistance*, first published in 1985. He sees the development of the movement as a "protest against massive population movement" in Jamaica. "For between 1943–1970," he writes, "the biggest movement of the population took place since the time of slavery, when over 560,000 rural Jamaicans were uprooted from their provision grounds by bauxite tractors and earthmovers." This dislodged large sections of the rural poor. It was into this ferment, largely animated by the Rastafarians, that Rodney connected himself to the activities of this group in 1968. Rodney identified them—correctly, Campbell argues—as a leading social force in the Black consciousness movement in the Caribbean.

Rodney's genius was not to "tail" the movement, or simply to nod and agree, but to bring his expertise as a historian and radical to the community. As Campbell explains, he did this in an "effort to lift the movement beyond the myths of Ethiopia and Haile Salassie." Rodney saw a possibility in the "racial expressions" of the Rastafarians a role they could play in freeing the region from foreign control. Campbell writes:

[H]e was fully aware of the negative influences of the movement, but he was sure that if the positive attributes could be harnessed, without complexes and without underestimating the importance of the positive contributions of other cultures, the Rastafari movement could be part of the dynamic regeneration of the working people in their search for complete freedom.[7]

In 1968, Kingston was a desperate place, to anyone who looked properly. The unemployed numbered approximately 150,000—a quarter of the population. A third of this number was regarded as permanently cut off from the labor market, a lumpenproletariat—what Fanon had described in 1961 as the supreme revolutionary subject. This "third" were involved in much of the city's already-notorious informal economy based in petty crime, theft, prostitution, and trade in marijuana. Quite a number were involved in the Rastafarian movement.[8]

The "groundings" in which Rodney participated were particular to the Rastafarian community. Hill gives a powerful description:

There were never flyers. There was nothing ever announced. Rastafarians evolved this ritual practice that Walter adapted to. And it basically consists of Rastas sitting around campfire, lighting a pipe, singing prises to his majesty, reciting prayers, but the thing that keeps fuelling it and driving it are reasonings. A topic will emerge, and different individuals will approach it and start to debate it.[9]

On Sundays, when these "groundations" would take place, Walter was a frequent speaker. They were not political rallies but ceremonies at which as many as three hundred people would sit around and talk. In these talks—some of which were later brought together in the collection *The Groundings with My Brothers*—everyone took turns. When it was his turn to approach a topic, such as African history, Black Power, or racism, he would speak clearly, fluently, and calmly. The talks were often at the Wembley sports ground, but he would also speak in other open spaces where people met, talked, and organized.

Alien to Rodney was any sense of superiority—and after all, superiority was what he was *expected* to feel, given that the entire middle-class training of the university was predicated on elitism. Then as now, hierarchy was deeply embedded in the university system, and intentionally so; students, administrative staff, other more junior staff, and auxiliary workers sit in clear and demarcated positions in the university pyramid. Thus, Rodney was subverting the whole, rotten structure when he taught as an equal alongside the poor and among the Rastafarian community in Kingston, learning from their extraordinary pedagogy of debate and politics.

Meanwhile, his teaching at the university continued, including through public lectures. Although Rodney was frustrated that he was not allowed to teach more African history on campus, he ultimately preferred "the meetings in the gullies." In fact, he regarded these venues—in the open air, with the poor—as the most fertile ground. The interaction was dialectical: Rodney learned as much as he taught, and the impact of others' lectures—or groundings—shaped and developed his own thought. He knew, as his collaborator and friend Richard Small wrote in 1969, that those he was speaking to "had already arrived at the conception that Africa has a history and they only required the illustration of that belief. People who believe that exist all over the island. Rodney did not organize them. They existed there before . . . and that is because of what Walter Rodney taught and what was done to him."[10]

At this time, Rodney was not engaged with any particular group or party, nor did he build any. He was well connected, though, and was widely known as a deft speaker with a committed and modest manner. He was frequently invited to lecture by Rastafarian community groups, and high school students, while also quickly developing a following on campus among his students and fellow activists. The appetites were vast: questions were raised about African history, decolonization, and Black Power, areas where Rodney had already given great thought.

A compelling portrait of one of these meetings is given by Rodney's principal biographer, Rupert Lewis, who attended Rodney's meetings when he was a young man. On August 17, 1968, Rodney spoke at a meeting commemorating the eighty-first birthday of Marcus Garvey—held at his shrine in Kingston. Garvey had been born in 1887 in St. Ann's Bay, on the north coast of Jamaica, and was a pioneer of Pan-Africanism and advocated the centrality of African history throughout his life. Lewis sets the scene:

> It was drizzling in George VI park and a youth was distributing copies of a resolution to be sent to the government protesting the banning on books by Stokely Carmichael, Elijah Mohammed and Malcolm X. It was a motley gathering of youths, Rastas, University students, UNIA Garveyites, New Creation Tabernacle members . . . curious individuals, Babylon [the police].[11]

Rodney spoke to the crowd, addressing them, he assured, not as a university lecturer but as a Black man from Guyana. He went on to criticize the university, its authorities, and his colleagues for refusing to engage with those outside of the campus. As he spoke, Lewis records, the Jamaican Special Branch—the country's intelligence service—took copious notes.

Lewis recalls a meeting in mid-1968 with Reverend Claudius Henry, a radical Black preacher who had recently been released from prison. Henry ran a church that was also a "self-help center" comprising a bakery, a farm, several houses, and a factory for making concrete blocks. The two men—Lewis and Rodney—were given a tour of the complex, and it was explained that Henry had about four thousand followers, with a thousand active members. Rodney did not speak but listened and learned—a vital part of his character and politics. Lewis writes, "[A]n important aspect of Rodney's activity in Jamaica was doing this—listening and observing and trying to understand the specific qualities of mass activity."[12]

Rodney was impressed with what he saw. Commenting in 1969—at which time he had been forced out of Jamaica for, among other things, "consorting" with Reverend Henry—he appealed:

> I must ask you to turn your attention also to another unique individual who champions the cause of the Black man in Jamaica and he is the Reverend Claudius Henry. . . . Rev Henry has gathered together a number of Black brothers and sisters, and they have turned themselves into an independent black economic community. In less than a year they have built themselves an attractive church and several dwelling houses. . . . They have proper plumbing and electricity, and in case the local supplies are inadequate they have their own water tanks and electrical generator.[13]

A Convinced Communist with an Interest in Black Power

We have seen how the Jamaican Special Branch took an active interest in Rodney's activities when he was a student at the University of the West Indies at the start of the 1960s. In January 1968, when he returned with Patricia and Shaka, the secret service was immediately on to him. In Michael O. West's definitive account of the activities of the Jamaican spymasters, he quotes their conclusion of Rodney's seven-year record of the young man, who, in their eyes, was a "convinced Communist with pro-Castro ideals, and latterly to have taken an interest in Black Power."[14]

While their accuracy varies, the reports from the spymasters provide insight into Rodney's activities. They recorded that he was impressed by neither the People's National Party nor the New World Group—one was the apparently radical opposition to the ruling party, and the other was a group of activists who were "too academic and not sufficiently in touch with the masses." Rodney had purportedly labeled both groups "reactionary." Rodney, the spies indicated, sought rather to circumvent existing political groups. "They wished," he said, "to meet the working people anywhere and everywhere in Jamaica. He expressed interest in the Rastafarians."

Rodney, the reports explained, had insisted on "a complete break with the capitalist system," and criticized the official Jamaican slogan, "Out of many, one people." The spies—operating, it seems, quite openly (attending meetings, taking notes)—note that Rodney argued the island was a "predominantly black and not a multiracial community. Therefore, they should be governed only by black people." They claimed that this objective "could be achieved only by revolution, adding that no revolution has ever taken place without a violent struggle."

There are many aspects of these reports that are interesting—as highlighted in West's brilliant research. At the same time, across the Gulf of Mexico, US authorities were involved in an intensifying repression of the Black Power movement across America. This would have been impossible for the Jamaican state and its apparatus not to realize. The "threat" from Black Power was international, and Rodney's activities proved it. As West writes, "U.S. diplomats not only closely monitored Black Power activities in Jamaica (and elsewhere in the Caribbean), but they also worked in concert with the Jamaican government to rein in Black Power movements and militants, even as the Americans sometimes took a jaundiced view of the activities of the Jamaican authorities."

Rodney's commitment to building coalitions of the poor threatened the heart and soul of the post-colonial regime in Kingston: "[H]e is potentially dangerous since he might succeed in bringing together various disaffected elements in Jamaica," the files reported. Rodney was the force, they believed, who might be able to cohere the disparate political energies and discontent into a meaningful movement, with communist-inspired Black Power at its core.

By September, the reports had become more hysterical and urgent. The intelligence service had "for some time" been pushing for Rodney's expulsion from Jamaica. They cited his "close association" with Reverend Henry, along with evidence that he was planning to speak at Henry's network of churches on the island and to Black Power organizers in Kingston. However, it was the potential impact on tourism that was of serious and grave concern to the spies; apparently, they had uncovered evidence that Rodney had been inciting Rastafarians to carry out attacks on tourists in the December season. Absurd and unfounded—in any documentation—as these claims were, the intelligence service knew that these allegations would ring the right bells in government circles. After all, tourism was, then as now, sacrosanct. Even US diplomats cautioned against overzealous reports, which were founded on no evidence and likely to be counterproductive.[15]

Whatever the lies and absurdities, the government had received what they wanted. Now, with the tourist industry under "imminent threat"—according to their trusty field agents—they moved against Rodney. They began to target the most coherent and brilliant spokesperson for Black Power in Jamaica, focusing on his consciousness-raising activities among the poor. Prime minister Hugh Shearer's cabinet met on October 14 and proclaimed Rodney as persona non grata. Even if the increasingly hysterical and fanciful reports about Rodney's subversive organizing had been read weeks before, the minister of legal affairs, Victor Grant, argued that "in this country there is neither black nor white nor pink. What we are interested in in this country is the quality of the individual, not the colour of his skin."[16] Prime Minister Shearer justified the decision three days later, on October 17, after riots had already broken out, claiming Rodney was carrying on "activities which constituted a danger to the security of the nation."[17]

Within hours of the ban's imposition, word had spread on the UWI campus. Students were enraged; their comrade and brother, who was in Montreal for the Congress of Black Writers (speaking on the political situation in Jamaica), would not be allowed to return. Wasting no time, they arranged for transport to take them to the prime minister's office on October 15. When the next day the buses and trucks did not arrive, the students attempted to march into town, but they were beaten back by police tear gas and baton charges.

The emerging dynamic of the movement—dismissively referred to as the "Rodney riots"—was impressive and served as a sign of Rodney's twin constituency, on and off the campus. Unable to entirely shed their elitism, students attending the protests initially came well dressed in their red academic gowns and carrying homemade placards. However, they quickly abandoned such academic decorum, picking up stones in what became an all-out fight with pro-government supporters in town.

The city supporters of Rodney included urban youth, the unemployed, and the groups with whom Rodney had been working and speaking since his arrival in Jamaica in January. West provides an excellent account of what happened next, once most of the student protestors had dispersed:

> Armed with stones, missiles they doubtless were more adept at de-
> ploying than the students, and Molotov cocktails fashioned from soda
> bottles and gasoline, roving bands of rioters scoured the business dis-
> trict. They singled out the holdings of international capital—prominent
> among them banking, insurance and oil concerns. Some rioters turned
> their wrath on the merchant class, everywhere a conspicuous symbol
> of oppression to the poor, breaking store windows and looting goods.
> Others burned the foreign-owned city buses, which, in addition to hav-
> ing a record of poor service, had recently increased fares.

While US government officials thought the rioting, hitting at the heart of the neocolonial fraud of independent Jamaica, was homegrown, the Jamaican authorities saw things differently. As far as they were concerned, this was a Cuban- and Black Power–inspired movement, the handiwork of "foreigners and their internal confederates," as government reports stated.[18]

Speaking in Montreal in the aftermath of the crisis, Rodney was clear: the uprising was not simply a "student riot," but something far more profound. Rodney saw it as Black people in Kingston seizing on an opportunity to "begin their indictment against the Government of Jamaica." According to his own account, fifty buses were overturned and destroyed. There were fourteen major fires across the city, and certain "known enemies of the people" were targeted, dragged from their cars, and beaten; shops were also identified and looted. Rodney wrote, "I gather downtown Kingston looks as if Hurricane Flora has just passed through." The rioting was a revolutionary act, reflecting a deep social malaise that suffused the entire structure of Jamaican society. The "violence," as it was labeled in the international press, was neither random nor wanton. The buses, for example, were run by a private company, the Jamaica Omnibus Service, which had seen repeated strikes and had recently hiked fares. "Now," he told the audience in Montreal, "imagine poor people in Jamaica standing in the hot sun, waiting on the bus, having to pay increased fares and while they are struggling . . . there is a whole set of guys flashing by in some cars longer than you can see out here in Montreal. . . . That little middle-class there, they love to show off."[19] The ban might have been the spark that detonated the fury underlying Jamaican society, but it was not the entire reason for the uprising. Rodney was careful to explain the issues involved and to make clear that the buses were burned for good and justifiable reasons.

The impact of this "rioting"—a popular rejection of both Rodney's expulsion and the entire edifice of a corrupt and backward independent state—was dramatic. Scholar and activist Jesse Benjamin notes that Rodney's "praxis was so powerful in 1968 Jamaica, at such a significant time, that he was expelled from the country in under nine full months, leading to the Rodney Riots or Rebellion, an event of national, Caribbean and arguably world historical significance."[20]

Nor were the events limited to Jamaica—Robert Hill, who was with Rodney in Canada in October 1968, records:

> October 1968 really constitutes a political divide in the modern history of the Caribbean, because it not only developed a protest movement in Jamaica but throughout the Caribbean, Trinidad, Guyana, Grenada, Antigua. It's as if what took place in Jamaica just . . . lit a spark, and that the modern political history of the Caribbean can be defined as before October 1968 and after October 1968. That is how important Walter was.[21]

The ruling Jamaica Labour Party government never recovered from the "Rodney affair."[22] The political crisis led to the PNP winning a decisive victory in elections in 1972—with a new leader, Michael Manley, trading on his connections to Ethiopia and the Rastafarian community. Michael, who took over from his father, Norman, was careful to distance the party from the previous leadership's complicity in Rodney's expulsion—even as he delayed lifting the ban. In fact, he would leave it in place indefinitely.

Rodney's Deportation

Declared a prohibited immigrant when he attempted to return to Kingston, Walter was rapidly deported, on the same flight back to Montreal.

During his brief return to Montreal, he was again with Robert Hill, who was also teaching in Jamaica and with whom he had also spoken at the Congress of Black Writers. Patricia, several months pregnant, was left in Kingston with Shaka; as details started to come through of the protests breaking out in Jamaica, Walter was anxious about her safety. Walter sent a letter to Patricia with Hill, who returned to Kingston soon after, arriving on October 20.

Arriving that Sunday evening, Hill went straight to Pat—knowing how worried she must be. Hill recalls:

> [M]y mother met me at the airport, and we drove straight to the campus and it was ringed by soldiers and police with machine guns aimed at the entrance. And no students, no one was allowed on or off the campus and I argued and insisted that I should be admitted. I was a student. I had every right to go to the university and I took the letter.

As we have seen, Patricia was a radical and a militant as well—part and parcel of her husband's revolutionary activism. At the time, she was a full-time student and had started classes in September 1968. Learning of the ban, she was worried for her partner, but also enraged; so when protests erupted, she joined the march. On the first day of action after the ban was imposed, Tuesday, October 15, Patricia demonstrated with the students as they tried to reach the city—as the group attempted to march from the campus to the town. No sooner had they come to the major junction outside the campus than police attacked them with tear gas. Patricia was temporarily blinded by the gas, and in the chaos, with demonstrators bent over, running for cover, and trying to help each other, she was injured as the protest dispersed. Several months pregnant with their second child, there was fear that she might miscarry.

When Hill tried to get the letter to her, Patricia was not in the family home in Trafalgar Gardens but under the care of Lucille Maturin Mair, the warden of Mary Seacole Hall. Patricia was in bed being monitored by doctors. Hill remembers, "I wasn't allowed to actually go into the room. I think they said she was resting, but I left the letter with someone I knew who was taking care of her." The situation was serious—"touch and go," Hill remembers. However, eventually Patricia's condition began to improve. As she grew stronger, and was no longer in danger, she was able to pack and make preparations to join Walter abroad.[23]

Always Grounding

Walter and Patricia finally met in London in late October 1968, before traveling to Cuba. Patricia remembers: "Shaka and I were expected to join him. John LaRose accompanied me to the Cuban High Commission many times, but we were unable to obtain a visa in a timely manner. During that period, air travel after seven months [of pregnancy] was not allowed, so we made the decision that Shaka and I should go on to Dar, which we did in December 1968."[24]

News of the ban had reverberations in other parts of the world. In London, for example, Eric and Jessica Huntley recalled in 1983, "[M]any of us who had participated in the Symposium [in Montreal] and others came together and organised protest action against the ban."[25]

The story of the publication of *The Groundings with My Brothers* is tied up with events surrounding Walter's expulsion from Jamaica. Before leaving for Tanzania, he left notes from the recent Kingston talks with comrades. Subsequently, a committee that included Richard Small, Dale Saunders, Earl Greenwood, and Jessica Huntley raised funds to print the collection. The committee also included Ewart Thomas, who edited the speeches that appear in *The Groundings*. In fact, it was upon the launch of this book that the publishing house Bogle-L'Ouverture was born.

The book—an astonishing, forthright denunciation of white power and centuries-old racism—was, to some extent, a departure for Walter. Walter was the consummate scholar, rigorous and focused, mastering the methods of academic work and research, and his work within his discipline had won him many supporters, even among those who did not share his politics. However, he knew when this training needed to be abandoned. This was his first widely circulated activist publication, and it was also a clear illustration of who he really was. Gone were the academic formalities and the University of London etiquette. Rodney also realized that as a Black man writing within the academic establishment, he had to be meticulous and thorough. He read everything; he digested and critiqued each book, thesis, and text, no matter from what political tendency it came—even if he was scathing about "bourgeois" scholarship, and entirely partisan in his approach to research, writing, and life.

His approach to study was thorough and entirely unsectarian. He continually learned as he went, on the basis of what he encountered. Jesse Benjamin gives a powerful description of the rigor of Rodney's thought:

How real and urgent his search for truth and answers was, but also how undoctrinaire and creative he was in his thinking. The groundings approach he already typified and then greatly refined during and ever after his Jamaican sojourn in 1968 was a very rigorous mode, one of self-reflection as to one's role and capacity in a given space, one of studying thoroughly the deep historical roots of each place, and then the process of decolonizing our thinking sufficiently to the task of liberation.

The archives at the Atlanta University Center's Robert W. Woodruff Library—where many of his papers and correspondence are held—attest to this astonishing curiosity. They include not only his correspondence and notes but also, for instance, an essay he penned on Buddhism. Rodney followed this broad array of interests into an examination of physics, the natural world, and the environment. Benjamin explains that

> he went wherever the questions and issues took him, and he was always independent in his thought, reading the original texts and forming his own analyses in the process, never skipping steps as a scholar, meticulous in his language and his argument. In his 20s he was openly contesting with the doyens of the field of African history and African studies in their peer-reviewed journals and remarkably holding his own.[26]

Rodney's experience in Jamaica in 1968 informed much of this approach, particularly when it came to listening and learning in humility. Even at this stage, many people commented on his ability to speak fluently and confidently without notes—not as an act of flamboyance or self-regard, but as a way of connecting directly with his listeners. Nor was his approach overly subject to prevailing trends in Black decolonial thought. Forthright and adamant though his Jamaica book was, it spoke of the incorporation of the Black Power movement into his work and thought—but also his contribution to its development. Benjamin explains concisely: "Rodney gives us a Marxism in which Black Power is central." In 1969, when *The Groundings* first came out, he was also declaring loudly and publicly his anger and celebrating the astonishing political movement that was Black Power, which was waking up the entire world. Robert Hill states the significance of Rodney's period in Jamaica in the correct terms: "His achievement . . . in 1968 represented . . . one of his foremost political legacies."[27]

However, the book's publication did not meet with universal acclaim, as seen in the responses of some of his academic friends and contacts. Many, no doubt, thought he could be contained within the walls of the academic establishment. One of his colleagues, the head librarian at the University of the West Indies, expressed this sentiment with alarming honesty, writing to Rodney on March 20, 1970, that his book *A History of the Upper Guinea Coast: 1545–1800* had arrived "with the author's compliments." Approvingly, the librarian, W. E. Gocking, "leafed through the book and found it to bear the marks of scholarship one would expect," offering his "humble congratulations on this happy issue of your researches." Gocking goes on to explain that he is unlikely to read the book closely but "knows others who will be eager to do so." Then he writes that the library has also "recently acquired" a few copies of

> "The groundings with my brothers" which I believe many are anxious to read—while they can. That's a little work of quite a different kind, being polemical rather than scholarly. Indeed, in parts I find it shockingly—and surprisingly—vitriolic; but that I suppose is its intention, alas. We are putting one copy of this also in our University Collection for historical reasons.[28]

Rodney obviously found the letter amusing enough that he saved and filed the letter. Interestingly, Gocking did not end up reading the monograph, but he did read *The Groundings*. Rodney's most significant books, read by thousands, were not written for the academy. Indeed, in the case of *The Groundings* the book was actually written *against* the university; its very purpose was to disseminate the talks, the dialogue, between Rodney and the poor of Jamaica about African history. These two souls of Rodney were complimentary, but also in conflict. The academic work, rigorous, "scholarly," and to some extent, "respectable," could find a home in university libraries, but his activist writings and work were predictably rejected and even despised as "dangerous." However, Rodney was never fully rejected by the academy. He was forgotten to some extent, and certainly pigeonholed, but his work was too thorough to be entirely "expelled" or dismissed. While there was always an attempt to divide his work and life between the "serious scholarship" and the polemical and "vitriolic," in reality, no such divisions were possible. All of this begs the question: What exactly had Rodney said in *The Groundings* that was so subversive?

CHAPTER 4

African History and Black Power

The preface to *The Groundings with My Brothers* was written by Ewart Thomas, a close childhood friend of Rodney. Thomas explained who the book is addressing:

> "Black" primarily refers to those people in the world who lack economic power and who do not control their own destinies, i.e. the oppressed; and "white" refers to the oppressors. Within this category of "black," there is a sub-category of people whose skin colour is "black," who are visibly African and who are easily identifiable (by the oppressors!). It is to these people that these lectures are dedicated in the first place."

Though the book was Rodney's first, published when he was only twenty-seven, it is also the foundation stone of so much of his work and politics. *The Groundings*, as Thomas writes, is an effort to "uproot" myths and lies about Africa and Blackness, and to correct the historical record. Rodney sought to do this as part of his lifelong project of addressing the deep and profound sense of inferiority of Black people, inculcated by generations of systematic racism, colonial and imperialist theft of land, *and* the "colonizing of the mind." Rodney worked furiously against these deadening habits of thought and self-awareness in whatever shape they took. In the Black Power movement, he saw a possibility to "implant" in the minds of Black people their history of revolutionary action and pride in an extraordinarily rich and complex African history and culture.

Thomas writes in the first pages of *The Groundings* that the process of awakening, or implanting, takes two forms. The first is a private or individual act, involving subjective logic and psychological needs—an act of knowing oneself (an idea similar to Frantz Fanon's belief in "recerebralizing" thought). The second form involves turning to the external world—the process of being political and achieving Black Power. This involves a collective and revolutionary realization of Black Power. This initial existential awakening is essential for the revolutionary act. Thomas argued that Rodney's words served to bring awareness and understanding of this: "If there is to be any proving of our humanity it must be by revolutionary means."[1]

In an introduction to the first edition, Rodney's friend Richard Small provides a disarmingly simple biography of Rodney as "of average height, articulate, gentle, quiet at times but with strongly held views, and . . . an unassuming presence." As noted in numerous other accounts, this "quietness"—Rodney's capacity to listen and to refrain from weighing in—gave his speech a particular force. Small goes on to explain that Jamaicans were ignorant of African history, in part because they were actively discouraged from studying it. Yet Jamaica, like much of Africa, was independent and in 1962 could proclaim its so-called freedom from colonial rule. Rodney set about correcting the gaping absences in official accounts of independence. In a post-slave society, Blackness is the key determinant—the measure of all things, the original foundation of a society based on slavery, where advancement is determined by how "non-black the blackest man can be." Therefore, Small explains, to gain a sense of oneself as being Black, and being proud of that Blackness, must be secured as the sine qua non for being a full human being.

As we have seen, the highly charged atmosphere of the late 1960s—in part on account of the radical and exciting ideas coming from North America's Black communities—had brought about an inflection point in political and intellectual debate on the island. Rodney was uniquely able to throw himself into these debates. He was already a historian of rising fame, with knowledge of Africa's history and contemporary trajectory, in addition to being an activist from the Caribbean. Small takes up the story: "He went to the middle-class clubs (groups of people searching for an identity) and he spoke about Africa. Within a few weeks the news of a man who knew about Africa, who would talk to anyone who wanted to hear him, spread."[2] Increasingly, demand for this man who knew about Africa spread beyond the privileged circles, to less respectable groupings across Kingston's varied urban space, and to villages and towns in the area.

Rodney was not the only prophet of Black Power in the Caribbean. Small reports how in Barbados it was expounded by a former boxing promoter, Eric Sealy. After being confronted by the island's poverty, Sealy gave up his main line of work and instead began to hold street corner meetings. By 1968, he was speaking about Black Power and its meaning in the Caribbean. The response Sealy reported was amazing: "20, 50, 100, 200, sometimes 3000 came to listen."[3] Likewise, in Trinidad, the unemployed—both schooled and unschooled—were part of this rising swell of Black Power. Student groups, Small wrote in 1969, were active in the social issues of the island. Similarly, the Antigua Workers Union called a general strike to force the country's elites to recognize it, indicating the rising tide of radicalism—one that reached into every aspect of political and social life.

The "Rodney riots" in October 1968 were part of this regional and continental trend. In turn, what was "created," Small explains, was a synthesis of what "Rodney taught and what was done to him."[4]

The Situation in Jamaica

The eclectic speeches that make up *The Groundings* were made over the nine-month period Rodney spent in Jamaica—many of them from the Sunday mornings he spent at the Wembley sports ground. The book's first chapter is one of these talks. Made on October 13 and subsequently presented on October 18th, 1968, at the Congress of Black Writers in Montreal, it is a statement on the Jamaican situation.

Written in a cogent and accessible way, the statement itself is an analysis of a society in crisis. The starting point of the "statement" is the 1938 riots and strikes in the country, when the sugar workers' and Kingston workers' strike paralyzed the country. Thirty years on, Rodney laments, little has changed, except for the intensified "oppression of our black brothers" by a class of exploiters—"local lackeys" of imperialism. Against the national myth proclaimed in the slogan "Out of many, one people," Rodney declares that a new phase is beginning for the "Black Humanity of Jamaica." The collapse of the lie of a harmonious and multiracial society reveals the hypocritical claim of the state regime to be a "representative in any way of the Black Masses."[5] It is the powerful Rastafarian brethren who have most thoroughly broken with Jamaican society and its national lies, he argues, and who have adopted a culture based on Ethiopian orthodoxy.

Looking at Black liberation in North America, Rodney pours scorn on Jamaica's ruling class, for banning "[b]rothers Carmichael, H. Rap Brown and James Forman"[6] and prohibiting the writings of Malcolm X and Elijah

Mohammed of the Nation of Islam. These acts have occurred, Rodney tells us, even as Jamaica is sponsoring International Human Rights Year.

Rodney decries the oppression of Black people, pointing in particular at the charges brought for the possession of marijuana—which then carried a minimum sentence of eighteen months. Since 1963 and "independence," the Black police force, Rodney notes, have proved themselves to be as savage as their white counterparts in New York. The prime minister has given the police authority to carry out "brutal methods" to confront these "criminals." "In eight months between August 1967 and April 1968," Rodney reports, "there were at least 31 people who were set alight by police guns. "[7]

As repression escalates, he observes, so does stagnation and poverty for the poor. In rural areas, "sugar estates" have gone out of business, leaving hundreds out of work. As life deteriorates, the government fails to make provisions for increased water consumption and electricity. In a cutting tone, Rodney perfected in his masterpiece *How Europe Underdeveloped Africa* (which would be published four years later) his analysis of how "the ramshackle nature of the neo-colonial structure has been cruelly exposed, and it was the very middle class . . . who recently complained most bitterly when they suffered simultaneously from water rationing . . . and no police protection for their property."

Yet it is into this "decay" that the Black masses have stepped, he observes, as the real arbiters of "the shape of things to come." The racial question is no longer buried; the Rastafarian brethren have pulled in a large number of Jamaicans interested in these questions, many influenced and inspired by the struggles of Black people in the States. Rodney is particularly excited by the literary manifestations of this renewed "self-expression" of Black people—pamphlets, newssheets, and so on. "These independent efforts are essential because of the complete control which imperialism and its local puppets maintain over the various established news media."

Excited by the emergence of new forms of workers' struggles that are not tied to the "reactionary trade unions," Rodney notes a "wave of strikes" and the appearance of independent workers' movements concerned with unity in action. In a pattern set by the two warring political parties, Rodney is hopeful that Black youth will reappraise the ways they are being used by the two parties, as supporters of the parties in 1967 "gunned each other down on the orders of the political bandits of the two parties."[8] It is with these "possibilities" of militancy and "reappraisal" that Rodney ends his statement, and the first chapter in *The Groundings*.

African History as Black Power

Rodney then plunges into the meaning he gives to Black Power, an urgent and necessary reassertion of an obliterated history. He is speaking to Black people, and he states that skin color for his brothers and sister is the most fundamental and important thing about them. At another time, in different circumstances, he writes, he would have liked to be color-blind, to "choose my friends solely because their social interests coincided with mine," but in today's world, no serious, conscious "black man can allow himself such luxuries."[9]

Of course, this text was not originally envisaged as a book; it was spoken words delivered for a radical audience in public lectures; it was part of the "community education" or, in a term from the period, "consciousness raising," in which Rodney engaged throughout his life. Rodney draws his lines harshly. "Black people," he writes, "are non-whites—the millions of people whose homelands are in Asia and Africa, with another few millions in the Americas."[10] Black people exist as the oppressed by a white world. Rodney comments, almost as an aside, that Black individuality is denied: "I've found out that a lot of whites literally cannot tell one black from another . . . it reflects a psychological tendency to deny our individuality by refusing to consider us as individual human beings."

Rodney takes his listeners through a historical survey—the process in which white power has asserted itself. In one country after another, where "whites" took power, Black people—indigenous populations—were marginalized as second-class citizens (in the colonization of Africa) or murdered in genocides of occupation (in the Americas and Australia). These processes in Africa followed on from "four hundred years of slavery" that transferred millions of people to work and die in the New World. Rodney concludes, "The essence of White Power is that it is exercised over black peoples . . . it is exercised in such a way that black people have no share in that power."[11]

After 1911, he reflects, white power faced increasing challenges globally. For this reversal, he partly credits the victory of the Russian Revolution in 1917 that put an end to Russian imperialism. Nevertheless, he asks, what sense is there to "Blackness" in a revolution won by the poor working class and peasantry, whose skin color was—for the most part—white? Equally, the Chinese Revolution in 1949—also named in the same paragraph—emancipated the world's largest "single ethnic group" from the white power complex. Rodney clarifies the first part of this seeming contradiction: "The Russians are white and have power, but they are not a colonial power oppressing black peoples. The white power which is our enemy is that which is exercised over black peoples, irrespective of which group is in the majority and irrespective of whether the particular country belonged to whites or blacks."

Here, Rodney uses Black Power, to some extent, as a device to get the attention of his audience and to make an argument. White power over Black people is not a universal rule, and "white power," as used here by Rodney, seems to specifically denote the colonial and imperialist world, with their racist power and rule over Black people and lands.

Reflecting the influence of dependency theory on his thinking, Rodney speaks about the "the nature of the relationships," as he says, "between colour and power in the imperialist world." Power in the world resides with white countries—the United States, Britain, and France, for example—which dominate and control Black countries and formerly colonized states. He also warns his audience not to be fooled by "independence" since "a black man ruling a dependent State within the imperialist system has no power." In Jamaica, Kenya, or Tanzania, this person or group is merely an "agent" of white power living in the imperialist metropolis.

In this talk, Rodney—with his reading, knowledge, and scholarship—moves effortlessly across the world, through Africa, providing examples of such "agents" or puppet regimes—indeed, there was no shortage of examples. The starkest of these was the Congo, whose independence was snatched away in 1960, almost as soon as it had been won. Yet the Congo was a "well-developed Congolese empire of the 15th century" that was brutally ripped apart by Portuguese slave traders; thus, they went from conditions of enlightenment and development to being regarded "as one of the darkest spots in dark Africa." Independence in the Congo was a sham, with white former colonial states intervening to install a palatable, acceptable agent of white power.[12]

Poverty and wealth also have a color code. Wealth, he argues, is a white commodity, and poverty a Black one. This division, Rodney explains, is built into the structure of the "imperialist relationship that enriches the megalopolis at the expense of the colony." Taking his listeners across the Atlantic to Central and Southern Africa, Rodney explains that Spain, and all of Europe, developed on the basis of looted gold and silver stolen from indigenous peoples. As Europe developed, fueled by pilfered minerals and slavery, indigenous populations in Central and South America were decimated and societies, cultures, and civilizations were "dislocated." In this global tsunami of suffering, Rodney says, it was Africans who suffered the greatest of Europe's crimes. In words that tingle and buzz even today, Rodney writes, "Europeans have climbed higher on our backs and pushed us down into the dirt."[13]

It is against this background that his narrative of Black Power emerges. In the United States, slavery created the wealth—the capital—that drove the development of industry and agriculture, making the vast country the foremost capitalist power. This wealth and power were built on the back of Black labor, even as today many Black people in the richest country in the world live at a "level of existence comparable to blacks in the poorest section of the colonial world."[14]

Relentless in his approach to teaching history, Rodney pulls the audience from the present back to the past. Black people in the United States, he notes, briefly held a modicum of formal power after the Civil War, when former slaves could vote as free citizens. As a majority in some states, they even elected Black representatives to help rebuild the South, promoting education for all. This, Rodney argues, is a paradigmatic example of Black Power, which was briefly alive and vibrant in a period known as the Radical Reconstruction. By the 1890s, however, its force was broken as the old ruling class sought to fully rebuild themselves, reinstating racism to break a left-wing populism that was struggling to wrest power from the rich. The renewed Black Power movement, Rodney argues, stands against the powerlessness.

Though he does not specify the shape US society will ultimately take, Rodney explains that some "form of co-existence with whites is the desired goal of virtually all black leaders, but it must be a society which blacks have a hand in shaping. . . . To get that, they have to fight." Charting the development of the movement in the United States, Rodney discusses violence and explains that while in the recent past—in the 1950s and early 1960s—it was common practice to "pray": "[W]e were on our best behaviour, we asked the whites 'please,' we smiled so that our white teeth illuminated our black faces. Now it is time to show our teeth in a snarl rather than a smile."[15] Violence, he argues, is a tool necessary to free yourself from oppression—from white power—but also to recover one's humanity. As a consequence, it cannot not be measured with the same attitude as the "violence of white fascists."[16]

Notable here is how deeply, almost instinctively, embedded Fanon's work on violence is in Rodney's. Fanon was by no means an apostle of violence; rather, he understood that in the face of an irredeemably racist society, the struggle to recover dignity and humanity would require a self-conscious, and frequently violent, assertion of Black personhood. Fanon argued that the process would lead to the "radical mutation" of Black people and repair the deep sense of inferiority as a result of centuries of bondage, slavery, conquest, and colonialism.

We can read Rodney's 1968 book as a companion volume to Fanon's *The Wretched of the Earth*, which had expressed the rage of the post-colonial world when it was published in 1961. *The Groundings* was Rodney's contribution to that rage, which was now most forcefully articulated in the Black Power movement.

Black Power and the Caribbean

Rodney goes on to discuss the consciousness of Black Power in Jamaica, particularly as it emerged at the University of the West Indies. The events that have inspired this interest, he tells us, are international ones: the "hangings in Rhodesia" (three Black Zimbabweans were executed on March 6, 1968, and others later in the year) and the murder of Martin Luther King Jr. (on April 4 in Memphis, Tennessee). He credits a handful of charismatic individuals for organizing such Black Power "activities"—a pantheon within which historians would ultimately include Rodney himself.

Black people, Rodney asserts, must take the offensive, rather than simply plead for fair treatment or concessions from white power. Why, he asks, should we be embarrassed or worried about offending the feelings of the oppressor? It was not Black people who carried out the worst atrocities of the twentieth century: "Did Black people roast six million Jews?" Nor was it Black people who killed the indigenous populations of the Americas and Australia, or who enslaved and killed millions of Africans. White imperialist society, as he formulates it in this talk, is incurably racist.

The Caribbean, he reminds the audience, is at the heart of this violence—an area of the Black world that is among the most oppressed. Here was a slave society where the legacy of human bondage still weighs down the population. Rodney then proceeds to the "lecture"; it is important to remember that these were not just polemical community interventions or rallying cries for Black Power, but educational engagements where Rastafarian community groups and militants would not only be informed of their history, but also invited to debate Rodney's contribution.

With his usual scholarly precision, Rodney begins by outlining the structure of his talk. He starts with slavery. C. L. R. James and Eric Williams, he explains, describe slavery in the West Indies as an economic, rather than a racial, phenomenon. Nevertheless, it was quickly racialized as white labor withdrew from the fields and Black people were confined to slavery. Out of this practice grew a set of scientific and social theories that stated the inferiority of Black people, who were destined to be laborers and slaves. West Indian societies became the highest, purest expression of this theory. According to Rodney, Black people also "became convinced of their own inferiority."[17]

Rodney then moves on to the subject of emancipation. In Britain, at the end of the eighteenth century, most of what could be extracted from slavery in the West Indies had been. In Rodney's words, "Slavery and the slave trade had made Britain strong and now stood in the way of new developments."[18] It was time to end the practice. In exchange, massive compensation was paid to slave owners, guaranteeing a supply of Black labor through the first years of abolition. Addressing his audience directly, Rodney says, "The Rastafari Brethren have always insisted that the black people were promised £20 million at emancipation."[19] Yet in the West Indies it was the exploiters, the slavers themselves, who were remunerated for the termination of the institution from which they had profited. Although the purchase and sale of slaves ended in 1807, making the trade illegal across the British-controlled Caribbean, it was not until the implementation of the Slavery Abolition Act in 1834 that the institution of slavery was actually banned. However, to center the role of the British Crown in these developments would be to conceal the rebellions and revolts—in Jamaica as well—that forced the pace of this abolition.

Rodney moves on to discuss "Indian indentured labor." Even if slavery had come to an end, the plantation system remained. In the years after 1834, he tells his audience, Black people increasingly left plantations to establish themselves as independent peasants. This resulted in a new demand for labor, which was satisfied by "importing" Indian labor under indentured conditions. At the end of slavery, indentured labor from India thus became a system of bonded labor whereby workers were recruited to work on sugar, cotton, and tea plantations or on infrastructure projects in British colonies. They were paid meager wages, or payment in kind, and promised return passage at the end of their contract, which was typically several years in length.

The labor crisis in one part of the British Empire was resolved by creating a crisis in another. Rodney writes how the impact of "British commercial, military and political policies . . . was destroying the life and culture of 19th century India and forcing people to flee to other parts of the world." Rodney exclaims at the hideous irony of this situation—a sensation you can almost hear reading the text. The West Indies, a site of dreadful suffering, poverty, and misery, "is a place black people want to leave not to come to."[20]

Further on, Rodney discusses how Britain found ways of prolonging "White Power in the West Indies." One key instance was the empire's crushing of an 1865 revolt led by Jamaican preacher and activist Paul Bogle in Morant Bay—a small town in southeastern Jamaica, about twenty-fives miles from the capital, that was proximate to several large sugarcane plantations. In what became known as the Morant Bay Rebellion, Bogle led a march for the just treatment for all Jamaicans—the culmination of local protests and action that had started weeks before. He was captured, tried, and hanged on October 24, 1865. Rodney explains how after 1865 the British government removed the Constitution of Jamaica and put the island under the direct control of the Colonial Office. Rodney draws attention to the distinction made by the British government by the end of the nineteenth century between white and Black colonies: in white colonies (Canada and Australia), the British Empire moved quickly to establish self-rule, while in the Black colonies (the West Indies and Asia), the British were "busy taking away the political freedom of the inhabitants."[21]

Next, Rodney proceeds to 1938—another year of revolt. Even though slavery had come to an end in the British Caribbean a hundred years earlier, the Black people of the West Indies were still rebelling against the unfreedom of a society that remained largely untransformed. In the context of the Great Depression of the 1930s, the British state was shaken by a series of mass uprisings and strikes in the Caribbean. These revolts reached a peak in Jamaica between April and June 1938. According to Jamaican activist Richard Hart, who was personally involved in the protests, they were organized in opposition to "[l]ow wages; high unemployment and under-employment; arrogant racist attitudes of the colonial administrators and employers in their relations with black workers; lack of adequate or in most cases any representation; and, no established structure for the resolution of industrial disputes by collective bargaining."[22]

Strikes and demonstrations infected every area; over a three-month period, each parish across the island was at some point effectively shut down, with sugar and banana plantation workers demonstrating from estate to estate. Violent clashes broke out with the police. Though a West Indian movement, the high point was Jamaica. When a Royal Commission was sent to the island to investigate the causes of the revolt, it found "conditions . . . so shocking," Rodney explains, "that the British government did not release [the report] until the end of the war."[23]

Discussing the West Indian population, Rodney is clear that his definition of "Black" includes both African and Indian. Making this inclusive point was important to Rodney; indeed, this aspect of his argument differentiated him from other Black Power militants. In the series of startling interviews conducted in 1975, published as *Walter Rodney Speaks*, Rodney discusses Stokely Carmichael's intervention in Guyana in 1970 in a tone of disapproval and disappointment. When Stokely visited Guyana in 1970, in speeches he gave he interpreted "Black" "in a narrow sense to mean African and hence anti-Indian." In what Rodney argues was an unhelpful intervention, devoid of local understanding or history, Carmichael employed an idea of Black Power that excluded the Indian. According to Rodney, Carmichael used "what was essentially an alien, that is, a North American, conception of what race was about."[24]

Some fear, Rodney explains, that "Black Power is aimed against the Indian." Yet when the same Indian was first brought to the West Indies, he experienced the same racial disdain. Nor was this Indian a figure of authority or power; on the contrary, he was regarded as a "hewer of wood and a bringer of water."[25] Rodney was already fully aware of the history of the Caribbean, and of the unity of these racialized groups in historical struggle. In fact, it would form the subject of his last great work, *A History of the Guyanese Working People, 1881–1905*, which sought to establish this historical unity once and for all, confronting the political divisions between the Indian and African populations. In 1938 the revolt across the Caribbean drew in Africans and Indians in Trinidad and Guyana. In Guyana, Rodney tells his listeners, it was actually triggered by the strike of Indian sugar workers. Even if there are members of the "white power structure" who are Indian (and African), this does not, he argues, change the reality that these populations suffer overwhelmingly from poverty, and that they have no real power.

However, Rodney makes an exception for the Chinese. According to him, although they were once laborers, they are now bastions of white West Indian power. Unlike the great advances being made by the Chinese Communist state, they are "to be put in the same bracket as the lackeys of capitalism and imperialism who are to be found in Hong Kong and Taiwan." The rupture with their laboring past is total. The same, Rodney argues, can be said of the so-called mulattos. He approvingly quotes Marcus Garvey's comment on the mulatto: "I was openly hated and persecuted by some of these coloured men of the island who did not want to be classified as Negroes but as white."[26]

While appealing for unity and the possibility of bringing together "browns, reds and so-called West Indian whites," the movement, Rodney argues, "can only keep the door open and leave it to those groups to make their choice." The Black Power he formulates is not an intolerant one in which the Black person simply seeks power over their own destinies; it is not opposed to a multiracial society "where each individual counts equally." Once there is the reign of equality, the very distinction between different groups will be lost.

This might seem like an almost liberal prescription for the racial ills of Caribbean society. Yet Rodney is careful to separate himself from such a perspective. What he objects to, he says, is the "current image of a multi-racial society living in harmony—that is a myth designed to justify the exploitation suffered by the blackest of our population, at the hands of lighter skinned groups."[27]

Rodney declares—speaking directly to Jamaican society—that the island is "Black." In crude terms, this was (and continues to be) the case. Rodney reports to his audience that while 77 percent of the population is "visibly African," every other group—apart from "the Afro-Europeans," at about 15 percent—are numerically insignificant. It is on these terms, on these figures, that Jamaica must be regarded as Black; all others should have the rights of individuals, but no privileges or wealth held since the birth of slavery.

The challenge against white power and its local—sometimes multiracial—elite is so entrenched that to break it requires a revolutionary step. In the Western Hemisphere, Rodney argues, only Cuba has managed to make this step by severing the chains that bind it to imperialism. Rodney refuses to see the region and its relationship to Black Power in simple color terms: when Cuba made a revolution, the majority of its population was "white," yet Stokely Carmichael, he notes, described Fidel Castro as "one of the blackest men in the Americas."

Even more explicitly, Rodney characterizes the Cuban Revolution as one in which "Black Cubans fought alongside white Cuban workers and peasants because they were all oppressed." Cuba, for Rodney, is the multiracial society he envisaged in practice: "Black Cubans today enjoy political, economic and social rights and opportunities of exactly the same kind as white Cubans." Secure in these rights and equal in their place in Cuban society, Black Cubans can "forget the category 'black' and think simply . . . as Socialist equals and as men."[28]

Race, therefore, is almost a transitory category in Rodney's thinking: one that may be dissolved once revolution and its accompanying transformations have occurred. The structures of white power, however, are real and require revolutionary Black Power to combat. There is something profound that lives behind Rodney's use of race; in his interpretation, it is a living and breathing force that can nevertheless be overcome.

Revealing his eclectic influences, Rodney cites the Russian revolutionary Leon Trotsky, asking the audience if the revolution in the West Indies will confirm Trotsky's definition of it as a carnival of the oppressed—a flowering of human possibilities as the poor rise up to take control of society for the first time.

Rodney condemns graduates of the University of the West Indies who, he claims, are fully part of the white imperialist system. Despite having black skin, he argues, they reproduce racist lies about Black people being lazy—lies that have been unchanged since emancipation in Jamaica, when Black laborers went to Central America to build the Panama Canal or to the UK to run the transport and health system. While "most of us do not go to quite the same extremes" today, he says, the situation has remained largely unchanged, with the elevation of a few individuals. Graduates were sold the myth of individual liberation, in Rodney's words, "personal progress measured in terms of front lawn and the latest model of a huge American car."[29] The choice is to remain as servants to this white power or break with it: a dramatic appeal to the students with whom Rodney was busily engaged in Kingston.

One task of Black Power in the West Indies, he observes, is to force the Black intelligentsia to serve the Black masses—within the university, students must overcome white cultural imperialism. Rodney says that "the brainwashing process has been so stupendous that it has convinced so many black men of their inferiority."[30] This is a condition inculcated since childhood. The Black girl plays with a white doll; the Black schoolboy asked to draw a human being can only sketch the picture of a white man or woman. This is hardly a surprise, he argues, since all textbooks and storybooks have only ever featured illustrations of Europeans. The Black person is simply invisible. This question was one to which Rodney would return years later, in the late 1970s, when he wrote *Lakshmi Out of India* and *Kofi Baadu Out of Africa*. The two children's books provided a story of Guyana's history, taking as their subjects, respectively, an Indian and African child.

According to Rodney, the very language used by Black people expresses a deep self-loathing. "Good hair," Rodney explains, "means European hair"; "good nose" means a straight nose; "good complexion" means a light complexion.[31] As absurd as these terms are, they continue to be used; Rodney argues, "whiteness" has a monopoly of beauty as Black is synonymous with darkness, aggression, and evil. From this separate situation, deeply rooted in the body politic of West Indian society is the necessity of Black Power and Black pride.

It matters little that these societies—now that they are independent—are run by a class of Black people or Indian people, since they produce and reproduce white values. Touching on the "tragic" divisions between African and Indian peoples in Guyana and Trinidad, Rodney laments that both groups are trapped in a European mindset. He explains, "When an African abuses an Indian he repeats all that the white men said about Indian indentured 'coolies'; and in turn the Indian has borrowed from the whites the stereotype of the 'lazy nigger' to apply to the African beside him."[32] No Black person can see another, except through the eyes of a white person. Brilliantly, Rodney concludes the chapters by claiming that Black Power in the Caribbean "must begin with the revaluation of ourselves as blacks and with the redefinition of the world from our own standpoint."[33]

Onward to the Past: African History

Even if the "groundings" are sometimes hyperbolic, this slim volume remains relevant, reflecting an incredibly sophisticated translation of Black empowerment and Black Power for the Caribbean situation. In some respects, all of Rodney's subsequent and most important works can be said to have their origins here. When colleagues and comrades complained about the influence of Black Power on Rodney's activism and work, they missed an essential point that Rodney had long grasped (see chapter 5 of *The Groundings*): the recovery of confidence and pride after centuries of injury, humiliation, and debasement—with elementary human dignity and history stolen—was the essential first step in the process of liberation and self-activity for Black people.

It is toward that stolen history that Rodney turned in chapter 4 of *The Groundings*. Africans living in the West, he observes, have been starved of their own history and the achievements of this history—part of an effort to maintain a picture of a barbarous continent and an enfeebled people. Then, in lines that should be cited at every mention of Rodney's life and legacy, he declares, "In order to know ourselves we must learn about African history and culture." Such a task—such "knowing"—has the direct, practical implication of creating unity among Africans across the world.

Rodney provides something of an ABCs of African history—which must have been startling for his audience. As the center of humankind, human beings "came into existence" on the continent almost two million years ago with human society reaching some of its greatest heights. On the River Nile were the kingdoms of Egypt and Meroë (in what is today Sudan) that developed and flourished long before the birth of Christ. Humankind, he argues, has "never rediscovered some of the technical skills which the Egyptians possessed." Europeans have refused to accept, as Rodney correctly observed, the elemental fact that Egyptian and Meroë civilizations were African. Their achievements were Africa's. Indeed, Rodney argues, the dark-skinned people of Meroë ruled over Egypt—a culture, Rodney argues, of a lighter complexion.[34]

Next, Rodney turns to Ethiopia. Here, he tells us, was the ancient kingdom of Axum, whose written language, called Ge'ez, "is still used within the Ethiopian church today."[35] Known for its fine architecture, Axum's ancient churches and pillars were carved into solid rock. It was in West Africa, he notes, that some of the greatest and strongest states developed over fifteen hundred years ago, lasting more than twelve hundred years. The kingdoms of Ghana, Mali, Songhai, and Kanem were all situated near the Niger River. Renowned for their trading and agriculture, they were also centers of learning and Islamic teaching; after all, Christianity had its East African home in Ethiopia, after a process of conversion in the early fourth century.

In addition to these states, each of which "achieved greatness before the arrival of the white man," were Benin and Oyo in West Africa;

Kongo and Monomotapa (in modern-day Zimbabwe) in Central Africa; and Bunyoro and Buganda in East Africa. Rodney explains that if these names seem odd and foreign, this is only because nothing has been taught about them. Addressing the themes of Black Power directly, Rodney says, "[I]f we want to call ourselves conscious Africans, then we must know the map of Africa, we must remember the names of these great African states, and we must find out as much as possible about them."[36]

Notably, Rodney resists the prevailing tendency to mistake all history with great states and civilizations; he goes on to argue that most Africans lived in small communities, and that these societies also need careful study. Large political states, he notes, do not automatically confer civilization—a reality to which the political systems in Europe and the United States testify, having destroyed many human values. Indeed, much of the greatest human value was developed, grown, and nurtured in the smallest African polities. In these places, principles of hospitality, respect, the central role of women, humane treatment of lawbreakers, and spiritual reflection were common. Though slavery has killed off much, he observes, certain elements of this culture have persisted.

He covers in some detail the development of agriculture, first in the Middle East, some ten thousand years before the birth of Christ, then spreading into Africa—the grasslands of Ethiopia and West Africa. Agriculture, he notes, was used to support a growing "urban," or settled, population across different regions of the continent. As methods of "taming" the environment for human cultivation and habitation advanced, these civilizations developed irrigation and terracing, as well as crop rotation—an early technique that ensured the continued fertility of the land, preventing soil erosion and increasing soil fertility and crop yield.

Similarly, Rodney explains that metalwork came to the continent not from the benevolence of the Europeans but from the Middle East. Such work was highly advanced in places like the Congo, an area famous for mining copper, while the Sudan became known for its ironwork. Concluding the chapter, Rodney argues that this is important for stressing ancient Africa as being in the "mainstream of human history."[37]

Why are historical facts, at the end of the second decade of the twenty-first century, still so important? For this book, the importance is twofold. First, in describing the development of Rodney's work and life the "groundings" form an important chapter; they mark a formative period in his life, and provide a window onto his political development and activism in 1968.

However, the second reason is more important. African history, culture, and society continue to suffer on account of stereotypes and racist clichés, and a deep sense inferiority still runs through Black and African society. The astonishing Black Lives Matter movement is, in part, a rage against these racist stereotypes. Indeed, Rodney's purpose for giving this history lesson bears repeating: he says such historical knowledge is vital because, as he puts it, "[w]hat we need is confidence in ourselves, so that as blacks and Africans we can be conscious, united, independent and creative."[38] Ripped out of their own societies and cultures by slavery, he argues, it is necessary for Black people to rebuild the confidence pulverized by conquest, colonialism, and, before it, slavery. Turning to the development of religion, literature, and art, Rodney argues, the continent can also be proud of its achievements. Though European history books tell us to look to early human art in France and Germany, for example, there are similarly extraordinary examples of early human culture seen in early rock art in Africa. What is more, Rodney reminds us, these examples of art are from a much-earlier period: 125,000 to 150,000 years ago. The same can be said of the great sculptures in wood, copper, bronze, and iron. "Black Africans have developed in the same way as all mankind," making their own contributions, adding their art, language, and culture into the human crucible. We are all, Rodney argues, "part of a single species."

There is a deceptively simple line—set in italics—*"skin colour by itself is insignificant."* In a manifesto, a series of public lectures on Black Power and Black and African empowerment, this is surely a contradiction. After all, skin color is of vital significance. However, Rodney is arguing that there is no difference, no inherent inequality of human value or worth in skin color, and that the tag of color signifies nothing. What does Rodney mean? He obviously did not believe skin color was insignificant, but that "by itself"—stripped of history and political economy—it was an empty concept that signified nothing. This is key to understanding Rodney's meaning, and why his point is not simply a reiteration of typical Western liberal humanist arguments about race. Rodney had set himself the task of real education—a contribution to the thinking of his brothers (and sisters), rather than simply a parroting of radical clichés. *The Groundings* was not an exercise in opportunism but a principled contribution to a people's education.

What is significant for Rodney is how color had *become* important— that is, how it had been constructed. White men and white power used "racialism" to marginalize and dehumanize Black people. The task now, he suggests, is to recapture and use race to "unify ourselves," breaking the racist hold of white power and structures (including its "black lackeys"). "So long," he explains, "as there are people who deny our humanity as blacks then for so long must we proclaim and assert our humanity as blacks."[39]

In the fifth section in the chapter, Rodney turns again to the Nile civilizations. Highlighting the role of women, he stresses women's centrality in the social system of the Kush and in other parts of the continent. "There were many great Queens of Kush," he points out, "and it is felt that Candace, mentioned in the Bible as Queen of Ethiopia, may really have been a Queen of Kush." Rodney draws on the vast breadth of his reading and research, conducted over the course of his childhood and youth in Georgetown and Kingston, and in London during his PhD. In his hands, African history was not an account of dead events, a scholar's desire for knowledge for its own sake, but a sword that could be wielded against racist lies, in support of a political movement. The importance of this history was vital, alive, and urgent.

The Groundings should be read not in the quiet of a library but spoken aloud to a crowd. Breaking into an urgent, declarative voice, Rodney declares—printed in all caps in the book—the "KUSH AND MEROE ARE PART OF OUR HISTORICAL HERITAGE AS AFRICANS."[40]

One of the most obvious observations of these lectures is that Rodney's attention to detail was impeccable; these were not polemical speeches, with a loose smattering of African history, but real, in-depth historical case studies, part of a profound and serious community education initiative. When it came to content, he made no compromises, speaking clearly and concisely to people who often lacked a formal education, exactly as he would to students in lecture halls or academics at conferences.

Brandishing History for Liberation

Curiously, chapter 5 of *The Groundings* starts self-reflexively, by questioning the approach Rodney took in his earlier lectures. Rodney explains that the impact of racism forces "us into the invidious position of proving our humanity by citing historical antecedents"[41]—at the same time that he notes its inevitability, since the white man has planted racist myths and lies to begin with. Such myths, after all, act as a block to revolutionary action. The task, Rodney explains, is not meant for a white gallery, but to enliven and free "Black minds." However, as vital and important as these tasks are, they cannot take precedent over the concrete "tactics and strategy" necessary—indispensable—to the achievement of liberation. It is the conquest of power that is the immediate goal, Rodney tells us.

Distinct from a liberal educator, who might see history as the prerequisite for any form of liberation, Rodney is clear that although the teaching of African history and languages is vital (noting that a recent proposal to teach African history and language was rejected by the Jamaican government), it is ultimately secondary to "the struggle that will not wait until . . . re-education."[42] Important though the "project of history" is, "if there is to be any proving of our humanity it must be by revolutionary means."[43]

Seeing through the contradictions of the expansion of African history teaching in North America, Rodney issues a warning to his audience: these efforts—or course offerings—are illusions. The US state can safely promote African culture and politics, secure in the knowledge of "white capitalist domination." Therefore, the teaching of African history is no panacea, no substitute for direct political struggle. Teaching radical history is not a threat if it is divorced from a wider consideration of power and the "raw reality of the American system." Rodney notes that there have been previous efforts at education of a forgotten history, but "today the revaluation of Africa's past is taking place within a milieu of social upheaval."[44]

Rodney argues that all elements of Africa must been seen: not only the great states and empires, but also the small communities and stateless societies that are often ignored or marginalized. As a consequence of the poor and racist teaching of African history, the lives of those outside the great civilizations, the city-states, receive short shrift. Yet, Rodney explains, these people, these communities, must also be written about and studied; African life in all its variety must be seen, researched, and recognized. Indeed, in these societies, principles of solidarity, mutual respect, and humanity frequently dominated—values absent from supposedly richer and more mature cultures and societies. Such principles of charity and compassion exposed these communities to European conquest; they were abducted into societies in which they could not comprehend the endless craving for profit and wealth.

Family ties and kinship networks served as social glue that linked vast areas, and both trade and travel were common. Though the Scottish explorer Mungo Park regarded the Djola of southern Senegal as primitive, he recorded that he could leave his belongings behind for great periods, only to return and find everything in exactly the same place. Rodney's narrative is far from a romantic account of "merrie Africa," but it is infused with deep reading and research—evident throughout the book. Talking about crime, Rodney says that there is no evidence of a jail or prison in early African society, or "stocks and fetters" (the staple punishment of medieval England), for example. It is from first-person accounts and archival material that Rodney's lectures were written, and these records show that European visitors of the fifteenth and sixteenth centuries were surprised, even shocked, by the humane nature of the penal system that existed. Frequently, religious belief reflected these values. The Yoruba, for example, could practice in the manner they chose, and there was a profound acceptance for those suffering from disabilities, who were placed under the protection of specific gods. This, Rodney muses, hardly constitutes evidence of darkness.

The great exaggerated racist myths, Rodney explains, present the continent as a place of uninterrupted savagery and primitiveness. Therefore, it has become important to emphasize the cities, states, and civilizations that have existed on the continent for thousands of years. However, all human life, large and small, needs to be embraced, respected, and seen.

The depth of Rodney's arguments, as presented in these public lectures, is astonishing. He takes on the European "egocentricity" that has created a fetish of its own large states and urban centers, from which they can apparently judge all other worlds and societies. Although these forms of human organization may be "outstanding," to use them as a measure of all human achievement and the "inherent worth of cultures and races," he notes, is the worst type of cultural arrogance.[45]

As Rodney states clearly, "It is possible to compare the Western Sudan between the fifth and the fifteenth centuries with Europe in the Dark and Middle Ages, and the comparison is advantageous to Africa on many points." Early European travelers to Africa noted these aspects, reflecting, Rodney argues, on the hospitality they received and witnessed in towns and villages—"the security of goods and persons in Africa"—and how it stood in contrast to the "depredations in Europe."[46] When comments on a particular custom were made, it was often because it delayed commerce. Rodney reports,

> One European denounced African hospitality in the following terms: "The law of hospitality is obstructive of industry. If there is provisions in the country, a man who wants it has only to find out who has got any,

and he must have his share. . . . Thus, whatever abundance a man may get by assiduity, will be shared by the lazy."[47]

Rodney was teaching history as an exercise in self-empowerment and self-respect but also presenting a striking tale in the morality of our societies—the absurdities and cruelties of "industry," "assiduity," and "commerce." Rodney was clear about this—how the supposed achievement of European society and thinking was in fact a catastrophe. In this respect, *The Groundings* is clearly preparation for *How Europe Underdeveloped Africa*, published four years later.

As Rodney points out, the apparent strengths of European development—its historical formations—are in fact the cruelties of a lust for wealth, which cast white men as "superior" in the "operative sense" and secured for them hegemony over the continent. For Africa, this was a catastrophe without end. Rodney explains to his audience, "Economies were disjointed and orientated externally; anarchy, injustice in the realm of the law, internal slavery and exploitation replaces public security, the human operation of the law and the solidarity of the family."[48]

Despite the visitation of such crimes on the continent for centuries, Rodney declares, indeed exclaims, "We did survive not only in Africa, but on this side of the Atlantic—the greatest miracle of all time!" Imagine how it must have felt to hear these words in Kingston in 1968—that *their* history was not simply a story of the plunder and murder on the continent, or of slavery and ruin, but one of astonishing survival and resilience. "And every day black people in the Americas perform the miracle anew."

Rodney's talk "African History in the Service of Black Revolution" was, in part, an effort to inoculate his listeners to the dangers of racism. They may be able to celebrate the achievements of great African civilizations, but what of "ordinary African life"? It is here that a "chink" exists for the propaganda machine to present contemporary Congolese and Nigerian issues, for example, as the outbreak of the "ancestral savagery of tribalism" once the civilizing white, colonial hand has been removed.

Rodney is careful to caution his audience against seeing African history as a "stepping-stone to the active regeneration of an African way of life." Although for him it essential that we revisit the continent's real history, it is just as necessary to "expunge the myths about the African past, which linger in the minds of black people everywhere,"[49] it is not a blueprint to how we should live now. The efforts being made on the continent to transform society—including in Tanzania—are as much an "exploration of the present as a recovery of the past."[50]

The fact that these talks were delivered with such power and punch by a twenty-seven-year-old is in itself impressive. But the sheer clarity and richness of content is even more astonishing. As one reads the text, the feeling is one of being engulfed by knowledge, freed of historical prejudice—to have heard these truths, delivered clearly, by the author himself would have been awe-inspiring.

The Groundings were a clear demonstration of Rodney's politics. As he explained at the end of the book:

> I would go further down into West Kingston and I would speak wherever there was a possibility of our getting together. It might be a sports club, it might be in a schoolroom, it might be in a church, it might be in a gully . . . dark, dismal places with a black population who have had to seek refuge there.

Once there, Rodney would do what he always did: sit down together with the attendees and "ground." As he recalled, "I have sat on a little oil drum, rusty and in the midst of garbage."[51] The process of these "groundations" was at its heart a dialogue: "[Y]ou learn humility because they are teaching you. And you get confidence too, you get a confidence that comes from an awareness that our people are beautiful."[52] Returning the following year to Tanzania, Rodney was humbled and enlightened by his experience in Jamaica. Nevertheless, he also carried with him the bitter memories of his expulsion by the "Black bourgeoise" of the island—evidence, for him, of their craven and empty souls.

CHAPTER 5

Revolution and History

With the birth of the Rodneys' second child, Kanini, in Tanzania on March 28, 1969, the family was now four strong. However, Walter would not see her for the first time until she was three months old, upon his arrival in Dar es Salaam in June 1969 following a long sojourn in Cuba. The second period in Tanzania would cement the family's long-standing and profound affection for the country.

Writing to Rodney in Montreal on November 4, 1968—only days after Walter's banning and the subsequent "Rodney riots"—Terence Ranger, a radical and important historian of Africa himself, wrote in his capacity as head of the history department at the University of Dar es Salaam:

> I hope one or other of the above addresses will find you. What are your plans? There is still a vacancy here—we have been soldering on all year with the largest student numbers and with only 7 lecturers. Let me know as soon as you can whether you would like to return and if so when. I don't want to rush you but it would be helpful to know soon because Isaria [Kimambo, the first African professor of history in Tanzania] and I will have to construct our ever-all staffing plan for next year very soon. . . . Isaria says he would love to have you back.[1]

On November 12, Walter received an offer from Marcia Wright, an American historian of Africa, who wrote from the Institute of African Studies at Columbia University:

> Without so much as a clue whether such an idea could be realized, either locally or from your side, I have started the bureaucratic machine which may produce an invitation to you to come to Columbia in the second half of next year as a Visiting Scholar. . . . What can I add to twist your arm? The stipend will be generous, New York will be almost

literally at your feet, and Columbia is going through some interesting phases. . . . I hope that you can be more than tempted.[2]

By the end of January 1969, further offers had been received, including one from Alfred Rieber—chair of the department of history at the University of Pennsylvania—explaining that "several of your friends and colleagues at the School of Oriental and African Studies have recommended you as possibly being interested in an opening which we have."[3]

It was not until halfway through 1969 that the paperwork was almost complete on Walter's post in the history department in Dar. On July 1, a letter explained, "[O]n behalf of the Council of the University College, Dar es Salaam, I am pleased to offer you the post of Lecturer in History at this College with effect from 1st July, 1969 or as soon as possible thereafter."[4] The position was an appointment for "preferably 4 years." On receiving the offer letter, Walter immediately completed the attached form (keeping one copy, which was kept in his records)—accepting the position and indicating that "[f]or the purposes of paragraph two of this letter, I wish to opt for a 4 year contract."

Within three days, a further letter was sent from the university to Rodney indicating, "The principal has allocated you quarters at House no. 28 Kileleni Road which is a three-bedroom quarter, with immediate effect. The rental is shs 140 per month, and the water charges 40 per month. . . . I hope you will be happy in the quarter."[5] The total rent was 1,680 shillings per year, which was, given Rodney's salary of 36,000 shillings, a very reasonable and affordable cost—quite unlike the extortionate rents on accommodation today in Dar es Salaam (a salary of 36,000 shillings had roughly the same buying power as US$40,000 today, but living costs were low, with annual rent equivalent to US$1,800). Indeed, Tanzania's capital is now the third most expensive African city for rental costs, after Johannesburg and Maputo.

Developments: Tanzanian Socialism

In the relatively short period that Rodney had been out of Tanzania, the country's contradictions had grown—along with the radicalism of its social movements. Even if many activists and scholars were skeptical about the country's plans to implement the progressive socialist agenda, as embodied in the Arusha Declaration of early 1967, they often believed that the country could develop the basis it would need to eventually break with capitalism. If Ujamaa was a crude populist movement, it was nevertheless a foundation on which they could build. There was both space and tolerance for the development of political ideas. What's more, there was even a consistent effort to bargain with President Nyerere—to debate with him, especially on "the Hill" (the term used to describe the hilly campus where the university was built) in the hope that, even occasionally, he would change his position. Under this fraternal pressure, they wondered, could Nyerere be compelled to shift from a rather idealized, Christian vision of socialist change to the fuller, meatier scientific socialism they supported?

The basis of Nyerere's thought and practice was a form of moral philosophy known as Fabianism. Originating in the UK and named for the Roman general Fabius Cunctator (whose surname translates as "the delayer"), the political tradition sought to bring about democratic socialism through modest and gradualist efforts. Nyerere's socialism embodied the notion that all people were regarded as "members of his ever-extending family."[6] Individuals, therefore, had a responsibility to be honest, and upstanding; if the peasantry already had such a morality, it was for the Tanganyika African National Union's leaders to match them. Similarly, capitalism was a "choice": something that was interpreted by individuals and stemming from their moral weakness or greed, rather than inherent in productive processes, as Nyerere's Marxist contemporaries contended. The Arusha Declaration spoke of transformation and an end to classes, but it did not offer much detail on economic structures and class dynamics in Tanzania—nor did it discuss the ways that society was indelibly marked by them.

In his 1968 *Freedom and Socialism* Nyerere wrote that the vital thing was the "extent to which we succeed in preventing the exploitation of one man by another, and in spreading the concept of working together cooperatively for the common good instead of competitively for individual private gain."[7] Where was the deep-rooted and thoroughgoing understanding of the contradictions between classes that dictated the relationship between "one man by another," as Nyerere put it? For Nyerere, capitalism and colonialism were synonymous; the former was brought in by the latter, and with decolonization and the right-nationalist attitude, the country could transcend the alien—and foreign—economic system.

Nyerere was not alone. Earlier in the 1960s, Ghana's first leader following independence, Kwame Nkrumah, had a conception of national development that discarded the notion of class; after all, for him the "formation of a pauper class is unknown, nor is there antagonism of class against class."[8] The liberation struggle in the 1950s had overcome differences in Tanzania; in independence the ruling party could generate similar unity and stall the dangerous formation of class antagonism.

However, without vital nuance and context, such criticism is ridiculous. Among the Left and student radicals, both at home and internationally, Nyerere was a revered figure. The struggle against imperialism that crisscrossed the continent was electrifying, and Nyerere was an outspoken figure in the struggle. Karim Hirji—one of Walter Rodney's comrades and a founder of the radical student publication *Cheche* ("spark")—wrote in 2010 that Neyerere's "diplomatic and material support to African liberation movements far surpassed that given by other African states . . . [while] the radical measures made Tanzania a beacon of hope, and inspired people struggling against injustice and exploitation everywhere."[9]

Thus, while the ideas of Ujamaa and the Arusha Declaration were relatively vague, there was an astonishingly warm and fraternal attitude toward Nyerere; indeed, he was welcomed as a comrade on campus. All the same, progressive intellectuals both on and off campus would criticize the utopian notions in Ujamaa, developing an analysis of how the country was intrinsically connected to global capitalist relations. *Cheche*, founded in the year that Walter returned, 1969, was one of the forums in which such debates raged. Zakia Meghji, another founding member of *Cheche*, was part of a new generation of radicals that included women and men. As Hirji recalls, "*Cheche* exposed the gap between the rhetoric and practice of socialism."[10] The publication drew in contributions by Walter and others, including his contemporaries at the university and renowned political economists Tamás Szentes, Issa Shivji, John Saul, and Yoweri Museveni (then a radical student leader in Dar).

Despite the magazine's efforts at rigorous and forthright criticism, aimed at thickening out the country's socialist development, it quickly generated the scorn of leading party officials and state bureaucrats. The magazine persistently challenged the flimsy analysis of state-led initiatives, as well as Nyerere's refusal to focus on class struggle while opting instead for a philosophy of individual moral choice. Nevertheless, for a brief moment, there was a fruitful exchange—heated though it was.

Nyerere invited members of the radical University Students' African Revolutionary Front to his private home for meetings and discussions.

This was no doubt in an effort to persuade them to tone down the criticism in the publication. As Hirji remembers, "The first one was in early March. He had again called us to his private residence . . . on 16 June 1970. What an encounter it was. Here were we, virtual nobodies, sitting down face to face with not just the Head of a State but also one of the most distinguished leaders in the world." The full account is irresistible and gives us an insight to the peculiar and politically intoxicating period:

> About ten of us sat in the living room, some on the soft couches, and others on the carpet. Mwalimu [an affectionate term, meaning "teacher" in Swahili, commonly used for Nyerere] emerged smiling, casually attired. . . . It was as perfectly informal and friendly a get together as one could visualise.
>
> Mwalimu began by saying, with a wry smile on his face, that he sought continued dialogue with the "true socialists." Then he dwelt on the difficult task of building socialism in a very poor nation. He told us he had tried to read the works of Karl Marx, but only after the Arusha Declaration was promulgated. It was not easy to comprehend Marx, he noted. But he had found Lenin more understandable.
>
> Then he asked us to raise what we deemed the main issues of the day. We first drew attention to the class character of the struggle for socialism in Tanzania. . . . We had to form strong alliances with the socialist nations. We also talked about participatory forms of government . . . .
>
> Mwalimu listened keenly to us. Now and then, he expressed his views. On alliances with socialist nations, he was sceptical. Otherwise, he seems to concur.[11]

It is not unheard-of for senior politicians seek to incorporate or even to buy off opposition—especially that of student activists.[12] However, this was different. At the same time that Nyerere wanted the students to become more cooperative, he was also interested in debate—encouraging them and seeking compromise. For instance, following a request made by students during the meeting above, he amended the university bill to ensure greater student representation in the institution's governing body. Even so, this was not a contradiction he was able to straddle for long. Enthusiasm for the Arusha Declaration, and the hope that TANU could be wielded as a genuine instrument of change, began to tail off. The numbers of campus Marxists and other supporters dwindled. The academic Patrick Norberg argues the "key shift" came with *Cheche*'s September 3, 1970, special issue featuring Issa Shivji's essay "The Silent Class Struggle"—an astonishing document that triggered the so-called Dar Debates (between Marxist-inspired intellectuals about the transition to socialism in Tanzania and across Africa) and provided the most systematic exposé of post-1967 economic changes to Tanzania.[13]

Given the importance of the essay to the development of radical thinking in Tanzania, and Rodney's own contribution to the debates it generated, it merits further discussion. In fact, the text that first appeared in the special issue of *Cheche* was so significant that it was republished as a standalone volume in 1974 by the Tanzania Publishing House, accompanied by responses from Rodney, Saul, Szentes, and Kassim Guruli.

When Shivji wrote the essay, he was a graduate student of law at the university and had been conducting extensive research on the post-declaration nationalization of companies in Tanzania. His work revealed the inner workings of these firms, including the Tanzania Tourist Corporation, as well as state wood and mining companies. His conclusions were alarming. As Shivji writes, "[N]ationalisation while being a necessary first step towards socialisation of the ownership of the means of production is *not* in itself socialisation. In other words, by nationalising a country does not break from the imperialist economy, it does not cease to be a neo-colony."[14]

Nationalization, Shivji concludes, has done little to generate disengagement of the national economy from the global capitalist system. In fact, he argues, it could work favorably for the state and capitalists, for "state ownership allows the bureaucrats to dull the consciousness of the exploited masses of the population thereby serving very well the interests of the international bourgeoisie,"[15] while the Left can be "suppressed" as extremists. Indeed, state ownership of the commanding heights of the economy had not led to worker or popular control—quite the contrary. As a result, nationalized British banks functioned through "management contracts" with international banks from other countries.[16] These agreements, Shivji explains, ensured "foreign partners" profited, and they protected the "regional interests and markets of the monopolies."[17] Shivji exposed an intricate web of capitalist or neocolonial measures through which newly nationalized companies organized.

The economic foundations of colonialism, Shivji argues, had not been overthrown; rather, they were entrenched in neocolonial Tanzania. The TANU's statements were commendable, but they would remain largely futile so long as the economic edifice of colonial state remained intact.

President Nyerere was correct in highlighting the poverty of the rural poor, but, unless the structures of economic control were challenged, the country would remain firmly imprisoned in underdevelopment and hopelessly dependent on foreign capital for investment in industry.

Even in the nationalized companies, a new class stratum had emerged: an economic bureaucracy (the "bureaucratic bourgeoisie") charged with running these giant state companies. Nationalization, Shivji shows, was not a serious challenge to capitalist interests—that is, to the project of securing steady profit and an acquiescent workforce. If this seems like a minor or even obvious argument today, it was not then. Indeed, at the time nationalization was seen as *the* path to socialist transformation in Africa—and elsewhere. Through his masterful analysis of Tanzania's political economy, Shivji, in the midst of the frenzy, stood apart and said, essentially, that it was a sham. While he still believed in the capacity of the TANU, the ruling party, and its most militant cadre, to break with international capitalism, his essay opened a debate of great and lasting significance. It also tantalized the reader with the specter of working-class politics: "[F]or a strategy like this to succeed," he concluded, "the working class must be surely and firmly in political power."[18]

Curiously, the article was viewed by many as a contribution to a national debate aimed at assisting the state and urging Nyerere, in particular, forward. Shivji was careful to explain that while Asian business owners—the comprador bourgeoisie—had largely lost out in the reforms, the new Africanized bureaucracy was in danger of assuming the same role. However, this new "caste" did not yet have the power to challenge socialist forces in the country. Nor did TANU have sufficient ideological clarity to see the danger that was unfolding, following on from the changes that had taken place. Shivji argued that two things needed to be done. First, the party had to be placed under the "ultimate control" of the vanguard in order to destroy the old social order. Second, in conjunction with this, was the prerequisite of disengagement from the global economy.

With the publication of the special issue, *Cheche*, Hirji argues, had come of age.[19] The time for fireside chats with Nyerere in his private residence was over. TANU bureaucrats were building socialism with capitalist means—an impossible paradox, so long as Ujamaa was condemned as a petty-bourgeois project that had to be transcended. Meanwhile, the reputation of the publication—and the students who produced it—grew locally and internationally; this was a socialist publication to watch out for. Issue 3 of the publication, which came out only six weeks later, included contributions to the debate from several student-militants.

What is notable about all of the subsequent contributions that followed the publication of Shivji's paper is how none of them challenged his fundamental thesis; for instance, Rodney wrote of "Shivji's 'invaluable contribution,' and how he 'provides convincing and disturbing evidence of the way in which the policy of nationalisation of foreign enterprises in Tanzania has been deprived of much of its sting.'"[20] He also celebrated his comrade's method of analysis—one characteristic of his own: "[O]ne must also commend Shivji for not inventing classes where they do not exist—a tendency of mechanistic Marxists."[21] Others, including Saul, commended the importance of Shivji's essay and its "power to stir discussion."[22] Ultimately, Shivji succeeded in setting a new trend in the parameters of the debate, deepening the radical critique of Tanzania. For a graduate student and tutorial assistant, this was an audacious and brilliant contribution. Rodney's intellectual collaboration with Shivji would continue, extending through the 1970s.

For a time, Rodney believed that Ujamaa could help Tanzania cut its reliance on trade with the West by shifting to domestic food production. His view stood in contrast to other more critical Marxist opinions in the country that rejected the idea that Tanzania was moving toward socialism. The Ujamaa villages, he believed, could become the building blocks of socialist development if TANU were clear about the need to modernize them with support from socialist countries. Thus, for a period, Rodney saw the main objective in Tanzania as the preservation of the Ujamaa villages.[23] Shivji, who was doubtful, challenged his comrades, including Rodney, to question Tanzania's socialist prospects deeply.

The Common Course

As we have seen, when Rodney first arrived in Dar, he was quickly baptized in campus politics. As Nyerere and TANU announced compulsory youth service for university students, there was a loud and furious reaction; "student intellectuals" wanted no part in the grubby business of participating in actual development on peasant farms, or in building projects. In October 1966, they protested under highly provocative banners praising colonialism and condemning the ruling party. The university's progressive scholars felt that they too needed to develop core changes to university teaching that could feed into the national need for radical change and break the deep conservatism that resided in the student body.

It was from such an initiative that the "Common Course," a bland title that disguised a lofty ambition, was born. As we saw earlier, the course emerged from the 1967 conference that sought to redefine the university, and the actual proposal, addressed to Nyerere and the vice president, was written by nine members of the faculty, including Rodney. According to the document, the university is not just a place of higher learning; rather, it "can and should play an important role in the development of socialism in Tanzania." However, its authors explain, the institution is hopelessly ill-prepared to do this, due to its fragmentation into "separate disciplines which provides the main obstacle to the development of an integral and coherent vision of man in history and society." Unreformed, the university might produce competent "technicians and technocrats" with specialist knowledge but no "comprehension of social development as a unitary process."[24]

Referring directly to the students expelled from the university for protesting against the new requirement that students serve in the National Service, the proposal states that they cannot be expected to return with a "change of heart" so long as the current "orientation and assumptions remain unchallenged." Framing their arguments in eerily contemporary terms, the Group of Nine calls for a "re-evaluation of the inherited disciplinary organisation and structure is a normal part of the overall process of decolonisation of education."[25] This exercise was all the more urgent at a time when an entire society was apparently engaged in breaking from capitalism.

The proposal challenged the most profound assumptions of university organization: "[T]he shattered and abstracted 'parts,'" it states, "must be reconstituted into their real totality, in terms of which they will be analysed and made meaningful."[26] Such a course would create an "awareness of the forces and structures constituting a social totality . . . to make possible a new way of thinking about Tanzanian (or East Africa?) realities and problems in all their concreteness and specificity."[27] If these hopes seem wild and unfeasible today, perhaps that is a reflection of the narrowness of our own period, rather than the hyperbole of the 1967 document.

The group envisaged an autonomous department of social analysis, which would initially draw on existing staff from other departments. The graduate from such a course would approach "his technical and administrative work from a much more than narrowly 'specialist' standpoint . . .

and relate his special area of operation . . . to a general understanding of social formation and social dynamics."[28] The group attached a draft curriculum of the proposed new department of social analysis, believing that the Common Course would comprise a third of the total time for every student in a three-year degree, producing a "vigorous socialist orientation" in their work after leaving the Hill.

The nine did not innocently believe that they could, as they teased each other at the time, build "socialism in one syllabus,"[29] replacing a deficient national and international political economy with radical pedagogy. However, they did hope that they could respond to the radical climate in the country, ushered in by Nyerere's Arusha Declaration, with an attempt to shift the country's intellectual organization at the university—to make the university fit for socialist transformation.

In the end, the heady ambitions of the full proposal were not adopted by the university, though some important aspects were cherry-picked from the report, and in 1969 a Common Course specifically for first-year students was set up. Its explicit intention was to challenge disciplinary specialization, and it was administered by the Faculty of Arts and Social Sciences. It was also the precursor to a Development Studies course that would be launched in 1970, compulsory for undergraduate students in the faculty.[30] From this initiative, another bloomed, and in July 1971 a new core course on East African Society and Environment (EASE) was established as compulsory for first years, replacing Development Studies. While its aims were not as ambitious as what the Group of Nine had envisaged, it was nevertheless a remarkable endeavor.

When John Saul delivered the last lecture for EASE in March 1972, he explained the origins of the course to the students as well as its central paradox:

> EASE is a dangerous course. In certain important ways it grew out of the student crisis of 1966 right here on this campus. There was much talk at the time about the necessity of having political education to transform you, the students, into potential political leaders of the construction of socialism. One catch though: you can't really effectively force people to be creative socialists which is what you really need for the real socialist construction.[31]

His final words to his students, spoken in part in Swahili, captured the spirit of the time, challenging them to answer: What would they do with themselves as members of Tanzania's petty bourgeoisie? Did they commit themselves to socialism in the "interests of world-wide revolution"? It was a decision they would now have to make. "I conclude then by saying: 'Nawatakia heri. Asanteni jamaa' [Good luck, and thanks, comrades.]"[32]

Comrades, Friends, Socialism, and the University

What did it feel like to live in Tanzania during these years? In fact, there were multiple distinct periods. The late 1960s were a high-water mark in the country's commitment to socialist transformation. The 1967 Arusha Declaration—which promised the wholesale change of Tanzania's colonial political economy—declared boldly that

> it is the responsibility of the state to intervene actively in the economic life of the nation so as to ensure the well-being of all citizens, and so as to prevent the exploitation of one person by another or one group by another, and so as to prevent the accumulation of wealth to an extent which is inconsistent with the existence of a classless society.[33]

The declaration was an unapologetic statement of a state-driven path to socialism. Hundreds of committed socialists flocked to the country.

Tanzania was not the only country to see an influx of fraternal labor, which was frequently contributed by radicals from the ex-colonial power. In the aftermath of independence and the withdrawal of the French from Algeria in 1962, approximately one million white settlers—the so-called *pieds-noirs*—fled the country. However, several thousand *"pieds-rouges"* volunteers came from Europe (and elsewhere) to fill posts in the civil service, in industry, and in agriculture. Later in the 1970s, in Mozambique—and to a lesser extent in Angola—*cooperantes* was the term given to Europeans who came to the country after independence, aiming to fill some of the technical gaps left by the exodus of white Portuguese settlers.

In Tanzania, these cooperantes were too numerous to list, though a few names will give a sense of the extent of this largely white influx: Giovanni Arrighi, Lionel Cliffe, Ruth First, John Saul, Peter Lawrence, Janet Bujra, Tamás Szentes, Robert and Ann Seidman, John Loxley, John Iliffe, Terence Ranger, Henry Bernstein; the list goes on. Suffice to say, this was a political generation that would define the radical agenda in their disciplines for years to come and would attempt to do much more outside the university, and in their books and articles. However, these cooperantes were not just a specific cadre of radical intellectuals, but also workers volunteering in various state projects.

Tamás Szentes is right when he explains, "[I]n those years, after the Arusha Declaration, Tanzania attracted a number of highly qualified and progressive minded scholars, obviously contributed enormously to the exceptionally good intellectual atmosphere in Dar." Many, though not all, were inspired by the politics of the government and the president's seemingly sincere commitment to socialism. Szentes puts it well: "President Julius Nyerere and his aim to develop democratically a genuine type of socialist system of society, different from those in the 'East,' had obviously gained not only wide-spread interest internationally, but also—among progressive thinkers—a great sympathy."[34] Even those who did not participate directly in the project spoke at events and conferences in the country—Paul Streeten, Dudley Seers, Samir Amin, Immanuel Wallerstein, René Dumont, and C. L. R. James, to name a few.

Peter Lawrence, then a young visiting scholar from the UK, explains: "There was a lot of excitement around Ujamaa and of course different interpretations of what it meant. Socialists from all over the world came because of solidarity, because of a belief that maybe the third world would mount the drive for world socialism and overtake the developed countries. A lot of romantic notions." He continues:

> I chose Tanzania because I had read the Arusha Declaration and thought it would be interesting to go there and do research that would support Nyerere's project. This was a poor country trying to do something different. I got to see a lot of the country and the differences in levels of development depending on which crops were grown and how valuable they were, and that was because I was seconded to the Development Ministry to join a team touring a quarter of the country in order to write the Regional Development five-year plan.[35]

This was not the normal academic route, nor were Lawrence's motivations typical. Intellectually stimulated and excited by what was happening in Tanzania, Lawrence wanted to make a contribution. To a generation of British Communist Party members in the 1930s, the Spanish Civil War was a defining moment, as cadre endeavored to support the struggle against Spanish fascism from afar or by traveling abroad to join the fight. Now, the most important developments in radical politics were taking place in the global South.

Dar was also the base for liberation movements, including the People's Movement for the Liberation of Angola (MPLA), Mozambique Liberation Front (FRELIMO), African National Congress (ANC), Zimbabwe African National Union (ZANU), and Zimbabwe African People's Union (ZAPU). These groupings did not exist in the city in separate silos; rather, there they mingled freely, often on the Hill. For many, Dar was the place where they first met leading figures in Southern Africa's liberation movements. Lawrence, for example, met Joe Slovo, Yusuf Dadoo, Alfred Nzo, Marcelino dos Santos, Josiah Jele (the head of the ANC office in Dar), and others in Tanzania in his first year. Nor were there the cooperantes only from North America or Western Europe; Tanzania was a melting pot of the North and South, East and West, and all of the distinctions between and within these regions. For example, as Lawrence explains, "[Y]ou could meet people from the socialist countries and discover the differences between them. I remember witnessing Szentes's frustration at the way an East German colleague was teaching Marxist economics in Soviet mode, thus exposing the differences between Hungary's more sophisticated Marxism and the mechanical political economy of Moscow."

Lawrence describes such daily contact with a veritable pantheon of comrades, long practiced in applying and discussing Marxism at a high level, as intimidating at times. As he recalls, he "was in awe of all these people," and soon realized "how little I knew about anything! And you would meet them by chance in cafés, hotels, on the campus or in friends' houses. And then I got to know people in government. . . . All very exciting!" One of the early cooperantes in Tanzania was Lionel Cliffe. By 1968, he had already been in the country for a number of years, had contacts in government, and was regarded as a trusted comrade. With Lawrence and others, he went on to found, in 1974, the *Review of African Political Economy*, the most enduring radical African studies publication anywhere in the world.

Tanzania was a base for socialist development internationally—though an uneven, patchy one. In Lawrence's words, it was the "Third World [that] would mount the drive for world socialism and overtake the developed countries." For a much-smaller group, Tanzania was a key international staging post. "The great thing about being there," he recalls, "especially when I started teaching, was that I thought I was doing something to build a socialist base—romantic and naive, but that was the same with others. And this was even after the student uprising of 1971, which we should have kept out of but were prevented from doing so because of our internationalism, which trumped any respect for nationalist sentiment."[36]

The protests to which Lawrence refers grew into a student movement in July 1971. Earlier, the Field Force had come onto the campus when it looked like the students were going to occupy the administration building. This led to a tense few months as the student union president, Simon Akivaga, was expelled from the country. Prior to the protests, the atmosphere at the university was tense. A new university—in name—had just been established in July 1970, breaking away from the University of East Africa, of which the Dar campus had been a subsidiary. The new administration had curbed freedom of association and press on the campus by banning student publications, such as the celebrated *Cheche*, and independent student unions in favor of youth party structures. Many others refused to be bystanders in this showdown with the university. To support Nyerere and his socialist project was one thing; to be a party sycophant was something else entirely.

The vibrant seminar scene at the university was exciting, involving students and teachers alike. However, the atmosphere was also extremely macho and competitive. Marjorie Mbilinyi remembers, "You had to be very courageous to give a paper in those kinds of settings." Following her presentation of a paper on education, she recalls, Abdul Sheriff accused her of sowing division; "At that time no one wanted to talk about anything that 'divided the masses'; don't talk about race, don't talk about gender. Yet here I was insisting that you must pay attention to patriarchal relations." Stressing the importance of intersectionality, even if people were not ready for it, she notes: "In those days we had the extremes of the extremes." Walter, she remembers, was far more sensitive to intersecting relationships, given his position on class, race, and the national question.

The attitudes at the university—the "extremes" about which Mbilinyi speaks—were deeply patriarchal. Mbilinyi recalls one female student, who was the top of her class, who received an offer at the end of the year to continue her studies as a postgraduate and work as a tutor. Her husband immediately went to the head of the department, explaining, "If you promote my wife, she will then get more education than me." "As a consequence," Mbilinyi explains, "they somehow blocked her promotion." The rescindment of the appointment triggered vocal opposition among female teaching and administrative staff, and eventually, the decision was overturned: the student was allowed to return to her studies and take up her appointment as a tutor. It was an important victory but one that illustrates the frequent sexism of the environment at the university, which endured, paradoxically, in a hotbed of Marxist politics and debate.

The battle to assert a women's agenda in this context was a difficult one; for instance, it would not be until 1978 that an all-women's reading group was established. However, female students and faculty were taking critical steps, as Mbilinyi explains: "We were organizing first for ourselves. It wasn't about them and us, as if we were privileged and going to save other people. We were fighting first our own oppression, but we were also sorting out our personal lives. We were reading Simone de Beauvoir and then what had been written in Africa." [37] The group, which became increasingly focused on Tanzania, applied for funding for various groups, including one centered on the peasantry, as well as others with focuses on poetry and education. The groups were made up of not only university graduates but also numerous others who had never attended university.

Remembering Rodney in Dar

As we have already seen, Walter and Patricia threw themselves into the political and cultural scene in Tanzania. Walter's friend, colleague, and comrade Abdul Sheriff, a historian who taught with him in the history department, remembers: "When he came here, he did not consider that he was really trying to get integrated. He always wanted to go back home—that is where his struggle was."[38]

For the staff who lived on campus—as most did at that time—engagement in collegial discourse was not a matter of making an appointment in a department office but of calling one another at home. If there was a problem, a query, a book that need to be borrowed, Sheriff would visit the Rodneys' campus home. "The standard thing in the late afternoon, at five in the afternoon, was to go and visit each other. There were frequently not even telephones, so you would not even call." This was true of many staff members, not just Rodney. "I remember going to his house and talking, and that was part of the recreation in some ways." Rodney was a great advocate of ska—a mixture of Caribbean mento and calypso music infused with American jazz and blues, and then reggae—and would explain to his guests, including Sheriff, why it was progressive.

As we have also seen, Patricia was never a bystander in the political and intellectual world of Dar; she was fully and completely engaged in its debates and transformation. Early on, it was clear what she would not do. While many of the wives of expatriate academics would gather during the day at one of their houses, for tea, coffee and biscuits, to discuss their husbands and gossip, Patricia, who sampled one or two of these "coffee mornings," knew that this was not for her. From the family's first visit in 1966, she was busy working. Patricia recalls: "I worked as a public health nurse with the Dar es Salaam City Council. That meant that our circle of friends expanded beyond the University Campus." This broader exposure, she notes, also meant an opportunity to advance her language skills: "My Swahili improved since I worked with mostly Tanzanians." Patricia was deeply rooted in Tanzanian life, as were the children, and she helped bring this world into the orbit of her husband's political and social universe— away from the rarefied atmosphere of the campus.[39]

Describing the atmosphere at the university and in the city, and the relationship between the two, Walter Bgoya, a Tanzanian publisher and friend of the Rodneys, explains: "At that time the university was a very active place . . . people went both from the town to the university and university to town, participating in lectures, discussion groups, and all kinds of activities." There were also quite a lot of social events, parties, and coffee afternoons, Bgoya recalls, though he was not always able to attend. When he first arrived at the Tanzania Publishing House in 1972, the company was in a poor shape and he was forced to work sixteen- or seventeen-hour shifts. Nevertheless, Bgoya remembers, "those parties were fun, a lot of fun. At that time there was a dance called the ska. Rodney was very good at it, he enjoyed it a lot. He became completely transformed doing the ska." The Rodneys' experience during this period extended and expanded upon the vigorous social and intellectual engagement of their first eighteenth-month stint.

Bgoya explains that despite this ability to be consumed by the music, the parties, and the moment, Rodney was a serious person. "He seemed to be very good at scheduling his work. When it was time to work, it was time to work. You could be partying next door and Walter would be busy working in the next room. . . . This was something I could never understand but that I admired a lot."[40]

He also applied this approach to his pedagogy. Mbilinyi recalls witnessing Walter's discussion with a group of students: "Right now," he told them, "you are here to study, you have to grapple with difficult texts, you have to learn. You cannot just go marching in the streets; you have to study, and you have to learn." Some of these readings, he explained, were going to be difficult, and this was their "challenge." For Rodney, this was the hard and "relentless" effort that was required in order to make sense of the world, to understand the past and to present it in an intelligible way for the purpose of changing it. "Strive," "work," and "understand" were his watchwords.[41]

Describing his colleague and friend, Abdul Sheriff explains that "his personality was such that he was very open, yet reserved in some ways . . . in that he didn't just talk rubbish. But he was open and encouraging to Africans doing their studies." Though Sheriff and Rodney got to know each other as friends, their main connection was as colleagues in the same department. Rodney was younger by a few years, but his experience, scholarship, and work made him the senior historian of the two men.[42]

Walter Bgoya became close to the family, attending the "Rodney parties" but also dropping by the household. He recalls, "It was a house where comrades got together and we drank, not alcohol necessarily, but coffee and tea, and we talked." Unlike the other radical expats, Walter and Patricia, gravitated toward Tanzanian colleagues and comrades, and the attendance at their famous parties reflected this. Bgoya puts it like this:

> Although it is very hard to articulate now, there was always in my view a kind of thread that ran through Walter's thinking. This white Western intellectual dominance at the university, no matter how progressive it was; there was always, in my view, a tinge of discomfort with Walter. He would always have preferred to have more African intellectuals, more Pan-African gatherings and so on.

Important racial questions were often subsumed by class analysis, the prevailing version of radical social theory at the time—what Bgoya describes as "street Marxist ideology." This "blindness" to race issues created certain problems.

Rodney and Bgoya also had friends in common. Ben Mkapa, a close friend of Walter's, was at that point editor of the largest newspaper in Tanzania, *The Nationalist*, and an influential figure in the country (later, from 1995 to 2005, he would become the third president of Tanzania).[43] Bgoya and Rodney both wrote for the newspaper.

Remembering Patricia, Bgoya explains "that she was very clearly a very good mum. I could see the dynamics between Walter, Patricia, and the children, with this hardworking, radical father. Patricia was also working as a nurse. It was a very nice home, where you thought good things were going on."[44]

The family had to confront certain contradictions that came with the university post. Though it was commonplace to have staff—to look after the children, help cook, and clean the house—Rodney treated them as equals. Though a ubiquitous practice, it left many feeling deeply uneasy. At the time, scholar and activist Janet Bujra was married to the Tanzanian academic Abdalla Bujra and living on the campus in Dar. She explains how unpleasant and contradictory it was to have "staff":

> Everyone had them . . . even some servants had domestic helpers. I hated it, but the pressure was great; people would come to your door, desperate for work, and since there were few labor-saving devices or organized childcare, you almost had to have help if you were teaching and working. Security was also an issue for some households. Husbands did not expect to help at all, so women either had to do it all themselves or hire help.

Bujra explains the tensions this caused between the couple:

> As a local, my husband did not question this system and wouldn't have supported me in not having help—I did resist at first! In the end, I just tried to find someone I liked and to whom I paid decent wages (paying a lot more was not acceptable) and gave proper time off (most people paid a pittance and expected them to work all hours—e.g., they would have to sit waiting in the kitchen after serving the evening meal so that they could wash up before going home). I shared some of the work—especially cooking and childcare. I always looked for female workers as I didn't feel comfortable with men, albeit they were in the majority amongst servants. Basically, I didn't want to be an employer, felt uncomfortable about giving out orders and I didn't like having to share private space. With most of those who worked for us, I had a companionable relationship; in one case, when I was alone with two children, we all ate together, but that was very unusual. . . . Many employers did help out in small ways, though, with secondhand clothing, school fees, medicines, etc.[45]

The Rodneys made no distinction between students and colleagues. Some of Walter's closest comrades were students, who provided the most challenging and profound critiques of Tanzania's socialist experiments. Chief among them was Issa Shivji, who would also attend the famous parties. "Walter," Shivji remembers, "was an exceptionally warm and generous man, very concerned." Echoing other friends' accounts, he notes that there was simultaneously a lighthearted side to his character: "Walter liked parties and dancing, and some of us, his comrades, thought that this was frivolous—this business of dancing. So while the party was going on, we would be sitting and talking and Walter would come over and say, 'What's this, man? Come on, dance!'"[46]

Another friend, Leith Mullings, arrived from the United States in 1970 as a graduate student in anthropology. The young Black researcher, then only twenty-five, was inspired by the movements taking place across the world and Tanzania, in particular. Mullings remembers Walter being at the "centre of a large group of intellectuals," involved in the debates about the type of society that was being built. The atmosphere was distinct and extraordinary; Dar was a city that was impregnated with the entire period, and "scholars flocked there from all over the world to try to participate in the new endeavour."[47] Liberation movements from other parts of the continent, and world, jostled with activists from the States who were on the run from the US government, in a political environment that combined Ujamaa, socialism, Black Power, and Pan-Africanism. The Third World was ascendant—or so it seemed. The American invasion of Vietnam, and the resistance it had engendered, was taken as proof of this fact.

Mullings was already teaching at the university when she met Walter for the first time. As she describes him, "Walter was really a star at the university. He was really a quick thinker and a prolific writer. People just milled around him, basically. You couldn't be there and not know Walter Rodney." She quickly became a friend and was invited by Patricia and Walter to the "Rodney party." Placing it in wider context, she recalls, "[P]eople were not only doing a lot of work and thinking hard, they were also, as African-descended people all over the world, living life to its fullest whenever possible."[48]

Acutely conscious of issues of race, prejudice, and politics, Mullings was a natural match for the family. Walter and Patricia easily gravitated toward her. "He was a tremendously warm person and very unassuming," Mullings recalls. "He was certainly very, very in tune with people of African descent in various liberation movements, from the United States, certainly the Caribbean. . . . He was easy to talk to and he was funny, a real pleasure to be around."[49]

As Rodney's archive in Atlanta demonstrates, he corresponded with a remarkably broad range of people, many of them nonacademics. The letters, some of which were sent before he published *How Europe Underdeveloped Africa* (*HEUA*), came from students, ex-students, and enthusiastic readers who were hungry for recommendations for books and articles and radical information. One letter dated February 4, 1973, was from Hassan Waziri, a prison officer at Keko Remand Prison in Dar es Salaam. Through a mutual friend, he appealed to Rodney to help him achieve his "long-term ambition to get into University for studies."[50] Another correspondent wrote on July 20, 1971, from Tanga in northeastern Tanzania, "Kindly favour me with at least one article to keep me enlightened, Brother, this darkness is thick. Send me the torch!"[51]

Every year, Rodney also received dozens of invitations to speak. On December 29, 1969, for example, the Makerere Students' Guild (MSG) invited him to deliver a talk to students the coming February at Makerere University College in Kampala, Uganda. Mulabya Taliwaku (later a senior diplomat for the country)—then "minister for national and Pan-African affairs" of the MSG—explained that "you will be doing Africa a big service if you accepted to come and talk to us because we are strongly in need of revolutionary water."[52] Rodney was again invited to speak—in August 1970—for the MSG's Africa Week, and to debate with Ali Mazrui: "so that you challenge," student activist Pao-Paul Wangoola explained, "his teeming bourgeois, reactionary ideas—which he has now Christened 'Mazruiana.'"[53] Rodney accepted the invitation, as he always tried to do. As such, Rodney was astonishingly busy.

By the end of 1970, the family had dug in real foundations, in terms of their friends, work, and life. The couple had even made an application for the purchase of a piece of land at Ubungo, an area northwest of what is today Dar es Salaam's central business district. The regional land officer wrote to Walter on November 16, 1970, about the "application for the piece of land at Ubungo . . . which you wish to develop as a residential and a poultry farm."[54] Tanzania and its projects were also the family's.

An Outspoken Advocate

Consistently radical, clear in his thinking, patient with students, and always prepared to speak his mind, Rodney was a celebrated figure on the campus. All the same, Dar's heady atmosphere, with a rare cocktail of activists, was not a straightforward utopia. There were acute contradictions in the politics of President Nyerere and the ruling TANU party, who encouraged and joined in with the debate—at the university and else-where—at the same time that they guarded vigilantly the frontiers of the states and the parameters of the discussions.

In his frequent speaking engagements, Rodney had an incredible impact. To capture some of this influence, it is worth recording the words of Karim Hirji, a student at the university and later a lecturer in statistics. Hirji met Rodney for the first time at a lecture on July 10, 1969—very soon after Rodney and his family had arrived. The name of the talk reflected his recent three-month stay in Cuba, following his expulsion from Jamaica: "The Cuban Revolution and Its Relevance to Africa." The event was sponsored by the University Students' African Revolutionary Front, of which Hirji was a member. Hirji explains that his own knowledge of the topic was sketchy, but Rodney filled in the gaps: "His captivating metallic voice and lyrical style transfixed the audience. He made us laugh and ponder at the same time. His exposition of US imperialism made the case for the essential relevance of the Cuban experience to Africa unimpeachable. I am sure that evening that Walter won over many wavering student minds to the cause of African liberation."[55]

Students gathered around Rodney after the meeting to continue the discussion and delve even deeper. After the discussion, his first meeting with Rodney, Hirji wrote in his dairy: "The most impressive and brilliant speech I have heard so far. One could almost feel the strong conviction and deep emotions from which he spoke. I am convinced that Comrade Rodney is one of the most devoted and brilliant socialists to be found anywhere." This was—for Hirji—the start of a friendship that would last for the remaining six years of Rodney's stay. Hirji writes, "I learned, struggled and laughed with this wonderful man on many occasions over a host of issues, and at a close level."[56]

Rodney continued to speak and lecture whenever he could, and his collaboration with USARF also intensified. However, in December 1969 his natural instinct for forthright and open discussion hit hard against the wall of the contradictions of the Tanzanian state. He was invited to speak at the East and Central African Youth Conference at the university, which was organized by USARF and TANU Youth League members, including high school students, who came to the university to help run the conference and print the conference papers. It took place during the midterm break, when the campus normally would have been quiet; instead, there was a frenzy of activity, discussion, and organization.

On the second day of the conference, December 12, Walter addressed a packed audience on the "ideology of the revolution." He spoke on Frantz Fanon's "Pitfalls of National Consciousness," the famous chapter in *The Wretched of the Earth*. In the chapter, Fanon is scathing about the "caste of profiteers" who assumed power across independent Africa, with no project of transformation for the new states, and were only too happy to accept the scraps thrown to them by the Northern elite. Along with the rest of the book, it is an excoriating takedown of post-colonial power that today still reads with scintillating urgency. In the hands of Rodney in Dar in late 1969, it must have felt like a firework display. Independence was an illusion—a cruel mirage of freedom—and real liberation was still desperately required.

The startling analysis electrified the audience at the university. Rodney also added his own invective to Fanon's: independence obtained through negotiations with colonial powers were nothing more than "briefcase revolutions." In this sense, these states were little more than impotent puppet regimes. The implications were clear: these pitiful neocolonial governments needed to be overthrown in a popular revolution.

Of the event, Shivji recalls: "It was a very militant paper about the African revolution and so on castigating the first independent regimes as petit bourgeois regimes that had hijacked the revolution . . . where the leaders went to Lancaster House, compromised, and came back with independence and this was not real independence."[57]

A first-year student, Georgios Hadjivayanis—who became active after hearing Rodney speak on the Cuban Revolution—was assisting in "cyclostyling" copies of the papers for distribution to participants; therefore, he had been unable make the conference in the city. That night, Hadjivayanis remembers, *Cheche* had planned to publish the collection of conference papers—Rodney's included—as a special edition. The copies were printed and ready to distribute. The day finished in exhausted euphoria in the university bar, with the "greatest gathering of progressive youth."[58]

The following day, however, the celebration came to a quick and bitter end with a rebuttal in the main organ of the ruling party's paper, *The Nationalist*. Allegedly written by Nyerere himself, the article was entitled "Revolutionary Hot Air" and targeted Rodney with vehemence. Though it opened by stating that "discussions of socialism even led by our critics is welcome in Tanzania," the article declared it completely unacceptable to appeal to "revolutionary violence" to "overthrow the governments of independent African states." Following Fanon's arguments, Rodney had explained that "armed struggle" was a logical means of obtaining freedom and that only this path signaled "real independence." In the late 1950s and early 1960s, Fanon had become enamored by Cuba's revolution and frustrated with the negotiated compromises he saw ushering in independence elsewhere in Africa. It was along these lines that Rodney argued real independence required an act of "revolutionary violence."

The editorial was clear: "[S]tripped of its verbiage, this means that 'revolutionary youth' should be planning for, working for, and actively supporting, the violent overthrow of All Independent African governments—presumably including the Tanzanian government!" Tanzania coexisted with its neighbors, many of them, arguably, in the "neocolonial" camp that Rodney had pilloried. For TANU, this was intolerable and dangerous. Indeed, there was a limit to the extent that a critique would be accepted. Those who would persist in this "revolutionary hot air" that risked being blown across "our borders," the article explained, would cause havoc and hatred toward Tanzania. Nyerere's response was a thinly veiled threat: "Those who insist upon indulging in such practices will have to accept the consequences of their indulgence."[59]

The initial reaction to the editorial, and the rumor about who had written it, actually energized the conference—as Hadjivayanis explains, "[W]e thought the conference having provoked such a comment was becoming livelier." However, when news spread later the same day that anyone distributing the paper would be arrested, the mood changed, and the students beat a hasty retreat. Two student activists, Hadjivayanis and Ramadhan Meghji, were charged with destroying the boxes of copies they had printed.[60]

Rodney, meanwhile, wrote a letter in response. It did not issue an explicit apology but rather clarified, in a carefully worded statement, the contribution he had made at the conference. It was a difficult line to straddle, between maintaining his forthright and radical opinions and respecting his role as "guest" in a country to whose politics he was sympathetic. Rodney explained that his paper "represented my own personal views, and did not pretend to speak for any party or movement inside or outside of Tanzania." He did not intend to flout party discipline and acknowledged Tanzania's need to maintain "good neighbourliness." Further, he stated that all revolutionaries should respect the principle of "non-interference in a sphere beyond one's experience." The work of "interference" is for the people in the country themselves; Rodney would cease to intervene if it was deemed to be "in conflict with Tanzanian policy."

To the most important criticism in the editorial—that Rodney was implicitly challenging the Tanzanian government—he responded: "I drew distinction between two types of African governments emerging in the 'post-independence period.' The first, in the overwhelming majority, had hijacked the African revolution, the second, who understand that the revolution will mean nothing 'unless it transforms the lives of workers and peasants.'" This was a deftly formulated restatement that praises the "Tanzanian revolution," but only in so far as it "transforms the lives" of the downtrodden—while making no compromises, and indeed, in his way, urging and pressurizing Nyerere further along a radical path. It was quite a feat for a public apology.

Rodney explains in the letter his own commitment: "[I]n my day to day endeavours at the University of Dar es Salaam and in numerous talks and writings here and abroad, I have supported the efforts of the Tanzanian people and government to build a socialist society." He also states that in 1967 he argued for a "defence of the Tanzanian revolution—through a committed people's defence force, the National Service." In conclusion, he says that his use of the terms "capitalism," "imperialism," and "neo-colonialism" should not be seen as masking a sinister intention; rather, these terms are ways of exposing a barbarous and dehumanizing system, "one," he argues, "which snatched me from Africa in chains and deposited me in far-off lands to be a slave beast, then a sub-human colonial subject, and finally an outlaw in those lands." It is under these circumstances, as a former slave stolen from Africa, that he asks to be allowed to "learn from, participate in, and be guided by the African Revolution in this part of the continent; for this Revolution here is aimed at destroying that monstrous system and replacing it with a just socialist society."[61]

Walter was not deported; far from it, his stature at the university grew as a result of the intervention. In his inimitable way, he had not only stood his ground against the government but developed an argument at the same time. The letter was accompanied with a photograph of Walter—smiling confidently at the camera, wearing a leather jacket, the large collars of his shirt open.

Rodney's attitude was, Shivji tells us, that "this is the point of view of Tanzanian comrades, and I will not interfere." This was the watchword for all of Rodney's activities in Tanzania and the basis of his—occasionally harsh—judgment of other foreign colleagues and comrades. By all means, he urged them, engage, intervene, participate; but the lead must come from Tanzanians themselves, to whom foreigners should defer.[62]

Writing *How Europe Underdeveloped Africa*

During this time, Rodney was astonishingly prolific. Over a period of barely five years, he discussed tourism, wrote articles on socialism and development, and produced scholarly papers on slavery, at the same time that he was developing courses (including one on the Russian Revolution), organizing fieldwork, and continually corresponding with friends, comrades, and colleges around the world.[63] He delivered lectures to the US-ARF Sunday self-education class, and enthusiastically threw himself into work on the development of cooperative villages and student-run farms. Along with colleagues and student comrades, Rodney also attended exhibitions on the war in Vietnam and the ongoing (and nearby) struggle against Portuguese rule in Africa and apartheid South Africa. Meanwhile, he was also an active father of three children—Asha, Patricia and Rodney's third and last child, was born in Tanzania in 1971. Not least in this herculean workload was the task of synthesizing years of historical reading and research into the mighty *HEUA*—which he finished at the end of 1971.

Even before the publication of *HEUA*, Rodney was constantly being solicited for contributions to journals, special issues on specific themes, and political publications. On November 5, 1969, for example, Paul Sweezy and Harry Magdoff—prominent American radicals who coedited the socialist magazine *Monthly Review*—wrote to him asking for a contribution to a special issue of the *Monthly Review* marking the centennial of Vladimir Lenin's birth. They had approached other writers and Marxists—including Louis Althusser, Amílcar Cabral, Eldridge Cleaver, Eduardo Galeano, Eric Hobsbawm, and Ernest Mandel. Rodney responded quickly and submitted the paper "Lenin on the Imperialist Partition of Africa"; Sweezy wrote to him on February 2 to express his thanks for the "very interesting and useful contribution," sending the fifty-dollar honorarium, as Rodney had requested, to "FRELIMO in your name."[64]

If there was one aspect in which Rodney was typical among activists and intellectuals in Dar, it was for his penchant to work collaboratively; it was critical that ideas and drafts of papers be discussed with comrades. If this approach to intellectual work applied to Rodney's articles and interventions for *Cheche* and *Maji Maji*, so too was it key to the development of his opus. There is no clearer statement of this approach than Rodney's own declaration, in the preface of *HEUA*, where he names comrades "Karim Hirji and Henry Mapolu," both students at the time, who "read the manuscript in a spirit of constructive criticism." Hirji remembers: "To this day, I boast that I was among the very first to read what has become a classic of African history. I remember the three of us sitting down week after week, two or three hours at a time, discussing one chapter after next in the close confines of the USARF office."[65] Rodney writes:

> [C]ontrary, to the fashion in most prefaces, I will not add that "all mistakes and shortcomings are entirely my responsibility." This is sheer bourgeois subjectivism. Responsibility in matters of these sorts is always collective, especially with regard to the remedying of shortcomings. The purpose has been to try and reach Africans who wish to explore further the nature of their exploitation, rather than to satisfy the "standards" set by our oppressors and their spokesmen in the academic world.[66]

These were obviously Rodney's own standards and principles, but they were also ones of collective (and political) work that he had learned while in Tanzania.

As a consequence of his book and his work on curriculum development at the university and across Tanzania, later generations of students at the university—in various faculties—had studied secondary school history that had been rewritten with the significant input of Rodney. He was given considerable responsibility for creating a new state-sponsored curriculum that depicted colonialism more accurately. In fact, in a sign of Rodney's deep and personal commitment to this project of "rewriting" the curriculum, upon Rodney's return to Guyana in 1974 he brought back boxes of files and papers related to this work. A considerable part of the Walter Rodney Papers held at the Robert W. Woodruff Library of the Atlanta University Center is made up of these documents—specifically, papers from master's students, whom he was still supervising, on the work of rewriting the history curriculum for secondary school students; the students had been set to the task of researching a new secondary school history curriculum, including work on important aspects of the country's decolonization.

In a sense, *HEUA* can be read as an extension of Rodney's work rewriting Tanzania's secondary school history curriculum. There was certainly an overlap in his intended audience: the book's exceptionally accessible style was written with a bright Tanzanian and African secondary school student in mind. Ultimately, the book would be read by an entire generation—in Africa and around the world—for whom African politics and history would never be the same.

CHAPTER 6

How Europe Underdeveloped Africa

In some respects, Rodney had spent more than a decade preparing to write his masterpiece, *How Europe Underdeveloped Africa*. His historical research had taken place in London—the heart of the beast, where this "unmaking" of Africa through the pillage of people, wealth, and history had been based—and then in the most radical country in newly independent Africa, Tanzania, where a new, socialist history and socialism were being forged.

Rodney was acutely aware of the pulverizing sense of inferiority of Black people, due in no small part to his experience with those he had met and taught in Jamaica and his students in Dar es Salaam. For those who now lived in Africa, and the large Black communities living in the Caribbean, North America, and Europe, the impact of European intrusion on the continent, the slave trade, and colonialism was devastating. Black self-esteem and pride had suffered these hammer blows, even as public school systems educated students about the "darkness" of the continent, while a hegemonic media narrative repeated over and over again a story of stupidity and underdevelopment.

Rodney's intellectual and activist mission was to correct the lies of official history and to give back to the continent and its people a proper account of how Africa had become "underdeveloped," poor, and dependent.

A Revolution in a Book

One of the striking features about Walter Rodney's masterpiece is its sheer audacity. The book is a breathless journey across the continent, over a period of five hundred years—jumping effortlessly from country to country and region to region, providing both nuanced analysis and general over-view. The idea for such a volume, and the confidence to undertake and complete it, could have only come from someone of Rodney's intellectual strength and self-assurance. Rodney was a young man when he started work on the book, which was published just before his thirtieth birthday.

Explicitly written for a general audience, the book ditches the normal protocol of footnotes and extensive references. It is a full frontal assault on the academic training he had received and the closely guarded protocols of scholarly life: peer review, references, deference to scholarship, and, most importantly, the purge of political content. Rodney had these elements of his learning explicitly in his crosshairs; in his words, he aimed to "de-feat . . . attack . . . and to circumvent" them. The book was also an attempt to step out of a form of writing and research that was "only accessible to certain kinds of people." As Rodney explained about *HEUA* in 1975,

> [T]his text was designed to operate outside of the university. It might get into the university, yes. I hoped it would. But it was designed to op-erate from outside in the sense that it would not to be sponsored by the people who considered themselves, and whom many others considered to the ones at that time who had the last word . . . on African history and African studies. The aim of this publication was to reach our own peo-ple without having it mediate by the bourgeois institutions of learning.[1]

The book sounded a thunderclap, not only in the academic establishment, who blustered loudly on its publication, but also among thousands of read-ers across the world *outside* of lecture halls and seminar rooms.

The text is free of these "burdens" and includes, at the end of each chapter, "brief guides to reading." For example, at the end of chapter 5, "Africa's Contribution to the Capitalist Development of Europe: The Co-lonial Period," Rodney notes that

> here again, few scholars have treated capitalism and imperialism as an integral system involving the transfer of surplus and other benefits from colonies to metropoles . . . thus, European or white American Marxists who expose the rapacious nature of modern capitalism within their own countries have not generally integrated this with the exploitation of Af-rica, Asia and Latin America.[2]

These comments are instructive of Rodney's own project writing *HEUA* (after all, he notes that "few scholars" have undertaken this vital work) and in guiding his readers to continue their own investigations. However,

Rodney also gives a critical caveat: beware of the literature, he cautions, pointing to the inherent bias, prejudice, and incoherence typical of bourgeois social sciences.

Rodney's normal practice was to exercise extreme "discipline" when it came to his scholarly work, leaving absolutely no space to be attacked for sloppy scholarship or for failure to undertake rigorous study of the topic. Issa Shivji, at one time Rodney's PhD student, describes a revealing incident: "Once I went to him and said, 'Walter, comrade, I am fed-up, this business of writing this PhD, quoting this and quoting that and having footnotes, is exhausting. Stopping us from doing the work we want to do.' He said, 'No comrade, this is important, this bourgeois discipline is important.'" It was not uncommon to hear this kind of statement from Rodney; after all, it had been his training in Georgetown, Kingston, and London. "We have to be doubly competent, twice as good as the bourgeois scholars," he told his comrades, "to beat them."[3] This is what serious Marxist scholarship was: a bloody war against a highly trained and hardened enemy.

However, *HEUA* was an entirely different project. Rodney's journal articles and historical scholarship required these exacting standards in the fight with an academic enemy, but now a different audience was the focus. This volume formed part of his activist contribution; like *The Groundings with My Brothers*, it was a serious volume but nevertheless intended for a general audience. Consequently, the format and style had to be different—something about which Rodney was adamant. On receiving the readers' comments for the manuscript of HEUA, Rodney declared to his friend, the Tanzanian publisher Walter Bgoya, "I am not going to make any changes, I have not written an academic book . . . to hell with these fellows who want to see footnotes and references."[4] The book, he stated, was not for "serious bourgeois historians" but aimed, in Rodney's words, "at a strata of literate Africans in universities, secondary schools, the bureaucracy and the like. They will have to judge whether it makes sense in the light of the present conditions in Africa."[5]

The book is clear about the theoretical approach Rodney was using and states this categorically early on. For example, in the first chapter, he details Karl Marx's method, stating that the nineteenth-century writer "distinguished with European history several stages of development."[6] He proceeds to describe a certain type of Marxism—prevalent at the time—in which humanity proceeds stage by stage toward socialism (communism). In this historical materialist trajectory, civilization begins with "simple bands of hunters with Communalism," proceeding to slavery, feudalism, and capitalism, a system of economic and social organization that concentrates "in a few hands of ownership of the means of producing wealth and . . . unequal distribution of the products of human labor."[7] Yet Rodney—as a historian—refuses any false solace. In his analysis, development is not linear; China, he tells us, "entered the feudal phase of development" early on, "virtually 1000 years before the birth of Christ."

Using China as a model for development, Rodney shows that development is not a forward march based on purely economic principles. The growth of beliefs, practices, and institutions in China—in what Marxists describe as the "superstructure," situated above the economic organization of society—profoundly "affect" a society's development. "In China," he writes, "religious, educational and bureaucratic qualifications were of utmost importance."[8]

Out of capitalism, Marx predicted socialism would emerge on the basis of a principle of economic equality, eventually leading to the development of a modern, technologically advanced communism. To this Marxist approach, Rodney adds a vital component: "uneven development." Marx had presented a version of development based on European society, seeing revolution and class consciousness as evolving from the contradictions embedded in class society—the collective organization of production in advanced capitalism, in spite of private control of production. Rodney writes, "What is probably of more relevance for early African development is the principle that development over the world's territories has always been uneven."[9]

This unevenness, Rodney cautions, means we must avoid seeing development as a simple process of "successive stages." Capitalism is intrinsically international—a world system—and as a consequence, it intensifies the unevenness at the center of human development. "Uneven development has always insured that societies have come into contact when they were at different levels—for example, one that was communal and one that was capitalist."[10] This provokes further development and new forms of social organization (as well as crisis). Such an "uneven capitalism," Rodney explains, inevitably diverges from the model of European development described by Marx in the 1850s and 1860s.

The book is suffused with Rodney's close study of the Marxist method, and especially his enthusiastic reading of Leon Trotsky's *History of the*

Russian Revolution. It was Trotsky's working out of the peculiarities of Russian history—what Trotsky described as "combined and uneven development," or the ways in which the sum of global social relations and development impact on less developed capitalist countries—that had a lasting impact on Rodney's own work. Writing in notes for a graduate course entitled Historians and Revolutions in the academic year 1970–71, Rodney commented that Trotsky was

> [n]o pedantic follower of Marx on Western Europe, he insists on the objective analysis of Russia, stressing the country's uniqueness and specificity. . . . Trotsky has the capacity to use Marxist methodology skilfully and creatively, so that he actually enriches Marxist theory. . . . The economic evolution of Russia skipped over stages such as craft guild, while technical stages hat had taken decades elsewhere were simply leapt over.[11]

Karim Hirji and Henry Mapolu—both comrades and student activists in the University Students' African Revolutionary Front—were, like many in their generation, influenced by Andre Gunder Frank's theory of underdevelopment. However, Rodney was not among his adherents. Hirji explains that Rodney added a great deal to their reading of Gunder Frank's work: "[O]ur understanding was of a mechanistic variety. Walter provided the complexity and dynamics. We critiqued the lower emphasis on internal struggle. The towering historian patiently paid attention to the two upstart students, and, in places, revised what he had written."[12]

Consistent with many activists and writers at the time, Rodney believed that there was a genuine socialist world in the 1970s that existed alongside capitalism. However, this world was also bifurcated, with competing blocs and distinct models of socialist development emanating from the two global communist superpowers—China and the Soviet Union. For a generation of Marxists, whatever the drawbacks of these models, actually existing socialism created an extraordinary pull. Rodney was not immune; though always critical, he saw the communist world that had developed alongside capitalism as a source of hope and potential for the Third World.

Rewriting a Racist History

What Rodney wanted to do was present a total picture of African history from the period *before* European intrusion through slavery and colonialism. The story, as Rodney tells it, stops before independence. The book was not a thesis on "dependency" but an effort to counter the crippling racist lies about Africa—ones that have remained remarkably unchanged. Rodney was not seeking to develop a critique of African nationalisms (he did that elsewhere); rather, he was generalizing from actual historical conditions on the contemporary development of the continent.

Rodney's starting point was to challenge an academic discipline infused with racist ideas and assumptions. When Rodney was studying at the School of Oriental and African Studies in the early 1960s, it was common to hear, among established historians, that Africa existed outside the realm of "proper" human history. Sub-Saharan Africa was childlike, without the necessary prerequisites of thought, criticism, and historical progress. As Rodney was completing his PhD in London in 1965, the Oxford-based historian Hugh Trevor-Roper published *The Rise of Christian Europe*, in which he wrote: "Perhaps in the future, there will be some African history to teach. But at the present there is none, or very little: there is only the history of Europe in Africa. The rest is largely darkness."[13] How could there be history on the continent, Trevor-Roper asked, if all that could be detected was the "unrewarding gyrations of barbarous tribes"?[14]

These racist assumptions about Africa are so deeply engrained that today it remains common for them to be repeated by both the right-wing press and politicians and left-wing historians. The former French president Nicolas Sarkozy, speaking to a Senegalese audience made up of diplomats, press, politicians, and students in Dakar in 2007, edified his audience: "The tragedy of Africa is that the African has not fully entered into history."[15] Similarly, in his otherwise-excellent *People's History of the World* (1999), the Marxist activist and journalist Chris Harman wrote little about pre-colonial Africa, and what he did write was astonishingly simplistic. Explaining the differences of development between Europe and the African continent in "climatic" terms, he succeeded in reproducing existing prejudices and made little use of the rich literature on Africa's real history—to which Rodney's own work is a crucial contribution.[16]

HEUA was written to challenge the excoriating racism that Rodney had found in academia, schooling, and society as a whole. From his own experiences in the Caribbean, in London, among the Left, and in the assumptions embedded in academic work, Rodney sought to counter this racism in a single book. *HEUA* also targeted deep feelings of inferiority—the great lie of a past without history—felt by students and activists whom Rodney had taught in Tanzania and Jamaica. The book was written for a Black audience—in the Caribbean and North America, as well as on the continent. That it was read by the white academy was to be expected, but their enthusiasm did not really interest him, nor did their criticism—though he engaged with the latter.

The book is remarkably sober; after all, Rodney was too serious a historian and Marxist to write a mere eulogy to the big states of the continent's past. Rodney was aware of the urgency of the book and the sense that it could only be written by him—infused as he was by African history *and* by the Black Power movement. In this respect, the 1972 book can be seen as a companion volume to his 1969 classic, *The Groundings*; the audience was the same and so was the topic. Rodney's contribution, written with the audacity of youth, is a survey of the entire continent over four decades—providing case studies and evidence of the violent inclusion of Africa into an emerging global system of capitalist production.

HEUA could not be further from an orthodox book on either Marxism or dependency theory (as Rodney has been accused). Indeed, Rodney was writing against the enormous weight of establishment historians and of contemporary criticism of Marxism; all the more impressive, he managed to do this without turning his book into a turgid critique. For Rodney, Marxism is a universal theory, and the complex and diverse elements of Africa's pre-colonial and colonial history *can* be explained within a Marxist perspective. However, the question of development must be undertaken with the correct historical approach. Rodney was defending Marxism not by way of theoretical polemic but with fulsome historical research. As such, his work was a challenge to the stubborn faith in progress found in many Marxist accounts.

Rodney was acutely aware that capitalism had neither brought about regeneration from the calamity of colonial destruction nor led the continent automatically to revolutionary transformation. Old civilization, societies, and communities were destroyed without a corresponding reconstruction. Real human development—the *possibility* of transcending capitalism—lay in a dialectical process.

In Rodney's dazzling historical account of Africa's tragic entanglement with Europe, there is a distinct sense that neither the past nor the present can be affirmed. Rather, the only way to secure real development for the continent is to break free of this abusive connection. Africa must chart a new path that neither glorifies the past nor presents it as a model for the future. But this will only happen if we understand history with the same rigor and thoroughness that Rodney displays.

Before European Slavers

The first part of *How Europe Undeveloped Africa* deals with African history prior to the arrival of European explorers and slavers. As it is through the book, Rodney's approach is forthright and honest, and this "prior" history he tells us reveals the "workings of the law of uneven development of societies."[17] There were the Ethiopian Empire and the smaller-scale hunting and gathering communities of the Congo Basin, the empires of the Western Sudan, and the Khoisan hunter-gatherers of the Kalahari Desert. He does not attempt to reproduce the "European experience"; rather, he observes that "stages" followed in some parts of the world were not replicated elsewhere. The purpose of the chapter, Rodney tells us, is to "establish that Africa in the fifteenth century was not just a jumble of 'tribes.'"[18]

Rodney explains that by the fifteenth century, "Africans everywhere had arrived at a conservable understanding of the total ecology—of the soils, climate, animals, plants, and their multiple interrelationships." From this derived a complex range of skills: animal trapping, house construction, tool use, identification and refinement of medicines, and "a system of agriculture."[19] Societies across the continent developed "guilds," associations of specialists that served (like those that would later appear in Europe) to pass on these skills. Rodney tells us, "At Timbuktu, there were tailoring guilds, while in Benin guilds of very restricted caste type controlled the famous bronze industry."[20]

In the centuries preceding the arrival of European traders, Rodney explains, there was an expansion of productive forces. He writes: "The principles of family and deferment to age were slowly breaking down. . . . The introduction of iron, for example, gave economic and military strength to those who could make and acquire it."[21] The general trend was for "communalism" to give way to complex forms of stratification—and, increasingly, of class division. This era of class formation, of transition, was also marked by the growth of state structures. At first these formations were weak and immature, but soon various states began to acquire greater strength, in turn increasing taxation, delisting labor, and developing repressive structures.

Rodney sounds a word of caution—the obsession with the "state" among European historians is, he writes, used as a measure of "civilization" "[t]hat is not entirely justified, because in Africa there were small political units which had relatively advanced material and non-material cultures."[22] The Ibo of Nigeria, as well as the Kikuyu of Kenya, did not produce centralized state structures, yet both had complex and sophisticated systems of political rule. Both were, in addition, expert agriculturists and ironworkers. The Ibo, for example, had long been manufacturing brass and bronze by the ninth century.

As discussed above, in this first chapter, the central category is "unevenness"; indeed, it is used again and again in the narrative. The huge variety of forms—communal, state, and stateless—that marked African societies in the centuries before the arrival of the Europeans each mingled, interacting with and impacting each other. The chapter zigzags across the continent with a restless, effortless confidence as Rodney weaves his way in and out of pre-colonial Egypt, Nubia, and the Maghreb, dipping into historical debates with "African nationalists and progressive whites" (along with the normal stock of establishment historians) and then back to examples to illustrate his central argument.

On Ghana, Rodney writes, "The origins of the empire of Ghana go back to the fifth century A.D. . . . Mali had its prime in the thirteenth and fourteenth centuries, and Songhai in the two subsequent centuries."[23] The Western Sudan, a region we now identify as West Africa, saw elaborate cotton cultivation, handicraft industry, and trade. Mining was also significant—with certain "royal clans," such as the Kante, becoming specialist blacksmiths. Throughout the account on Western Sudan, Rodney is mindful of the racist echo of the white academic authority. For example, Rodney targets the British historian E. W. Bovill for his description of the "silent or dumb" barter in Ghana's pre-colonial gold industry, which involved the banging of drums that called out natives from holes in the ground, where they lived "naked." As Rodney writes, "[T]he only thing dumb about the trade is what he writes about it."[24]

Upon arrival, the Europeans were aghast at what they found. The Portuguese, finding their way to the Gambia River, saw how gold was traded and "marvelled at the dexterity shown by the Mandinga merchants."[25] These merchants carried scales inlaid with silver and suspended from silk cords. Within the Mandinga were the Dioulas, a group of professional traders who were adapt at crisscrossing Western Sudan. Traversing coastal areas of Gambia, Sierra Leone, Liberia, and the Ivory Coast, they traded kola nuts from Liberia, gold from the Akan (in modern-day Ghana), and leather from Hausaland. Nor was the trade limited to the region; goods from Egypt, the Maghreb, and the Mediterranean coast also entered Western Sudan, crossing the Sahara.

Another civilization Rodney identifies is Zimbabwe, whose multifaceted brick "city" developed "appreciably" in the centuries before the European intrusion. By the fifteenth century, an empire had emerged, named "Monomotapa" by Europeans. The site of "Great Zimbabwe" remains to this day, near the modern Zimbabwean city of Masvingo. The vision of the surviving stone ruins is electrifying; the main structure is a tower almost one hundred meters long and eighty meters wide, with walls fifteen meters high and eight meters thick. Its bricks are placed one on top of the other, without cement, and have stood undisturbed by the interruptions of the proceeding centuries. Rodney notes, "[O]ne European archaeologist is reported to have said that there was as much labour expended in Zimbabwe as on the pyramids in Egypt."[26] This might be an exaggeration, he says, but the development of the empire of Zimbabwe (of which only "Great Zimbabwe" survives) would have required the mobilization of huge amounts of labor.

The "greatness" of these pre-colonial societies required another fantastic effort: the need, on the part of colonial and imperial authorities, to explain these "anomalous" developments. Rodney records, "When Cecil Rhodes sent in his agents to rob and steal in Zimbabwe, they and other Europeans marvelled at the surviving ruins of the Zimbabwe culture, and automatically assumed that it had been built by white people." A Black civilization, they reasoned, had to have been built by the genius of white settlement—presumably visiting architects and designers from London and Paris! Rodney—forever the temperate historian—warns against "wonder" at these developments, the very expression of which is a symptom of our racist education. Rather, we need to assess these developments with the "calm acceptance that it was a perfectly logical outgrowth of human social development with Africa, as part of the universal process by which man's labor opened up new horizons."[27] "Great Zimbabwe" was not some sort of superhuman oddity; rather it was a development built on the soil of centuries of advanced agriculture and mining.

The task of the Marxist historian, Rodney notes, is not to celebrate but to appraise calmly. He writes, for example, that in Zimbabwe, "there was no single dam or aqueduct comparable to those in Asia or ancient Rome, but countless small streams were diverted and made to flow around hills."[28] This was evidence, in other words, that indicated sound knowledge of scientific principles. Interestingly, Rodney's approach never lets the reader sit still for long. As such, the pleasure of reading about the hubris and stupidity of Cecil Rhodes, or the achievements of Zimbabwe, is quickly undermined by a clearheaded assessment of Africa's uneven development prior to the arrival of the first Europeans.

On the basis of these the racist accounts of African barbarity and European civilization, Rodney writes an entirely new history of the continent—one that profoundly muddles the "stages" of history preferred by a certain type of Marxist history and conventional accounts. Africa before the arrival of Europeans was a complicated mix of societies and cultures, classes, and conflicts.

Most accounts of those who first visited the continent from Portugal, Holland, or England saw in West and East Africa development that was comparable to the societies they had recently left. Rodney cites a Dutch visitor to the city of Benin, who remarked:

> The town seems to be very great. When you enter into it, you go into a great broad street . . . which seems to be seven or eight times broader than the Warmoes street in Amsterdam. . . . The king's palace is a collection of buildings which occupy as much space as the town of Harlem, and which is enclosed with walls. There are numerous apartments for the Prince's ministers and fine galleries, most of which are as big as those on the Exchange at Amsterdam.[29]

Yet no sooner do we have this comparison then Rodney reminds us against the "self-delusion" that all things between Benin and Holland were equal. "European society," Rodney writes, "was already more aggressive, more expansionist, and more dynamic in producing new forms." Picking up from the quote above, Rodney clarifies the historical account: "[I]n the galleries of the exchange at Amsterdam sat Dutch burghers— the ancestors of the modern bourgeoisie of industry and finance . . . this class in the fifteenth century were able to push the feudal landowners forward or aside."[30]

European Exploration and Slavery

HEUA does not provide an "orthodox" account of "underdevelopment" through African history. The influence and impact of European contact—on the structure of trade, slavery, and, later, direct penetration—on African societies was catastrophic and marked a rupture with the past. However, it was the dynamic and intricate meshing of forces that triggered developments on the continent that engaged African agency. Indeed, Rodney provides a full class-based history of the continent under the impact of European commerce. Nowhere in Rodney's account does he describe a simple process of external control of Africa's entire socioeconomic trajectory—far from it.

In a telling explanation of his perspective, Rodney writes, "Modern African nationalist historians correctly stress that Africa had a meaningful past long before the coming of Europeans. They also stress that Africans made their own history long after coming into contact with Europe, and indeed right up to the period of colonisation." This approach, which pushes African agency to the center of the picture, is not, he tells us, incompatible with one that emphasizes the central "transformatory" role of external (i.e., European) forces involving the trade in slaves, ivory, and gold. In order to align this "combination" of seemingly distinct approaches, Rodney cautions the reader that they must see the external (and mostly European) influence on the continent until 1885 as extremely uneven, with the coasts impacted to a far-greater degree than the hinterlands. While commerce affected aspects of African life profoundly, certain political and ideological "apparatus" were left untouched. Finally, in Rodney's words, "dynamic features of independent African evolution and development continued to operate after 1500."[31]

The idea that African history somehow stalled with the arrival of Europeans is a self-evident absurdity; however, it was nevertheless altered in deeply disturbing ways, as independent paths to further development were stifled. The point remains that Rodney's account does not line up with his critics' depiction of his book as positing a one-dimensional, straightforward "underdevelopment," free of agency, class dynamics, and independent activity.[32] However, it would be equally ridiculous to argue that European contact benefited Africa in the pre-colonial period; indeed, slavery, from its emergence in the fifteenth century, was a hammer blow to the continent.

Rodney explains, "[S]lave trading led to the commercial domination of Africa by Europe, within the context of international trade." Yet it is also true that even with this domination—from which the continent would never be the same again—in areas of Africa (south Central Africa), there were societies that could pursue an independent path, determined, in Rodney's words, by the "interplay between African people and the African environment in the particular localities." Rodney is also clear that even in those regions where there was direct contact with European traders and slave ships, African political authorities were not "displaced."

European ideological penetration of the continent was also limited in this period. There were attempts made to "access" Africa by missionaries, but most were consigned to, as Rodney describes, "blessing Africans as they were about to be launched across the Atlantic into slavery." Rodney's full description of the "autonomy" and agency enjoyed by African polities is worth quoting at length—and remembering:

> So long as there is political power, so long as a people can be mobilized to use weapons, and so long as a society has the opportunity to define its own ideology and culture, then the people of that society have some control over their own destinies, in spite of constraints such as those imposed as the African continent slipped into orbit as a satellite of capitalist Europe.[33]

In his discussion of slavery, Rodney challenges the simplistic formulation, made by Senegal's first president, Leopold Senghor, that the slave trade swept Africa like a bushfire and left nothing standing. Rodney argues that there is a better metaphor, one that suits a proper historical account: "The truth is that a developing Africa went into slave trading and European commercial relations as into a gale-force wind, which shipwrecked a few societies, set many off course, and generally slowed down the rate of advance."[34]

Beginning with the coastal societies, society after society, state after state, were dragged into the slave trade. However, at all stages, the penetration of the trade was met with resistance. In Dahomey in West Africa, in the eighteenth century, the king attempted to oppose the European slave traders; as a consequence, the society was denied European products, which by this point had become important. Realizing that Dahomey's development and the slave trade were in contradiction to each other, the king, Agaja Trudo, organized raids on European forts and slave camps that lasted from 1724 and 1726. As a consequence, the trade was briefly reduced to a trickle.

Agaja failed in his efforts to persuade Europeans in allowing the state to develop "new lines" of economic activity; but at the same time, Rodney notes, the European slavers also failed to crush the Dahomean state. By 1730, the slave trade had resumed—though on a much more restricted basis. In Angola, the Portuguese used direct military intervention to seize political power; it was in reaction to this aggression that the state of Matamba was founded in 1630, with Queen Nzinga as head. Matamba's formation was an explicit effort to coordinate resistance to the Portuguese slavers—with the state only losing the battle for control in 1648. Rodney reports, "So long as it opposed trade with the Portuguese, it was an object of hospitality from neighbouring African states which had compromised with European and slave trading." Matamba did not have the power to stand alone. By 1656, Queen Nzinga was forced to resume negotiations with the invaders.

Other examples of resistance in *HEUA* tell the same story: one of resistance to the European slave trade, which was eventually broken as most parts of the continent became drawn in. In the early eighteenth century, the Baga people (in what is modern-day Guinea) lived in small states. In 1720, Tomba, one of the leaders of the Baga, tried to secure a coalition of states to stop the slave trade. However, Rodney writes, "[h]e was defeated by local European resident-traders, mulattos and other slave trading Africans."[35] European traders formed their own alliance to break the resistance and ensure that Tomba and his Baga followers continued in their ascribed role as suppliers of captives.

In addition to the gradual incorporation—"underdevelopment"—of Africa, and the inevitable collaboration with the trade, were the enormous benefits accrued to Europe. Rodney speaks of the exploitation of Africa and African labor as a "source for the accumulation of capital" to be reinvested in Western Europe. He writes, "The African contribution to European capitalist growth extended over such vital sectors as shipping, insurance, the formation of companies, capitalist agriculture, technology and the manufacture of machinery."[36] The Atlantic trade was also an arena for technological competition between European states—the Dutch adapted the Portuguese and Spanish caravels, small and swift sailing ships used for exploration of the African Atlantic coast in the fifteenth century, with the British adapting Dutch technology to become the leading sailing nation. As Rodney says, "The Atlantic was their laboratory."[37]

Some of the wealthiest cities in Europe were those "slave ports" of Bristol, Liverpool, Nantes, Bordeaux, and Seville. Connected to these ports, Rodney tells us, "there often emerged the manufacturing centers which gave rise to the Industrial Revolution." The first center of the Industrial

Revolution was Lancashire, whose advance—as the avant-garde of this revolution—was reliant on the growth of Liverpool.

The list of major capitalists who benefited directly, securing their "primitive accumulation of capital" from the slave trade, should still shock us today. David and Alexander Barclay were involved in the trade from the 1750s before setting up Barclays Bank. Lloyd's of London went from being a small "coffee house" to becoming one of the largest insurance houses, achieved by, in Rodney's words, "dipping into profits from slave trade and slavery."[38] Beyond these "direct" links are other ones—American produce, Rodney writes, was a result of African labor. "Sugar from the Caribbean was re-exported from England and France to other parts of Europe to such an extent that Hamburg in Germany was the biggest sugar-refining center in Europe in the first half of the eighteenth century."[39]

The slave trade, he notes, was clearly not the sole factor in the development of Western Europe from the fifteenth century. In England there were the enclosures of commons that drove the peasantry off the land, forcing more and more into urban centers and emergent industry—yet it was the African trade that hastened these elements. "That is why," Rodney explains, "the African connection contributed not merely to economic growth . . . but also to real development in the sense of increased capacity for further growth and independence."[40]

African rulers, who could see the distinct advantages of European technology (which Europeans were constantly stealing from one another), sought to acquire these advances for their own internal development. These "requests," Rodney tells us, were "deliberately ignored." For instance, the Ethiopian court in 1520 requested Portuguese assistance with the expansion of Ethiopian industry. These requests continued into the eighteenth century, as seen when Trudo of Dahomey appealed for European craftsmen to work with their own tradesmen, sending an ambassador to London to lodge this petition. Rodney writes, "The Asantehene Opoku Ware (1720-1750) also asked for Europeans to set up factories and distilleries in Asante, but he got no response."[41] In response, Africans took creative initiative, finding ways to bypass European industry. For example, Asante society under Opoku Ware took imported silk, carefully undid it, and combined the thread with cotton to make kente cloth. Rodney concludes, "[T]here would have been no difficulty in such African societies mastering European technical skills and bridging the rather narrow gap which existed between them and Europe at that time."[42]

Further efforts were made to acquire the means to make firearms and gunpowder; after all, wars were being fought with these imported and traded European weapons. In Dahomey, an expression emerged that emblematizes these desires, "He who makes powder wins the war." Rodney remarks, "Of course, Europeans were also fully aware that their arms technology was decisive, and there was not the slightest chance that they would have agreed to teach Africans to make firearms and ammunition."[43]

Toward the end of the chapter on African society until 1885, and almost as an aside, Rodney writes a few pages on the ama-Zulu and Shaka—a Zulu leader born in 1787 who is regarded as one of the great warriors and leaders of his era (and whose name was adopted by Walter and Patricia's for their first son). As head of the small clan of ama-Ngoni (a people who trace their origins to the Zulu), within a few years he had reorganized it into a great fighting force, and soon—through warfare and political maneuvers—he had united the ama-Ngoni, previously divided into independent clans, into a single force. Rodney reports, "It was a tribute to the organisational and agricultural capacity of the society . . . that it could feed and maintain a standing army of thirty thousand men, reequip them with iron weapons."[44]

Rodney repeats the story not to retell the greatness of Shaka—who is often presented as some sort of unique hero warrior, unparalleled in African history—but in order to explain that his achievements, the development of the Zulu people, were possible because no one came to "civilize" them. (In fact, in 1876 a much-diminished force of the ama-Zulu defeated the British in the Battle of Isandlwana.) Under the propulsion of internal dynamics, and adapting from previous innovations, Shaka was capable of reorganizing, uniting, and innovating on an impressive scale. There is a model here of "autonomous" development, Rodney tells us, without the brutal intervention of European slavers and gunboats. The great nineteenth-century achievements of the Zulu people in technological development, social organization, and warfare were possible because of the relative autonomy of the Zulu nation, free from external interference.

Concluding the chapter on pre-colonial contact and African history, Rodney explains that it is important to follow the development of Europe and the underdevelopment of Africa, but, in his words, "to understand how those two combined in a single system—that of capitalist imperialism."[45] The effect of this single system on the "comparative economics" of the two continents is that while there was a "slight difference" when

Portuguese sailors arrived in West Africa in 1444, by the time "European robber statesman" sat down in Berlin in 1884 and 1885 it was a huge gap.

These gaps were not just between nations and continents, but also, crucially, between classes. Within Britain, Germany, and Holland, for example, there was the stark polarization of wealth, Rodney explains, "between the capitalists on the one hand and the workers and a few peasants on the other."[46] There was thus unevenness between *and* within the nations of Europe.

The "scramble for Africa" that led to colonialism—the direct occupation and control of the continent—was facilitated by the long period of pre-colonial trade. Political domination followed the pulverization of the continent over hundreds of years. Though there were slave forts and small European settlements, Europe had been incapable of penetrating deep into Africa. Technological development by the end of nineteenth century ensured that the continent could now be conquered and occupied—though not without considerable difficulties. Rodney is correct to point out that the "[b]reech-loading rifles and machine guns were a far cry from the smooth-bored muzzle loaders and flintlocks of the previous era. European imperialists in Africa boasted that what counted was the fact that they had the Maxim machine gun and Africans did not."[47]

Yet, even during the pre-colonial period, when African societies made efforts to develop, they were savagely stamped on. In Egypt, Muhammad Ali, who ruled between 1805 and 1849, used the relative lack of European interference in this period in North Africa to attempt to manufacture its own cotton, as well as glass, paper, and other goods. Rodney writes, "Egypt was not to be used as a dumping ground for European goods which would undermine local industry, so that protective tariff walls were set up around Egypt's 'infant industries.'"[48] This did not lead to isolation; rather, Ali hired European experts to advise his government and traded with the rest of the world. These ambitions clashed with those of British and French industrialists—who sought to produce raw cotton by all available means, but for whom it was inconceivable that Egypt would become an industrial competitor. European banks and financiers succeeded in transforming the country into an "international beggar" by the second half of the century—with the country largely mortgaged to European capital.

In conjunction with these methods, the period also saw, Rodney tells us, a dramatic escalation of "white racism," with Britain characteristically leading European nations in this respect. For example, when the Fourah Bay College in Sierra Leone sought affiliation with Durham University in

1874, the London *Times* newspaper apparently declared, "Durham should next affiliate with the London Zoo!"[49]

In much the same way a class of Africans was to become key to the perpetuation of European domination and rule under colonialism, during the pre-colonial period of "trade," many Africans had already become "middlemen" in commercial roles—working as a "comprador" class serving European interests. A new trading group made up of children of European or Arab fathers had played this role for years in Africa and the Caribbean. In Senegal, for example, this "mulatto" class lived in the trading ports and cities, such as Gorée, Dakar, Saint Louis, and Rufisque.

Commenting on the role of this "comprador" class during the transition to colonialism, Rodney writes, "One of the most striking features of 19th century West African history is the manner in which Africans returned from slavery under European masters and helped in the establishment of colonial rule."[50] In many respects, it was the softening up of the continent over centuries of the "pre-colonial" trade, and Africa's integration into an emergent global capitalism, that had made full colonial conquest possible.

Colonial Conquest

Rodney's approach to the European conquest and control of Africa has shaped an entire body of research on the relationship between the North and what was known as the Third World. However, Rodney does not spend very much time looking at the resistance to full colonial intrusion into the continent. Rodney's concern, rather, was with the mechanisms of control established over the course of occupation, as European powers faced enormous resistance on the continent. Resistance *and* existing economic and political development had to be uprooted by the occupying powers. In Algeria, for example, the territory in what eventually became a French département took eighteen years from 1830 to be fully integrated (in fact, Algeria was not one French département, but three). The French confronted extraordinary resistance from the native population—who needed or wanted none of French "civilization." When integration finally took place, the Arab-Berber population (or *indigène*) were not accorded French citizenship and remained subjects with few rights.

The experience in Algeria, as across the rest of the continent, was in large part an effort to drive pre-colonial society back. Therefore, trade, schooling, and human development were systematically underdeveloped by French colonialism. In an important historical account, the radical Algerian writer Mostefa Lacheraf explains these developments powerfully:

> Algeria was no barbarian country inhabited by illiterate people with anarchic or sterile institutions. Its human and economic values attained a high level. . . . Patriarchal, agricultural and civic lifestyles coexisted . . . throughout there was a marked sense of energy and industry: in maritime and artisanal techniques, in para-industrial methods, in city organisation, in the commerce with Africa and across the Mediterranean, in a system of intellectual values which was strongly impregnated with legal traditions, formal logic, more or less rationalist theology, with Arabic and Maghrebine folk traditions . . . a widely diffused culture, generalised through its written and oral expression. . . . Algeria in the earlier 19th century displayed far fewer deficiencies, far more chance of progress in relation to the civilisation of the period and the general movement of free peoples than it did by the end of the century, stripped of its millions of hectares of forest, robbed of its mines, of its liberty, of its institutions and thus of the essential prop and motor of any collective progress.[51]

Schooling, which had been widespread when the French arrived in 1830, was almost completely wiped out. By 1950, the United Nations Educational, Scientific, and Cultural Organization reported 90 percent illiteracy among the Algerian population.[52] Under the impact of the invasion, millions of Algerians lost their lives by direct killings, displacement, and the collapse of food security. Communities were forced off the land and fertile agricultural regions taken over for the cultivation of vines for the export of wine to Europe. Algeria's population fell to approximately 3.5 million in 1852, from 6 million in 1830. Still, the French did not have an easy time—nor did any of the colonializing powers. Pacification of Algerian resistance was never guaranteed, even with the superior weaponry and technology of European power. From 1830 to 1871, there were only a few years without fighting.

Elsewhere on the continent, the pattern was broadly similar. When it comes to these developments, Rodney's account is rich in examples and detail. As he illustrates, regions that were self-sustaining in food production were compelled to turn themselves over to cash crop production for export to Europe. By the late nineteenth century, whole fertile areas of West Africa century were transformed, under the impact of direct force and colonial taxation, to start producing ground-nuts (in Senegal, Nigeria, and Chad, for example) and cocoa (in Cote d'Ivoire and Ghana, for example). A catastrophic change in food production, combined with a series of El Niño–induced droughts and famines, in the context of colonial agricultural transformation, led to a series of what Marxist historian Mike Davis calls "late Victorian holocausts."[53] Across India, South America, China, and Africa, local populations were wiped out. European development of African food systems thus deepened the continent's underdevelopment.

The Congo serves as a graphic example of these processes—the incorporation that became full-bodied colonialism. The Berlin Conference of 1884–85, a gentlemen's agreement among the European powers, officially recognized the Belgian King Léopold II as the legal head of the euphemistically named International African Association of the Congo, soon renamed as the Congo Free State. The stated aims of the new Belgian colony were to abolish slavery—indeed, war would be waged against Arab slave traders for this purpose—and to promote free trade. These pretexts were frequently used by European powers as justifications for colonial occupation and invasion.

Rodney tells us that over the course of colonialization, the metropolitan power profited enormously—an argument that bears repeating. Even today, we often hear that colonialism was not a profitable endeavor, and one of minimum lasting impact. Rodney was clear about the balance sheet, and he provided a forensic account of the political-economic mechanisms of colonial power. His description of the role of currency in the colony is illustrative of both the processes of underdevelopment and Rodney's systematic approach.

Coins and notes, he tells us, were initially issued by private banks. For Britain, this function was soon taken over by the West African Currency Board and the East African Currency Board, set up in 1912 and 1919, respectively. Yet currency issued by these boards had to be secured by sterling reserves, which directly earned money from the continent. Rodney explains:

> The manner in which the system worked was as follows. When a colony earned foreign exchange (mainly) through exports, these earnings were held in Britain in pounds sterling. An equivalent amount of local East and West African currency was issued for circulation in the respective colonies, while the sterling was invested in British government stock, thereby earning even more profit for Britain. The commercial banks worked hand in hand with the metropolitan government and the Currency Boards to make the system work.[54]

These reasonably complex financial networks had as a common objective the enriching of Europe and the parallel and connected impoverishment of Africa. To put some figures on these reserves makes the example completely clear. In the small colony of Sierra Leone, by the late 1950s, sterling reserves had reached sixty million pounds. Yet in 1955, the UK held 210 million from the sale of cocoa and minerals from the Gold Coast (today's Ghana). Rodney explains that "Africa's total contribution to Britain's sterling balances in 1945 was 446 million pounds, which went up to 1,446 million by 1955."[55]

If there were any lingering doubt about the continent's contribution to Europe's twentieth-century wealth and development, Rodney describes the "exacting tribute" Belgian extracted from its colonies. Once Belgium was occupied by Germany in May 1940, a government in exile was established in London. The costs of running that exiled government were financed entirely by the Congo—the country's principal African colony. Rodney cites the colonial secretary of the exiled government, who explains: "[T]he Congo was able to finance all the expenditure of the Belgian government in London, including the diplomatic service as well as the cost of our armed forces in Europe and Africa, a total of some 40 million pounds." The country's gold reserves could be left untouched; thanks to the Congo, not a single dollar had to be borrowed. Rodney goes on to note that, following the war, the surplus of earnings by the Congo in currencies other than the Belgian franc were all amassed by the National Bank of Belgium.

Though the exact financial approaches used by different European powers varied, the pattern of extracted wealth was the same. Whether this siphoned capital came through government currency boards or commercial banks, colonial powers succeeded in "earning" billions in foreign exchange from the sale of raw materials. "Colonialism," Rodney concludes, "meant a great intensification of exploitation within Africa."

A word needs to be said on the focus Rodney takes in the book—specifically in chapter 5, which deals with Africa's contribution to European development. What is striking about the chapter is the astonishing detail of his analysis of this period of political economic history. Though the book was written for a general (African and Black) audience with little familiarity with this history, he does not skimp on complexity or detail. Apart from the very occasional exclamation, Rodney's style is lucid and clearheaded throughout—uncompromising but never polemical.

Rodney details not just the "takeover" of African territory by a specific European power, but also the intersection of private companies in this process, often across national borders. For example, Portugal was too poor to fully exploit its Southern African colonies of Mozambique and Angola, and consequently opened both colonies to foreign, frequently American, capital and finance. Meanwhile, the Belgian Congo also sought American finance to exploit the country's rich uranium deposits.

American involvement on the continent after the Second World War accelerated this process, and the Marshall Plan—a huge injection of US funding to war-torn Europe—Rodney writes, "allowed Americans to buy controlling shares" in companies that were exploiting African resources.[56] America was edging out old colonial powers on the continent—an acknowledgment that would have had chilling resonance among Rodney's Caribbean and American readers.

Elaborating on the intersection of political and economic forces in the underdevelopment and exploitation of the continent, Rodney writes:

> To fully understand the colonial period, it is necessary to think in terms of the economic partition of Africa. Unlike the political partition of the nineteenth century, the economic partition had no fixed or visible boundaries. It consisted of the proportions in which capitalist powers divided up among themselves the monetary and non-monetary gains from colonial Africa.[57]

Nor was actual possession of colonies a barrier to profiting from colonial plunder. Rodney's account is a deep description of the exploitation by private capital, mining companies, banks, and multinationals, who enjoyed the "fruits of exploiting the colonial and semi-colonial world" as a common treasury for metropolitan capitalism as a whole.[58] The section in the book on the multinational Unilever is a tour de force, articulating the exploitation of the continent by private capital and the relationship of private companies to the colonies, African peoples, and Northern metropolitan powers.[59]

Another striking feature of chapter 5 is Rodney's section on the "nonmonetary" benefits of colonialism. Here, he writes about the elaboration of "organizational techniques" of capitalist firms and their various uses of the continent. He cites a range of examples, from the contribution of African troops in the twentieth century's two world wars (including the use of African troops to suppress anti-colonial uprisings in other parts of the world) to experiments in genocidal techniques (as in Italy's use of poisoned gas against Ethiopians following their invasion in 1935).[60] We can add to Rodney's list of "nonmonetary" benefits Germany's pre-1914 genocide against the Herero and Nama people of South West Africa.

What emerges from the book is not only a clear illustration of this epoch of exploitation in Africa, but, crucially, how this exploitation was central to the birth of the entire capitalist system. Simultaneously, this exploitation created new social forces that had begun to emerge from the dramatic mutation of African society under colonial occupation. These were inherently contradictory, involving neither the total liquidation of the past nor a clear project for the future.

Dependency Theory

Though Rodney was influenced by dependency theory—which saw the drain of wealth from the global South by the North, as the principal engine of underdevelopment—it did not overwhelm his greatest book, nor was it his overarching framework (we should not mistake the title of *HEUA* for an analysis). Along with Andre Gunder Frank, Paul Baran was the other main thinker of dependency theory; both argued that the North accumulated capital by exploiting and draining or transferring the resources of the global South. The writer and activist Chinedu Chukwudinma describes how "[t]hey saw development in the centre and underdevelopment in the periphery as opposite sides of the same coin."[61]

Founded on the notion of a drain or transfer of wealth, it presented an overly deterministic theory—that there was an absolute and continuous transfer of wealth from the global South to the North, and that this stymied development in the modern period. In the 1960s and 1970s, dependency theory was a major influence on a number of classic, radical texts; perhaps the best known was a "companion" book to Rodney's *HEUA* by Eduardo Galeano, *Open Veins of Latin America*, published at almost exactly the same time.

The actual processes that dependency theory speaks about were both built into the structural relationship between dependent ex-colonies in the South and North powers, and also consciously and repeatedly reproduced by political forces. Thus, "dependency"—and "underdevelopment"—was an unavoidable and central aspect of the relationship developed over generations between the North and South. These relationships, however, were not historical peculiarities, existing in one unpleasant period in history, to be superseded by a liberal and well-meaning free market capitalism. Indeed, the "dependent" structural relationship continues into the twenty-first century. [62]

This is not the only story on the continent, though; in fact, Africa presents a variegated reality, with efforts at industrialization (such as in Ethiopia and Angola) and development that do not uniformly fit the description presented in the examples above. The picture of the world market as uneven—and Africa as a weak and peripheral rule taker—remains unchanged.

Nevertheless, the approach has received some justified criticism. Though dominant in the 1960s and 1970s, by the 1980s the theory was substituted by the Left as largely irrelevant to the study of development. Dependency theory, it was now argued, was excessively deterministic with its insistence that growth in the periphery of global capitalism was simply impossible—locked in, as it was, by the crippling relationship with the North. The extraordinary ability of Southeast Asian countries to develop has to demonstrate some of the misconceptions of such a fixed approach to development, which was posited by the early proponents of dependency theory. One of the most forthright Marxist critics of the theory was Nigel Harris, who, in the 1980s, pointed to the rise of Newly Industrializing Countries. Their progression indicated, he argued, that the global economic system "does not lend itself to the simple identification of First and Third, haves and have-nots, rich and poor, industrialized and non-industrialized."[63]

An alternative approach is offered by the Marxist writer Esteban Mora, who argues that we should not only be looking for a connection between "drained" countries and countries who "drain" others, but also for a relationship of *mutual* profiting between an international bourgeoisie—who can be found in all countries, North and South. Mora argues that dependency theories cannot capture the totality of the relationships in the international market. While inequalities and unevenness in the world market exist, with both strong nation-states and weaker ones, this is a division based not on countries or regions, or on geography or ethnicity, but on relations of production. In other words, we must unearth the mechanisms of "mutual profiting" across all regions to see a class-divided world market. The world market, he posits, is part of an international system of states where *every* single state is an agent of capital.[64]

In this formulation, the world market is inherently uneven, marked by rules that are rigged against certain regions and a distribution of wealth and power that expresses these inequalities. Yet the mechanisms of global inequality involve the mutual profiting of a global ruling class across every region of the world.

By no means does Rodney's use of dependency theory overwhelm his book. Unlike many Marxists before and since, Rodney never belabors his theoretical approach, and he does not present a ready-made framework into which he slots a historical narrative. As a consequence, much of the criticism of Rodney's "dependency theory" is incredibly crude and is based on perception rather than reading his work. *HEUA*, for example, was remarkably free of a conceptual model imposed on the historical story. Rodney was aware that dependency theory falls down on the question of class divisions in a Marxist sense; indeed, Frantz Fanon's work was an important influence on him, specifically his analysis of the emerging bourgeoisies in Africa—the "caste of profiteers," as Fanon described them—which is repeated throughout *HEUA*. It is simply disingenuous to paint Rodney as a crude advocate of dependency theory, for nothing could be further from the truth.

Rodney argued that Marxists should see the process of capitalist development as involving the theft and colonization as part of the expansion of productive capital as a whole. Theft in one part of the system is one of many interconnected elements of the inherently combined and uneven development of capitalism. Chukwudinma asserts that dependency theory insists industrialization must be stifled, *and* that the data today shows that industrialization in Africa has been reversed.[65] Rodney explains historically how that fact was possible. This is an entirely consistent conclusion for Marxists.

Rodney did not regard capitalist accumulation as simply a transfer of surpluses from Africa to Europe.[66] He saw how capitalism depended on the constant transformation of productive forces, but he sought to understand these processes historically—in their immense unevenness. There is a distinct narrowness in certain criticism of Rodney's work, and to non-Western revolutionary traditions in general, that cripples a richer historical understanding of capitalism and development.

Conclusion

Much more can be said about *HEUA*; of particular interest is the final chapter, which deals decisively and thoroughly with the "supposed benefits of colonialism." One of the remarkable sections is the one on education, which captures Rodney's own passion for teaching and learning. He grasps the tension of colonial authorities and their need for a layer of trained Africans to run lower levels of the administration, or to work in trade, and the genuine and popular enthusiasm for general education. Rodney refuses to entertain the liberal notion that education was a gift of colonialism. In fact, he is scathing on this point: "If there is anything glorious about the history of African colonial education, it lies not in the crumbs which were dropped by European exploiters, but in the tremendous vigor displayed by Africans in mastering the principles of the system that had mastered them."[67] Where schooling was provided, the colonial authorities were frequently propelled further than they were normally prepared to go by popular sentiment and pressure.

There are many criticisms of Rodney's book—and indeed his entire output—some of which come from the Left. I have intentionally not dealt with them in detail here, because to do so would be to obscure the book's enormous and continued relevance. Much more can be gained from reading the book than by dismissing it for its "inaccuracies" or theoretical weaknesses. *HEUA* is replete with the intricacies and tensions of this relationship, structured and determined in many respects, but also contradictory and open to challenge. The book speaks of Northern, or European, societies as class-bound, riven with their own grotesque inequalities—though on an entirely different scale than the situation faced by the African working class and peasantry.

Rodney's account might lack a certain emphasis on agency—the emergent class forces that were vital in challenging colonial authorities— but he was writing a book of ferocious and important ambition and he could not include everything. Yet it is true that his emphasis at the time, as an enthusiastic supporter of Nyerere and other socialist leaders on the continent, might have left him blindsided to critical questions of class and agency. However, as we will see, his thinking on these issues developed and was enriched by later experience and reading, and once more he became an outrider criticizing state and petty-bourgeois projects of development that offered nothing to Africa and the Caribbean.

There is one matter on which it is worth commenting: Rodney's attitude toward existing socialist regimes at the time. Like most of the radical Left of his generation, Rodney was relatively uncritical about socialist states, specifically the Soviet Union. He saw the Soviet Union and Eastern

Europe, which he refers to throughout the book, as representing a genuine socialist alternative and playing a largely progressive role in the continent's recent colonial past; he also implicitly credits them with presenting the continent with a model for its own development (though he does not say explicitly this). His critics are warranted in pointing out that he was mistaken in this belief, and though he was critical of Stalinism—as made clear in his writings on the Russian Revolution—he never fully moved away from this position.[68]

In any case, to dismiss Rodney's most important work because of various asides he makes to the Soviet Union and Eastern Europe—or other crimes of ideological impurity—would be sectarian folly that has little bearing on the work itself. The reality is that it is hard to label with any accuracy a man like Rodney; no sooner are these criticisms made than they are refuted. At the end of *How Europe Underdeveloped Africa*, Rodney appeals to the action of "peasants and workers"—now, he writes, that explicit foreign rule and exploitation have gone, a clearer appreciation of exploitation and imperialism is possible. The masses can finally determine their own future. In his concluding words, "[t]hat is the element of conscious activity that signifies the ability to make history, by grappling with the heritage of objective conditions and social relations."[69] This struggle is immeasurably assisted by Rodney's 1972 book.

CHAPTER 7

A Book to Change the World

By the time he took over the directorship of Tanzania Publishing House in 1972, Rodney's close friend Walter Bgoya had already worked in the Foreign Office, with stints in Ethiopia and China. In the 1960s, the publishing house functioned much like other aspects of the economy, partly controlled and owned by foreign money, and run by Europeans; 40 percent of the company was owned by Macmillan, while the National Development Corporation held 60 percent. However, this dynamic was beginning to shift.

One of the most important projects the publishing house ever produced was Rodney's *How Europe Underdeveloped Africa*. When Bgoya first arrived at Tanzania Publishing House, having established that there would be no interference in his decisions about what to publish, *HEUA* was already at the page-proof stage. The book was printed through a co-publishing arrangement with Bogle L'Ouverture, a small, radical London-based publisher that Guyanese activists Jessica and Eric Huntley had set up in 1968 to produce Rodney's *Groundings with My Brothers*.

Initially, the book sold only "quite well," Bgoya explains, "but 'quite well' meaning modest numbers. I don't remember how many copies we had initially; I think we might have had three thousand copies, though I am not sure. Three thousand at that time seemed to be the magic number for publishing."[1]

Bgoya had met Rodney before 1972, but it was only with the appearance of the book and his promotion to director of Tanzania Publishing House that they really go to know each other. Only in 1972, when Rodney came into the offices to discuss the book, did the two men sit face to face—separated by the proofs for the book.

Rodney's life quickly became shaped by the book's publication—if he was already a well-known, outspoken, and sharp-witted socialist, rapidly he became the famous author of a book that challenged the historical record, debunked racist myths, and confronted a global economic system that had dragged a continent—and people—into the abyss.

Reaction

On the event of the book's publication, there was still a considerable amount of work to be done. Unlike Rodney's previous historical work, this was a book, an activist intervention—or movement book, as they were known at the time—that required an audience. Anthony Ferguson of the Caribbean Unity Conference wrote to Rodney on November 17, 1972, soon after *HEUA* has been published:

> The Caribbean Unity Conference has sent out complimentary copies of How Europe Underdeveloped Africa (64) per the list you gave us. These were accompanied by the enclosed letter. . . . In addition, we have taken two hundred and thirty-five (235) copies to be sold in the Washington D.C. area. We have also been urging the book's adoption as material for class study, not only at Howard University but also at another area college, Federal City College.[2]

As this correspondence indicated, Rodney was directly involved in the distribution of the book, liaising with activist groups, universities, and the publisher to ensure that the copies, in the right numbers, arrived and were sold to a receptive audience. Other correspondence also speaks of copies designated for sale in neighborhoods or at activist events and community meetings. This was not simply a volume to be read and taught on a university course; it was meant to be read by activists, and in the street.

The letters of praise and engagement were considerable and came from remarkably diverse sources. At one level, in the years after first publication of *HEUA*, Rodney received letters from the continent's radical intelligentsia. For instance, on April 3, 1974, Rodney received a letter from the Nigerian novelist Wole Soyinka, who was "on the verge" of taking over as editor of the magazine *Transition*. "Sometime last year," he wrote, "I ran into your 'How Europe Underdeveloped Africa.' I liked it enormously."[3] In a letter that Rodney received in early 1973 from the editor of the African studies journal *Ufahamu*—based at the University of California—Teshome Gabriel wrote to Walter about a "roundtable" discussion that he wanted to start in the pages of the journal, partly triggered by the "ominous silence" on the book by "Western academicians, journals, etc." As part of this endeavor, he had written to a number of leading scholar-activists, many of them who had responded positively to the invitation to engage with the book's arguments.

The exiled South African revolutionary Ruth First wrote with enthusiasm, "It is seminal in that it places the continent in a setting that the prevailing conventional view is bound to exclude no wonder it was not 'officially' noticed." The militant and writer then excuses herself from writing for the *Ufahamu* "feature": "I'm not sure that I have a great deal to add to his general historical account, and thus much to contribute to a Round Table feature already heavily subscribed by excellent contributors." The radical historian Basil Davidson also expressed his "excitement" at reviewing *HEUA*, as did Keith Buchanan. Labor studies scholar Peter Gutkind commented opaquely that he was willing to join the discussion: "I am delighted to hear that you pay some attention to the new Rodney book—an angry but interesting book."

Then, intriguingly, Gabriel reveals that "the Ghanaian Student Group" were studying the book and preparing a "collective review." Meanwhile, the "Ethiopian Student Union here in LA" was also doing a "collective review" focusing specifically on whether or not "the thesis in HEUA also applies to Ethiopia." Ethiopia had experienced only a brief period of formal colonization, by Italy between 1936 and 1941. Obviously in some sort of discussion with the Ethiopian students, Gabriel reported, "[E]ven on Ethiopia the argument of the book is valid, that until WWII or until the intrusion of Foreign Capital Ethiopia could be said is undeveloped rather than underdeveloped."[4]

The "round table," Gabriel explains, would appear in the next issue of *Ufahamu*—which it did not, though there were further contributions to the debate on *HEUA*. Ultimately, the full consideration of the book—with the list of authors Gabriel mentioned—was held up, a situation later explained by the urgency of producing a special edition on Amílcar Cabral, the Marxist leader of the liberation movement in Guinea-Bissau and Cape Verde—who had just been murdered.

Two points Gabriel makes are worth further discussion. The first is his reference to the "ominous silence" that has greeted Rodney's book— even though this is in a letter sent in March 1973, months after the book's first appearance. Its reception, by any standard today or then, does not quite warrant alarmist descriptions of "ominous silence." After all, the uptake and interest in the book was healthy—even if certain academics were studiously ignoring the volume. I suspect the editor of *Ufahamu* was expressing his own frustration—of a sympathetic radical scholar—that a book of such mighty importance had not yet stopped all the clocks.

The second interesting point is connected to the first. The feedback Rodney was receiving from Ruth First, Basil Davidson, and other colleagues and scholars who he respected was incredibly positive—almost overwhelmingly so. Yet for the rest of his life Rodney would receive messages, letters, and comments from the African and Guyanese working class—the audience he *was really* addressing—praising his book for inspiring them.[5] One reader "an African (of Kinshasa) studying in the USA" wrote how *HEUA* fell into his hands. The correspondent categorizes the book as "one of the two" on African problems that has "inspired me very much"—the other being the Dakar-based Marxist economist Samir Amin's *L'Accumulation à l'échelle mondiale* (Accumulation at a world scale), which first appeared in 1970. The book was a sustained critique of the theory of underdevelopment as presented by conservative economists and a growing class of theorists of development, whose ruling proposition was that "underdevelopment" was simply "delayed development."[6]

In place of such orthodox theories, which remain remarkably unchanged today, Amin made a case for dependency, noting, like Rodney, that these were not mutually and equally competing spheres of the global community, but parts of the world locked into an exploitative relationship. For Samir, the world was divided between "core" and "periphery"; countries in the North, or in the core, for reasons of colonial history and modern imperialism, locked Southern "peripheral" states into an unequal relationship.[7] They were forced to sell primary exports—crops and minerals—at prices determined and fixed in the core, and were thus unable to break out of "dependency." The two volumes celebrated by the Congolese fan of *HEUA* were thus complementary: one was a historical account of how capitalism had underdeveloped Africa, and the other was an account of Marxist political economy within a framework of dependency theory.

The author goes on to offer Rodney advice. Since, he argues, "most of our people don't read very much," the next edition of the book should make use of "graphics summarizing the main ideas; this would, I think, help the people digest them more easily." He then praises the book: "Thank you very much for publishing that book. I am sure it will make up a lot of African minds—at least those which remain African."[8] The writer then asks if he can continue his studies under Rodney's supervision in Dar es Salaam, and if there is some paid work or "job somewhere" that will help him pay for his studies.

In February 1976, Rodney received a letter from another reader, a Ghanaian living in Canada, who explains that since reading *HEUA* he has been "recommending it to anyone within sight." The book, he declares in capitals, should be "read by every 'student' . . . in every underdeveloped country." He goes on to state his "fervent" "wish . . . to engage myself more meaningfully in the search for human alternatives."[9]

In August 1973, Rodney received a letter from a reader in Lagos, Nigeria, who, although he had only just bought the book, could not

> afford the luxury of waiting until I go through [the book] before dropping you a few lines. Looking at the front and back cover, I am sure it will contain the message I want. My main aim of wiring is that I want to inform you that you are one of my heroes. . . . I just think I must get involved in Black revolution. This is what I want to live for. . . . I am only twenty and entering the University of Ibadan next September.

The reason for writing, he explains, was to secure from Rodney a commitment to stay in "constant communication." The excitement of the period—the hope in Black empowerment, revolution, and freedom—jumps off the page.[10]

Earlier in 1973—on March 17—Rodney received (and filed) an airmail letter from José Dominguez, an Argentinean living in London who had also just read *HEUA*, for which, he wrote, "I congratulate you and I am very grateful for the information and analysis that your book provides." He stated that the problems and struggles of the Africans

> are either disregarded or silenced by the press of my country. . . . I must say that I have found your book quite by chance. Aside from a wish to congratulate you, I would like also to ask you to get in touch with a publisher in some Spanish speaking country . . . we are almost 300 hundred million Spanish speaking people, and what you say in your book . . . is of great importance for us all. Therefore, there should be a Spanish translation as soon as possible. Our comrades will be grateful for it.[11]

Not bad for a book that had only been published the previous year. Indeed, such fan mail from nonacademics was direct evidence of the influence the book was beginning to have on the audience that mattered most to Rodney.

On November 14, 1976, the Congolese intellectual and activist Jacques Depelchin wrote to Rodney about a review of *HEUA* written by a "comrade-student," and the possibility that the review would be published in the *Review of African Political Economy*. Depelchin explains that the paper was originally submitted as part of a third-year course on Africa, responding to the prompt "Write a Marxist critique of W. Rodney's *How Europe Underdeveloped Africa*." The paper was presented at a seminar where, Depelchin reports, the

> consensus was that the critique was valid and timely. Some participants tried to point out that the book ought to be understood also in relation to your subjective position (exiled West Indian). In general, it is fair to say that those who wanted to temper the criticism tried to draw attention to the timing of when the book was written.[12]

While a slightly overelaborate report on a student's critical paper, the letter points to the impact that the book was beginning to make. Not only was *HEUA* being used in teaching; it had also been elevated to the status of an exam or paper question, shaping debate—as it has continued to do.

More typical was a letter received on March 5, 1973, from a reader in Montclair, California, who wrote:

> [A]fter reading your book . . . I could hardly hold myself back from writing to you a note of thanks and gratitude for the good work you have done and we the people hope you will keep on the . . . wonderful work. Brother you are beautiful and gracious. Your writing is so good that I can't put the book down—I sleep with it. I hope everybody in Africa or every African in the world reads it.[13]

The book had clearly succeeded in pushing furiously against the tide of racist history. Indeed, its readers' starry-eyed accounts demonstrate that the effect of encountering such a volume, so accessible and clearly written, was nothing less than revelatory—especially outside the university seminar.

On July 20, 1976, the assistant headmaster of a school in Tanzania, S. K. Aboagye, sent a letter to Rodney through the Tanzania Publishing House. "Your book HEUA has so inspired me so that I cannot help bothering you in-spite of the fact that I am neither heard nor known to you." The correspondent was seeking Rodney's support; he wanted copies of his books, a reading list, and contacts that would deepen his interest in politics and developments in Africa. He was assured that the "future of Africa lies in socialism."[14]

HEUA had created a storm of emotion in his readers, and its impact, clear in this correspondence, was as profound among Afro-Caribbean activists and students in America as it was among those living on the continent. This was essential, proving what Rodney had always known and had spoken about as a twenty-six-year-old in his public "groundings" in 1968: there was, in fact, a fundamental emotional and political solidarity among all Black people.

However, not all of Rodney's political readership was in the United States or Africa. On December 5, 1973, an American reader staying in Italy had written: "I have just finished reading . . . HEUA and I am moved to write you of my enthusiasm and gratitude for it." Praising Rodney's writing, he continued: "I am sure you have heard . . . of the effective lucidity and simplicity of your writing style. Even more impressive to me, however, was the comprehensiveness of your thought in dealing with your subject." The result, the author says, was a "thoroughly convincing and devastating indictment of the long and continuing process of Western exploitation of Africa." This writer was a Marxist and "actively engaged" in the American Socialist Workers Party (SWP)—an orthodox Trotskyist organization. In fact, it was through this group, at a party bookstall in Berkeley, California, that he had encountered the book. A year after publication, the book was selling in activist bookshops across the Left's ideological field, in different parts of the world. If there was ever a book that had found its time, this was it. Keen to deepen the contact and to meet the author of the volume that had been so inspiring—even transformative—the correspondent appealed for a future meeting in Tanzania and an interview for the SWP paper, *The Militant*. "Thank you again," he wrote, "for what you have done to assist the struggle everywhere."[15]

The archive does not tell us whether Rodney responded to this—or any of the other—letters; only in rare cases did he copy and store his replies. However, so prodigious was his correspondence and work, and so seriously did he take his readers' comments, that it is hard to imagine that Rodney did not reply to each of these letters.

The process of writing for Rodney had always been collaborative—the result of work written up from speeches, drafts shared with comrades, and criticism constantly sought. One correspondence in particular illustrates this point. At the end of 1972, Rodney received a letter from Leo Neuwens from Belgium. Neuwens had been part of a study group that had traveled across the continent, and while in Tanzania he had been given a copy of *HEUA* by the economist and activist Marc Wuyts. Writing about the study group as a whole, he explains:

> Although obviously written for the African student—and perhaps just because of that—it left a very deep impression even on our European minds . . . your analysis has made a major contribution to our understanding of Africa. . . . I am convinced your book and your analysis should be brought to the white European student. Its knowledge is of a vital importance and necessity for us also, if we want to understand underdevelopment from its roots onwards.

The letter writer goes on to say that there are others who have "tackled" these questions—politicians and African writers—but none have done it with such clarity or from "an African point of view."

Neuwens urges Rodney to consider a Dutch edition, which, if published cheaply enough, would be certain to reach a "solid number of our students and pupils." After all, as Rodney states in the preface of *HEUA*, this is one of his principal concerns—"to give as many people as possible the opportunity to get acquainted with the African view on European colonialism." Neuwens offers to "prepare" the translation and arrange its publication and distribution. He then writes: "I dare to ask you this only because I believe that the reasons you forwarded in your book for writing it, are genuine and true. For there is hardly any profit in translating and publishing a book in the Dutch language, unless you want to sell it at a high price." He then requests the rights for translation—promising not to change a word in the text.

Rodney's reply came quickly—within a little more than a fortnight. "Your letter was most welcome and stimulating." He answered Neuwens's offer of a Dutch edition: "[I]t seems . . . that we have a common view on most essentials, and personally I would be quite happy if you undertook the translation and arranged for publication in Belgium (and possibly Holland)." Though the book's translation rights were held by Bogle L'Ouverture Press in London, the appearance of a Dutch edition, Rodney explained, was unlikely to affect their commercial interest in the English version. He explained that he would write to the publisher indicating his support for the proposal and recommended that Neuwens do the same. The book, Rodney argues, was indeed

> intended primarily for Africans, but its circulation was never meant to be exclusively confined to Africans. Those of us here in Dar es Salaam and other parts of Africa who share these views would be most happy to see them widely disseminated throughout the world and particularly in the metropoles with whom (for good or for bad) we are still closely integrated.

If this type of engagement was typical—detailed responses to requests, enthusiastic engagement, and criticism (as we shall see, Neuwens challenged Rodney to clarify several points in *HEUA*)—then it is hard not to imagine that most of the letters also received similarly fulsome and fraternal responses.

Early Criticism

In the 1972 letter from Anthony Ferguson mentioned above—which he addressed "Dear Brother . . . "—the Caribbean Unity Conference member engages Rodney directly in some detailed comments and criticism. Writing as "one revolutionary to another," he explains that he has read *How Europe Underdeveloped Africa* and is studying, "with Mzee C. L. R. James, Nyerere's document's on Decentralization, line by line." (The "document" discusses an ongoing debate in Tanzania in the early 1970s and speaks to problems of planning development, including difficulty centralizing decision making and a chronic shortage of resources, trained personnel, equipment, and organization.)

Ferguson then explains that after all of this study and reading, "I have come to the conclusion that your equating Russia with socialism is a mistake." The result of this conflation, he argues, is "that you have written off the atrocities of the Stalin regime, the Khrushchev regime, and the bureaucracy as it is now under Brezhnev." These are grave errors, he notes, and ones Rodney needs to correct, especially as a "Third World intellectual"; after all, according to Ferguson, people in the Third World are beginning to break from Stalinism, increasingly aware that the differences between Russia and the United States "are not that great."[16]

In the 1972 letter in which Leo Neuwens offered to take charge of translating and publishing a Dutch language edition of *HEUA*, he also requested clarification on a couple of points. The first is Rodney's argument that the slave trade ensured the "stagnation" of the continent's general development, widening the gap between Africa and Europe. Neuwens asks: If Europeans were able to even get to Africa and other continents, does this fact not prove that the "gap" in development was already significant? In respect to technical advances and trade, the gap, Neuwens suggests, was greater than Rodney's analysis would indicate. He asks—presumably wanting an answer to these questions before he starts the translation—if it wouldn't be more accurate to say that both continents could be classified into the feudal mode of production, with Europe "going towards the end" and Africa "rather at the beginning of it." He then—rather presumptuously—tells Rodney that it "would be wrong to underestimate the already existing gap or even to create the impression that at that time there was hardly any gap at all."

Neuwens moves on to his second objection. Taking up Rodney's example in the book of the Zulu state, which, Rodney argues, was unaffected by the slave trade, while the continent "left to itself" attained a high level of development. Yet, Neuwens argues, "this civilisation was nearly exterminated by a handful of Boers"—who could hardly be considered part of the European elite. When these two groups—Zulu and Boer—met, it was the smaller group that won. Eager to press his point, Neuwens asks whether this does not prove that the "gap has been widening" between an African group developing on its own, and a European group also developing on its own. His conclusion is that answers to Africa's underdevelopment must be sought not only in Europe's contribution to it, but also within African societies themselves.

Finishing the letter, which is notable for its honesty and inquisitiveness, Neuwens writes:

> My father is a worker and most of my family are. . . . I worked myself to pay for my studies. Yet in my family, nor in any other worker family as far as I know, has coffee been introduced for daily consumption only after powder-coffee had been invented [an argument made in *HEUA*]. In fact, on the European market, Nescafe, are not cheaper than coffee beans: it is just easier and more quickly served.

Unless Rodney, he asks, has figures to prove this to the contrary, he asks if this can be deleted in the Dutch edition he offers to prepare.[17]

Rodney's reply came quickly—within a little more than a fortnight: "Your letter was most welcome and stimulating. Within the field of African history, a thesis such as mine would meet with criticism of the type that has a bourgeois world-view as its premise." Commenting on the necessity of such intervention and constructive commentary, he argues, "[I]n all disciplines relating to African studies, any progressive scholar is likely to find himself even more isolated than is the case for Socialist scholars generally." This isolation, Rodney states, may generate stagnation—on whatever path was initially intended, therefore meaningful "dialogue such as that which you have undertaken" is essential.

These are significant comments. Rodney is stating clearly—to a correspondent who has carefully presented certain criticisms of *HEUA*—that whether or not the book has been written for him—a white worker from Europe—his engagement with it is essential. Neuwens had stated clearly that he is from a family of Belgian, Flemish-speaking workers. Rodney pays attention and takes his criticisms seriously.

On the request for the change in the text on the question of coffee, Rodney explains that "in the USA and other parts of the world with which I am familiar, the blends of ground (and not 'instant') coffee are more expensive. In any event, the fact that instant coffee is 'easier and more quickly served' . . . is related to the cost, when one considers the percolator and the time involved." It was over the colonial period, Rodney explains, that consumption of tea, coffee, and cocoa first took place, and among the poorer income groups. He suggests a slight change in the sentence objected to by Neuwens, in which the discussion of coffee takes place.

With remarkable grace—and ease—he deals with the other points Neuwens raises. One the question of the Zulu and the Boers, he explains that the Boers were "essentially pre-capitalist." In the early nineteenth century, both had certain "spheres of influence" in Southern Africa, and it was the British—not the Boers—who crushed Zulu power late in that century. The Boer victories, Rodney corrects his interlocutor, were achieved over hunting and gathering societies that had long been in existence before the "epoch of Shaka."

On the issue of "relative stages of development" and where on the "feudal mode of production" both continents resided at the start of the slave trade, Rodney explains that he agrees entirely with Neuwens. While Neuwens asks if there were not indications of a further stage—"perhaps mercantilism as a transitional period from feudalism to capitalism" while Africa was "influenced by the previous stage of communalism"—Rodney again agrees and accepts that his own description—in the book—might have understated the gap that Neuwens talks about. He explains that these processes—before they could be felt in people's lives—took centuries to be realized. To ensure clarity on these questions of emphasis, Rodney argues for maximum response and discussion—a process he thanks his Belgian interlocutor for starting.[18] As we have seen, it is only through Rodney's correspondence that one can truly grasp his rigor, fraternal approach to scholarship, and openness to criticism.

CHAPTER 8

Class, Race, and Politics in Tanzania

Throughout the writing of *How Europe Underdeveloped Africa*, Walter had taught, designed new courses with his colleagues on the Hill, and, once more, become a father, with the birth of Asha in 1971. It was his extraordinary focus that gave him the time to complete this enormous historical undertaking. Patricia describes how he would work on the manuscript of *HEUA* while Asha slept on his lap—reflecting both his characteristic focus and care for his children. Still, there were great distractions. One noisy dispute, which has continued to hang in the air for the last fifty years, was on the question of race.

Rodney was not simply an adherent of the radical movement for Black Power but also someone who had helped shape its expression and politics in the Caribbean. He had earned this role, not least with his expulsion from Jamaica over his involvement in a mass program of education, out of which his extraordinary *Groundings with My Brothers* emerged. He was a leading intellectual at the university in Dar es Salaam, and more widely—lecturing and speaking to activist groups throughout East Africa.

Rodney was acutely aware of his role in Tanzania: he was a guest. He was clear that his position as a socialist was to intervene, and to participate in debates, but that this involvement had to acknowledge his place in the country. Tanzania's political transformation—its own project of socialism—was ultimately a matter for communities in the country and region itself. As Rodney expressed in 1974: "I can make my contribution here, but I will never be able ever to grasp the idiom of the people. I will not be able to connect easily."[1]

Unlike other visiting comrades, Rodney understood that he needed to be extremely sensitive when it came to how he operated at the university.

Eventually, Rodney would leave, with his family, and so would most of the other comrades. In the end, Tanzanians would be left to continue the debates and struggles in the country. It would also be, at a basic level, Tanzanians who had to fill the posts at the university, in the civil service, in government departments, and in schools and technical colleges. Europeans, whatever their political allegiance and commitments, would have to go.

The various political complexions of the visiting Left, their motivations and idiosyncrasies, were labyrinthine; they did not come from a single tradition, share a unified political perspective, or agree on how to intervene in Tanzania's transformation. Peter Lawrence, for one, recalls the conditions in the country upon his arrival in 1968, including the complexity of the Left among the various expatriates, their involvement in Ujamaa, and their relationship to Tanzanian comrades and colleagues:

> There wasn't a distinct Left grouping, though I remember that [Giovanni] Arrighi, [John] Saul, [Lionel] Cliffe, and other like-minded people tended to have coffee and tea at around the same times of the day. . . . I can remember an American, Bill Luttrell, who was married to a Tanzanian and who together with a Tanzanian, Simon Mbilinyi, started an Ujamaa *shamba* [cultivated plot of ground] on some land given by the university and tried to get other academics involved. It didn't last long, partly because non-Tanzanian academics were not much good at agriculture in practice, and also that no one was prepared to live on the shamba to protect in against wild animals that lived in the outer campus. So the Left comprised many who were enthused by Ujamaa (especially non-Tanzanians) and the Marxist Left, some who took the view that this was Tanzanian business and they were there to do a job—that would have been the Communist Party line—and those, like Saul, Cliffe and others, who thought in terms of more active political solidarity and were critical of those for whom being there and doing a job was solidarity enough. Then [there were] the Left critics of Nyerere and the idealism of Ujamaa, and those who saw the unreality of socialism in one poor country in the age of imperialism. I think people like Lionel, who had already been in East Africa for eight years by then, saw political solidarity as supporting the Tanzanian Left, while Saul saw this as actively leading if necessary, rather than listening. I took that line too, which got both him and me into trouble over faculty reorganization. And Rodney took a critical view of this because we hadn't taken enough Tanzanians with us. Lionel, who was on his way out at the time, having been replaced by a Tanzanian, also took that view. He was closer to

Walter (although the Sauls and Rodneys were neighbors on the campus and had been good friends).[2]

There were only a few Communist Party members from the UK, but there were quite a few East Europeans whom, according to Lawrence (then also a British Communist Party member), could best be characterized as enjoying their time away from their state socialisms. He records that "politically, they were hopeless—except for [Tamás] Szentes of course."

As Lawrence argues, Rodney—with others—understood the role he had as a lecturer at the university had to, in large part, be about creating the conditions for this "replacement." When, in 1974, Issa Shivji asked Rodney to stay in the country, he refused. Tanzania could never be his home—not completely.

Rodney worked toward these objectives in a number of ways. Firstly, as an intellectual, he threw himself into the work of redrafting the country's high school history curriculum. Tanzanians had to have a good and clear sense of their history and the history of the continent. Ultimately, this would prove the overriding intellectual commitment in his life. This project of rewriting the history curriculum had taken up a considerable amount of his time while he was in Dar, and then after his return to Guyana.[3] For a young generation, Rodney was preparing the ground for a sustainable, just, and thorough understanding of the country's independence—its position in the world order, and the continent's "historic tasks" for the future.

The second groundwork took place at the university, which, he argued, also needed to be transformed. Indeed, this was a central question with which faculty members and students were engaged: How could an essentially colonial institution be built to service the needs of a new nation?

Race and Politics on the Hill

Surrounded by trees and flowers, a central road winds its way through the University on the Hill, or Mlimani ("the mountain" in Kiswahili). Smaller roads and cul-de-sacs lead to large bungalows, built in the 1960s, with gardens that circle the houses. Set back from the main road are the faculties, lecture halls, dining rooms, and student accommodations. Between the different departments—most of them long, two-story buildings, with offices on both floors—are a series of pathways that meander through the lush green hills of the campus. Today, the university has a population of more than twenty thousand students, and the infrastructure staggers under the impact of years of restructuring and underfunding. However, during Rodney's days at the university, the notion of "the Hill" expressed not just the verdant hilly beauty of the campus—still visible today, despite decades of austerity and sweeping budget cuts—but also its isolation and privilege from the hardships faced in the city and country. The air on campus was rarefied; its debates seemed distant and obscure to the struggles going on in the country and continent below.

This could not be more clearly illustrated than in a debate that took place in a meeting of the Faculty of Arts and Social Sciences on November 24, 1971. A faculty committee had been set up to investigate changes to the curriculum, and its recommendations included a new direction in undergraduate teaching. Committee member John Saul—a prominent Canadian socialist at the university who remained a vital and radical critic of devastating neoliberal reforms that ripped across the continent in the 1980s and 1990s—saw resistance to progressive changes from less radical expatriate colleagues, now joined by returning Tanzanian academics; the latter had no enthusiasm for changes in the curriculum that could be perceived as undermining their expertise.[4] Saul has since argued that the debate over the report—which was in the end rejected—pitched those who wanted to challenge and reform the "academic infrastructure" (work that had been started with the Common Course) against resistance from within the "professoriate." According to Saul, the defeat in the highly divisive and angry faculty meeting was a turning point—confirming that radical efforts at reform in the university (and perhaps elsewhere) had crashed on the rocks of philistinism. Tanzania's grand adventure at radical reforms was being extinguished. "It was now to be only a matter of weeks before a number of us, Tanzanian and expatriate, black and white alike, were sacked and more or less forced to leave the country."[5]

Saul's account, still fresh with the anger of the meeting itself, is partial, and the nature of the dispute complex. Given the lofty claims made for this fork in the road, it is worth examining the issues behind it in some detail. Sitting in the large Council Chamber was the entire teaching staff, including Saul, Peter Lawrence, John Loxley, Walter Rodney, Simon Mbilinyi, Archie Mafeje, and Abdalla Bujra. Some were white North Americans and Europeans, while others were Tanzanian colleagues or from countries on the continent. The meeting was charged with discussing and considering the "recommendations on Faculty re-organisation programmes for 2nd and 3rd years, drawn by a Faculty Committee." The minutes to the meeting are short and include no details of what actually happened, apart from a tantalizing comment in "Any Other Business," that "[n]oted with regret the manner in which some members of staff reacted to criticism during the early part of the Board proceedings and expressed concern at that kind of behaviour during Board proceedings." The meeting was lengthy: it opened at 2:15 p.m. and concluded at 6:40 p.m.[6]

On one side of the dispute was Saul, who had drawn up the report with Peter Lawrence, Archie Mafeje, and others. On the other side were some of their Tanzanian colleagues supported by Walter Rodney—the so-called professoriate.

Kighoma Malima, a lecturer in the economics department, wrote to the dean the following day to explain that he was "profoundly horrified" by the way the meeting was conducted. "Faculty Board Paper 12.1 was rejected by the Board, not on the grounds of its merit but on grounds of RACE."[7] Malima clarified that the committee that had drawn up the report was white except for one member, who was considered—in the meeting—"almost as a traitor." Despite these accusations, the chief academic officer and the dean were silent. Why did they not speak up, Malima asks, "at a moment when your leadership was desperately needed?" Earlier in the month, the faculty board had elected the committee, on which, Malima recalled, "six Tanzanians including yourself were asked to serve in the committee and they refused!" How seriously then could such racial criticism be made, only weeks later, when the report was being submitted?

Opposition to the report—challenging the integrity of disciplines and recommending serious changes to the curriculum across the faculty—was impassioned, with a variety of voices being raised. At some point, Walter expressed his support of the Tanzanian colleagues who were objecting to the report. According to Saul, he made a "very opportunist and highly rhetorical brand of black-nationalist racism" directed at several leading members of the committee; in turn, Malima criticized him for his "racialist and anti-socialist remarks." The result of these heated exchanges and accusations—in which Rodney reacted powerfully to what he perceived as a rejection of criticism being made about the "reorganization" by Tanzanian colleagues—was a walkout by members of the committee. Other members of the faculty, in the meantime, endorsed Rodney's objections, including Abdulla Bujra and Anthony Rweyemamu. The debate was, then, Peter Lawrence argued in a letter to the dean on November

29, "structured on racist lines." Resigning from his position on the faculty board, along with John Loxley, Lawrence argued that the dean failed to "rule Rodney out of order for blatant racialism," yet he had "ruled me out of order for trying to tell the Faculty Board that it had been 'deceived, manipulated and fed false information.'"[8]

What was fundamental—Lawrence argues—was that "racial intimidation was carefully used by those in the Faculty who have always opposed reorganization, in order to suppress any rational discussion of a programme which might affect their departmental self-interests." The "racial factor" was used against expatriates, Lawrence argues, while the struggle for progressive reforms is "always a political and not a racial one." Days later, the fury from the faculty meeting was still raging, and it would last much longer.

Saul refused to resign. In a letter dated November 29, he explained, "I have decided not to yield to Dr. Rodney's racialist intimidation, explicitly sanctioned as it was by Mr. Leshoai, Dr. A. H. Rweyemamu and Dr. Bujra, and tacitly sanctioned by yourself and the Chief Academic Officer, among others." Saul was furious:

> Unlike Dr Rodney I do not patronise Tanzanians by assuming them to be incapable of engaging as equals in rational debate with others of any race nor do I see any need that they be protected from such debate by demagoguery and deceit. Were I a Tanzanian I do not know which of Dr Rodney's premises would offend me more—his racialism or his paternalism. I choose not to assume that any Tanzanian who finds himself in agreement with an expatriate (black or white) is somehow a tool or puppet of that expatriate.

The real position, Saul argued, that should be taken was ideological—and in this Rodney had failed. For example, Saul writes, on the political question of reorganization, Malima "found himself in agreement with Loxley, Lawrence, and Saul, and Rodney with A. H. Rweyemamu!" In a valedictory statement, he concludes, that "[f]or more than six years I have given the very best that is in me to that effort of which the President speaks and, if I may be forgiven this personal note: I find myself more committed to the future of the Tanzanian socialist experiment than to that of any other system of which I have experience." Ultimately, he argues, "it is Tanzanians, outside and inside this institution, who are deciding the direction of the movement. . . . [I]n the long run Rodney, Saul and the rest, effectively powerless and rightly so, represent merely some minor footnote to the struggle for Tanzania's future."[9]

These letters were copied to all the relevant parties—each member of the faculty, as well as senior management at the university—and inevitably news of the meeting spread quickly across the Hill. Rodney, who had been promoted to senior lecturer at the start of 1971, read the denunciations of his behavior at the meeting (carefully filing the documents in his personal archive) and responded to the dean—J. F. Rweyemamu—on November 30.

Rodney condemned the accusation, writing, "Curiously enough, the open letters which charge me with having made racist utterances at no point repeat what was supposedly racist." Rodney was not backing down; he notes that the minutes provide no "references to the statement" and explains that "[a] few Europeans, who would describe themselves as 'Leftists' and 'Progressives,' have been acting in an arrogant, manipulative and hegemonistic manner in refusing to consider or contribute to what the majority of Tanzanians think is correct." Things had changed, Rodney argues—and it was incumbent on the university, and its "Leftist" staff, to see these changes. Four or five years before, he writes, it might have been "permissible and inevitable that an issue such as Faculty re-organisation should be settled by a predominantly European committee. Today, that is untenable." Whatever the circumstances, and whether the proposed curriculum reorganization and faculty changes were progressive or not, Rodney was arguing that a decision to make fundamental reforms should not be decided by a white and expatriate committee. This was at the heart of Rodney's frustration and, it seems, the reason for his outburst during the meeting.

Rodney was acutely aware of the fact that there could not be racial neutrality when some voices were silenced by arguments about progressive-versus-conservative politics. Race was a sharp dividing line, of urgent and pressing political relevance, to every decision. He was approaching the issue from the point of view of historical injustice, which was still—in the early 1970s—being played out powerfully in "socialist" Tanzania. He writes, "The full implications behind what I said go much further, relating to the centuries-old domination of black people by white." This was not a "racial" argument but a historical and political fact—the legacy of this history, the deep sense of inferiority still felt by Black people, operated in the world at large, in the microenvironments of faculty meetings, and in university organization. It mattered who was making the arguments.

It was not that Rodney imposed a Black Power narrative from the Caribbean and North America on Tanzania. Rather, he was a historian—on the verge of publishing *HEUA*—and he knew the deeply felt crisis of Black identity after centuries of enslavement, imperial and colonial occupation, and oppression. His colleagues showed an egregious lack of racial awareness. However, Rodney was prepared, as he stated in the letter, "to pursue in a meaningful and constructive manner our disagreements in the Faculty Board meeting."[10]

The incident exposes much that was difficult, contradictory, and problematic about the Dar years and how utterly distinct the experience was for Black and white expatriates. To Rodney, the white expatriates, from whom he mostly kept his distance, were back-slapping, beery, and boastful—left-wing, maybe, but all the rest of the baggage was there too. How deeply were they actually embedded in African local politics, and who were the Black people that they remembered within their magic circle? Rodney was an astute observer of the racially stratified social setup, which clearly vitiated the radical and revolutionary tenor of Dar and Tanzania under President Nyerere. He was—as we have seen—furious at what he saw and at the insensitivity to racial issues (so often falsely juxtaposed with real political or ideological positions).

These issues exploded across the table, blowing apart even the normally generous limits to dispute in academic meetings at the university. Accusations and counteraccusations were made. To tell a Marxist that they were behaving like "colonialists" would have cut deeply—"yet this is what happened," Lawrence recalls. Decades later, Lawrence's concedes the dispute to Rodney: "In retrospect, we played it badly because we looked like a left version of colonialism."[11]

The dispute involved not only a falling out among faculty members but also among comrades and friends.[12] Their struggles, after all, were meant to be the same; their aims, hopes, and ambitions for Tanzania and Africa identical. To have Rodney's eloquence, his intellect, and arguments aimed at a fellow traveler must have hurt. Indeed, to be told that their behavior was "colonial," imbued with white superiority, privilege, and entitlement, would be hard to forget. That Saul remembered the incident so well is probably a symptom of this.

Lawrence seems particularly sensitive to these issues and to what Rodney was attempting to explain to the "visiting" white comrades in Dar es Salaam. As he recalls,

I think Walter was trying to tell us that we need to listen and understand where the Tanzanians are. He always thought Saul should have understood the politics better than he did. . . . But it wasn't our place to tell Tanzanians what to do even if we were echoing Nyerere. Race was, and still is, a big issue and because we haven't been on the receiving end of white racism, we are less likely to understand what it does.

Rodney understood—perhaps better than any other "expatriate" comrade in Dar at the time—what race really meant. It was not simply an invented category, clouding analysis and somehow getting in the way of class analysis, but a living and breathing reality (born of a dreadful and long history). Rodney knew that the experience—in Africa and the Caribbean—of being on the "receiving end of white racism" was a fundamental and defining one. If you were a European, white Marxist, no matter how impeccable your analysis, it meant that in certain circumstance one had to either understand what was being said, or shut up and stand down. In a word, he demanded that they listen—something that the radical Left has never been very good at.[13]

Today, these issues continue to be of critical importance: How can we be racially aware as white radicals and also operate as Marxists, sensitive to the realities of exploitation and class and racial determinations? This is the central question—one that was not asked by those expatriate comrades in the meeting in Dar in late 1971 of themselves, or by generations of others today. As Peter Lawrence observes fifty years later, "I think we thought we knew the answer—ignore the racial issue because we were color blind, weren't we—and act as though we were fervent Tanzanian followers of Ujamaa."[14]

One of Rodney's most startling contributions—what scholar and activist Jesse Benjamin has referred to as "a Marxism in which Black Power is central"—was how, as a Black man, to be racially militant and racially conscious, and also simultaneously and fully sensitive to the parallel and complementary realities of exploitation and social class. This synthesis is what makes Rodney's work distinct and brilliant: his life and writings remain vital to a generation of Black people whose lives are still destroyed by racism and violence, and who are still attempting to topple this system. He managed to bring together the necessity of racial awareness in the charged settings of the newly independent Caribbean and Africa with a Marxist analysis of the development of capitalism in the Third World.

Though Rodney's work and life were subject to shifts and turns, on this issue his role was transparent. Torn by this dichotomy—essentially, how to integrate a militant racial consciousness and also function as a

Marxist sensitive to exploitation and class analysis—Rodney achieved a remarkable synthesis.

Navigating Liberation

Tanzania (and Dar es Salaam, in particular) was *the* base for Africa's second wave of liberation movements. It is impossible to understand the period and Rodney's involvement outside this context. The continent's most pressing debates, its factional divides, and its vital political organizations and activists were all at one time or other (and often at the same time) on Rodney's doorstep in Dar. No serious scholar-activist could function in the capital without some involvement in the furious arguments of Africa's liberation, which were being fought, won, and lost in the country.

However, as we have seen, it would be an illusion to view late-1960s Tanzania as some sort of socialist nirvana. As Rodney described the country in his Hamburg lectures in 1978, Tanzania was a desperately poor and underdeveloped country.[15] Many of those in Dar, at the university, were perfectly conservative and viewed the world without the radical lens of the Left. In fact, many of the battles at the university pitted the Left against the Right—or at least those opposed to the radical Left. In this sense, there was much opposition to any Marxist approach to education. To circumnavigate these institutional blockages, courses were run—including Development Studies and East African Society and Environment. While all students had to attend this course, for many it was not regarded as a proper academic course. Lawrence explains the dynamic at work: "Insofar as a Marxist approach fulfilled a nationalist purpose, then it was okay, but the idea that it should support Tanzanian socialism was not universally approved of." Some of these intellectual initiatives were driven by non-Tanzanians, which became a source of resentment for the Tanzanian staff members. Lawrence goes on:

> Rodney's position was one of identifying first with Tanzanians and only second with socialists. . . . Rodney saw the issue of race much more centrally than we white foreign lefties did. We thought we were doing what Nyerere wanted but maybe the local academics and others had a different agenda and a different politics, and we didn't understand that.

Added to this mix were radical students who explicitly questioned the presence of expatriates. Walter Bgoya, for example, also argued that

Frantz Fanon's last book, *The Wretched of the Earth*—which dealt with the question of liberation and the struggle against racial oppression and colonial control, and first appeared in Tanzania in 1965—played a part in these debates. Widening the context, Bgoya argues that these debates were also reflected in the liberation movements based in Dar and how these organizations were aligned. He argues that South Africa's Pan-African Congress (PAC)—founded in 1959 as a radical "Africanist" group critical of the African National Congress (ANC)—attracted the support of many Tanzanians. This support (at least from certain groups of Tanzanians), Bgoya argues, was due to the presence of "white" comrades in the ANC (and to the propaganda that the ANC was infiltrated by the US Central Intelligence Agency). In addition, he argues, "many Tanzanians" had doubts about whether white people should be allowed to participate in the various nationalist movements, including the People's Movement for the Liberation of Angola (MPLA) and the Mozambique Liberation Front (FRELIMO).

The PAC had many active representatives in Tanzania, who could press their arguments powerfully. Bgoya remembers a few, in particular, including David Sibeko, a member of the PAC's presidential council and responsible for foreign affairs, who was murdered in 1979 in Dar. He was a loud and charming man, heavyset, with an impressive presence.[16] There was also Gora Ebrahim.[17] These figures were very present and active in Tanzania's political scene, and Bgoya, who was close to them, could see their influence. When PAC Chairman Robert Sobukwe died in South Africa in 1976, power shifted decisively to its organization in exile.

President Nyerere was generous to these liberation movements, refusing to take sides. The division between the groups was acrimonious and sometimes violent, occasionally spilling over into the street. Nyerere's position, Bgoya explains, on the dispute between the ANC and PAC was that it had to be resolved by South Africans themselves. As Bgoya describes the situation, "It takes a long time to decide who was wrong and who was right, and sometimes it's not a question of who was right, but [of] who wins."

Overall, Bgoya argues, there was a tendency to regard the presence of white people in liberation movements as a negative. Did Walter Rodney have the same view? There is no clear answer to this highly speculative question. However, Bgoya believes, "by the thrust of his arguments and his work on Black history one would tend to think that he would sympathise with some aspects of this opinion." Bgoya stresses that it was not just the presence of white people, it was also their leading role in certain liberation movements.[18]

Walter never used the discourse of race without nuance, but nevertheless saw that it had real and lasting impact on the lives of Black people. On July 26, 1972, Ray Tricomo, a graduate student in the United States with whom Walter had spoken during his trip to Michigan State University, wrote to him. The importance of the meeting is apparent in his letter: "After your talk, I came up to, we were introduced . . . In our necessarily brief conversation, I first asked you whether or not a European even had a right to work in the United Republic of Tanzania? You countered my question with a question, 'What did I have to offer?'" This response, Tricomo explained, "carried more hope than anything I have heard or seen before."[19]

Speaking about the general atmosphere among the radical Left at the time, Abdul Sheriff—the Tanzanian historian and friend of Walter's—notes: "[T]his kind of pushiness, dismissing people with slogans tended to fragment the left—which was already divided, along Trotskyist, Chinese socialist, Soviet communist lines. We were fighting each other, quite often we didn't have problems with the right-wing, it was with each other." It was this politics, Sheriff argues—these "intra-left divisions"—that was problematic, and the expatriate colleagues had clear positions in these debates.[20]

Black Politics in Tanzania

Tanzania was not an island separated from wider political changes and arguments. Quite the contrary: as the radical capital, at that point, of the continent, it attracted the attention of militant Black lecturers and students from North America. The Black Power movement, and the unique way Rodney intervened in it, resonated loudly in Tanzania. The Urban Center for Black Studies in Poughkeepsie, New York—part of Vassar College—contacted the head of history in Dar, copying in Walter Rodney, on November 23, 1970, about "a group of black female students" who were traveling from the United States in June 1971. The center had only just been formed, in a storm of publicity, after a student occupation demanding a Black studies program in 1969. The explosion of Black studies across North America at this time came about from the movement for Black Power from the 1960s—and the radicalization of that movement. In Jamaica, as we have seen, Rodney was a leading part of this movement.

At each step along the way, every victory was hard-won; even with the ascendancy of Black politics and revolt, established institutions, universities, and research centers had to be dragged kicking and screaming to respond. The situation at Vassar College is a case in point. Claudia Lynn Thomas, one of the Black women leaders of the revolt that led to the foundation of the Urban Center for Black Studies, recorded the experience of the Black students' protest in her memoir. From October 30 to November 1, 1969, Vassar's main building was occupied by thirty-four Black female students, demanding that the center be set up and become a fixed part of the college's curriculum, with core funding, along with a dramatic increase in Black student admission.

As Thomas recorded in 2006, one of their

> stipulations was the appointment of a nucleus of qualified full-time Black studies faculty . . . that separate housing be open to Black students coming to Vassar, that an African-American Cultural Center exist and that the Urban Center for Black Studies remain part of the Black studies academic program. If I had harbored any lingering doubts about the validity of the take-over, they were now erased.

No student involved in the occupation was arrested or expelled, and every demand made by the students was met. Thomas concludes: "The Black studies program at Vassar College became a model for colleges around the nation. Its faculty included prominent scholars, and Dr. Milfred C. Fierce directed the program with a style unique to his sincerity, candor and expectations of students. As students of Black studies, we researched our national and international history."[21]

Under the leadership of Fierce, the new program organized a trip to Tanzania for a group of students—including Taylor and numerous others who had been involved in the occupation at the end of 1969. He now wrote to the University of Dar es Salaam explaining, "We plan to be at the University for three weeks or so and we would like to divide our program into three one week phases: African History, Contemporary African Politics and Seminars on the Liberation Struggle in Southern Africa."[22] In the end, the group of eighteen—all women except for Fierce—made the trip, which lasted six weeks in all and concluded with visits to Kenya, Uganda, Nigeria, and Ghana. The students were between nineteen and thirty-one years of age. It was Rodney who put together the program on African history for the group, and he greeted the students when they arrived in Dar in the summer of 1971.

On April 25, 1972, while Walter was lecturing and writing in the United States for a short period, he received a letter from Fred Brooks, the director of a radical nonprofit called Pan African Skills, who wrote from the organization's office in Dar. Brooks mentions a film about famed Black activist and scholar Angela Davis, which he says, "we have shown . . . around Dar." Davis was then making international headlines as she awaited trial for her alleged connection to an armed occupation of a courtroom in Marin County, California. Brooks, writing to inform Walter of developments in Dar, told him, "We have got to call a big rally because we want to plan something that will coincide with the conclusion of her trial." Newspapers in Dar, including *The Nationalist* and *The Standard*, had been, he reported, following the case very closely.[23]

Similar demonstrations had taken place in Vietnam, China, and Cuba; however, in Tanzania's domestic political scene, the issue of Davis's trial—the plight of Black people in America—was marginal. To miss this point is to misunderstand a central aspect of the period: although events in the United States were peripheral to Tanzanian politics, Black Power resonated with Africans and the diaspora around the world.

Public Lectures, Ideological Classes, and Comradeship

Issa Shivji recalls the exciting intellectual and activist environment in the early 1970s, which included visits by US Black Power figures, as well as the former Guyanese prime minister and leader of the People's Progressive Party:

> Outside the lectures, we had public lectures organised; this is a time when C. L. R. James visited, organised by Walter. We were visited by Stokely Carmichael, by Cheddi Jagan of Guyana, and the liberation leaders also used to come onto campus. These leaders always had their ears open, asking, "What is the university saying?" They paid particular attention to what was going on.[24]

Nor was the university at this period a communist jamboree, with students marching in unison to public lectures singing "The Internationale." Students and staff were divided by multiple issues and discussions within the left camp, and neither of the liberation movements camped out in the country nor the Tanganyika African National Union's militant-sounding declarations had their exclusive attention. As in the international Left, there was dissension on the role of the Soviet Union, China's communist path, the historic role of Trotsky in the Russian Revolution, and the position of the peasantry and workers in the struggle against capitalism (to name a few).

Apart from a minority of politicized students, there was also a great deal of apathy on campus, when it came to the question of revolutionary socialism. In his radical student days, Yoweri Museveni—now the widely hated president of Uganda—had looked to Tanzania as a paradise of struggle and was determined to study at Dar. His impressions on arriving, recorded in *Cheche* in 1970, express his disappointment, giving a vivid picture of life on the campus:

> I arrived at the College in July 1967. I was, almost immediately, disappointed. I found the students lacking in militancy. Many were hostile to socialism, and some, even to the question of African liberation. There was no clear social commitment on the part of the broad sections of the student body. Most of our extracurricular time was taken up by frivolous activities: drinking, dancing and watching decadent Western films. I remember one occasion when I was really most unhappy. This was the time when Chief Albert Luthuli died. A service in his honour was organsied at the Arnatoglou Hall. Transport was provided to all the students who wished attend the service. Alas!!—only a handful of us turned up—the majority being students from Southern Africa. Apathy towards, and ignorance of, many vital questions regarding the interests of the African people were the rule of the day.[25]

Similarly, Shivji remembers when, in his words, "we sabotaged rag day. Students would go into the streets dressed in dirty clothes for charity . . . so USARF, after discussing the whole question of charity in capitalist society, decided to sabotage it."

To confront liberal tendencies among students and develop radical cadre, every Sunday there would be "ideological classes"—frequently attended by thirty or forty students and specifically organized on Sundays to counter the pressures to attend church services. These classes were administered and led by students. However, in the melting pot of the university at the time, faculty members would attend as well. Rodney, for one, was a constant presence. As Shivji explains, participating from the "ground up" was instinctive for him: "Although Rodney by then was a professor of history, well known and popular with students—he used to give lectures on the social and economic problems of East Africa—with John Saul, Lionel Cliffe, all of them were invited." In spite of his reputation, Rodney's relationship with the students was not a hierarchical one. "You must understand" Shivji stressed, "that he was a comrade giving lectures; the relationship of us with Rodney was one of comrade. We didn't talk to him or address him as a professor." Many students knew him simply as "Walter." Shivji gives an impression of the university at the time as a crucible of intense debates, in which there were practical efforts to mold a critical and committed student body.

Shivji remembers a trip to Somalia in 1973 organized by a progressive Somali student, in which Rodney participated. Somalia in the early 1970s, was in the midst of its reconstitution as a one-party Marxist-Leninist state under the presidency of Siad Barre, with the support of the Soviet Union. Traveling in a group of about seven, Shivji recalls arriving in Mogadishu: "This was a time when Siad Barre had declared Marxism-Leninism. Where we were taken was very hot. There were revolutionary songs; everywhere you went you would see the pictures of Marx, Lenin, Stalin. There were literacy programs, the adoption of the Latin script from Arabic." The group was given a tour of revolutionary Somalia—or at least a country that was now embarking on a program of progressive reforms. The small party of visitors exchanged information with Somalis about what was happening locally and in Tanzania. As a group of radical students and scholars, they also gave lectures.

Though it was not an official visit, the group was treated like state guests. Shivji remembers:

> Walter was very impressed. I remember distinctly, toward the end of our trip, Siad Barre invited us to his palace; we had dinner there. After dinner, Siad Barre told his assistants to bring a big map—one of his themes was the idea of a "greater Somalia" that included Djibouti, the north frontier in Kenya. From what I remember, some of us were not exactly impressed and took Barre with a pinch of salt, as an army man.

Though no disagreements were expressed in front of the new president, in the group differences of opinions began to emerge about his politics. For their part, the Somalis who were studying in Dar and had traveled with the group expressed a degree of skepticism at some of Barre's declarations.

According to Shivji, the group was divided between those who tended to orient to the model of socialism exported from China, championed by

Mao, and Rodney, on the other side, who saw the Soviet Union's rapid industrialization and state-led development as a model for the underdeveloped world. Siad was also pro-Soviet, and while he would break with the Kremlin almost a decade later, he was at that time unwavering in his support for Moscow. Shivji explains:

> Rodney was impressed by Siad, and I could understand why. Coming from the background that he did and seeing something like that, clearly, on the face of it, left transformation of the people, with the involvement of the people. So for someone coming from a Afro-Caribbean, African American background, from those heavily discriminatory societies, these kinds of developments in Africa obviously gave him hope that something was happening.[26]

It would, however, be a mistake to see Rodney's attitude in revolutionary Mogadishu in 1972 as an indication of his uncritical support for Soviet-sponsored governments across Africa. No doubt he was making a judgment based on some of the positive reforms that he had seen for himself. Rodney was deeply engaged in some of the most serious criticisms of what was happening in Tanzania, not least of which was Shivji's penetrating study *The Silent Class Struggle*. Ultimately, Rodney was ill suited to banging the party drum—or at least to maintaining a regular beat.

Though there were not abrupt turns in Rodney's positions, until 1973 he broadly supported the Tanzanian state as an instrument for developing socialism and saw the peasantry as its fundamental base. Though he never discarded the central idea of Marxism as the emancipation of the working poor, his emphasis was elsewhere. As Fanon had argued more than a decade before, the African—and Tanzanian—working class was too small and too narrowly spread across the country to lead a revolution.[27]

Even while he was teaching in Dar, Rodney received invitations to teach courses in North America. From February to June 1972, for example, he served as a visiting professor at the Center for Afroamerican and African Studies at the University of Michigan. His official role was "Martin Luther King Writer-in-Residence" at the College of Literature, Science, and the Arts, where he was based with his entire family. He was paid $7,500.[28] Even though it was an official visit, Rodney and the family had aroused sufficient suspicion from the authorities for their travel documents to have been taken into "custody" when they arrived from Tanzania on February 17.[29] The family seem to have been forced to stay in the country until August, even though Walter had requested a return of the documents so they could leave on June 26. The discomfort of US authorities upon receiving such a well-known radical on their shores was palpable. Patricia remembers: "I was in the US several months before Walter and the children and Mashaka (who lived with us in Dar and who traveled with us) arrived. Walter was not allowed to travel outside of the US during this period, so I attended his good friend Ewart Thomas's wedding in Toronto, Canada, by myself."[30]

The Sixth Pan-African Congress

The dizzying array of activities in which Rodney was involved is exhausting even to read. As an activist, he wrote and published constantly; as a visiting lecturer, he spoke regularly to student groups, while developing new courses for master's students at universities in East Africa and the United States, as well as maintaining an impressive level of correspondence. Promoted to senior lecturer at the University of Dar es Salaam in 1971, by March 16, 1973, he received notification of his further promotion to associate professor in the history department.[31] His colleague and friend, the historian of Nigeria Elizabeth Allo Isichei, wrote to him on June 13, 1973, with "congratulations on becoming a professor! Okwudiba Nnoli was passing through recently and told us about it. It is a very well-deserved promotion."[32]

In 1974, an important event took place that required all of Rodney's political authority and reputation—and intellectual might. The Sixth Pan-African Congress, the first to be held on the African continent, was to be hosted by Tanzania from June 19 to 27. The radical "call" of the congress was framed clearly in the language of Black Power:

> The 20th century is the century of Black Power. It has already been marked by two dynamics. First, a unified conception of all peoples who have been colonized. They are known by friends and enemies as members of the Third World. And the most significant members of the Third World are those who strive for power to the people and Black Power to the Black People. On the other hand, white power, which ruled unchallenged for so long during this very century, is marked by unparalleled degeneration, first by two savage and global wars such as the World had never before seen. The same mentality prepares for a third war. Its barbarism unpurged, European power strives at all costs to maintain

that domination from which the formerly colonial peoples are breaking. That is the world white power seeks to maintain at a time when the colonial peoples have begun one of the greatest movements toward human freedom that the world has ever known. The SIXTH PAN AFRICAN CONGRESS . . . is part of that movement.[33]

This was language that would have been familiar to Rodney and that could almost have come from his own pen. However, before the congress was even held, it was riven with disputes. One of these concerned the inclusion of Caribbean opposition groups and parties. It was a question of central importance. In the Pan-African world, many new states had become independent over the previous two decades—including large parts of the Caribbean and most of the African continent. Yet these new governments were in many cases heavily criticized as failing to deliver real independence or presenting a sham socialism. The "call" stated: "Upon this policy which Africans are carrying out with arms in hand, the Sixth pan-African Congress must draw a line of steel against those, Africans included, who hide behind the slogan and paraphernalia of national independence while allowing finance capital to dominate and direct their economic and social life." C. L. R. James was heavily involved in drafting the "call," and in a letter to "My dear Walter" on May 18, 1974, he explained: "I had a large share, in fact, a substantial share in its preparation. Whatever its deficiencies it offers a base."[34]

Invitations went out to leaders of these states but not to every opposition group. Before long, there were resignations from the organizing committee, including James, a close friend and mentor to Walter. The objective of the conference was to help further deepen the liberation of Southern Africa, end economic exploitation and dependency, and fulfill political independence. Perhaps the last of these objectives was the most important and controversial.

Despite these noble intentions, the congress, as June 1974 approached, saw a real and acute divergence. On the one side were those who wanted to include government delegations and states from the Pan-African world; on the other were those—Walter prominent among them—who strongly rejected this approach and saw the Congress as a forum for opposition groups and radical political movements, and thus as a resolutely nongovernmental activist event. In the name of Black Power, liberation movements in Southern Africa and elsewhere had to be defended; anything else was meaningless. The congress was eventually, as historian Hakim Adi writes, "transformed into one dominated by governments . . . and ruling parties of 'Black states' were invited, whilst their opponents were barred from attending."[35]

James and Rodney withdrew their support. Indeed, what else could they do? Black Power was not, for them, "Black states"; it needed to intersect with class and internationalism to have any future. Was this not the lesson of the collapse of Portugal's dictatorship in April of that year, which had seen the liberation struggles in Angola, Mozambique, and Guinea-Bissau cripple the decaying Portuguese state, with a militant working-class movement taking to the streets? Political and class forces had to be united.

In the paper prepared ahead of the congress in April 1974 and circulated to comrades and friends in Africa and the Caribbean, Rodney argued that Pan-Africanism was a weapon in the struggle against imperialism. He lamented the continent's colonial borders, arguing that if Africa remained fragmented, it would continue to be vulnerable to Western companies keen to plunder its wealth and imperialist states ready to invade. He argued powerfully that Pan-Africanism of "the petty-bourgeois states became a sterile formulation . . . incapable of challenging capitalism and imperialism."[36]

Rodney's paper was an astonishing and thorough class analysis of African independence and the nature of class struggle on the continent— from which liberation and Pan-Africanism was missing, fifteen years after formal independence. Walter's friend and comrade the historian Robert Hill described it well: "Walter brought to bear a class analysis that was unrivalled for its clarity and its uncompromising nature."[37] What was emerging in the plans for the congress was a state-led jamboree, and one that need to be resisted: "[T]he realities of state power," Rodney writes, "have predetermined that when the Sixth Pan-African Congress meets in Dar-es-Salaam in June 1974 it will be attended mainly by spokesmen of African and Caribbean states which in so many ways represent the negation of Pan-Africanism." Rodney posed the dilemma sharply: "[I]n the light of the above considerations, any African committed to freedom, Socialism and development would need to look long and hard at the political implications of participation in the Sixth Pan-African Congress." If these militant Pan-African movements were to participate, then "the recapture of the revolutionary initiative should clearly be one of the foremost tasks of the Sixth Pan-African Congress."[38]

In the end, six hundred participants were present at the congress, including representatives of twenty-six African states. Underlying the tensions was the simple fact that because it was hosted in Tanzania, the state—even a nominally progressive one—would opt for continental and international diplomacy, alliances, and governmental delegations. If President Nyerere had condemned Rodney in 1969 for using his base in Dar to issue statements of revolutionary "hot air" against neocolonial regimes on the continent, he was now even more adamant. The state was the last word—and no fundamental criticism could be broached.

Bgoya explains some of the disputes: "[T]here was a big issue about who comes to the conference. The Tanzanian government wanted a congress with the representatives of governments . . . while the hardcore Pan-Africanists wanted a people's Pan-African Congress, with as little government as possible and more popular participation."[39] These were issues for the continent and also for the Caribbean, and most of these "hardcore Pan-Africanists" were opposition parties. For the ruling TANU party, there were divisions—the party wanted an all-inclusive congress, but also did not want to appear to be bringing in radical oppositionists intent on overthrowing the governments and their representatives present in Dar. Rodney was precisely the type of person they did not want to attend.

Recalling several years later, the Nigerian poet and novelist Wole Soyinka, who was present at the congress, wrote about Rodney: "[I]f my memory serves me correctly, more than one Caribbean government had, through their representatives, indicated that their delegations would quit the Congress if Walter Rodney participated in any capacity." Rodney's absence was not due to illness, as many have since contended; he had long since recovered, Soyinka argued, from a bout of malaria. Rodney knew he would not be permitted to attend but nevertheless would join James in boycotting the event. "Yet," Soyinka argued, "the 'progressive' government of Tanzania had succumbed to the blackmail of reactionary Caribbean governments to keep out this radical scholar from such a gathering."[40]

However, an important addendum needs to be made to this account. The records show that it was not so much Rodney following James's lead and joining the boycott, but rather the opposite: Rodney had penned the above-cited condemnation of the congress before it had taken place, and it was in fact this move that forced the hand of others—including his senior comrade James. On May 19, Robert Hill—or "Bobby," as Walter called his collaborator—wrote that the document he received from Walter was "immediately copied and circulated." The "Institute"—presumably the Institute of the Black World in Atlanta—Hill reported, was planning to print and circulate "five thousand copies" to its mailing list. In addition, "a sister in Louisiana has already begun circulating a hundred stencilled copies in her area. Some brothers in New York are also printing it up to circulate on the East Coast." Apart from anything else, this was an impressive distribution network.

Hill was enthusiastic about the document, writing, "[Y]ou did not pull too many punches about our generalissimo friends." Then he explained that he had mailed the document to "strategic people," including James: "I expect that he will be squarely sandwiched between your position and the official position. . . . My best sense is that it will be your position that will chiefly divide the forces at the Congress, and that should be as it is." He explained that Guyanese president Forbes Burnham had already extracted a promise from Nyerere that he would not allow the congress to become a platform for anti-Burnham protests. James had apparently "patched" it up and ensured there was the assurance needed from the Tanzanian ambassador to the United Nations.

But the point remains: Rodney provided a radical left critique of the congress, from the perspective of class and class struggle, that drove a wedge between the official position held by Nyerere and a militant and principled one. James was compelled to break with the congress, which he had spent years organizing, because of the position Rodney had taken, stated, and published. James was thus challenged by his former student to break from the compromises he was seeking to build in the run-up to the congress—trying somehow to bridge the divide between militant anti-government delegates and official government ones. Robert Hill was clear: the activists were looking to Rodney "to carry a strong revolutionary line against the official fandangle."[41]

What was left of the congress without the Black Power Marxists was hollow, futile even. Delegates were treated to long-winded speeches, some of which were not even delivered in person. Ahmed Sékou Touré, Guinea's once-lauded anti-colonialist, had, according to Soyinka, recorded a "three hour" speech that was played to the hall. Nyerere delivered his own long speech, with sycophantic delegates declaring that both speeches should be considered the basis for discussion at the congress. Tedium prevailed. As Soyinka records: "The takeover, the victory of governments was complete."

Anti-apartheid and anti-colonial movements survived the purge, but those opposing Joseph Mobutu and Hastings Banda, the presidents of the Congo and Malawi, respectively, were simply dispatched with. Even Soyinka was instructed—after a message had been sent by the Nigerian government—not to speak. This was post-colonial power on graphic display in a single toothless, state-led congress.[42]

Socialism from Above

Julius Nyerere had put a great deal of effort into cultivating his image as a people's president who took solitary walks on campus and who debated openly and democratically with his critics; even his security detail was small, with a motorcade of one. In reality, however, Nyerere's politics was a far cry from such romantic visions. He was a deeply contractionary figure who always defended the interests of the ruling TANU and opposed any genuine struggles from below, which were seen as a threat to the integrity of the state.

In his memoir, John Saul reports on Nyerere's "high-handed assistance" to Sam Nujoma in Namibia. Nujoma, who would become the first leader of the independent state of Namibia in 1990, was then under fire from critics in his own movement, which was seeking independence from South Africa. Nyerere, Saul reports, protected Nujoma from criticism "by conniving in the arbitrary jailing of democratic claimants in SWAPO-in-exile."[43] SWAPO—the South West Africa People's Organization—is the synonym for the Namibian liberation organization founded in 1960. Worse criticisms were to come—including Nyerere's smashing of strikes at Mount Carmel Rubber Factory, or when the Tanzanian government made an important policy statement in 1973 called Mwongozo, a charter of workers' rights reviving the radical aspect of the government's Ujamaa and socialist policy. When workers themselves attempted to implement rights that were supposedly safeguarded by Mwongozo, their actions generated fear and repression by the government.

Other examples abound, including the ruling party's suppression of the Ruvuma Development Association (RDA), which created seventeen self-governing villages from 1963 to 1969, but whose autonomy and success became a threat to politicians who banned the RDA and sought to bring the initiative under party control.[44] The shine was coming off Tanzania's people's president and the state's championing of Ujamaa.

Many also rubbed up against Nyerere's rough side; Rodney himself had seen his host's limits when he spoke of Fanon's theory of revolutionary change in late 1969, and later when he had seen how the TANU wanted to choreograph the Sixth Pan-African Congress into a state-led jamboree of post-independence leaders, bullies, and murderers. Earlier, Rodney witnessed the invasion of the campus by the Field Force Unit in 1970 when the student leader, Simon Akivaga, originally from Kenya, was, in Saul's words, "dragged at gun-point down the cement stairs of the central administrative building then tossed like a sack of old clothes into an army vehicle and sped away to expulsion from the university and from the country."[45] Another example was the savage beatings of student protestors in 1978—long after Saul and Rodney had both left.

When a prominent university historian, Arnold Temu, had the courage to speak up and criticize the government's response, he too was dismissed, sacked from his job and told to leave the country—forced to forge a precarious career outside Tanzania. When he met Saul in 2001 in Dar es Salaam, he explained to his interlocutor that he had "sworn to himself not to return to live in Tanzania as long as Nyerere was alive." Saul writes that "[h]e thus offered a perspective on 'Mwalimu' and his 'democratic sensibility.'"[46] Across Tanzania, Nyerere's former loyal allies, fellow travelers, and comrades were still drawing the lessons; it had, after all, taken some years for the true nature of regime to reveal itself.

Each of these acts exposed the shallowness of Nyerere's democratic and socialist declarations, let alone any claim to be empowering the poor in the struggle against their exploiters. Saul explains that this was because he "took the potential challenges of 'nation-building' much more seriously than he ever took the imperatives of class struggle and socialist construction in Tanzania!"[47] Saul is both right and wrong; surely a deeper criticism would see the impossibility of "building socialism" in Tanzania alone, or anywhere else, in the context of the pressures of global capitalism.

When there were genuine efforts to transform society from below in Tanzania, these were systematically broken. Make change by all means, the ruling party seemed to say, but it must be directed and limited by state authority. The sort of socialist transformation that Rodney and Saul both wanted could not come from Nyerere's Tanzania, and, in different ways, they both left the country with the same lesson. But what did they propose in its place?

Many, if not the overwhelming majority of Rodney's comrades and interlocutors, saw in Mozambique—which in 1974 was close to independence—a popular and radical alternative to the revolution that had run aground in Tanzania. Could the national liberation movement in Mozambique, FRELIMO, be trusted as a "vanguard party" to serve the interests of the popular classes, or would the better path be for the working classes to power popular transformations in their own name? Many radicals leapt from liberation movement to new government, in a game of leapfrog, hoping to find a state that would somehow resolve the challenge of social transformation. For many, including Saul, Mozambique was the next stop.

However, the new state was invariably confronted with the old problem. At the third congress of FRELIMO in 1977, when the party officially swung behind Marxism/Leninism, many threw themselves with great gusto behind the project of socialist change from above being declared in the capital of Maputo. Ruth First, the exiled South African revolutionary, was hard-nosed about the failures of independence in the 1960s and 1970s. Writing in 1970, she argued that decolonization had been little more than "a bargaining process with cooperative African elites."[48] But she remained an enthusiastic advocate of some of these "projects" on the continent. In 1975, she wrote to her husband, Joe Slovo: "I must say I'm thrilled to bits. Tanzania is one thing, but Mozambique! Wow."[49] As critical as she was of efforts at transformation from above, two years later she moved to Maputo to contribute to exactly this project.

In the late 1960s and early 1970s, Rodney's attitude toward Tanzania's socialist experiment was broadly favorable—always critical, but supportive. Karim Hirji, a student and friend of Rodney's, explained that Walter leaned "towards the hope tendency," and that progressive forces in the country had to enhance the "work against the reactionary ones, but within the current political set-up." The struggle at this time—1970—Rodney argued, was against the bureaucracy who opposed and obstructed the initiatives and projects of Nyerere's Ujamaa. His student comrades—Shivji, Hirji, and Henry Mapolu, for example—were more critical and had started to craft a thoroughgoing critique of the state and Nyerere's apparent socialism.[50]

In 1972, in a classic statement of his support for Ujamaa and Nyerere's projects in Tanzania, Rodney published the article "Tanzanian Ujamaa and Scientific Socialism" in *African Review*. Like all of Rodney's writing and work at the time on Tanzanian socialism, it is a serious and considered endorsement. Rodney does two interesting things in the article. Firstly, he draws a clear line between the "African socialism" celebrated by Senegalese president Léopold Senghor and others, and Ujamaa. However, they had similar elements prior to 1967, and Rodney argues that from the Arusha Declaration to Mwongozo, there was a real commitment to (rural) socialist transformation. The second interesting feature of the article is Rodney's impressive effort to connect "scientific socialism" to Ujamaa, through a historical account of the development of Marx's work in prerevolutionary Russia. Although Rodney's position would later shift, there is still much that warrants study. For one, his support—crafted in careful study—for Nyerere's Tanzania is clear. Rodney writes:

> Tanzanian *Ujamaa* has begun to make the decisive break with capitalism. The evidence lies in the *Arusha Declaration*, in the *Mwongozo*, in the Tanzam railway, in the nationalization of certain buildings and in virtually every act of Tanzanian foreign policy. Tanzania *Ujamaa*, limited as it is in actual achievement can substantiate the claim to be the ideology of the majority of Tanzanian producers in the countryside and the towns.[51]

Even then, however, Rodney was beginning to shift his position, gradually and surely; indeed, in his response to Shivji's far-reaching and powerful analysis on class and capitalism in Tanzania, Rodney was increasingly favorable. Just two year later, in 1974, Hirji recalls that Rodney was close to turning his back on the Tanzanian project. In Hirji's words, "[H]is views on socialism in Tanzania retained a modicum of hope. But now he accepted that a reactionary bureaucracy was wresting control of key institutions of the state."[52] In a lecture Rodney delivered in 1975 at Chicago's Northwestern University, called "Class Contradictions in Tanzania," he discusses the tensions in the country after the implementation of the Mwongozo guidelines. Rodney's "modicum of hope" was still present, and he had not yet made the decisive shift away from the projects in Tanzania. As he explained in his conclusion:

> It would be difficult at this time to make a prognosis about the immediate resolution of the said contradictions—whether progressive tendencies or more reactionary tendencies will win out. I have a certain confidence, perhaps, a confidence tinged with hope, that the trend will in fact lead, even in the short run, towards the resolution of these

contradictions in favour of the progressive elements among the working peoples.[53]

It is worth contrasting Rodney's sure and full shift in position on Tanzania's socialism with that of his teacher and comrade C. L. R. James. Hirji describes James's lectures and talks in Dar in the late 1960s and 1970s as brilliant but largely "static" with regard to Tanzania's projects. For a time, James and Rodney shared a favorable position on Tanzania's trajectory, but there was a crucial difference between the two men. Hirji writes: "[U]nlike his erstwhile mentor, Walter's stand was a dynamic one. He learned from practice. He paid attention to the facts, the life of the common person and the views of other comrades." James, by contrast, had not paid enough attention to the shifting facts of Tanzania.[54] Though Rodney had been positive, full of hope and energy for Tanzania's transformation, he changed his position (and had the courage to do so). Hirji is absolutely correct when he explains that "[i]n Tanzania, he started off with much hope, came to realize the primacy of popular struggles, and went on to implement that in practice in his place of birth."[55] Walter Rodney, with his own brilliant and distinct arguments, faced a profound predicament of agency and revolutionary change—who exactly would power the socialist transformation that he wanted to see? Indeed, it was one that he would not resolve so long as he remained in Dar es Salaam.

Leaving Dar

By summer 1974, Walter felt he had reached the end of the road in Tanzania. Moreover, he and Patricia both wanted their children to experience life and childhood in Guyana, and Georgetown in particular—where they had not only friends but family. There were other factors that pushed them hard to leave. Walter was quickly arriving at the conclusion that Nyerere's path to socialism had been exhausted; his criticism of the state's efforts to reform the country and find an "appropriate" Tanzanian path to socialist change, which Rodney had started to develop himself, was an important element in the decision. Issa Shivji's demolition of Tanzania's early post-Arusha efforts had influenced many who had previously been sympathetic to Nyerere and the ruling Tanganyika African National Union.

Many who had been associated with the University Students' African Revolutionary Front were beginning to break with any hope that

Nyerere's TANU could be reformed. USARF was forced to shut down by the government on November 9, 1970. Even if the vision of Marxism it celebrated contained its own limitations (and omissions), it had rejected nationalism, believing that socialism was only a viable project on the international plane while providing a thorough challenge to Nyerere's hopelessly compromised Pan-Africanism. Pan-Africanism, in Rodney's view, should present a socialist vision for the continent, not only an anti-colonial one (and a government-led one at that, as Rodney argued in 1974). Interestingly, when USARF was banned, it was criticized as promoting foreign ideologies—namely Russian—and their publication, *Cheche*, was criticized for being named after Vladimir Lenin's *Iskra*.

However, even for USARF—and many of those associated with it—more radical versions of national liberation fell within a perspective that did not vary fundamentally from Tanzania. On this dimension, FRELIMO, the liberation organization leading the fight against the Portuguese in Mozambique (which shares a long border with the southern edge of Tanzania), was the preferred organization for many USARF activists. Liberation, in their view, could only take place by guerrilla struggle, led by an armed organization from the countryside; FRELIMO was friendly to USARF comrades and shared the analysis produced in *Cheche* and later *Maji Maji*.

Activists from the university and USARF went on quasi-military field trips to liberated spaces in Mozambique, producing a pamphlet to challenge "reactionary propaganda against FRELIMO in Tanzania."[56] There simply was not, even among the left-wing critics of Nyerere, a perspective that criticized the armed struggle. In fact, it was frequently presented as the sole way to fight for real liberation—whether that was simply anti-colonial or socialist in nature. For them, the only real road to freedom *required* an armed movement.

Penning his document about the Sixth Pan-African Congress in early 1974, Rodney already knew that Dar could not become his permanent home—nor could it continue to serve as a guide to political action. In his last months in Dar, he thought seriously about the years he had spent in Tanzania and reached the same conclusion as Tanzanian scholar Chris Peter and politician Sengondo Mvungi in 1986, who argued that "the death of USARF [at the end of 1970] nipped in the bud the growth of a real revolutionary left in Tanzania."[57] The signs were already there, for those who cared to see them. The country was on the verge of a rapid descent into authoritarianism, which would escalate through the 1970s, leading to the widespread suppression of workers' struggles. During that time, Rodney would become a vocal critic of the regime in Dar.

In 1971, the Mwongozo guidelines, issued by TANU to encourage popular involvement in Ujamaa, led to a response by workers with occupations and strikes in state and private businesses and factories. However, these efforts at popular control were broken by the state. The post-Mwongozo wave of workers' struggles, and the state's response, was the subject of extensive analysis by Shivji—scholarship on which Rodney would draw in one of his final courses, taught in Hamburg in 1978.[58]

By 1974, the family had become deeply embedded in Tanzanian society and culture—all three of their children spoke Swahili. Though the family was tempted to stay—and professionally speaking, it would have been easy, since Walter was a popular and respected colleague and comrade—ultimately, Walter and Patricia could never consider the country home. Walter had to consider carefully where he could position himself to make a political difference, where he could help shape struggles taking place that might empower another world. For Walter—and Patricia—this could only be Guyana.

In 1975, Walter reflected: "I could have become a Tanzanian citizen, and indeed thought about it seriously. The question is, what does that really mean? You change your legal status, you become a new national and, therefore, hopefully you open both to the advantages and disadvantages of being a national of that country." But beyond their legal status—which could easily be revoked, as Rodney reflected—there were other more significant obstacles and challenges. "It is much more than a legal definition that makes one effective," he explains. "[O]ne must have a series of responses and reflexes that come from having lived a given experience." Walter spoke, for instance, of visiting a marketplace for food and supplies and his inability to "bargain in the Swahili manner without being perceived as an outsider."[59]

Yet, he goes on, to do this requires a proficiency in Swahili that is a lifetime task—to be truly embedded in the language, beyond the niceties of greetings. This deeper understanding is essential, Walter explains, to "master the higher level of perception which normally goes into a culture. And I didn't believe that I could afford that." The world from which he came drew him back with incredible force—his home, as a revolutionary and a man, would always be the Caribbean.

CHAPTER 9

Returning Home

Soon after the Sixth Pan-African Congress, Rodney left the country; Patricia and the children had already departed in May. Walter Bgoya, who had grown close to the family, was sad to see them go; nevertheless, through the publishing community and occasional personal messages, he would remain connected to them. In London, Rodney would regularly visit the office of Bogle-L'Ouverture, where he would hear updates on his friends in Guyana.

Walter and Patricia's departure from Tanzania was one they had planned for a long time—even if it became mired in uncertainty. When Walter had taken up his initial appointment in Tanzania in July 1966, these plans were, as we have seen, upended, and the family had returned to Tanzania after Rodney's expulsion from Jamaica. On October 31, 1972, Walter wrote to "Mr. Karram," the registrar at the University of Guyana, explaining, "I have been advised to forward my *curriculum vitae* directly to you." He had been told that the head of the history department had indicated that there was no vacancy but that there was a post available as director of Caribbean studies—a position Rodney asked to be considered for, while also hoping to apply for an "appointment as professor of History." He writes that though he is contractually obliged to be present at the University of Dar es Salaam for some of 1973, he could leave in December.[1] It seems Rodney did not receive a response—though, like many academic positions, it is often contacts within the university who provide information about positions or inform colleagues and friend about vacancies.

On May 14, 1974, Rodney wrote once more to the university, this time to "Mr. Peter Ramkissoon," the assistant registrar. He stated: "It appears from your letter of 2nd January 1974 that I am required to re-apply for any given post, in spite of my standing application of 31st October and your own reply of 29th December 1972, which stated that my application was 'on file' and would be considered when there was a suitable opening." Rodney had been informed that an advertisement had appeared in the *Daily Chronicle*, a Georgetown newspaper, in April, for the "post of Professor of History." He wrote: "I am formally responding to this advertisement." In a strange and dismissive response sent to him in Dar—on a standard stenciled form—he heard back on August 20, stating, "I wish to advise you that you have not been selected."[2]

Rodney's hope of an appointment had been clarified in a personal letter, dated May 22, 1973, from his friend Clive Thomas, an academic at the University of Guyana. In a conversation Thomas had with the vice chancellor, he was assured that Rodney would be "offered a job" at the university. "I asked him to review the correspondence so far and write to you as clearly as he can indicating the position. He has promised to do so, and I will give him a reminder." The vice chancellor apparently also "absolutely assured me (!) the politicians have not been involved at all, nor does he expect that they would, as there can be no question of your coming back." However, apparently there were forces within the university and the department of history who were working against Rodney's appointment. Presumably, Robert "Bobby" Moore was one of these—he had taught Walter history years before, and now when Thomas spoke to "Bobby," "about your application, [he] claimed he *never knew that you had applied for a job*." Thomas explained, trying to get to the bottom of what was going on, that "I am avoiding him whilst I get a feel of who, if anyone other than 'Bobby' is lying to me." Rodney, for his part, was determined to return, whatever the forces arrayed against him.[3]

Guyana was going to be the family's home; Shaka, Kanini, and Asha were discovering it properly for the first time. The capital—baptized Georgetown by the British in 1812, in honor of King George III—was the administrative center of the port and colony, and had about twelve thousand inhabitants. In the half century since the Rodneys' return, the city has grown rapidly and today has a population of about 235,000—roughly one-third of the population of the country. Though the city was marketed as the "Garden City of the Caribbean," it was, and remains, a place of poverty and squalor for thousands. Open sewers, rubbish strewn in boggy canals, and informal, basic housing for the poor, stand in contrast to a number of elegant colonial buildings downtown. One contemporary observer of the city noted, in 2018, that despite these striking contrasts, "The city maintains nevertheless a particular charm due to its street life, the commercial streets and the very young and mixed Indian, African, Amerindians, Venezuelan and Brazilian population."[4]

Upon the family's arrival in this poor yet vibrant city, there was little time to adjust to the move from Tanzania before Rodney was thrust into the limelight. Almost immediately, Walter became the source of national controversy. The situation was alarming, and even though there were many offers of work (as we will see), doubt overshadowed their prospects for properly settling in Georgetown. It remained unclear where Walter would work and how they would establish stability.

Yet there was hope and expectation among Guyana's activist community, and more widely. The longtime Pan-Africanist militant Eusi Kwayana describes the mood ahead of Rodney's return home: "[T]he whole country was looking forward to Dr. Walter Rodney, even before he set foot in Guyana. From the time he was banned from Jamaica and came to the notice of the public as a son abroad, he was a very popular figure in the imagination and hearts of the Guyanese people."[5]

In spite of the uncertainties of work, the family returned. By the time Walter arrived, the children were already in school, and Patricia was working with the Georgetown City Council. She was hired as the matron of a day care center in East Ruimveldt, not far from where the Rodneys lived for the next six years.

By September 1974, Walter's cold-shouldering had become known as the "Rodney Affair." On September 18, he issued a public statement. "It is with considerable reluctance," he writes, "that I am addressing myself to the news media at this point in time" regarding a "government created problem." He explains in the statement that it is "now well-known that my appointment was approved through the regular academic channels and that it was disallowed for supposedly political reasons." Absent from the country for fourteen years, he writes, he had played no active role in national political life. It was now time for the government to explain itself.

Rodney made clear his commitment to return and teach in Guyana: "My professional training was carried out at the expense of the people of Guyana and the British Caribbean. To be denied the opportunity to pursue my profession at home is tantamount to being condemned to exile and hence to be cut off from direct access to the community which was my sponsor." Even in this determined political statement, commenting on what had become an international issue, his commitment to Guyana and the Caribbean resounds. He concludes: "I shall not be intimidated.

But once more it is necessary to emphasise that it is not a matter of mere personal predicament or personal resolve."[6]

With their intervention to prevent the appointment of Rodney, the government had generated a storm of international protest. From the UK he received a letter from Ms. Duncan, who had been an adoptive "mother" to the couple when they lived in London from 1963. She wrote to Walter from Tufnell Park, North London, on September 4, telling him: "[R]egarding your affairs . . . arrangements have been made for the next meeting at Conway Hall and we intend to do some picketing at the last meeting." Expressing concern for "Pat and the children," she writes, "as I close this letter, I am asking God's Blessing be with you always."[7]

Arrival and Reactions

With support from Walter's and Patricia's parents and other relatives, the family began to acclimatize to their new life in Guyana. The children, however, missed Mashaka (their caregiver in Dar), their friends, and the freedom they had known in Tanzania. The children found it strange that people did not normally greet each other in Georgetown, and they were sometimes teased in school because of their names.

The job situation forced on Rodney by the regime in Guyana meant that he was obliged to take up international offers of employment. The family of five lived, for a time, on Patricia's income and Walter's overseas teaching and research contracts. In 1979, Patricia returned from studying in Jamaica and was denied her former job: she was informed that she was "overqualified" for that position. Now both of them were unemployed. She had interviewed and was offered several other positions, but those offers were quickly withdrawn. In May 1980, she began work as a research assistant at the University of Guyana. In spite of the deliberate attempts by the government to continually harass and intimidate them, the family was attempting to build a healthy and safe environment for their children.

Walter was in almost constant motion—moving between continents, accepting temporary teaching positions, applying for grants, and sending his CV to colleagues or high schools (and even if there was not a "vacancy," requesting that it be "filed" for a possible future post). On one of these trips to the United States in 1979, he met with the Kenyan student Jembe Mwakalu, whom he had met briefly in Tanzania in 1972—a former student leader at the University of Nairobi. On July 22, Mwakalu wrote to Walter, who had returned to Atlanta—his frequent base when in the States. After pleasantries, he wrote:

> Now down to serious discussion. It struck me deeply then to learn you had no job. It is disappointing. It is nevertheless part of the struggle to disarm progressives and divert their attention from profound social crisis. By holding you down to the search for bread and other basic means for survival, it is hoped, I presume, to frustrate you and / or break your will. I know *they* are mistaken. Please let me know how and where you are. . . . I'd like (with others) to send you something to buy bread with. My friends are students too and children concerned about Kenya, Africa and oppressed peoples world-wide.[8]

This is an astonishing letter. It was both a fairly accurate analysis of Rodney's situation and an expression of deep solidarity and concern—with a practical offer to help. By preventing Rodney from working at the university, Forbes Burnham had hoped to exile an unruly subject. While he failed, the toll on the family was immense.

In the months after the position at the university had been rescinded, there was a constant tide of concern from comrades, colleagues, and friends—each inquiring after the family's well-being. On February 10, 1975, months after the Rodneys had arrived in Georgetown, Patricia and Walter received a letter from Edward Alpers, who they had known in London. "Ned" had also studied for his PhD at the School of Oriental and African Studies under Richard Gray, in the same years as Walter, and then worked for two years in Dar. He wrote, "I was profoundly disturbed to hear of the circumstances in which the Government moved against you, Walter, although I was not particularly surprised that they did." Alpers, who was then teaching at the University of California in Los Angeles, explained:

> The Committee of Concerned West Indians has been circulating its flyer about your case here, as elsewhere, but I don't expect that Burnham will be any more moved by international protest than were the rather more anonymous French authorities who caused the termination of Suret-Canale's post in Paris.[9]

In a warm and familiar tone, Alpers asked, "What are your plans then? I heard recently that you are devoting yourself full time to politics. . . . Presumably, if you get this and reply, it has been decided to give you a certain amount of leeway, although safely away from the University and a normal means of support. Are you working, Pat? How are the children?"

The letter is intimate and kind, recalling their children playing together in Dar—Shaka and Joel—and photos taken in 1973 of the two boys, and how Joel "still lingers over them." He gives news of Abdul Sheriff, a mutual friend from Dar, who had recently visited.[10]

Concern for the Rodneys came from comrades internationally, but it was also provided practically by local groups. In late 1974, Navin Chandarpal, the president of the University of Guyana Students' Society (UGSS) wrote to Walter expressing "complete disgust" "with the actions of the Board of Governors on the question of your appointment."[11] Walter was then invited to run a ten-lecture series for UGSS on "aspects of capitalist and socialist development"—which included lectures on the French Revolution, the Russian Revolution, and the Cuban and Chinese Revolutions. A UGSS magazine, *The Student*, from January 1975, advertises the Support Fund for Victimized Members of the University—focused also on Mohamed Insanally. A prominent opponent of the regime and a lecturer at the university, Insanally was a leading figure in the Guyana National Liberation Front. In July 1973, the university's board of governors decided not to renew his contract—he was in effect fired. The two men, Rodney and Insanally, were now in a similar position. *The Student* reported that

> on Friday 24th January 1975, the UGSS held an impressive ceremony to mark the commencement of lectures by Dr. Walter Rodney and Mohammed Insanally. . . . The President of the UGSS, Navin Chandarpal . . . brought the audience up to date with the incidents relating to the refusal of the board of Governors to employ both Dr Rodney and Mr. Insanally. He said that this was a calculated attempt by the "present regime" to prevent progressive elements to lecture at the university. However, the UGSS has decided to have both lecturers at UG in keeping with the resolution which was adopted by students at the beginning of the academic year.

This was a bold and courageous act by an organized student body, and an open and daring snub to the government and the board of governors, who had effectively declared Rodney persona non grata at the university. The students declared that a course *would* be run by excluded professors—who would teach them the radical history that the regime wanted to keep out of the university. The article reports:

> The last speaker was Dr. Rodney. He pointed out that what is termed the "Rodney Affair" is an issue which goes far beyond his appointments.

. . . . Burnham's statement reported in a Caribbean press that the Government did not deny him employment is one of "patent absurdity"—an insult to the Guyanese people. How can this be so when the Board comprises higher government and party officials. He made it clear that he would not use the University as a political forum. His course, however, will be taking a definite ideological trend.[12]

Rodney was enthusiastic—though the university would not, he stated, be used as a political forum, he saw these lectures as an important opportunity for a radical riposte. He would not be silenced. In a letter to Chandarpal on January 6, he confirmed his availability to speak and expressed his desire that "the lectures would be open to all students and possibly to the public."[13]

Within a very short time, letters and invitations started to arrive—both as acts of solidarity *and* opportunities to pull in a rare and radical voice to their universities and colleges. In October, James Turner from the Africana Studies and Research Center at Cornell University wrote acknowledging a letter and proposal he had received from Walter: "We would like to extend to you an invitation to join us as a research fellow. The purpose of which would be to prepare the data you have collected in Tanzania into a publishable monograph to be printed as part of our monograph series." In addition to this "unpaid" position, Turner also invited Rodney to accept a position "as a visiting Associate Professor for the Spring semester. We are prepared to offer you a salary of $5,000." For this—the equivalent of about $24,000 today—they expected that he would be with them for six weeks to two months to "conduct a seminar."[14] The offer was clearly intended to provide Walter an opportunity to earn an income and continue his research.

A month earlier, Walter had received a letter from James Millette at the department of history at the University of the West Indies in St. Augustine, Trinidad. News of Walter's situation had traveled fast. Millette wrote:

> Would you be willing to consider SERIOUSLY a position at St. Augustine, or do you particularly want to be in Guyana? I suspect you want to be there, and there alone, but I want to know. If you are agreeable, I shall then open up the question of bringing you here . . . there is a post at the Senior Lecturer level in the field of Caribbean Studies. . . . I propose that we fill it and appoint you to it, IF YOU AGREE.[15]

Millette's instinct was, however, correct: Patricia and Walter's decision to return to Guyana was definitive. It was their home.

Even if Walter had not been prevented from taking up a post at the University of Guyana, and was forced to pitch for work, short lectureships, and visiting research positions, as a scholar, he would have traveled to some degree. Now, however, travel had become essential to his continued employment. Despite the travel and work, Rodney remained a family man, intently focused on his children and partner. Patricia recalls how every Friday evening he would have a "family meeting" with his children to review their homework and ask them questions about their progress at school and what the week had been like for them. In their family, there was no rigid wall of adulthood separating the lives of parents and children; Rodney involved his children in his work, taking them to the archives with him and, as Patricia recorded in 2016, whenever possible he even took his children on international, regional, and local trips. Often, he would take them to Linden—the center of the country's local bauxite-mining industry, and an important area of political organizing.[16]

Black Studies and Rodney

As a noted Pan-Africanist, scholar, and activist who had helped to breathe political and historical life into Black Power in Jamaica, Rodney was an obvious choice to anyone who wanted to develop academic programs in Black studies or politics. Robert Chrisman, the editor of *The Black Scholar*—one of the first journals of Black political thought in the United States—wrote to Rodney on February 4, 1975, about a retreat in San Francisco Bay Area in March. The aim of the retreat, called "The Pan-African Movement: What Is to Be Done," was to focus on the prospects of the Pan-African movement and, in Chrisman's words, "the significance for liberation struggles in Africa, the United States and the international Third World Community." Promising to pay for travel and costs, Chrisman urged Rodney to attend. A few months later, he wrote again to "Walter" explaining that "we were all tickled to get your letter of May 26th. We enjoyed your participation in our retreat very much and felt that you made a profound contribution to our understanding . . . of race and class, nationalism and Marxism." The letter and Rodney's paper, which he had enclosed for publication in *The Black Scholar*, had, Chrisman reported, "brightened our day."[17]

As we have seen, one of Rodney's principal bases in the United States was Atlanta, and specifically the Institute of the Black World (IBW), which officially opened on January 17, 1970. The history of Black and Africana studies (the study of people, politics, and culture of Africa, and the African diaspora) in the United States is worth a minor detour, since Rodney played a part in the development of these fields. From the late 1960s, across the US, Black student groups began to insist that universities and colleges set up Black studies programs; as we saw in the example of Vassar College, it was frequently through the militant activism of Black students that new courses and centers were established. In a major study of the period, Winston A. Grady-Willis explains that these centers, courses, and programs were "one of the most tangible and significant manifestations of the Black Power phase of the larger human rights struggle."[18]

Across the United States, it was directly as a consequence of student and community action that Black studies started to gain ground. Frequently, demands were made not only for a transformed curriculum but also for the provision of separate residence, targeted financial support, and widening access for Black students. For instance, Grady-Willis records, "At Cornell University an armed contingent of the Student Afro-American Society occupied the school's administration building in 1969, an action that led to the establishment of the Africana Studies and Research Center."[19] Atlanta, where Rodney was a prominent and regular visitor, was part of the same wave of action.

In April 1969 a group of students at the Atlanta University Center attempted to raise their concerns to the board of trustees. When this effort failed, they locked themselves in with the board members. Grady-Willis notes that "[t]wenty-nine hours and an informal agreement later, student activists unchained the doors and released their dazed hostages."[20] Within a remarkably short period, embryonic programs were established, and approval for a Black studies program was conceded. New Black faculty members were appointed to head these programs, and wider recruitment of students was promised.

Perhaps the most prominent of the centers that emerged from this ferment was the IBW, which was first envisaged in 1969, and formally opened in 1970. According to its statement of purpose, the institute had at its heart a project aimed at the convergence of "Black intellectuals who are convinced that the gifts of their minds are meant to be fully used in the service of the Black community. It is, therefore, an experiment with scholarship in the context of struggle."[21] Though explicitly focused on the whole African world, there was an initial stress on America.

The statement of purpose was accompanied by a program that sought to lay out the objectives of the institute. It included "developing new materials for teaching Black children," "[f]orming creative linkages with other concerned activists and scholars in the global African world," "sponsoring seminars, workshops and conferences," and "launching a publishing program." The program concluded with a commitment to creating a "new cadre" of men and woman trained in the scholarship of the Black experience and wedded to the "struggles of the Black world."[22]

Each of these objectives were shared by Rodney; indeed, both the institute's influence on his own work *and* his imprint on the institute itself were clear. The IBW set itself apart from mainstream academia, in that it was not just a center of Black or Africana studies, but a place where the dominant perspectives about the world could be challenged and alternatives built. One of Walter's close friends and comrades, William Strickland, saw the IBW as a place where certain Marxist notions could be challenged—specifically the tendency on the radical Left to downplay the role of race in the United States. The approach of the institute was irreverent toward both mainstream thinking *and* popular conceptions of radical theory and practice. As an intellectual environment, it was creative at the same time that it was subversive.

In the summer of 1969, prior to the IBW's formal establishment, Atlanta activists and scholars organized a workshop for students with a conference on Black studies. The atmosphere was electric. The world was being reshaped by activism, and new areas of study were blossoming. As Grady-Willis explains, the period was "marked by the eclectic cultural and political movement of Black Power."[23] Rodney, we must recall, was not simply a brilliant though peripheral visiting scholar to these gatherings; he was an intimate part of the movement's flesh and bones. As we have seen, his *Groundings with My Brothers* marked his extraordinary contribution to Black Power in Jamaica in 1968, and was an original, if not a founding, statement of the formation of radical "Africana" or Black studies in the region. The book became required reading in training sessions and community programs. The conference program included talks by C. L. R. James, Robert Hill, and Rodney—who had arrived via Uganda dreadfully ill with malaria.

Its fusion of activism with scholarship meant the environment at the IBW spoke to the urgency of the period and was unlike other academic hubs. Joyce Ladner, who would become a close friend of Patricia and Walter, was a senior research fellow at the Martin Luther King Center for Nonviolent Social Change in Atlanta and spent a year at the Institute from 1969; she noted that it was "the single most productive year of my academic career. . . . I wrote more. I taught. . . . I had this incredible energy personally, and yet it was such a collaborative environment."[24] From the start, however, there were severe problems related to funding; as Vincent Harding, the first director, lamented, there were "fantasies" about the "millions of dollars of American guilt money" pouring in. It never happened, and there was, for the entire life of the institute, a constant and ferocious struggle for funds.

The political environment was ripe not just because of the astonishing struggles taking place in the United States with the Black Power movement, but also on account of the extent of political upheaval in the Caribbean, Southeast Asia, and Africa. There were several popular lodestars: the Cuban Revolution and the mass demonstrations against the American war in Vietnam, but also the gathering battle for independence and socialism in Guinea-Bissau, Mozambique, and Angola. Amílcar Cabral was an immensely popular figure; as a leader of nationalist forces in Guinea-Bissau, he sought to apply Marxist theory to the "African revolution," refusing easy formulations. He too was drawn into this extraordinary political awakening.

Activism informed the spirit of the IBW, ensuring it remained infused with the energy of the time. As Grady-Willis explains:

> Propelled by grassroots activism in poor and working class Black neighbourhoods in Atlanta and throughout the United States, a core group of college students and intellectuals in the city took it upon themselves to transform the academy . . . the IBW, a movement-centred think-tank located in the house that WEB Du Bois had occupied decades earlier. There . . . an engaged Black intellectual life and discourse began to flourish in international dimensions.[25]

One of several initiatives of the IBW in which Rodney was deeply involved had been its second-ever Summer Research Symposium, held in 1974. Organized under the theme "Black People and the International Crisis: Where Do We Go from Here?," the symposium included lectures on the struggles of Black people in the United States and abroad, and the history and political economy of the "international crisis." Over a six-week period in "public lecture forums," recordings were made of each session, which were then made available, distributed for "classroom, workshop, community and religious-group study" on "C-90 cassette tapes."

The "technology" was relatively new, having only been used in the United States from 1964; thus, the distribution of these cassette "courses" by the IBW was highly original. One of these cassette tapes included Rodney speaking on the "politics of the African ruling class"—where, the program notes, "Rodney sketches a general picture of the present state of affairs on the African continent, concentrating on the ruling class, which although a minority, determines the destiny of millions of people."

In exchange for his role in the summer school, Rodney received "a check for $448.16"—about $2,000 today. In July 1976, the director of the IBW, Vincent Harding, wrote to Rodney asking him if he would serve on the institute's board of directors, which meant overseeing the programs of the IBW and "establishing goals objectives priorities and strategies." On the "brink of the 21st century," Harding explains, "we are trying to . . . raise the right questions, to put forward the best possible analyses of the Black condition and American and world society and to do whatever we can to press our people and this entire society. . . . . Towards fundamental transformation for . . . all humankind." Rodney had been nominated to serve on the board because of the "respect and admiration of the Black community here and abroad," which would bring credibility and legitimacy to the IBW; Harding explained that the "entire staff" hoped that he would agree to serve the institute.

Walter readily agreed to join the board, which would meet once a year. Funding had been precarious from the start, and one of the challenges to which board members had to put their minds was the IBW's "immediate financial problems." Rodney, engaged in his own long struggles to keep mind and body together, and to support his family, was asked in a letter on October 27, 1976, "if you know of any sources where we might get small emergency grants ($1000–$5000)" or if members could "(1) contribute whatever he/she can during this period ($100–$250 had been pledged by several Board members) and (2) write to 5–10 of their friends and associates asking them to make a tax deductible contribution before the end of the year." Considering Walter's circumstances, this was probably not the most appropriate letter to send—yet it expresses well the perilous state of finances of Black studies, which had led Harding to end his July 29 letter with the words "[i]f we can make it through the rest of the summer."[26]

Travel: Income and Political Work

Rodney's astonishingly varied activities required almost continual travel—both for work, in the narrow sense of earning an income, and for open political work. However, the two were inevitably linked: wherever he went, he talked about the struggle in Guyana and spoke to solidarity groups, Guyanese exiles, students, and workers.

Invariably controversial, Walter's talks frequently appeared in the papers. Early in February 1975, the radical Trinidad-Tobago newspaper *Tapia* published a report by Syl Lowhar on a lecture delivered by Rodney called "Socialism, Pan-Africanism and the Caribbean in Trinidad." "Rodney's visit," Lowhar explains,

> was long overdue. For long the brothers and sisters had studied his
> Groundings looked forward to welcoming him in their midst. . . .
> Someone observed how ironic it was that this former UWI lecturer,
> now hustling, scrunting freedom fighter, would have to speak from a
> lectern in the Trojan Horse, the gift which the Americans gave to the
> country when the 1941 Chaguaramas base lease was re-negotiated.

As usual, Rodney spoke without compromise. On this occasion, Lowhar wrote, he was "lavish" in his "attack" on the "pseudo-socialists who are to be found everywhere in the Third World. Even Tanzania's President was not exempt. He branded Nyerere's African Socialism as petty bourgeois nationalism that was neither African nor socialist . . . everyone is now a socialist he said. That everyone felt the need to identify with that ideology was the clearest recognition of its validity."

The attack on the so-called pseudo-socialists in the Caribbean was intentional—and would have hit close to home, given that the islands of Trinidad and Tobago are less than 7 miles off the coast of Venezuela and about 375 miles from Georgetown. Rodney targeted an entire class that he saw as holding back progressive change in the region, and across the Third World, while serving the interests of US power. Lowhar continued in his account of the lecture: Rodney argued that "all these pseudo-socialists . . . have the ideology of self. For them, socialism is a stepping-stone to gain. Rodney saw them as so much debris, as obstacles in the path of the development of genuine Socialism." To the surprise of those in attendance, Rodney identified himself with the petty bourgeoisie. Yet, he noted, they could "exempt themselves" from this stigma by serving the interests of the working class. He was challenged on this point by "a young Indian graduate . . . who pointed out that only the workers can lead a socialist revolution. Intellectuals like Rodney can only betray it."[27]

Later in 1975, in November, Rodney was speaking as a guest of the student federation at the University of Waterloo in Ontario, Canada, where he spoke about the Third World. He explained that in the last decade, "the volume of Marxist literature has increased and so have the number of intellectuals willing to acknowledge themselves as Marxists." However, Rodney argued, "there is still much argument that Marxism is a 19th century philosophy in a 20th century world, people are discovering that the political questions of today are being asked by Marxists. The question of multi-national corporations controlling the Third World economies were first asked by Marxists."[28]

In 1976, on November 11, the *Stanford Daily* reported on a talk Rodney gave at the university that analyzed the situation in Southern Africa. The analysis, he argued, was not simple, since every contradiction is represented. "When one grasps the contradictions as a totality," he observed, "Southern Africa is automatically a revolutionary situation . . . each conflict is sufficient cause for revolution, but together they are explosive." The reports explained that Rodney compared the situation to "just before the overthrow of Czarist Russia." Discussing US involvement on the continent, Rodney claims that the "US stepped into Africa as a 'neo-colonist' police-force, ensuring the continuation of colonialism when European imperialists were unable to do so." Then, according to the report, Rodney turned his attention to the Soviet Union and how

> the nationalistic Pan-Africans want to keep both the US and the USSR out of Africa and let the Africans do it themselves. Meanwhile, the internationalist Marxists fear both capitalistic and Soviet imperialism and believe the latter is the greater threat. Rodney disagreed with both views. The US is already entrenched in Africa and can only be removed with the aid of non-capitalistic countries and their arms.[29]

The article was accompanied with a photograph of Rodney speaking, mid-sentence, in a leather jacket and smart, high-collared shirt; light from the auditorium reflects in his glasses, his face is relaxed and calm.

If Rodney's life of an activist was already difficult, now he was being pulled simultaneously in different directions—constantly pitching for research funding and traveling for seminars, conferences, and workshops, while also participating in almost-nightly meetings and informal talks to groups of workers and comrades. Through all of this, it would have been easier to take permanent work outside Guyana, but this was never something he and Patricia seriously considered. Indeed, as we have seen, they both felt a deep emotional and political connection to their home and felt it was their responsibility to bring their children up in Guyana and to join in efforts to transform the country and the lives of the poor.

As part of this effort, on November 13, 1975, Walter wrote to "Sister Hazel Campayne," headmistress of St. Rose's High School in Georgetown. He explains:

> This letter is a follow-up of our recent conversation in your office, during which I enquired about the possibility of part-time employment at St. Rose's High School. . . . As a University undergraduate and subsequently, I studied courses which qualify me to teach to the equivalent of "A" Level the following subjects: 1) History, 2) Economics, 3) Economic Geography. . . . . My "A" Level qualifications include English Literature and Spanish; and I would hold myself available to teach these two subjects. . . . I understand that there are at the moment no vacancies, but this formal application would be place on record and could be considered if the need arises.[30]

Teaching in a high school would probably have been regarded by Walter as important, even vital work; after all, he had spent time helping to develop the high school curriculum in Tanzania, work that he had brought back with him from Dar es Salaam to complete. At the same time, he was under increasing pressure to look for other avenues of work and income. In the end, the need for his services did not arise at the school, and Walter continued to work on short contracts overseas.

The Rodneys continued to resist efforts to draw them out of Guyana. In May 1976, Walter was offered a position teaching African history at Addis Ababa University in Ethiopia, recently reopened after the country's revolutionary struggles. Merid Wolde Aregay, chairman of the history department, wrote: "All members have recommended that I approach and try to interest you in coming to Addis Ababa. . . . You are fairly well known to Ethiopian students. You know their revolutionary fervour." Of all the offers that Rodney received after 1974, this would have been one of the most attractive. In 1974 the regime of Emperor Haile Salassie was overthrown in a revolution, events which Rodney would have followed with interest. Aregay urged Rodney: "[I]f you cannot absent yourself from your present post for long, the Department will be prepared to make any arrangements that may satisfy you." In August, Rodney was offered a visiting professorship for the following year at the Ahmadu Bello University in Nigeria—as the head of history explained: "[M]any of us here have read your books and articles and feel that you can contribute towards the type of teaching and research orientation we want established in the department." Rodney responded promptly that he was not available, because of "political responsibilities in Guyana."[31]

Letters of support and solidarity continued to arrive from comrades and friends. Congolese activist and scholar Ernest Wamba dia Wamba responded to a letter of Rodney's in an intimate reply on July 31, 1976: "I am also glad to hear that your domestic situation is in good shape. The primacy of internal contradictions commands that our domestic situation be the starting point and the ending point with the whole world in between (singularity-generality-singularity). If this point is shaky then we have difficulty trying to focus."[32] Indeed, Rodney's "domestic situation" was foundational to his life's work.

In July 1976, Pierre Y. Paradis from the Canada-based International Development Research Centre informed him that his application to the center had been successful, and that he was being granted a research associate award. The plan was to conduct research on the "colonial political economy of British Guiana," from 1884 to 1934 (research that eventually became *A History of the Guyanese Working People, 1881–1905*). Rodney submitted a proposal, in July 1977, suggesting a start date of September in 1977, and an affiliation with the Institute of Commonwealth Studies in London, where he would be based with his family. The award, confirmed in a letter on August 18, would total CA$27,100 (around US$86,000 today). The amount might seem generous, but certain things had to be accounted for: the entire family was traveling; the return to London (where the colonial archives he needed to consult were based) for the party of five cost almost CA$10,600; and the duration of the research period was long, from April to September 1977. Typical of research grants, every penny had to be reported, and Rodney kept scrupulous records.

Upon their arrival, Rodney's schedule of travel to archives and universities across the UK was ambitious: regular trips to the newspaper archive in Colindale, and travel to the Lancashire Record Office, the Essex County Record Office, libraries in Oxford, the Liverpool Record Office, and public and university libraries in Glasgow and Edinburgh, as well as the Scottish Record Office. It was a period of intense and painstaking work, traveling (frequently alone) across the UK to spend time in archives by himself—the peculiar solitary work of a historian, which in Walter contrasted with the dramatically social and public work of a revolutionary activist. The official statement of proposed work submitted to the Canadian research fund the previous year did not reflect his real objectives; Rodney sought to present a historical account of the emergence of working-class unity between Black and Indian workers in Guyana. Activism was once more at the heart of his historical work.

The family returned to Georgetown, and Rodney was once again writing to former colleagues in search of other opportunities to speak and teach. The archival collection in Atlanta shows Rodney's meticulous budgeting for the research trip to the UK—a stipulation of the Canadian grant but also consistent with his own penchant for careful organization and planning. There was not a category for "discretionary" expenditure, or family costs, so the hunt would have been on for work as soon as he touched down in Georgetown. Writing to George Jackson, who Walter believed to be the dean of the Essex Community College, on September 23, 1976, he explains: "I am functioning as an independent researcher and I lecture from time to time in North America. . . . I wondered whether it would be possible to get a paid speaking engagement at Essex Community College . . . during the first week of November." Rodney suggests that he speak on the situation in Southern Africa but understands that "[i]n recent times, budgetary constraints have become all-powerful; so that if you cannot act it will not be too surprising."[33]

Within a few weeks he received a response. Writing from Howard University and the School of Social Work, George Jackson clarified: "I am aware of some of your problems but am glad to see that you are still a Black scholar. Unfortunately, I am no longer the Dean at Essex. Black scholars are not welcome there." Instead, he forwarded Rodney's request to a colleague, Judith Miller, then director of Black studies at Seton Hall University, in the "hope that they might be able to use your services."

Jackson expressed pleasure that Rodney was "still a Black scholar." Yet, remaining so was never a choice for Rodney; it was an identity tied inextricably to his political and revolutionary activity, for he knew that history (in the right hands) was an indispensable tool to craft activism that could change the world. History and research were the air he breathed, and he could no more surrender them than hand over his heart and lungs.[34]

It is important to state that upon the Rodneys' return to Guyana, they did not find themselves in a period of desperate foraging for work. Of course, Rodney had wanted a permanent position at the university, which was snatched from him as he arrived home from Tanzania. Perhaps the best account of the period is provided by his wife, Patricia: "We were never desperate for money. Walter wanted to work; that was his right, and he also raised funds during his trips for the Working People's Alliance. But I had a job until I returned from the University of the West Indies with a bachelor of science degree in 1979. . . . Every other position I applied for after that was blocked by Burnham."[35] The family coped and coped well.

When speaking in the Caribbean, he was often forced to be circumspect—which was certainly the case when it came to his planned lecture at a conference called "Contemporary Ideologies and the Christian Faith," hosted by Trinidad's St. Andrew's Theological College. As Idris Hamid, director of the college, explained in a December 18, 1976, letter, the conference would "seek to provide an opportunity for study of the 'Contemporary Ideologies' such as Socialism, Capitalism, Marxism and their socio-political manifestations." Rodney was asked to deliver four lectures, starting with a "survey of Marxist philosophy." This was clearly more than delivering a "research paper" at an academic conference— the usual format for such conferences. Instead, Walter was required to "teach" and then stay on for the entire duration "as a resource person." All costs and a "modest honorarium" would be provided. However, Rodney was advised by Hamid on January 22 that to "avoid any problem" on arrival he should "indicate to Immigration . . . that you are here to *attend* a Seminar and not to give any lectures." The speaking permit required would "delay" or "prevent" Rodney's participation. Interestingly, on the program of the conference there is no mention of Rodney's name—indeed, its inclusion might have set off fireworks in Trindad and alerted the authorities to his presence.

After the conference, on April 12, Idris Hamid wrote to Rodney once more, this time addressing the letter simply "Dear Walter." He enthusiastically offers his thanks: "On behalf of the Caribbean Ecumenical Programme and the participants of our seminar . . . we wish to thank you most sincerely. . . . Your lectures were very stimulating and informative and were appreciated by all. We were also happy to have your wife with us." As we have seen, Patricia was not an extra on the Rodney show, but participated actively in the world of activism and academic conferences.

This small indication that Patricia traveled with him to Trinidad for the duration of the conference between February 15 to 18, in addition to the far-longer period she and the children spent in London in 1977, shows how deeply integrated they were in his activities.[36]

Living, working, and surviving as an "independent scholar" required diligent organization: visiting lectureships and conferences and research fieldwork had to be organized months, and occasionally years, in advance. The Rodneys' trip to London in 1977 had to be set up in September of the previous year to tie in with the Canadian-funded research he was planning to conduct over this period. W. H. Morris-Jones, director of the Institute of Commonwealth Studies, wrote to confirm "that you will be arriving in April, I am arranging that your three meetings should take place on 17 and 31 May and 14 June at 5.00pm. . . . The Institute of Latin American Studies will be combining with us on this operation, as well as the Centre of African Studies at SOAS."[37] In a sense, this would have marked Walter's return to Bloomsbury and the University of London, where he had studied for his PhD years before.

During his period in London, Walter ensured that he also spoke to activist groups—indeed, this was among the most important of his engagements. On June 25, he received an invitation from Ikhenemho Okomilo of the Pan-African Association of Writers and Journalists in Britain to speak for thirty minutes on the subject of "the Black writer in a white racist society." "As you may know," Okomilo writes, "we are a poor and newly formed organisation and the maximum fee we could offer you would be £10." An enthusiastic thank you "for the most interesting talk" was sent in July.[38]

In early 1978, Walter was once again organizing his year of work, travel, and teaching. This time he was headed, as a visiting professor, to Hamburg, where, as we will see, he was to deliver a pathbreaking lecture course on modern African history and political economy. Plans for the course had already been put in place the previous year; on February 18, Rainer Tetzlaff, a radical German scholar and activist who was coordinating Walter's visit, wrote to provide certain administrative details, including "monthly pay to the amount of DM3500" (approximately $27,000 today)—a high monthly figure. Nevertheless, it was, once again, one that had to include all expenses—not least the extortionate airfares from Guyana to Hamburg. In addition, this was the only significant salary that year for the family; every penny had to be carefully budgeted.

On March 6, Tetzlaff wrote to Rodney with details of flights with British Airways, leaving Georgetown on April 5 and arriving in the afternoon the next day in Hamburg—the cost was an astronomical 1,487 Deutsche marks (equivalent to $12,000 today), one way, to be deducted from his monthly "salary." Although the era of international air travel had arrived, it was still almost entirely the domain of rich. If one were funding their own travel, either they did not travel far or they took a boat. The only way Rodney was able to travel was if he was funded by a university—and his hefty $27,000 salary was quickly diminished.[39]

When news spread that Rodney was in Hamburg, he received invitations to speak from other universities and scholars. On May 11, Wilfred Röhrich, a political scientist at Kiel University, invited him to present a seminar to students on "African problems"; a student would collect Rodney, and he would be invited for a "drink to a nice place in Kiel with my tutors and some of my students" after the course. Rodney accepted—rare were his refusals. In June, he also presented seminars at the Free University in Berlin.[40]

Even while Rodney was in Hamburg, he was fielding requests and invitations sent to Guyana. The celebrated economist and historian Immanuel Wallerstein wrote on May 25 to ask if "Walter . . . would be interested to become an Adjunct Professor" for six weeks to teach and work at the State University of New York in Binghamton; he would be joining other Marxists, including Perry Anderson, Giovanni Arrighi, and Ramkrishna Mukherjee. This position would run for three years, and he would receive a stipend of $5,000 and round-trip airfare (about $20,000 today). There would be about nine hours of graduate and undergraduate teaching a week, with supervision of students.

Many thousands of miles away, the message was conveyed to Walter—perhaps by Patricia—and he called, as Wallerstein suggested, on "reverse charges." Wallerstein in turn wrote to him again to suggest dates for his visiting position in either October and November that year, or January and February the following year. Wallerstein suggested the former dates; when the weather was better, he would teach "Africa in world-system perspective" and the "historical sociology of the plantation system." Wallerstein signed off, "I'm delighted that you will be coming." Confirming in August, he wrote again, suggesting, "Frankly, why don't you start from scratch and compose your own [reading] list." The official, bureaucratic letter from Binghamton was sent on September 6, with full confirmation of the three-year position as adjunct professor of sociology effective from September 1 and ending August 31.[41]

So started a fruitful, though truncated, collaboration—though it was only a matter of months before it would be tragically cut short.

CHAPTER 10

Building the Party

There was no wall of steel separating the teaching and research trips Walter made to the United States or Europe from the political work he undertook in Guyana. After all, the center of his world was the liberation of Guyana. Each time he visited Washington, DC, Atlanta, Los Angeles, New York, Hamburg, or London, he lobbied, organized, and fundraised for the Working People's Alliance (WPA), of which he was one of the leaders. While founded in Guyana, the left-wing organization's work was international in scope. In July 1976, one comrade, Josh McClendon, who was based at Howard University in the mid-1970s, reported to Rodney on the group's aim

> to inundate the Guyanese and West Indian communities in Washington, New York, and, hopefully, in California with the political educational materials from the WPA, thus widening our constituency. The case for scientific socialism must be taken over, built and be advanced by the WPA as it goes through its party-building programs. This will be a means of staking out a distinct proletarian identity at home and abroad.

Indeed, communicating with party comrades at "home and abroad" was an important part of the WPA's—and Rodney's—work. Through his enforced travel, he had the opportunity to promote the party's programs, build support for WPA groups internationally, and, crucially, raise funds. In this sense, the pain and separation forced on the family by his regular travels, often for very long periods, had also become indispensable "political work" for the WPA.

McClendon, a WPA activist in the United States, gave his opinions, reporting on this "party work"—of support groups and new members—in a letter to Rodney in 1976. "Consolidating the structures of a Vanguard Party, of course, entails even more than those efforts marginally performed at present," he wrote. "Apart from fund-raising, we are planning to launch, soon, a Caribbean Liberation Support Committee which might better, organisationally at least, promote the programs of WPA." Josh explained that some books—"the Lenin volumes"—were being sent to the party in Georgetown by boat (to save money), and that they would likely arrive at the end of July. The rest of the letter describes the activities of a committed "exiled" party worker, collecting money, organizing reading groups, and raising awareness of the struggle in Guyana. McClendon continued:

> Our personnel are few, but in time we should be growing in numbers and intensifying our work. Our study group, the one formed after you left, is going fine with about 25 people. It is international but not yet organized for political work under one banner. We're taking time to groom and to set things up tidily. Meanwhile a few of us are working with the Guyana National Association and are succeeding in politicising the group, making it aware of the farcical PNC [People's National Congress] socialism and the need for scientific socialism.

Signing off the letter, McClendon wrote: "[T]he PNC is talking now of ultra-leftists and of saboteurs in the mining industry. Clearly, their ideological position is revealed in these attacks, further they're recognising that the WPA is a force to be dealt with. Fight them! We're behind you all the way, comrades."[1]

So commenced a period in Rodney's life of full-time political activism. In some respects, it was the practical consummation of everything he had been working toward in his adult life. He threw himself into political organizing as an activist who enthusiastically got his hands dirty in the daily nitty-gritty of building WPA branches in working-class areas and speaking to bauxite, sugar, and rice workers. He popularized political material as a necessary and urgent task of party building—a difficult and undervalued skill, retelling vital lessons from Guyana and Africa's past, explaining that the unity of Indian and Black workers had existed in the past and could again. Rodney thus brought his understated brilliance to the work of revolutionary organizing in Guyana.

The Political Stalemate

To understand the political world to which Rodney was returning, it is necessary to survey what had happened in the years he had been away.

Though he had been following events in the country through correspondence, conversations, newspapers, and books, he had to be in Guyana to get a real sense of what was happening—and how he could intervene.

Walter had already left for his studies in Kingston when the People's Progressive Party (PPP), for whom he had campaigned as a boy, won the election in 1961 with a small margin. Despite the fact that the party had gained almost double the number of seats of the People's National Congress, the aftermath of the elections had seen terrible racial violence, with mass demonstrations headed by the PNC, and a general strike. After a few weeks, British authorities stationed in the country intervened, with the governor announcing a state of emergency. In the racial divide of the country, the PNC garnered the support of the Afro-Guyanese population, about a third of the country's population at the time; though the PPP was officially multiracial, its electoral constituency came from the Indian population, who then made up almost approximately 40 percent of the population.

The PPP leader and then premier of the country, Cheddi Jagan, received the hostile and paranoid attention of the Kennedy government from Washington, who labeled him a communist. The Central Intelligence Agency compelled the UK to assist in a program of political sabotage inside the country in the early 1960s, using, among other means, Forbes Burnham and members of the PNC to destabilize the country. Burnham had split from the PPP and formed the PNC in 1958; he was a smart, though brutal, political operator who spoke about the radical empowerment of Guyana's Black population and socialism while receiving funding from the CIA.

Cheddi Jagan was born in Guyana in 1918 to parents who had come from India. His father was a bus driver, a career for which he would have been regarded as a lowly member of the Indian middle class. Despite few spare resources, the family sent their son to Queen's College in Georgetown—the same elite school where Rodney would be educated a generation later. An exceptionally able and bright student, Jagan attended college in the United States at Northwestern University. After graduating in 1942, he returned to Guyana the following year with his future wife, Janet Rosenberg, who Cheddi had met when he was studying dentistry; the American was then was a student nurse at Cook County Hospital, a public hospital in Chicago. The couple married on August 5, 1943, and moved to Guyana in December of that year.

Ten years after the "coup" led by the British colonial administration against the first PPP administration, similar processes were again at work. Elected in 1961, the British were nervous about granting the country independence with a radical leader and party in government. Two years later, the British, under pressure from the United States, carried out a constitutional coup that ensured that Jagan's PPP would not be elected. The British were mindful of US interests and recognized that British Guiana (as Guyana was known before independence in 1966) fell under the US sphere of interest, no matter Britain's hefty commercial interests in the sugar industry—estimated at $400 to $500 million (approximately $4 billion today).[2]

In astonishingly candid communiques between Washington and London in 1962, US secretary of state Dean Rusk explained to the UK foreign secretary Sir Alec Douglas-Home:

> I have reached the conclusion that it is not possible for us to put up with an independent British Guiana under Jagan. . . . The continuation of Jagan in power is leading us to disaster in terms of the colony itself, strains on Anglo-American relations and difficulties for the Inter-American system. . . . I hope we can agree that Jagan should not accede to power again.

However, this was going too far, proving too crude even for the British government. The response from Douglas-Home asked: "[H]ow would you suggest that this can be done in a democracy?"[3] Fear that another Cuba was about to break out on the United States' doorstep was too much to countenance in Washington.

Despite such initial reluctance, the British knew what side their bread was buttered on. It was not long before they accepted the US edicts. The plan was multipronged, involving a carefully orchestrated program of destabilization and changes to the electoral system. Historian Mark Curtis explains:

> The CIA helped to organise and fund anti-Jagan protests in February 1962, which resulted in strikes and riots, and during which, in fact, the British sent troops to restore order. But the centrepiece of the CIA's cover operation was funding the general strike that began in April 1963 and lasted for 80 days. Using $1 million allocated for the purpose, CIA agents gave advice to local union leaders on how to organise and sustain the strike and provided funds and food to keep the strikers going. This strike was publicly cited by British officials as evidence that Jagan could not run the country.[4]

At the same time these activities were taking place, the US and UK governments were hatching other plans. In March of that year, the US consul general in Georgetown, Everett Melby, confirmed an agreement between the US and UK governments: a shift to a proportional representation (PR) system for the colony, it was decided, would be the best way to unseat Jagan, replacing the PPP with "a more democratic and reliable government."[5]

We can be fairly confident that this "more democratic" language was merely a disguise for what was really taking place: a barefaced electoral scam to make it more difficult for the PPP to win elections. Later in 1962, the US president and UK prime minster were in direct communication. Kennedy approved the plan hatched by the British and expressed his gratitude: "[T]his problem," he remarked, "is one in which you have shown a most helpful understanding of my special concern."[6]

The plan involved bringing the political leaders of British Guiana to London to force a solution to the political instability, rioting, and strikes and to set up a new electoral system based on PR, which would, in their estimation, work as a ballast to racialism. For a colonial government who had spent decades fostering such racialism, this was a hideous joke. The actual coup took place in October 1963 at a seemingly benign constitutional conference; elections, the attending delegates determined, would be held under a new system of proportional representation, with the promise that the country's population of about half a million, including both its large Indian community and smaller African community, would receive their just and proportional share of political power.

Though Jagan and the PPP rightly complained at this open attempt to drive the party from power, they held on to the illusions that an incoming Labour government in the UK would overturn the PR plan. These hopes, however, came to naught, and in October 1964, the new Labour administration in London would neither accelerate the plans for independence, nor replace the new electoral system. The coup was signed, sealed, and executed.

Elections in Guyana were held in December 1964, and though the PPP won a larger share of the vote, and more seats, Forbes Burnham's PNC formed a government with the United Force (UF). The chicanery continued almost unabated after 1964. The Office of the Historian at the US State Department released documents in 2005 that detailed clearly the extent of the continued intervention in Guyana. In the words of the report, "The U.S. Government acted on a covert political plan to defeat Jagan by funnelling secret financial support, campaign advice and expertise, and other assistance to the two main opposition parties."[7] Though in the 1964 elections Jagan's PPP secured most seats, the PNC and the UF together won more seats and were thus invited to form a government. The UF was a conservative party led by Peter D'Aguiar, a businessman who drew his support from the small Portuguese population, while attempting to build a constituency among the Amerindian population. Immediately after the elections, Jagan refused to step down, and he had to be removed by the governor. Seeing the PNC and Burnham as the most popular anti-Jagan party, the United States distributed films and publications blasting the PPP, slashed most aid to British Guiana, and rejected Jagan's requests for senior meetings with US officials, in an effective effort to undermine him.

Forbes Burnham, an avidly pro-American leader, took power at the end of 1964. Born in 1923 into a relatively prosperous Afro-Guyanese family, Burnham was the only son in a family of three children. His father was the headmaster of a Methodist primary school just outside Georgetown. Burnham did well in school and won a scholarship to study for a law degree at the London School of Economics, graduating in 1948—mixing with a generation of nationalist figures in London, including Ghana's Kwame Nkrumah. He was one of the founders of the PPP in 1950, becoming the party's chairman, with Jagan as the party's leader. Burnham split from the PPP in 1955, forming the PNC three years later.

The United States continued to provide financial support to Burnham, his party, and his political allies in the UF party—as well as the state in general, the police, and the unions; declassified US documents provide detailed evidence. As a key area of potential unity in Guyana's working class, the country's unions were targeted by the United States in its efforts to shore up Burnham's divisive power base and maintain the country's racially divided class structure. There was even a "small management group" formed to keep Jagan out of power, made up of the presidential special assistant for national security affairs, the ambassador, and officers in the Department of State and the CIA. The US encouraged an earlier date for independence using a combination of racial prejudice and cunning. A memorandum between members of the "management group" explained on July 14, 1964:

> With the British in British Guiana and the East Indian population growing, there is always the chance that the British will change the rules of the game (e.g., coalition, a new election). In this regard, it is probably true that Jagan feels he still has a chance so long as the British

are around. With the British gone, Jagan himself may decide to bug out. . . . The chances for violence probably won't increase significantly with independence. Generally speaking, the East Indians are timid compared to the Africans and, without the British to protect them, they might be even more timid. Also, it is conceivable that a British military presence could be maintained even after independence.[8]

Curtis's response to this is scathing. He writes: "Now that the acceptable leadership had taken office, Guyana could be granted independence, which proceeded in 1966. The Anglo-American constitutional coup to remove the nationalist threat had successfully countered the democratic voice of the unpeople of British Guiana."[9]

After independence in May 1966, the country, henceforth known as Guyana, received US support for road building and certain "development projects," as well as food aid. Though the cynical coalition between Burnham and D'Aguiar, leader of the UF, barely held together, the United States fought hard, until the end of 1968, to maintain this state of affairs. The loyal watchdog of US interests in Guyana, Burnham met with President Lyndon B. Johnson on repeated occasions in 1966. Declassified documents also show that the US approved funds to ensure that the Burnham–D'Aguiar coalition won the December 1968 elections.

The die had thus been cast since 1964. With ethnic violence and division overwhelming the country, and a pseudo-left, "Black Power" premier in Burnham, the country became a carnival of reaction—one that led many activists to leave independent Guyana in despair. WPA activist Rupert Roopnaraine remembers the period:

> I had become so disenchanted with what had happened in Guyana in the 1960s. When I left there in 1962, February, it happened, the burning of the city [PNC/Burnham-led demonstrations against the government] on 16 February 1962, led to dozens of businesses destroyed by fire and looting. . . . When I left in 1962, I did not even wait for exam results to leave. I left even before the exam results came out.[10]

It was a progressive and radical generation who left. The news that reached Roopnaraine throughout his voluntary exile in the 1960s would have done nothing to reassure him. On the contrary, as he described in 2012, he "felt that the way in which Guyana had developed in the 1960s, what had happened then, really removed any possibility of progressive politics that was non-racial." This was the politics of *"Apan jaat naa bhu-*

laiba," which in Bhojpuri (a Hindi dialect spoken in Guyana) translated as "Don't forget your kind"—an idea that had become ingrained in Guyana by the mid-1960s.

In the 1970s, Roopnaraine studied in the United States, where he rekindled his earlier friendship with Walter; the two men had known each other as children in Georgetown. Their conversations convinced Roopnaraine, in his words, that "there was a real movement . . . a real possibility, that space was opening up." "Walter," he concludes, "persuaded me to come home and I did."[11]

Following independence and the PNC victory in the 1968 elections, with the United States ignoring to Burnham's use of fraudulent absentee ballots, the country became increasingly divided by race. This was in no way mitigated by Burnham's decision, in 1970, to declare Guyana as a republic committed to socialism and nonalignment. His pseudo-radicalism extended deep into activist circles, inside and outside the country; for example, unlike the government of Trinidad and Tobago, Burnham refused to ban the American-based advocate of Black Power, Stokely Carmichael. In fact, at a rally on December 12, 1968, the prime minister endorsed the Black Power movement, describing it as "the consolidation and strengthening of the rule of the black man and the brown man over the resources and destinies of Guyana."[12]

The PPP and its supporters, long bludgeoned by the ruling party, now extended limited support to the PNC—on the basis of the "adoption" of a more radical-sounding politics. Efforts among different groups on the Left that eventually came together to form the WPA in 1974 emerged, in part, from these frustrations and a determined effort to break from the sectarian past—the prolonged nightmare of the country's decolonization.

The Origins of the WPA

To meet these challenges of division and racial conflict, a new organization had to be built. Efforts at building unity between Guyana's main communities were taking place amid the country's worst racial strife—many years before Rodney returned to Georgetown. One gathering of left-wing writers was the New World Group, which was an informal group of intellectuals, writers, and activists from the anglophone Caribbean. Established in Guyana in 1963, as the country grappled with its legacy of racial division and underdevelopment, the group published its formative "Working Notes towards the Unification of Guyana." The list of members was impressive—and Pan-Caribbean, including many of the region's most acclaimed writers and activists, among them Norman Girvan, Syl Lowhar, George Lamming, and Andaiye (formerly Sandra Williams).

Committed to rethinking the region's politics, the group became a home for radical thought; indeed, their orientation was to thought, not action. When Rodney was asked to join the group in Jamaica in 1968, he declined, saying, "[A]ll this . . . [is] interesting but I'm not really into all of that. I am going to go into the ghettos . . . [to] ground with the Rastafarians and this is what we need to do, learn from the masses."[13] In Guyana, the New World Group focused in on the central weakness of the Left, which they diagnosed as rooted in the racial divide between Indians and Africans, as well as in Burnham's propensity toward corruption and election rigging.

The disillusionment extended to PPP, which members of New World regarded not as a socialist organization but, in the Guyanaese scholar Nigel Westmaas's words, "a curious amalgam of a labour and business base drawn from the Indian population."[14] If the New World did not see their role as organizing resistance to the country's racial polarization, they could clearly see the predicament faced by Guyana's poor. From 1966 to 1970, Burnham and the PNC's domestic and foreign policy almost exclusively followed the prescriptions of the West. Guyana's voting record at the United Nations, for example, in this period was identical to that of the United States.

Though Burnham tacked left from the late 1960s, Westmaas notes, most astute observers saw the PNC's newly discovered radicalism as simply "opportunistic," largely provoked by domestic issues. As racial violence and division continued to escalate through the 1960s, other groups were formed to challenge the state's politics of divide and rule. One of these, established on the campus of the recently founded University of Guyana, was an organization of radical students and faculty members called Ratoon. Westmaas writes that Ratoon, formed in 1969, mobilized "a strident anti-imperial voice" to condemn "foreign penetration of the economy while providing support for labour struggles."

Invited to speak by Ratoon, the Black Power leader Stokely Carmichael addressed an audience in 1970 at Queen's College—Rodney's alma mater—explaining that Black Power was only for people of African descent.[15] Clive

Thomas, a Ratoon activist, had tried to convince members, especially Indo-Guyanese activists, that this was not the organization's position—but his efforts met with limited success, and most had walked out.

Each of these groups represented efforts by activists, through groups, meetings, and publications, to press for unity—some of which were successful, and others were not. These early "foundations" of unity—the "new politics," as Westmaas calls them—were assisted by joint, united action. The shooting of Ratoon member and university lecturer Joshua Ramsammy in October 1971 was another spur to action. Ramsammy was in his car outside the Guyana National Cooperative Bank when gunmen approached and fired several shots. He was rushed to the hospital where he underwent an emergency operation—performed on him by his brother, a surgeon at the hospital. Ramsammy lived, but the attempted assassination provoked an enormous antigovernment backlash.

The Movement against Oppression (MAO) was yet another organization established to challenge the PNC's political impunity and brutality. In the aftermath of the assassination attempt on Ramsammy, a united front of twenty-four organizations was formed, including PPP members and the MAO, to discuss an end to the terror. All of these efforts to combat the PNC government and break down racial divisions in the country took place before Rodney had come back to Guyana. However, his presence in the country would soon help to accelerate these moves toward class unity and opposition.

The WPA, formally established in 1974 as an alliance of four distinct working-class organizations, from the start saw itself as a revolutionary coalition, rather than a reformist one. The WPA was founded by the African Society for Cultural Relations with Independent Africa (ASCRIA), the Indian People's Revolutionary Associates (IPRA), a small Maoist political party formed in 1969 called the Working People's Vanguard Party (WPVP), and Ratoon.

One interesting document in the Atlanta archive is entitled "The WPA and the anti-imperialist socialist revolution." Anti-imperialism was the oxygen to any socialist politics in a region controlled by the United States. The document, arranged from drafts during the 1974 discussions of the founding of the WPA at a conference in 1976, reads today like a party statement. It states boldly the WPA's revolutionary objectives, focused on organizing among the popular and working classes of Guyana (though it noted that other classes may play a role). "The motive force of the revolution," it reads, "is the struggle of the workers . . . towards socialist objectives and against pseudo-socialism."

However, the document continues, the struggle of the popular forces has been overshadowed by ethnic and racial factors. Yet now, "a proletarian internationalist outlook in these conditions . . . will offer the solution to this problem." This "founding statement" emphasizes—and we can almost hear Walter's sing-song voice—the importance of "studying the people's struggles . . . teaching the danger of reformism in present day Guyana and promoting the revolutionary unity of the working people."[16]

Later, in 1974, when Rodney had returned to Guyana, he was drawn into a solidarity campaign for Arnold Rampersaud, a taxi driver accused of murdering a Black police officer in a PPP area on July 18, 1973. That August, he was remanded to the prison in Georgetown on trumped-up charges. Rampersaud was a PPP activist and a taxi driver, thirty-five years old and a father of five children. Together with Eusi Kwayama (the leader of ASCRIA) and Maurice Bishop (who became prime minster of Grenada in 1979), Rodney helped to lead the campaign for justice.

It was at the end of his first trial in 1975 that a broad-based Arnold Rempersaud Defence Committee was formed, and a worldwide campaign with considerable international support began to demand his freedom. The Defence Committee comprised members of opposition political parties, trade unions, and religious groups; they claimed that Rampersaud was being persecuted for his political beliefs. The campaign, which involved public meetings, demonstrations, and picketing, inspired a widespread demand for a fresh trial. In December 1977, after four years in prison and three trials, Rampersaud received a verdict of not guilty. The committee had clearly illustrated the power of unity as different groups and communities came together to demand justice for an Indo-Guyanese activist.

At an open-air public meeting during the second Rampersaud trial in 1976, Rodney declared: "No ordinary Afro-Guyanese, no ordinary Indo-Guyanese can today afford to be misled by the myth of race. Time and time again it has been our undoing."[17]

By far the greatest inspiration of the "new politics" was a spike in working-class activism. Though co-opted and brutalized by the racialized politics of the PNC in the 1960s, in 1970 bauxite workers went on strike in Linden, the second largest city in Guyana, about an hour's drive from the capital. At that time, bauxite remained Guyana's most important revenue earner. In 1969, the industry had approximately five thousand employers, with the ore having taken over sugar to become the largest export of the country—earning 60 million Guyanese dollars, then almost half of total exports (approximately US$4 billion today).

Though bauxite miners were previously loyal to the PNC, tensions were emerging. Supported by ASCRIA, the strike, in Westmaas's words, "terrified the PNC because strikes suggested losing workers to [the] other side."[18] The strike led to the rise of the Organization of Working People (OWP), which Rodney and the WPA acknowledged had taught them a great deal about "workers' political culture"—saving schemes, hardship funds, and so on. This worker-led, rank-and-file, bauxite-based organization would become a prominent element in the mass labor actions of the late 1970s.

As a mass rank-and-file organization, the influence of the OWP on a period of great labor militancy in the 1970s cannot be exaggerated. One of the first OWP publications explained the group's position—much of it on questions of morality and comradely conduct:

> The OWP recognises that in any genuine working-class movement the highest discipline of all workers must be demonstrated. . . . No workers must seek to enrich himself. . . . If any worker is found to be exploiting other workers he or she must be expelled. . . . Workers should treat the problem of a fellow worker as the concern of all. . . . No worker who acts in the capacity of a Workers' Representative must accept Management offer of supervisory position during the period of service to workers. He must first serve his full period as Workers' Representative.[19]

Put simply, the OWP emerged as the voice of workers in bauxite mining in the 1970s; it was a formidable rank-and-file body, in a sector that had seen an astonishing level of militancy since the 1940s, always led by unorganized workers. The OWP was the latest in a line of grassroots worker organizations that by the mid-1970s had effectively replaced the Guyana Mine Workers Union (GMWU)—a co-opted, corrupt, government-backed union.

Much of this action was "wildcat"—a term adopted from the British trade union movement to describe unorganized, worker-led strike action. This wildcat action had become a staple feature of industrial life, with workers in the mining sector struggling hard against their own trade union representatives. The major union in the bauxite mining towns and communities was the Guyana Mine Workers Union, and it had, through the 1950s and 1960s, become increasingly remote from its members—with headquarters in Georgetown, and prolonged rank-and-file efforts, many of these preindependence, to bring corrupt officials to justice (or simply to open their books for an official audit). Odida Quamina, a former mineworker, wrote in 1987: "Wildcat, unofficial or illegal strikes had become the most popular forms of industrial action through which the workers expressed their grievances."[20] He was not exaggerating. Official statistics record that between 1962 and 1970, there were forty-seven strikes in the bauxite industry, yet of these the GMWU had only called two—the first in support of the Trade Union Congress's call for a national general strike in 1962 in opposition to the government's budget proposals and the second, in 1963, against the Labour Relations Bill.[21] Forty-five of these were wildcat strikes; efforts by the government (and others) to co-opt the largely Black workforce in the mines were, to put it mildly, pathetic.

Further action took place in the countryside, encouraged by a generalized militancy. In late January 1973, a land rebellion on the sugar belt on the east coast of Demerara stimulated a new growth in cooperation among the different groups that would shape the WPA. Unity in action, it seemed, was more powerful than any bureaucratic efforts to forge a new politics. The action included the mass squatting on land in Demerara by a multiracial coalition and support base. Terrified, the state intervened violently to evict the squatters. ASCRIA, confirming its split from the PNC, even called for an insurrection of the landless across all races, which led to further radicalization and action against foreign and local employers and landowners.

By 1974, the PNC announced so-called "cooperative socialism," an action that only enflamed the rebellion of workers and the landless who deepened their resistance to the state.[22] The elements of unity across class and ethnicity, seen from the early 1970s, began to coalesce in a more organized and radical form. The "left turn" of the PNC state—ironically taking some of its socialist rhetoric from Nyerere's Tanzania—was a fake anti-imperialism, an effort to win over elements of the popular classes, while shoring up its support base. Indeed, the regime had long been trying to present itself as the true heir to socialism in the Caribbean; as early as 1966, Burnham's PNC had launched an international public relations campaign to present itself as "revolutionary socialist," standing alongside the great struggles of the day in Vietnam, Angola, and Mozambique, and with the US Black Power movement. This strategy had served the PNC well, for it had succeeded in silencing certain international voices.

At its 1974 party conference, held at Sophia Plantation, the PNC announced what became known as the "Sophia Declaration," which declared the paramountcy of the party. As Burnham explained at the conference, "It was also decided that the party should assume unapologetically its paramountcy over the government which is merely one of its executive arms." The entire operation of the state, its various departments and institutions, would now—to much unapologetic fanfare—fall under control of the party. The direction of travel was clear to anyone who cared to look; in 1973, Burnham had announced: "God says that before you were, I was. The party says to the government before you were, we were. The government has got to be in our system a subordinate agency to the party." These were not unusual political tendencies at the time, and the Sophia Declaration merely stated what was fashionable across many so-called left ruling parties around the world, exported to a large extent from the Soviet Union and Eastern Europe.[23]

The 1971 nationalization of the bauxite industry did little to stem worker militancy. The Demerara Bauxite Company (DEMBA), Guyana's largest enterprise with five thousand employees and sales of approximately US$60 million per annum, was nationalized on July 15, 1971, and renamed the Guyana Bauxite Company (GUYBAU). At the time, these were common developments in many parts of the Third World, with a majority stake taken by the state. However, little changed for the workers of these "new" parastatals. Quamina writes, "The immediate post-nationalisation years (1972–76) were pregnant with various struggles for control; and influence within the bauxite industry and its communities."[24]

From 1972, various groups of the Guyanese Left came together to discuss a common program for the country. This was work done before Rodney's return, but he followed the developments closely. The establishment of the Race Commission, an initiative of IPRA and ASCRIA, had visited African and Indian villages to discuss unity and livelihoods.

It was from these combined actions among workers in their workplaces and through militant land occupations, campaigns, and support groups that the WPA was formed. As we have seen, the coalition was formally launched in 1974 from these strands of organizing and struggle. Initially, it was just what it said: "an alliance" of different organizations. (However, in 1979 it would be established as a formal political party.) One of the statements in the founding of the multiracial alliance was a commitment to create a "workers and farmers' advisory service" to give workers assistance.[25]

In its founding statement, the WPA announced that it stood for the "revolutionary unity of all subject and liberated peoples" and "for an economy which will be controlled by the working people for their own benefit . . . in which every citizen has the right to work and in which exploitation and exploiting classes are abolished." Importantly, the WPA also stressed that it would "address . . . the historical exclusion of Amerindians from the political process."[26]

If official "independence" in 1966 had been buried under a mass of racial violence and political terror, with US funding and support, the 1974 birth of the WPA tantalized Guyana with the prospect of real liberation.

Elections and Revolution

Interestingly, participation in electoral politics was not the WPA's original motivation; rather, it sought education and social action. Due to the many different opinions and perspectives among members of the alliance, holding it together was a balancing act that was not always successful; members occasionally pulled out, withdrawing their support.

The electoral issue was less simple than it might seem, and the internal debate over this question went to the heart of what the WPA was. If the WPA was a revolutionary organization, then to many it seemed irrelevant for it to participate in elections to a rigged, parliamentary system, in which real economic power was not part of the electoral contest. Indeed, a party might have influence among groups of workers in certain workplaces, plantations, and mines, but not necessarily in neighborhoods and communities. Among WPA membership, "the question of elections" was passionately discussed.

These issues were fleshed out in a draft perspective paper on just this question, held in the Rodney archive. The paper is undated, though it was likely written late in 1979 (ahead of a national poll scheduled for 1980), neatly typed with key phrases and words underlined. It is quite probable it was written by Rodney: it has his typical clarity, with little time wasted on rhetorical or stylistic flourishes, and a rigor of analysis characteristic of his pen. The whole document deals in a serious and thoughtful way with questions that most radical and revolutionary left organizations, at some point, must confront.

The seven long pages of closely typed analysis contain approximately five thousand words and start with the assertion: "We state frankly that *we are not an electoral party.*"[27] However, whether to stand in elections is a tactical decision, not one of principle; it is, the perspective document states, "never absolutely predetermined one way of another." The task of the WPA is to "study and analyse the social, political, and historical situation in Guyana." Across the Caribbean, the decision about standing in elections by the Left has varied, the paper notes. As an example, it cites the decision—which it supports—of the New Jewel Movement in Grenada and of the United Labour Front in Trinidad to contest elections.

The WPA was established to "generate the broadest possible grouping of forces of the socialist, progressive, and patriotic type" while ensuring the "active expression of the popular will of the revolutionary masses" guided by their central organization. The WPA must respect, the report continues, the "spontaneous struggle of the masses against the well-entrenched neo-colonial and bureaucratic state." The main field of struggle is among "self-organised workers," of whom the paper lists a few examples: "Linden mine workers, Corentyne school-teachers."

A serious consideration is the involvement of foreign forces—imperialist interests—that would work hard against any possibility in elections for a party to be elected that stands against the WPA's objectives. "In the last ten years," the paper continues, "we have learned more and more about specific CIA intervention in Guyana in 1963 as well as their general technique of penetration in Latin America."

Yet there is a tension in the document—one that no doubt reflects a real ambiguity that existed inside the WPA on the question of elections. On the one hand, elections were not—and would never be—where real power was decided; recent experience in the country had demonstrated this clearly (in 1963, and a decade before in 1953). Yet, on the other hand, if the "working class in Guyana" were to "step up activities," then it might be possible "to ensure that the registration and the conduct of elections have at least that degree of 'neutrality'" necessary for reasonably fair elections.

The PNC government had deeply eroded the possibility of open and democratic politics; the paper reports how in September and October 1977, public meetings had been disrupted by PNC thugs, as part of a far-reaching campaign against public displays of democracy. The government had used the Public Order Act, brought in by the colonial authorities in 1955, to "counter the struggle against colonial rule." There was no fundamental space for democratic organizing, a condition that deepened the WPA's suspicion about the ability of elections to unseat the ruling regime.

In 1976, Burnham had already urged the WPA—and its "fraternal organisation the OWP"—to stand in elections and to "match words" with action. Yet the WPA focused instead on "socialist education and worker mobilisation"—more effective, the report pointed out, than matching words in futile parliamentary debate. The PNC would have preferred for the WPA to be "filled with illusions about the parliamentary role," which would have diverted their energies from working-class mobilizations. Instead, the paper continues, WPA had set itself the task of "scientific ideological education of the working class so that elements of this class would strengthen themselves for the leadership of the society." But the paper nevertheless asks: Is there room "to move into the arena of electoral politics?"[28]

Though the paper comes down firmly against standing in the country's national elections, there is an ambiguity on the question. "We say that the electoral road at this stage of the development of our movement would represent not a broadening of our activities but a deflection from our original commitment . . . the cost would be too great in terms of neglect of basic aspects of working class education and mobilisation." The alliance's raison d'être was to deepen working-class self-confidence and self-organization. Given the limited resources, comrades, time, and equipment, there was a need to focus exclusively on this objective; indeed, education and mobilization were the central elements of party work.

Finally, the paper argues that the WPA should not stand in the elections; doing so would change the WPA's entire political culture and sow illusions and hopes in "changes at a general election," "rather than in building a participatory socialist democracy based on . . . [workers'] contribution to production." The paper states that even in a "functioning bourgeois democratic system," it leaves "multi-class winners to look after the workers' interests and to emancipate them from above." This vision of democracy is nonsense, it explains, with the population only coming "alive politically at the time of a general elections." There is no real democracy in this model of democratic practice.

The forthright and passionate tone of the report is worth citing in full. Condemning "bourgeois elections," it states, "Years of mass revolutionary work are side-stepped, abuses are tolerated, and all hopes are placed on those five minutes at the ballet box once every five years." Under any definition of real participation in decision making, this is an eviscerated democracy—a bleak, hollowed-out democratic charade that plays out every few years in the United States, Britain, and Guyana. It is, the report argues, a repetitive electoral cycle that results in an endless circulation of the elite and those who serve them. Rodney, of course, rejected this model, arguing that it offered the working class and poor of Guyana nothing.[29]

The document is scathing about the electoral pantomime, but there is a whiff of ambiguity. It states that the "major electoral parties . . . have in their turn proved insensitive while in power, leaving a trail of racial bitterness." Yet the WPA welcomes the recent statement of the PPP expressing interest in "building a government of national unity comprising progressive elements." Does this mean there would be a "government of national unity" distinct from the bourgeois electoral system that the report has just roundly condemned? Since the WPA, in the words of the report, "believe that the working people of Guyana can forge such unity independent of the electoral system," what role could there be for the alliance in such a "government of national unity," which would presumably involve contesting elections?[30] In this sentence there seems to be no possibility of being part of a government of national unity, based on the existing electoral system, since the WPA is founded on the premise of developing a workers' democracy.

Rodney's call for a government of national unity in his 1979 article "People's Power, No Dictator," remains a slightly ambiguous demand; indeed, it is one that has been criticized.[31] Still, the paper provided an illustration of the lively debate on the electoral strategy by the WPA in the late 1970s.

By contrast, Jagan's PPP was an electoral party, a machine engineered to win elections. Though its militants were trained in the politics of the Left, PPP members did not engage in popular political education. Even as a much younger man, Rodney felt that the PPP was not, and could not, lead the necessary radical pedogogical work among the poor; its entire preoccupation was the electoral game. Rodney, in contrast, recognized that as an intellectual, for whom there was inherent danger of becoming alienated from the working class, he needed to redouble his efforts to listen to, and learn from, the concerns and realities of working-class life. Rodney encouraged members of the WPA to, like him, travel regularly to villages to meet people, and to visit plantations and factories to discuss the conditions of work among workers. He went to learn, but also to teach—something he did across Guyana. His biographer Amzat Boukari-Yabara explains, "[H]e gave history courses open to everyone outside his house."[32] The entire structure of political organization was in contrast to the PPP.

Reflecting on the history of the WPA, in 1979 the document states, "[F]orces have emerged which can lead to genuine national liberation and genuine self-emancipation of the working people."[33] In the struggles that have taken place, African and Indian groups deepened their class consciousness, and "exclusivism in racial terms has had to give way to serious political analysis and political work." The document continues with a list of activities in which the WPA was engaged since its founding—all activity took place away from the electoral cycle and was based on building from the bottom up:

> The historic recommendation by the sugar unions that 25 percent of the Sugar Levy should be placed into a fund for paying a cost of living allowance to all Guyanese workers whose weekly wages were below the minimum. . . . The campaign . . . in defence of urban and rural housewives and workers in support of bauxite workers . . . WPA support for the Corentyne teachers; The solidarity strike of the two sugar unions, GAWU and NAACIE, with the striking bauxite workers in December 1976 . . . the solidarity march of the OWP with Arnold Rampersaud during his second trial . . . the formation of the loose grouping of four unions . . . taking a class approach to the whole question of workers' democracy.

These examples, the paper concludes, represent "a significant development for true democracy."[34] With the growth and extension of these activities and movements, the working class could contribute "in its own name" to the development of the country. The document ends with a clarion appeal to another type of worker-based democracy, founded on the workplace, the mine, the plantation, and the factory, where true democracy can flourish. This is a model of democratic practice that runs exactly counter to the forms of decision making offered in Guyana's elections.

Rodney was especially innovative in his approach to organizing— both in ridiculing Burnham and in championing forms of struggle outside the narrow and limited constraints of the rigged "Westminster model" Guyana had inherited from its former political masters. Guyanese scholar Perry Mars, looking back on this time, explains that the WPA advocated "people assemblies" with popular participation at the center—schemes that were not exclusively Guyanese, but used in other parts of the Caribbean. Countering those who saw the future in "free and fair elections," the WPA in this period had a far-larger conception of democracy—stemming from workers' participation from the bottom up. "Workers' assemblies" would ensure popular participation and be largely economic institutions organized where the working poor were based: in sugar, bauxite, and transport. In turn, these would be "storehouses of workers' power."[35]

Some commentators have questioned the WPA's model in one area in particular: women's rights. There was, in Westmaas's words, "little active consideration of woman's rights inside and outside the organisation."[36] Apparently, women were poorly represented in party structures, with little offered on women's liberation in the WPA publication *Dayclean*. Yet this is a problematic assessment for women held many prominent positions in the organization, directing and leading the work across the country and internationally, alongside their male comrades.[37] It nevertheless remains open to question whether there was a major weakness on the question of women's rights.

The WPA was not dogmatic. Indeed, their revolutionary positions were clear to anyone who paid attention, and they were open to "progressive" alliances. In 1977, for example, the PPP proposed a joint "National Patriotic Front" government. The WPA were suspicious, anxious that these were just further electoral games. Though they backed the proposals, they expressed a number of reservations and subsequently produced their own program for national reconstruction. The radical program advanced by the WPA insisted on not just the removal of the PNC but a period in which all democratic organization in society would be fully represented. As Lincoln Van Sluytman of the New York WPA support committee wrote in 1980: "This period of self-organisation, particularly of the working class would best create the foundation in the Guyanese context, for the socialist transformation of the future. Toward realizing the program, the WPA has joined with the PPP and the Vanguard for Liberation and Democracy—a coalition of groups that span the political spectrum—in the Anti-Dictatorial Alliance."[38]

By 1979, the WPA would become a formal political party, stepping up its challenge against the state. The WPA was an imaginative Marxist organization that formulated new approaches to doing politics, creating different methods to organizing that were culturally sensitive and historically appropriate. The genuine coalition of grassroots organizations that had given birth to the WPA in 1974 offered real solidarity and hope to the poor. Under Rodney's influence, it would be the working poor themselves who would struggle for and take control of a new society.

Building the WPA

Rodney came alive in his political work among the poor—a fact noted by his closest comrades. His longtime comrade and friend Rupert Roopnaraine, who had helped build the WPA with him, recalled a man whose very essence only really found expression when speaking to the working poor.

> Here was a person who really got nourished by the mass movement. I remember Walter saying to me that there was nothing that gave him more nourishment than the trips taken to teach the bauxite workers political economy. He always came back very energised with this contact with ordinary working people who were progressive and on a revolutionary path. This is what really energised him as an activist.[39]

Exactly the same "energy" fueled Rodney's political work in Jamaica with the poor in 1968; these "groundings" were his true raison d'etre. The WPA—in the hands of Roopnaraine, Rodney, Clive Thomas, and other leading members—was a revolutionary organization that saw its role as one of preparation. In the formulation of the documentary filmmaker and writer Clairmont Chung, "One prepares. One educates. One waits"—for an insurrection.[40] Roopnaraine explains that they were "attempting to equip ourselves, essentially ready ourselves, and ready the masses for an insurrectionary attack on the state. I make no excuse for that."[41]

Roopnaraine's personal trajectory followed many of the contours of Walter's. He had grown up in a political family; his parents were activists in the PPP. He too had been an activist, handing out leaflets and organizing as a boy and as a young man. He had left the country to study in Cambridge in 1962; disillusioned with the political struggle in Guyana, he decided when he left that he would not return—he was bright and highly educated, and a promising tenured academic career beckoned. In 1970, Roopnaraine was a scholarship student studying for his masters and PhD in literature. Yet he had begun to question his life in "exile," as he later called it, remote from the major revolutionary wave beginning to transform the world.

One particular trip he took had a profound influence on him, sowing the seeds of doubt about his academic life: "I had . . . gone to Portugal on my study leave and had been on the streets of Lisbon during the time of the Portuguese revolution of 1974. . . . In the summer of that year they had the most progressive government of Portugal."[42] That government, led by Vasco Gonçalves, had ended all of the country's colonial wars, signing independence treaties with the rebel movements. It was supported by many of the mass movements of the revolution. Witnessing a country—whose language and literature Roopnaraine had studied—in the midst of a revolutionary transformation was an intense experience. He also encountered Rodney's work—his high school friend from Georgetown—in Lisbon. "In that period," he explains, "the Portuguese translation of HEUA . . . was in all the bookshops. . . . It was the period when they were talking about the Africanisation of the Portuguese revolution. The Portuguese armies that went to Mozambique and Angola to fight against the African liberation fighters came back completely infected by the guerrilla movements."[43] It was amid this period that Rodney's book had its greatest exposure.

Roopnaraine left Portugal and returned to the United States, where he was completing a PhD, but something had broken in him: "I can tell you, to leave revolutionary Lisbon and back to upstate New York was a bit of a culture shock. I began to get very edgy at Cornell and felt I had come to the end of my usefulness in the States. Really, I could not see myself becoming a tenured academic professor in an American university."[44]

Inspired by the revolution in Portugal—and its "partner" revolutions in Africa—Roopnaraine considered going to Mozambique, having met activists in Lisbon. But he was more interested in pursuing possible work in Cuba. In 1975, when Roopnaraine was still in New York, he met Walter, visiting from Guyana, who explained what was happening in Georgetown. For both Roopnaraine and Rodney, the urge to return to Guyana and participate in revolutionary organizing there was guided by similar instincts. Roopnaraine finally returned to the country in 1976 and was appointed to a teaching position at the university in 1977—a time when he became closer to the WPA.

It was another friend who had discussed with Rodney the possibility of returning to Guyana. As a professor of economics, Clive Thomas had worked at the University of Dar es Salaam, on Walter's urging. Thomas claims that he was instrumental in persuading Rodney to return to Guyana: "But when I was in Tanzania," he explains, "I managed to convince Walter of one thing. I told him that there is a limit to which, if you are not a national of the territory, not born there, or not a full citizen, you can really participate in the social, economic and political life of the country. I urged him to come back to Guyana."[45]

Thomas was clear about the great possibilities of the time, when revolutionary change felt like it was within reach. He writes: "We really were doing things that were different from what had happened previously, historically, and thought our generation would make a difference. So many people of our generation were motivated to do something toward the development . . . of the West Indian people."[46] Thomas and Rodney had come fresh from the developments in Tanzania, and Roopnaraine from Portugal, via New York. They were surrounded by the *success* of revolutionary movements and experiments, from Cuba to the second independence in Africa and the overturning of the dictatorship by a mass movement in Portugal, which had been inspired and directly influenced by the anti-colonial revolt in Guinea-Bissau, Mozambique, and Angola. These great revolutions—or revolutionary "rehearsals"—it seemed, were theirs for the taking, if activists simply reached out and grasped the opportunities.[47] A generation from a diverse range of left-wing positions was enlivened by the hope of political change. As Thomas puts it, their stance during the period was not only defensive: "We had a more assertive, positive, proactive view that we could make a contribution to civilisation."[48]

The party was funded from members' contributions—not large donations from international donors and NGOs. This made fundraising a laborious but activist affair, involving campaigns for individual donations and newsletter subscriptions. The work was tiresome, but it allowed the group to implant itself deep in the soil of Guyana. Though the WPA—not formally a party until 1979—courted groups (and even governments) for funding, these often came to nothing. Thomas recalls:

> [W]e wanted finance, we wanted funding equipment, and we were still publishing with a Cyclostat [stencil copy machine]. We never got a printery or a printing press. We were really, if you look at the mechanics . . . a party that was 90 percent financed by the contributions of the activist group. You're talking about tens of dollars and twenties. You're not taking about any million-dollar effort.[49]

The WPA looked for inspiration and a political model in other countries in the Caribbean and Africa—in Grenada, Cuba, and Zimbabwe, for example. However, they also had a keen desire to do things their way. Maurice Rupert Bishop was a revolutionary and the leader of the New Jewel Movement in Grenada—a Marxist party that sought to transform Grenadian society and that came to power in 1979. Bishop's political trajectory was similar to a small and bright generation of Caribbean radicals, politicized by the Cuban Revolution in 1959 and educated on scholarships in the UK. As it had for Rodney, Cuba's revolution pressed itself deeply into the young man's consciousness. He recalled some time later: "In fact, for us it did not matter what we heard on the radio or read in the colonial press. For us, it comes down to the courage and legendary heroism of Fidel Castro, Che Guevara. . . . Nothing could overshadow this aspect of the Cuban Revolution."⁵⁰ Similarly, the ideas of Fanon, and later Nyerere, became central to Bishop's political education. Yet, for all the noble politics and promises, these governments gave little away. When Bishop came to power, he made statements, but "he never," in Thomas's words, "sanctioned any support for the WPA once he was in power."⁵¹ Nor did Fidel Castro or Robert Mugabe, when Rodney sought his support for the struggle in Guyana in 1980, during his undercover visit for the independence celebrations in Harare in April of that year. Bishop, for his part, would be removed from power—and shot—in 1983.

Cuba also did nothing to support the WPA. Forbes Burnham knew how to play the game—and the game was cynical statecraft. He worked hard not to be isolated. He posed as the good, respectable socialist, keeping at bay the extremists. Thomas notes, on Cuba, that even they "certainly never isolated him, and they were a big part of the scene because Russians were not very active in Guyana matters. Fidel, even though he was closely affiliated to the PPP because he belonged to the Communist group, still did not break ranks in any significant way with Burnham."⁵² It was the same story with Manley's so-called socialist government in Jamaica—Manley approached Burnham for help with his economic crisis in the 1970s, which eventually saw him call in the International Monetary Fund and World Bank for financial assistance.

As the above examples show, support from these apparently fraternal and radical governments was not forthcoming to the WPA, however much they asked. Rodney would have already known the reality of these politics and how offers of "support and solidarity" were, in the words of the UK strike leader Jayaben Desai, "like honey on the elbow—you can smell it, you can feel it, but you cannot taste it."⁵³ The revolution had to come from within, and the only true allies were the workers and poor themselves. Yet the alliance was still small and young and was not able to respond to every outbreak of political and industrial action. Thus, the WPA was unable to seriously build solidarity with sugar workers during their 135-day strike in 1978, which was ultimately defeated. In spite of its achievements, the influence of the WPA had not yet penetrated across the entire country beyond the capital, some towns, and certain mining regions.

Notably, the WPA's politics of working-class unity arose during a period of violent sectarian violence and division. One account, by a young WPA activist named Abyssinian Carto, provides a particularly vivid portrayal of the life of a party militant during the high point of political action, in 1979. Carto had been involved in the Movement against Oppression, established to fight police brutality in the poor Georgetown neighborhood of Tiger Bay, where young Black men were being targeted and killed by the police. The neighborhood was also the site of the headquarters of the party publication, *Dayclean*, edited by Moses Bhagwan. (However, the newspaper was printed in Trinidad by Tapia House, as there were no printers in Guyana prepared to risk the regime's wrath.)[54] In a country whose racial divisions were being fueled by politicians and the ruling party, the priority for the Left was to bring its movements and opposition together. Carto explained in 2012 that Rodney was a central part in this effort: "I think the multi-racialness of the WPA allowed us to intervene in a very profound way. If the WPA was not present during that period of time, I do not know what direction the politics would have taken in Guyana."

Carto recalls how extensive the network of Burnham's intelligence system was, stretching deep into poor communities. He remembers: "[I]t would not be unusual for somebody who is a vendor, someone selling sweet mangoes, to be connected with them. Or someone just liming [hanging around] on the corner, or bridge, working as an informant looking at your movements, when you are coming out or going in and so on." As the decade reached its end, police repression and raids escalated. "[B]y that time," Carto explains, "the death squad had been formed as part of the police force." Though not acknowledged, activists knew that the "Special Branch" carried out political assassinations against so-called criminal elements on the fringes of society. In short, it was a brutal period, during which the stench of murder hung in the air. [55]

The role of the WPA, and Rodney, was to organize and politicize; political education was key, as it had been for Rodney's entire life. As we saw with the "groundings," he was a brilliant and fluent speaker who did not dazzle his listener with his wit and analysis but empowered them in their own capacities. To do this, to communicate, Rodney used the Caribbean art of ridicule.[56] He nicknamed Burnham "King Kong"—to denote a man who desired to be king but was simply a raw beast. Another term he employed in his talks was the so-called "Burnham touch"—the opposite of the "Midas touch"—by which everything Burnham touched turned to shit. Rodney employed mockery to devastating effect.[57]

The Bombing

Even if the Working People's Alliance did not contest elections, it was engaged in all of the major events of the day. In 1978, the national elections, which had been due in October, were in disarray after a rigged referendum in July had "endorsed" the creation of a so-called Constituent Assembly. In order to allow time to draft a new constitution—one which would give broad new powers to an "executive president"—elections were postponed until 1979. As the influence of WPA grew, so did the repression.

A word needs to be said about the campaign against the Constitutional Amendment Bill, which was put forward in 1978. Where necessary, to gather maximum support against the PNC, the WPA formed strategic alliances with opposition groups and parties. As Eusi Kwayana, a leading WPA activist at the time, would later testify:

> This was another manifestation of the close working relationship—a united position of the PPP and the WPA in the . . . struggle against the intentions of the then administration to carry out constitutional changes which were rejected in mass by the Guyanese people; and both parties were looking for the appropriate forum as part of their efforts to mobilise the population . . . we all joined hands together to oppose the Referendum.

The informal coalition against the referendum brought the leadership of the PPP and the WPA together in a "cordial and strategic collaboration."[58]

On Wednesday, July 11, 1979, at 3:00 a.m., a bomb destroyed the offices of the Ministry of National Development and the Guyana Sugar Corporation—an event that led to the arrest of Rodney and three other members of the WPA. Abyssinian Carto was nearby. He recalls: "I heard this loud explosion and then the skies lit up. . . . It happened in the morning, after midnight. . . . I went to look at it, as did many people. In Guyana fires fascinate people and they came from all around."

At about 6:00 a.m., police officers raided the homes of eight political activists, all but three of them members of the WPA. Later in the day,

Burnham announced that he suspected the WPA was behind the arson and that he had ordered the arrest of the three leading comrades, including Roopnaraine and Omowale, along with five others, including Karen De Souza and Bonita Harris—supporters and activists of the WPA.[59] Rodney was detained at La Penitence Police station, just outside the city, and the others at Eve Leary, the Police headquarters in Georgetown.

The party quickly mobilized a response, mounting vigils at each of the detention facilities where their comrades were being held, which lasted until midnight. The bauxite rank-and-file group—the Organization of Working People—also met to condemn the arrests, as did the University of Guyana Staff Association (Roopnaraine was head of the English department). If the state believed that the arrests would intimidate the movement, they were wrong. In fact, the opposite happened, as diverse groups mobilized, and politicization deepened.

The next day, the WPA extended its resistance across Guyana's borders. Activists and comrades in the UK, Canada, the United States, and throughout the Caribbean started to petition Burnham's government. Telegrams were sent denouncing the detention of the eight, and activists began pickets outside the Guyanese embassy in New York and, the next day, the high commission in London. The national radio broadcast remained silent on the arrests, but Radio Antilles—based in Montserrat—broadcast the news, which seeped into the country.[60]

On Friday, July 13, the legal machine started to turn on. The state had begun to feel the heat of both internal mobilizations and international protest and condemnation. According to a November 1979 account, "A combination of rising militance within Guyana, growing international protests and a possible court confrontation . . . forced the government to lay charges, however trumped up, and to release those not charged." By Saturday, July 14, Rodney, Roopnaraine, and Omowale were in court, charged with arson; the other prisoners were charged with lesser crimes or released. Bail was granted for each of the accused, and they were ordered to appear again in court in August.

The burning intensified pressure on the WPA, with the PNC leaning hard on the organization. Yet the court case against the WPA activists charged with arson became a rallying cry inside and outside Guyana. Though Carto did not attend himself, he remembers how "there was always little crowds of people surrounding the court, watching, listening and talking politically about what was happening in the country, what the trial meant . . . what needed to be done."[61] On July 14, the men were freed on bail. Their supporters outside the court erupted in celebration. Primed for violence, the police took their revenge on the crowd. As Carto explains, "[W]alking down Brickdam with the crowd following behind . . . toward Brickdam police station, the thugs came out and started wading into the crowd and attacking, beating people."[62] Bernard Darke, a Jesuit priest who had been born in the UK and a photographer for the fiercely antigovernment *Catholic Standard*, was stabbed to death by activists of the progovernment, Christian militia the House of Israel. Carto explains:

> That sudden explosion of violence when those thugs came out . . . these men were coming with sticks and one of them had a bayonet that killed Father Darke . . . It's like a slow-motion thing where you can see everything. You can see a blade of glass. . . . Everything becomes so perfectly clear to you. That was the amazing thing about it. So, in the midst of people in different directions and trying to avoid being beaten and attacked, you see things unfolding.[63]

The House of Israel was a curious militia. It was led by David Hill—or, as he called himself, "Rabbi Washington"—an African American who had settled in Guyana but was wanted by the FBI for criminal activities. He was one of a number of the "gang leaders" who had been given sanctuary by Burnham, granted facilities and finances to set up as a religious sect while working principally as a guard dog for the regime.

The connections between the House of Israel and the Guyana Defence Force (GDF) were widely known. However, these links were irrefutably shown in a 2016 report. Documentation from June 24, 1979, shows that there was "an appreciable quantity of arms and ammunition including 19 G3 rifles, 19 G3 Bayonets, 1500 7.623 ammo, 10 Browning pistols and 500 9mm long rounds which were taken from the GDF," handed to the House of Israel, and chargeable to the PNC.[64]

The bombing, the repression, and the trial took place against a background of growing militancy in the working-class movement. A period of great radicalization was about to break out—what Roopnaraine refers to as the "those heroic months of the revolt," a high point in the popular resistance that was underway in the country in August, September, October, and November 1979.[65]

The Great Revolt

In 1979, wildcat strikes and work stoppages continued to escalate. Such actions were launched by the WPA in what they referred to as a "civil rebellion" against the PNC's dictatorship. In August and September, unofficial action rippled through the mines in a powerful thirty-four-day strike. The management complained afterward that it was "not too difficult to calculate, in money terms, the actual revenue loss resulting from lost sales due to the strike. One such estimate puts the figures at approximately US$15 million . . . what is difficult to calculate, however, is the amount of customer goodwill lost."[66] The strikes, led by the OWP and WPA, were incredibly political; in turn, workers were described by the PNC as antinationalists, anti-PNC (for workers who had historically rubbed along with the PNC, this was a sign of the times), and destabilizers who were striking for political and subversive reasons. Brutality and strikebreaking were the order of the day—with scabs receiving high praise and generous handouts for their part in nation-building later in the year. The president of the GMWU—who was also moonlighting as president of the Guyana Trades Union Congress—was even given an Arrow of Achievement for his services in 1979 by the government.

Unlike the previous ones, these strikes were intensely political, coinciding with the organizing of other movements and coalescing in a broad wave of coordinated action. During a three-month period beginning in July, there was a succession of actions, followed by state repression—one after the other. The WPA opened its membership to hundreds of African and Indian youth who were eager to join. As a consequence of the new membership, the WPA created education study groups, called "nuclei," where recruits studied radical literature, including Vladimir Lenin's *What Is to Be Done* and Amílcar Cabral's *Party Principles and Political Practices.*[67]

According to Carto, during these weeks and months,

> [t]here was a really deep sense of this thing about struggle. It was more than a spiritual awakening for me . . . but it's more taking a religious path, it's a very profound transformation that happens to you. It's where that understanding of life and death becomes so clear. Particularly when dealing with a state as this one, where we can die or be killed. . . . And you are dealing with a state that has already shown what it can do, its level of violence, its capacity to kill. I don't think it's because we were

brave people, I believe we just reached that point in our lives where we said we are not taking this anymore.[68]

There was a great sense of pride in being part of a collective movement that sought to transform society—and, for a time, seemed to be winning.

Although it was a period of terror, brutality, and murder, during which meetings were broken up and activists were hounded across the country, it also held out the possibility of a new future. Collective defiance through protests, illegal meetings, and the distribution and sale of the paper *Dayclean* immediately identified their participants as enemies of the state but gave activists and supporters of the WPA an immense strength. Carto did not describe himself as a particularly "brave" man but was inspired with radical, even foolhardy courage. At one demonstration that year, he describes how he was arrested, dragged to a bus, thrown in, and threatened by an armed policeman. "I told him to go on and shoot me . . . . This is not because I wasn't afraid or being brave. It was just that I had reached that point where I said, 'If you want to kill me go ahead and do it.' And I told him, 'You must be sure that I am dead, because I will come and look for you.'"[69] About twenty-five had been arrested with him, and they were taken away, singing protest songs and shouting anti-Burnham slogans. The group of activists were taken to a field outside the city, where the police could beat them with impunity. However, they had organized themselves such that when they came off the bus, they quickly found pieces of wood and armed themselves; they were determined not to run. The police were faced with a group that not only included children but was now also armed, possessed of an iron determination. In the end, there was no confrontation; the police left, and the demonstrators made their way back to Georgetown.

Throughout this period of heightened struggle and intense politicization, Rodney received invitations to speak around the country. On May 30, 1979, Seeram Teemal, a sugar worker and militant of the National Association of Agricultural, Commercial, and Industrial Employees (NAACIE), wrote to Rodney with a request: "[T]he members of NAACIE at Uitvlugt Branch are requesting that you pay them a visit to give an address at their general monthly meeting on Tuesday 19 June, 1979. The meeting will be kept at the Uitvlugt Junior Staff Club and will start at 4.15pm." Uitvlugt, a village situated on the west bank of the Demerara River, was named after Ignatius Uitvlugt, the owner of a giant sugar plantation during the Dutch colonial period of the seventeenth and eighteenth centuries. Teemal explained to Rodney that the topic of address would be up to him, but "it would be appreciated if you could speak about the current situation facing the Guyanese working class. The audience will comprise all categories of sugar workers from Uitvlugt Estate."[70] In his speeches, Rodney addressed Indian sugar workers and African bauxite workers with the same message, and the same approach.

Similar mass meetings were being held across Guyana, and when it came to organizing speeches, strikers and protestors would settle for no one but Rodney. As we have seen, he was a brilliant orator who left the listener with a sense of their own abilities—their thinking enlarged by a lesson or historical point. Roopnaraine, for one, claimed in 2014 that Rodney preferred the smaller "educational" meetings, groups of five or ten workers with whom he could discuss politics and history.[71] But these were the days of mass rallies, and mass oppression.

On Tuesday, September 4, the WPA held a meeting at Vreed en Hoop, on the west bank of the Demerara. Within four minutes of the meeting starting, PNC thugs stormed the stage, smashing the public address system. Undeterred, Rodney clambered onto the back of a lorry and attempted to address the crowd. We do not know exactly what he said on the back of that lorry, but based on the content of the other speeches he gave between 1977 and 1980, we can assume it was a message of unity and history. The content might, for example, have resembled a speech he gave to the North American Congress on Latin America:

> Who benefits from the division of the working class? I was struck on one occasion reading an old book on the history of Guyana by a planter way back in slavery times, corresponding with friends in England. And they asked him, "How come you manage to control so many slaves when you are just a handful even though you may have guns? If they were to rush you all at one time, they would overwhelm you." But the planter was quite confident in his response. "Not to bother," he wrote, "the trick is that we keep them divided." You see, exploitation is always carried out by the few over the many. . . . And the only way that the few can maintain themselves over the many is, the many must be divided.
>
> If the working class is to realise that power which comes from the fact that they are the ones who produce, whether it be in the fields or in the factories, on the docks or on the buses, they will obviously have to strengthen the basis of their own organization. Classes take power to

the extent that they are organized to do so. You don't just walk off the street and take political power or take power over your daily life. You have to organise.[72]

Rodney did not get a chance to finish his speech; a Land Rover driven by a regional PNC bureaucrat reversed into the lorry, as the police and PNC militants continued to smash up the meeting—people scattered, chased by the police swinging their truncheons. Clearly the regime was targeting the executive of the party. Roopnaraine piled party members into this car and tried to escape; they were eventually forced to abandon the car and run, while the vehicle was looted of money and equipment and set on fire.[73]

Rodney managed to escape on foot. Biographer Dwayne Wong (also known as Omowale), in a compelling account, though frustratingly without any dates, writes about a similar attack on a WPA rally in 1979. Once more, Rodney and other comrades were forced to run, stopping, hiding, assessing how far they were from the police, and whether they were still being followed. Eventually, they hid behind a house and played cards, waiting for the police to leave. Anthony Ferguson recalled that Rodney used the opportunity to deliver a lesson on African history.

> I think it was about Rastafari or Africa or something else, but he started talking . . . very simple, without pretension . . . just talking very loosely about some historical incidents in Africa. Of course, it was very profound and to us and we were listening with a lot of interest . . . it was sort of unreal, here we were simultaneously hiding from the police and getting a history lesson from Rodney.[74]

The PNC state continued to bring down a hail of repression. In October 1979, Burnham spoke to leaders of his party, declaring: "The gauntlet has been thrown down. . . . We have picked it up. The battle is joined. We asked no quarter, and we shall give none. We shall use every weapon at our disposal. Let there be no weeping or complaints." A formidable orator in his own right, the president was issuing a threat to a mass movement that challenged its very existence. Meanwhile, the party's authority was already tottering; the referendum on a new constitution the previous year had been openly rigged, with a reported turnout of 15 percent, while the PNC had claimed a 70 percent vote in favor.[75]

There was layer upon layer of crisis—political, industrial, and economic. To many observers, the regime looked as if it would not survive. On the brink of bankruptcy in late June, the country had received a three-year loan of $81 million from the International Monetary Fund. Economically, the problem had been sparked by the rise in oil prices and a precipitous drop in the world market price for sugar. Once more, the country's extreme vulnerability to price changes on the international markets was exposed.

By late 1979, the opposition led by the WPA was seen—even by the mainstream international press—as the most significant force in the country. Joseph Treaster of the *New York Times* provided a compelling account:

> The new Working People's Alliance is seen by many as having achieved a breakthrough. For the first time, diplomats and some Government officials say, a political party is drawing significant support from both blacks and East Indians.
>
> The party, which contends that it has no individual leader, but is run by an executive council of 19, has led the way in calling for the Prime Minister's ouster, and a loose coalition of older parties of traditionally limited appeal, as well as a number of prominent individuals, has come together in its wake.
>
> Through the summer the alliance has been drawing large crowds, sometimes numbering in the thousands, to rallies in the parks and on street corners.

As the WPA reached its apogee of political action and leadership of the mass movement, the government targeted the party—not only with the iron fist of repression but also in rhetoric. Hamilton Green, the minister of health, labor, and housing, described the WPA during the crisis as consisting "of a small group of the lunatic fringe whose only objective is to disrupt and to destroy."

These extraordinary months of mass action saw remarkable unity among Black and Indian workers, who stood together in both strike action and WPA-organized meetings and rallies. Carto communicates a vivid sense of the excitement at the time:

> [I]t was amazing to go to public meetings during this . . . time and see black people and Indian people standing up together. For the first time they were listening and looking at each other as brothers, comrades, that there was some common bond. We come from different religions and different races and stuff like that, but we really are not different.

This unity, unusual and vital in post-independence Guyana, was one to which Rodney had made a noteworthy contribution as one of the WPA's main drivers of united working-class action. Carto goes on to explain: "When Walter was reasoning with them, he had a way of, when he spoke, talking to them, taking their lives personally and identifying with them and seeing, listening, asking, 'What are your fears as an Indian about black people? What are your fears about black people as an Indian?'" [76] We should stress that during this organizing, Rodney consistently talked and wrote about "the role of women" in meetings and one to one conversations with workers and with his comrades in the WPA.

Throughout the late 1970s, the party's radicalization had spread like wildfire, embracing a creative divergence of thinkers and revolutionaries. At the advent of the 1980s, the WPA's program was inspired by the writings of the Russian revolutionary Leon Trotsky and advocated a "revolution in each country as permanent." Thus, the WPA embraced the idea that an authentic revolution would extend beyond national borders. [77]

Writing Unity

Since 1974, Rodney's formidable life force had been spent in Guyana, forging in activism and historical work the unity of these twin oppressed groups. This extended to his research trips to the UK, and his extensive reading and archival work, which was eventually published as *A History of the Guyanese Working People, 1881–1905* (the first volume of a planned multivolume study). With it, he sought to challenge the official narrative that pitched Indian and Black people against each other. The Caribbean novelist and writer George Lamming later wrote, in 1981, how Rodney sought "with colleagues of his generation to cut through the miasma of race which had been nurtured with such mischievous care and which served to obscure that fundamental unity of interests that might otherwise have advanced African and Indian labour in a decisive struggle to control their common destiny." [78]

Carto recalls that in the process of writing the book, Rodney would bring his draft chapters to meetings with comrades and "go over them and have a discussion about the different chapters . . . there were people who were working on it, actually typing it up and putting things together. And he would reread and decide . . . what he liked in it, and what needed to be taken out, or he would disagree with the person editing it." [79] Carto actually played a part in the book, credited in Rodney's acknowledgments: "Colin Carto (Abyssinian), for map work." [80]

Rodney's way of writing was deeply collaborative; drafts of chapters were discussed with comrades, circulated for debate, and edits encouraged by a team, who would make suggestions and accept corrections. In many respects, these patterns of working mirrored the comradely approach to scholarship he had practiced in Dar, where he had frequently shared drafts with students and activists he was close to—Issa Shivji, Henry Mapolu, and Karim Hirji, in particular. This was not writing for promotion or self-aggrandizement, but entirely and exclusively for the movement.

There is no better celebration of Rodney's approach to history and writing than in Lamming's magisterial "Foreword" to *A History of the Guyanese Working People*. Lamming writes:

> His scholarship was sure, but it was also a committed and partisan scholarship. He believed that history was a way of ordering knowledge which could become an active part of the consciousness of an uncertified mass of ordinary people and which could be used by all as an instrument of social change. He taught from that assumption. He wrote out of that conviction. And it seemed to have been the informing influence on his relations with the organised working people of Guyana.[81]

A History of the Guyanese Working People

By 1980, Rodney had spent years developing what he planned as an exhaustive history of the Guyanese working people, beginning from the end of slavery in 1838, the growth of "free labor," and the increasing dependence by major sugar planters on unfree, indentured labor from India.

The book focused on the post-emancipation period, and how Caribbean societies—specifically Guyana—lost their central place in the process of capital accumulation. However, Rodney explains, their "dependent integration into the world capitalist system remained a significant feature." As ever, these peripheral colonial economies were buffeted by periods of crisis and boom taking place in metropolitan states. Whether the Guyanese poor were aware of these forces or not, their lives were fundamentally marked by them.[82]

A History is a beautifully and meticulously written book—with painstaking detail and background that explains, in a convincing and calm tone, the development of working-class unity and possibility. If the logic of late-nineteenth-century Guyanese political economy was to drive groups together, as Rodney writes, "planter propaganda concentrated on the difference between reliable Indian indentured servants and unreliable African villagers, [while] it obscured the fact that common socioeconomic circumstances produced similar responses—irrespective of race."[83]

Rodney never cheapened his prose for a rhetorical flourish, or to beat a radical drum; he was writing a serious volume on the making of the Guyanese working class, and the use of an imported, indentured labor force who could be compelled to do the work that African workers would not.

The book begins with a history of the immense environmental struggle to wrest from Guyana's coastal environment land that could be used for cultivation. By the turn of the nineteenth century, there had been an enormous battle, led by Dutch engineers and experts, to dam land along the coast—which had been a mangrove swamp—for cultivation. As a consequence, a strip of land of about 1,750 square miles, out of Guyana's total surface areas of 83,000 square miles, was "rescued," with the original inhabitants of Guyana, the Amerindians, preferring inland locations.[84]

Maintenance of these dykes and dams was excruciating—for the colonial treasury, but most of all, for the slave and indentured labor needed to maintain the dam walls and dredge the canals. Though nineteenth-century plantations purchased steam-driven drainage pumps, the "capital debt" was crushing. What is more, funds for maintaining the pumps were in short supply, and coal for running them was imported and prohibitively expensive.

Rodney shows how the environment interacted with colonial production such that the "enormous influence" of "flood and drought" impacted the lives of working people. The working poor would find themselves out of work in periods that were "extremely dry" as estates cut back on their allocations of "task work." Thus, droughts in November and December saw a drop in the level of water, meaning that boats—"punts"—could not transport cane from the fields to the factories; in consequence, cane cutting and grinding stopped. Equally, when the rain was excessive, work was often halted. In the prolonged seasonal droughts and floods, workers suffered, and often had little to eat or drink.

Rodney gives an example of this combination of human and environmental forces. Sophia Ross, a woman from Hopetown village, was convicted in November 1884 for trespassing on Plantation Bath. She had been trying to get water from the estate trench to "satisfy her thirst"; the alternative was to walk for miles in the heat to obtain dirty water. Rodney explains, "[T]his seemingly petty conviction highlights the toil and trauma involved in so basic an operation as securing supplies of drinking water."[85]

These seemingly extraneous details, in a book on labor, were central to framing Rodney's history. He writes: "Sea defence, drainage, and irrigation were problems demanding the scientific intervention of civil engineers. They were also being tackled within a specific set of class relations. The hands that dug the canals and the feet that trod the dams were taking an active part in the class struggle which would eventually mould the Guyanese people."[86]

While the book is a detailed case study, Rodney never loses sight of the role of global political economy in shaping the country's history. He explains how British Guiana's connection to the world economy was driven by the production and export of sugar. The fate of British Guiana's people, he writes, "was not only heavily influenced by the general movement of commodity prices but the specific market performance of the varieties of cane sugar which originated in the colony."

In 1884, for example, prices plummeted, so a ton of sugar had fallen to $69.84 from $107.26 the year before—reaching a record low of $46.09 per ton by 1896. The collapse in prices was caused in large measure by the dumping of large quantities of state-supported European beet sugar—with Germany in 1886 "dumping" almost eight hundred thousand tons of sugar on the UK and the United States. The wild fluctuations in prices were devastating to planters, many of whom went out of business. For the workers on these plantations, however, it was a question of raw survival. Once more, the world economy was ripping through colonial British Guiana.[87]

The impact on the lives of the poor was terrible: "[C]apitalist slumps and market crisis struck at the very fundamentals of working-class existence—namely the right to work and the right to earn a living wage." As estates and plantations closed, workers were thrown out, and between 1892 and 1900, forty-one estates were dismantled. Rodney writes, "All categories of workers as well as peasants together bore the burden of reduction in wage rates, diminution in earnings, and increase in indirect taxation that were features of this crisis-ridden period."[88]

In the second chapter, Rodney deals with the evolution of the plantation. The end of slavery, he writes, did not defeat planters—at least not those who kept ahead of the curve, invested, and remained firmly in control of the new post-emancipation dispensation. Yet both planters and former slaves had to deal with a new world; the planter hated the untrammeled free labor of the post-slavery period, and former slaves resented the alienation from ownership implicit in the free labor system. In 1838, an "apprenticeship" scheme was instituted to ensure that workers were tied to specific estates—a system that was detested. There were protracted sugar strikes in 1842 and 1848, Rodney reports. He writes that in 1842,

> sugar workers coordinated their opposition in a strike that lasted for twelve to thirteen weeks. Less than three years after being emancipated from slavery, the new wage-earning class was acting in certain respects like a modern proletariat and the first recorded strike in the history of the Guyanese working class was a success, leading to the withdrawal of the planters' labour code and the continuation of the moderately increased wage rate.[89]

Economic and labor tensions persuaded planters to secure "immigrant laborers" whose conditions of indentured service fixed them to a single employer. So similar was their situation to the former, recently abolished system of slavery, that in 1838, when the British first attempted to institute indentured service, they were forced to scrap the system; witnesses reported Indian arrivals being treated in exactly the same manner as Africans had been under slavery.[90] Despite these early misgivings, the system of indentured labor was extremely popular. Bonded to work at a specific location for a number of years at a certain rate, thousands of workers arrived on British Guiana's shores. Between 1851 and 1871, a total of almost 230,000 Indians arrived in annual shipments.[91]

The shipments of indentured laborers amounted to a curious export and import trade between the colonies of the British Empire—one that reflected the different economic, political, and environmental conditions throughout the empire. In the 1880s and 1890s, British Guiana was the main destination for emigrants from India. Driven to accept "indenture" by drought and famine in India, agents and recruiters enticed the poor with the promise of prosperity across the world. Life for them was frequently brutal, lived hand to mouth. For example, in the tough year of 1896, Goolijar, a spokesman for immigrants, announced, "Times were very hard . . . we cannot live on the wages we are getting; our stomachs are not being filled."[92] Though they received housing and, for the most part, food and return passage at the end of the period, life was unrelenting. Accommodation was poor, and disease and death common.

The system was cruel—indeed, a barely disguised form of slavery. Rodney cites Peter Ruhomon, a Creole Indian historian who asserted that "no trick of sophistry or twist of logic . . . can ever avail to defend the system of semi-slavery paraded under the guise of indentured immigration, under which Indians were brought to the Colony to labour on the sugar plantations, in the interests of a powerful and privileged body of capitalists."[93] To defend this "semi-slavery," any infraction was severely punished. In 1881, 3,168 indentured workers were defined as criminals for fighting with their employers on the plantation; 532 were "dispatched to prison," while 1,577 others were issued large fines, which frequently resulted in their imprisonment.

In contrast, Rodney observes, "village labor" was far removed from the conditions of indentured servitude. The free village movement of the mid-nineteenth century—which had seen African plantation workers achieve partial independence by residing outside the "nigger yards" in the estates—had secured for them alternative subsistence and meant that they could bargain or specialize in certain work. Rodney writes how "[t]he independent task-gang under the leadership of one of the worker members was . . . a post-Emancipation development."[94] These "gangs" would move from estate to estate and negotiate with the management over wages, conditions, and the specific "task." This "village labor" won a large number of "skirmishes" in the confrontation with plantation bosses. Impressively, elected village councils in this period were genuinely popular and democratic bodies.

Evidence of the "success" of organized "village labor" meant that between 1881 and 1905, factory work was exclusively the domain of village labor. The lowest grades of work paid accordingly and involved cleaning trenches, forking, banking, and weeding—and it was in these jobs that Africans were only rarely found. However, cane cutting, punt loading, and digging trenches, work that offered many times the amount in wages, were the activities of African workers.[95]

In chapter 3, Rodney writes about the small farming sector. The chapter, like the book, is a remarkable celebration of the resistance and survival of working people. Quite apart from the organized strikes in the early post-emancipation period, the remarkable fact of "small farming," Rodney notes, is noteworthy on a historical scale. Freed enslaved Africans often left the plantation and tried to survive on small parcels of land away from the agony of wage labor. Work, which was seasonal—and occasionally on workers' own terms—was sought two or three days a week. The frustration with "freed labor" that sparked these sorts of reactions by the "Creole

Africans" provided the impetus for indentured labor from India, China, and Portugal.

However, indentured labor, Rodney tells us, was not always the stable social base for sugar production. Once the period of "indentureship" had expired, either the laborers would be returned at considerable cost or, as often happened, they would stay. The emergence of a "Indo-Guianese" peasantry was assisted by planters opening up lands for "time-expired immigrants," which was preferable to facilitating a mass exodus from the colony. Still, the 1880s saw large-scale repatriation to India, continuing until the turn of the century. The colony sought to stem this wave by offering free land grants on the condition that the right to repatriation was surrendered.

Rodney notes that for the "peasantry"—as much as it existed in the post-slavery period—the late part of the nineteenth century saw efforts to diversify. Planters increasingly offered parts of their estates to immigrants for other opportunities than wages on the estate itself; for instance, land was leased for rice farming, a compromise seen as safer than allowing the labor force to "disperse across the colony."[96] This created what has been termed a "paddy proletariat"—who grew rice for their own and local consumption, but was still reliant on wages from sugar cultivation on the estates. Rice for export became increasingly important in the early twentieth century, but it was the remarkable adaption of cultivation techniques that inspired Rodney.

Rodney is full of praise for the "ingenious" irrigation practices of Chinese immigrants, who, he writes, were "'liberating' water through bamboo stems from the state supplies." He cites an account of a plantation manager who noted in 1881, "In lot 72 or Hong Kong they have peculiar arrangements that I have not seen anywhere else for husking and cleaning their rice, of which they have about 100 acres in cultivation."[97] These techniques were quickly taken up by other communities.

On the question of the "peasantry," Rodney is circumspect, painting the picture in all its complexity: "In practice, there was an ever-increasing number of villagers who were either landless or owned insufficient land to engage in peasant production. The majority of the rural population acquired the status of tenant farmers. For instance, at Bagotville in 1896, the five hundred 1/4 acre lots were owned by about 250 persons, while the total village population was 2,403."[98] The struggle for survival conquered all. The fate of the poor was tied inextricably to the collapse of sugar cultivation;

thus, estates that no longer produced the crop made arrangements with "villagers" to rent land. This had the effect of "holding back" the development of an independent landowning peasantry among the Creole Africans.

The exhaustive, meticulous work in Rodney's *History* is evident throughout the volume, though in this respect perhaps chapter 4, on "differentiation," stands out. The entire volume deals specifically with the last two decades of the nineteenth century; as Rodney explains, this was a time of "economic differentiation," when the decline of sugar saw the growth of other commodities and exports, including timber and diamond and gold mining. With "peasant farming" on the rise, British Guiana became more differentiated. Since the Dutch had settled on the use of coastal agriculture in the mid-eighteenth century—which involved the complex task of building dams and dykes—little use had been made of the hinterland. Rodney writes, "[P]lanters viewed the hinterland as a potential competitor for labour and sought to dissuade free blacks from moving in that direction in the 1840s, just as they had earlier sought to forestall slaves from escaping into the bush."[99]

The colonial economy was lopsided, deformed, and uneven—making little use of local resources, especially Guianese sources of timber, and preferring imported goods and materials. Only later in the nineteenth century were native woods used for construction and local building work. In harvesting the local wood, Rodney writes, the "rights of the indigenous Amerindians were totally subordinated to those of coastal business interests."[100] These Amerindians were forbidden, for example, from felling trees over a certain girth. The pull of scarce labor from timber to gold mining was a real threat—with the metal offering higher rewards than the hard work of logging. Rodney records ten thousand persons passing through the goldfield each year from 1891 through 1893. Labor shortage had been an old problem in the slave colony—with gold mining shut down by the Dutch in the late eighteenth century to prevent labor shortages in coastal plantations.[101]

Rodney offers a powerful description of the life of Creole Africans during this period: "[A]ccustomed to artisan work, day labour on the sea defences or the village roads, provision farming, the making and selling of cassava . . . and the huckstering of foodstuffs—in addition to their days of estate labour." Added to this was occasional gold and diamond mining— activities, at different times of the year and often simultaneously, that only barely managed to sustain a precarious existence.[102]

Rodney's conclusions are undoubtedly correct when he writes that this kaleidoscope of labor of former slaves meant that they did not simply become peasants after emancipation. Rodney's own words summarize his argument brilliantly: "They became instead potential members of a free labour force and were amendable to numerous forms of labour. Pressures generated by international depression caused Indian workers to use rice farming to enhance monetary earnings, while Africans resorted to the bush for their survival and created a new economic sector." The pressures of the international economy in British Guiana, to which Rodney refers, meant the plantation economy cast a shadow from the coast deep into the interior; all life was subjected to its vicissitudes.[103]

When Rodney turns his attention to the stratification of communities after slavery, we see a society evolving, fracturing, and mutating at a rapid pace. From the 1840s, the Portuguese received certain assistance from planters that was denied to Creole Africans; quickly, the Portuguese were encouraged to carry out the functions of retail distribution, and they established monopolies in these areas. Equally, with access to credit, the Chinese immigrant workforce also rose to the position of a middle class, working in shopkeeping, woodcutting, and entrepreneurship on the goldfields. By the end of the century, a developing Chinese middle class in towns across British Guiana had begun to emerge—sometimes the class even managed to purchase their own plantations.[104]

Certain privileges allowed some individuals to overcome prevailing stratification (of race, class, and gender), while others were unable to do so. Rodney summarizes the experience for ex-indentured Indians: "[A]ccumulation on a small scale by immigrants on and off the estates constituted the first movements of the process of social stratification within this community."[105] The expansion of education was also a development that began in the late nineteenth century with "creole laborers" placing a great value on their children's education. Education was often provided through church and state, and though limited, it enabled Black people who finished primary school to advance further and progress to careers, for instance, in schoolteaching. The consequences of this advance were predictable. As Rodney writes: "[T]he upward mobility of the black and brown middle class brought them into conflict with white incumbents in jobs that indigenous persons identified as rightfully theirs. In many instances, it seemed all the more galling to the new educated elite that positions were filled by incompetent or inexperienced Europeans whom native Guianese had to teach or prop up."[106]

In the last two decades of the nineteenth century, the middle class was growing more confident. Increasingly dissatisfied with the lower-ranking roles of teacher and clerk—and church minister—they began to rise further to professions in medicine and law. Rodney warns us not to see these achievements as the satisfaction of personal interest; rather, as he writes, educated churchmen and headmasters were "socially significant . . . [in] that their mobilisation helped guarantee the reproduction and expansion of the middle class as a whole."[107] Rodney's last work is a towering feat of social history. Indeed, few Marxist historians have managed so successfully, and with such precision, to combine a vision of history from above and below.

In chapter 5, Rodney writes how the political power of the planters that had been insurmountable had begun to break down in the last quarter of the nineteenth century. This transformation was brought about by changes in technologies of sugar cultivation, the falling price for the export crop, and reorganization of plantation production. Under the blows of sugar price collapse, estates were becoming larger through amalgamation; one example was Thomas Daniel & Sons, of Bristol, who reincorporated as a limited liability company in 1886. Plantations were now often run by managers, rather than directly by families.

In their efforts to escape the planters, villagers in British Guiana managed to exercise a degree of agency and personal choice. Rodney writes how "villagers in British Guiana were uniquely free, judged by the standards prevailing in the West Indies."[108] In London, the *Times* described the phenomena of British Guiana's communal villages as "little bands of socialists"—referring to the cooperative authority of these post-emancipation villages. The authorities kicked back with efforts by the colonial state to "incorporate" them into central government control—attempts that were not always successful—and in many places, conditions by the 1880s had only grown worse.[109]

Reformers' disenchantment with developments in the colony challenged the colonial authorities. With this in mind, the Reform Club was established in 1887—with mass petitioning and public meetings. Though the leadership was clearly and resolutely middle class, the club appealed to a broader base of British Guianese society. The target for their campaigns was, Rodney writes, "mass grievances . . . [of] the emergent middle class." The colony's varied press was engaged in the effort to urge a more aggressive tempo of reforms and change. The movement, lasting until 1892, was influenced by the poor—common artisans, small cultivators, and laborers.[110] Serious energy was put into campaigning for a lower "monetary barrier" for enfranchisement—from six hundred dollars per annum to as low as three hundred.

There were other objectives, including the opening of crown lands, state support for small industries, development of the interior, and the expansion of Creole civil servants, as well as improvements in medical and educational services. Rodney notes at the end of the chapter how the refusal to register a Black doctor led to countrywide activism, until an act in the legislature in 1890 was passed allowing him to work. The popular front of the Reform Club generated wider politicization, and Rodney championed its achievement.[111]

There is a detectable change of tone as the book moves into chapter 6, where Rodney discusses "struggles" and early forms of resistance among the Indian and Creole African populations. This is where the author's passion resides, and it is clear in the change of pace; he writes as a committed scholar, meticulous in his detail and historical research, but resolutely on the side of those taking action.

Rodney starts by debunking the "myths of docility": if this was historic nonsense in the period of slavery, he observes, so it was with indentured labor too. For these workers—bound by a strict contract of work to a single employer—there was a "dialectic of accommodation and resistance," Rodney writes.[112] Throughout the years he surveys, indentured labor was regularly brought before the courts—"itself proof of restlessness, absenteeism and noncompliance."[113] One indication of discontent is seen in the annual reports of the immigrant agent-general—who was responsible for the conduct of indentured labor, organizing their arrival and allocation. Between 1874 and 1895, 65,084 indentured immigrants were convicted of "breaches" of contract.[114] These workers, reprimanded en masse, responded by demonstrating their discontent. In the 1880s, it was not uncommon to see fifty or sixty indentured laborers brandishing shovels and forks in Georgetown as they attempted to take their cases to officials.

Such action followed, to a large extent, the vagaries of sugar prices on the international market. Thus, by the time the sugar price collapsed in 1884, indentured workers had begun taking more regular and militant action. Rodney reports that thirty-one "strikes and disturbances" occurred in 1886, fifteen in 1887, and forty-two in 1888."[115] Among the many accounts Rodney details, he focuses on a militant indentured laborer—a man called Bechu, a Bengali, who arrived to work on Plantation Enmore in 1894. Unfit for hard labor, he was given domestic and light duties. He became a labor activist who defended the rights of his class, writing to the press and lobbying on behalf of fellow workers. "His denunciation included substantial allegations of immoral exploitation of Indian females by overseers." As Rodney notes, "Bechu's exposures sometimes led to remedial actions such as the dismissal of offending overseers"[116] An activist of iron will, Bechu was twice tried on libel for accusing the Enmore manager of causing the death of an immigrant laborer, who was turned away from a hospital.

Rodney records Bechu's words: "[T]he immigrant system is as sacred as the old system of slavery in former days, and for one in my humble position to have ventured to touch it with profane hands or to have dared to unveil it is considered on this side of the Atlantic to be a capital and inexplicable offence."[117] Denounced by planters as a "high-caste" Indian, Bechu was victimized; such laborers were regarded as uppity and unreliable—rabble-rousers stirring up trouble.

Clashes with planters and authorities escalated through the 1880s and 1890s, and into the new century. On May 6, 1903, an "indentured gang" marched to New Amsterdam, where they argued that management on the plantation had refused to accept a compromise wage. The manager succeeded in getting a driver to testify that the workers had threatened his life, ensuring that they were charged. In the end, Rodney writes, "six workers were killed and seven seriously injured. . . . they were shot down outside the Magistrate's Court . . . whence they had proceeded to seek justice." The so-called ringleaders were sentenced to terms in prison.[118]

Rodney explains that taking action was easier for "village workers," since their relationship with the estates was not bound with other conditions arising from "tied housing" and the general bundle of indentured circumstances. In this sense, the situation was "classical," with the class struggle centered on "free workers" and plantation managers and how much could be "extracted from the labourer."[119] There was both open struggle and also "hidden" forms of resistance. Rodney listed some of these "tricks," which included "accidental breakages" or "leaving pieces of iron on the cane carrier,"[120] each of which would stop production.

At the turn of the century, organized action often came with the development of groups that catered to the needs to workers; as Rodney explains, "[W]orkers association and friendly associations had come into existence."[121] Priority has to be given to "Friendly Societies and Lodges," he writes—bodies that played a direct role in welfare and in advocating for workers' rights. However, the "class struggle" had to be fought with "whatever limited weapons were in the hands of the working class."[122] In this period, the main expression of the struggle was in spontaneous action—one example of which was the anti-Portuguese riots of March 1889. In response to the wounding and subsequent death of a Black man, the riot targeted Portuguese businesses and shops. As Rodney explained, it "erupted against the most accessible agents in the hierarchy of exploitation—not the plantation capitalists nor the big import-export firms, but the small shopkeepers."[123]

One of many astonishing aspects of the chapter was Rodney's ability to straddle the Atlantic—to draw on comparisons and working-class action internationally. His celebratory tone is evident when he discusses the impact of British Guianese workers on the "tremendous struggle which was then being waged on the English labor front. The historical dock strike began in London in September 1889." The strike in London was covered by the press in the colony, along with other aspects of the new unionism that was breaking out in the metropolis. Rodney explains, "When the press in Guiana spoke of 'an epidemic of strikes' in 1890, they pointedly adverted to both the local and international dimensions of this epidemic."[124]

Rodney was never one to make tenuous historical connections. Therefore, his celebration of the affinity of the English and British Guianese working class needs to be stated clearly. He writes:

> The much-published strikes of dock workers at places like the London West India docks must have brought to the fore the similarity of class interests and hence the possibility of stepping up the local class struggle through strikes. When the *Royal Gazette* first reported the London dock strike, it noted that "West Indians will be interested in being reminded that intimately associated . . . upon the Dock Director's Committee is Mr. Neville Lubbock." It may seem purely coincidental that Lubbock needed to travel to Guiana one year later to supervise one of the areas in which his capital extracted labour surplus. But the links between the exploitation of English dockers and West Indian plantation workers were not accidental. If the *Royal Gazette* found the connection intriguing, the sugar estate employees of Mr Lubbock's Colonial Company and other Guianese workers were certainly capable of deciding to

follow the lead of the London dockers.[125]

Forever realistic in his assessment, Rodney explained that the condition of "proletariat organisation" in British Guiana was weak and underdeveloped. At that point, there was no body that consciously united the British Guianese working class.

Rodney is realistic about the limits of "popular front" organizing in the 1890s—which meant that the "new middle-class spokesman compromised considerably with the planters with who they were sharing the legislature."[126] As labor struggles escalated, however, the colonial state was clear about the need to respond: the police in the early 1890s were reorganized into a "semi military force."[127]

Further support and solidarity came from the UK; after all, as Rodney explained, the two countries—despite the unevenness of their relationship—shared much in terms of class interest and radical politics. The church was not a neutral arbiter, as seen with the arrival of Reverend H. J. Shirley to take charge of the New Amsterdam Mission Church. He used the pulpit for militant organizing, on which the British Guianese press duly reported. Shirley spoke powerfully: "All the labourers and all the employees of the colony from the clerk to the coolie should FORM TRADE UNIONS so that no employers should be able to dismiss a man for asking simple honest justice . . . exercise the right of free speech, and agitate, for it is both legitimate and imperative."[128] Demonized as a "socialist demagogue" by the authorities, Shirley nevertheless persisted. Rodney explains that the reverend entered the colony "with a class consciousness developed in England where the modern proletariat was carrying out trade union and party struggles. His real contribution was not so much the denunciation of existing ills in Guiana as his emphatic call for the self-realization of working people through agitation and organisation."[129]

Teachers, who had constituted what Rodney describes as a quasi-vanguard status within the working class, used the platform of the *People* newspaper (formed in 1901) to help set up a People's Party, or People's Association. According to Rodney, "The People's Party was a proto party with well-defined positions; and its leadership sought to use the limited constitutional arena to advance popular demands." Yet Rodney advances a word of caution at the end of this chapter—one that echoed through the decades to the struggles he was directly leading in the late 1970s: "The political leaders who had agitated and organised a 'mass' base were far from achieving . . .

the degree of power required to neutralise the planters or to alter the manner in which Guiana was buffeted by international capitalist forces."[130]

Chapter 7 deals directly with the question of race, trying to address whether Guyana is a "society," in Rodney's words, in which "racial division and conflict have been in the ascendancy over consensus and class action." Rodney's survey of the period covered in the book concludes: "[M]y contention is that the case for the dominant role of racial division in the historical sphere has been overstated, and that scholarship on the subject has accepted without due scrutiny the proposition that Indians and Africans existed in mutually exclusive cultural compartments." Rodney argues that there has been a tendency, among historians, to reflect back "racial conflict" from independence in 1966 to earlier history. It is, he argues, a lazy historical approach that is "indefensible when the assumption is made that all previous development was nothing but the unfolding of the theme of racial conflict."[131] If such an approach is taken, then everything in the past can be read as a precursor to racial conflict—a version of predestination which has nothing in common with proper historical research and writing.

Rodney states that there was a "racial dimension" among the Guyanese working people in the nineteenth century—establishing itself in state-aided Indian migration, residential separation, and the "slow rate of diversification of the colonial economy." Yet there were relatively few significant interracial conflicts between different groups in the period before the 1906 elections. These seemingly mild-mannered conclusions are astounding; Rodney knew he was standing much of Guyana's history on its head. Reading the book, there is little doubt that he was correct.

The final chapter looks at the riots and protests in 1905—often referred to as the "Ruimveldt Riots," because workers in Plantation Ruimveldt were the first to die in the action. The protest movement spread from plantation to factories, from sugar boilers and porters to building workers and cane cutters. It was, however, the Georgetown-based stevedores who sparked the protests on the question of wage rises. The action, which extended from November 28 to December 6, reached an apex on the third day. As Rodney describes, on

> 30 November, masses of people took to the street in Georgetown. Those who were on strike set out to persuade others of their fellow workers to likewise cease labour. Sometimes force was required. Thursday morning, domestics were dragged out of private houses, while workers at the Railway Goods Wharf were threatened and pushed off the site. By

afternoon, crowds roamed the business centre, and some looting took place at pawnbrokers and jewellers. Most businessman hastened to close their premises.

The colonial state responded quickly and with force, reading the riot act—literally—"around 6.00 pm that Thursday at four different parts of the city of Georgetown."[132] Most of the country's sugar- and wealth-producing areas were impacted, including the sugar estates of East Bank Demerara, which saw shootings and disturbances on December 1. Managers were chased away by strikers, and plantations were robbed of their food stocks. The porters of Diamond Plantation demanded, on December 2, that their wages be increased from thirty-six to forty-eight cents per day. Rodney writes, as wave upon wave of action spread, that "for the first time in decades managers were forced to sit down by their own employees. At Schoonord and Versailles, the managers were prepared to negotiate."[133]

The state, terrified by the scale of the uprising, scrambled two admiralty vessels: the HMS *Diamond*, a 3,000-ton cruiser, was quickly dispatched from Barbados, and another came from Trinidad. Combined, the two ships had a force of almost 600 men. The first task of the arriving force was to round up and arrest the instigators of the strikes in West Bank Demerara.[134]

As direct military intervention got underway on the sugar plantations, desperation set in, and the strikes on the waterfront in Georgetown collapsed. The background of the strikes, Rodney tells us, has to be viewed in the context of the "sustained and unrelenting pressure brought to bear on the living standards of the working people since the depression of 1884."[135] Rodney paints a bleak picture of suffering and hardship in the two decades before the riots: "When the rains fell, Georgetown residents waded among floating feces; when casual labourers obtained two days' work per week, the entire earnings could barely cover the rent and keep away the bailiff's cart; when mothers gave birth, they stood a 30 percent chance of burying that child before the first year was up given an infant mortality rate of 298 per thousand."[136] This was life in British Guiana: brutal, short, and relentless.

However, it was not just domestic issues that generated the rocket fuel need for an uprising of this scale. Indeed, Rodney was clear that there were other aspects in the rising levels of worker self-awareness at play. He writes, "The stevedores of 1905 represented the highest expression of worker consciousness derived from the struggle both on and off the plantation." These dockworkers were at the nexus of the colonial import-export economy—loading sugar for export for shipping firms associated with the massive joint stock sugar companies of the era, such as Booker Brothers, Sandbach Parker, and H. K. Davson.

Through contacts with an international group of seamen and coverage in the national press, dockworkers were aware of struggles elsewhere in the world. Rodney writes that the stevedore strike wave in 1890 followed "on the heels of the great London dock strike of the previous year. This process of class education through glimpses of international experience must have continued in the years that came after. The stevedores and the clerks of the shipping firms were amongst the first to hear, read and discuss news from the outside world."[137] More than any other year in recent decades, 1905 marked a great turn in popular struggle. The press in Georgetown carried "lengthy accounts of the 1905 Revolution in Czarist Russia."[138]

However, the working class on the docks lacked organization—which could have helped cohere their movement and strikes. Efforts at building a popular cross-class organization in the 1890s had not been sustained; therefore, the rebellion in Guyana in November and December 1905 was a great, spontaneous action, with no structures that could guide and direct the movement in workplaces, plantations, and on the streets.[139] Compelled under the sheer force of popular sentiment to negotiate, these plantations were forced by the governor, Frederick Hodgson, to back down. Wage increases would not be made on the back of a mass movement; if there was any doubt about this, Hodgson sought to dispel it with personal visits to several important estates, accompanied by troops from the visiting vessels.

Among the aspects of the revolt Rodney details is the role of women. He writes that "women from all levels of the working people were involved in the 1905 riots. Court records do not substantial the slur that even those arrested were all rowdies, viragos, prostitutes, and the like. One encounters reference to a 'badly-clad lady of the centipede class' [a gang name for those who apparently resorted to violence in Georgetown]."[140] Women also participated in the uprising in East and West Bank labor struggles—one, Dorothy Rice, was part of a delegation from Plantation Ruimveldt that put the case for the workers to authorities.

Rodney rarely felt the need to labor his theoretical approach with long quotes or biblical references to Marx, Engels, or Lenin. In his last book, the only Marxist "authority" he cites is Trotsky, where the Bolshevik leader observes that "there are always leaders, even when there is no overt organisation and even when the personae are left nameless as far as historians are concerned." As evidence of Trotsky's point, Rodney observes: "A reading of the official and newspaper reports shows that within the masses on the streets, there were individuals who stood out as bold and decisive."[141] One of Rodney's sources, Hubert Nathaniel Critchlow, was a docker who persuaded his fellow workers to wait to strike until there were more ships in harbor and their bargaining position was thus stronger. In West Bank Demerara, it was Phillip Washington of Uitvlugt who was regarded as a strike leader. Rodney notes that during the Ruimveldt shootings, the police were ordered to target and kill strike leaders.[142]

Though the strike and action did not see an entirely unified Indian and African movement, for reasons already laid out, Rodney was clear that the governor was wrong to convey the impression, in his letters and telegrams, that the action saw Africans attack Indians. "The apparent racial split," he writes, "was a reflection of the division of labour which still tended to concentrate Africans in the estate buildings or—in the fields—only as canecutters."[143] The technique that was later used to drive the communities apart—such as using Indians to police Africans and vice versa—was not then one of state control. In fact, Rodney explains, "the wage demands by strikers resulted in management promising wage increases for both *African and Indian workers*"—a reality that was deliberately overlooked by Governor Hodgson, who tried to portray the riots as the grievances of a single group.

The extent of the uprising cannot be understated; for a few days, it threatened the entire edifice of the colonial state. The police, overpowered, were unable to make arrests and hardly able to protect the governor himself. So significant was the movement that colonial power was forced to seek the reinforcements of British troops stationed more than five hundred miles away. Yet there was something more enduring, Rodney writes, than the days of the uprising itself:

> What the government found difficult to handle was the remarkable estrangement of the people. Their rejection of colonial authority lasted, not for days or weeks, but for months, and in some respects their resistance was better coordinated. . . . and the People's Association was revived to draw together the grievances of men and women. . . . On 29 January 1906, artisans and workers packed into the Town Hall . . . to unite a series of demands into a petition sponsored by the People's Association.[144]

The uprising also seemed to impact the popular press locally. Increasingly, its reports from far and wide described an international terrain of struggle. Rodney explains that each "new outbreak of fighting in Russia" was reported, as were the African uprisings in Natal and socialist protests in London. Each and every one of these international struggles "found a place," he observes, "in the local press to the exclusion of what the governor considered more 'interesting' news and with the consequences of creating what he described as an 'artificial' situation of unrest."[145] So unsettled were the times that the colonial power regarded it as necessary to "detain" a British warship for months after December 1905.

Rodney's last book, published posthumously, is one of the high points in postwar Marxist history. Its achievements—sadly limited to a single volume—remain immense, charting the making of the Guyanese working poor. Focusing on the last decades of the nineteenth century but casting a historical gaze to the entire post-emancipation period, it leaves us with a compelling picture of "working people," in all their brilliance, humanity, and complexity. This "making" took place in circumstances of a colonial state and economy with specific and constraining features; Rodney systematically lays these out, while always leaving room for agency and movement. A real people emerge, divided, ethnically compartmentalized, but with the capacity and willingness to act, despite great hardship. The 1905 rebellion was that moment—one to remember, record, and celebrate.

Understanding the past in order to shape the future was Rodney's intention in his last, extraordinary book. In it, he never sidelines the specificities of Guyanese history and political economy, and he is always careful to stress the weaknesses and peculiarities of the country's conditions. The book reflects his conviction that only from such a historical vantage could the Guyanese working people begin to understand their own past, and how the conditions in the present had been made.

As we have seen, during the late 1970s, Rodney's focus was intently fixed on the struggle of the WPA and the political developments taking place in his home Guyana. However, he simultaneously remained occupied with ongoing lectures and teaching abroad—pursuits to which we shall now turn.

CHAPTER 11

From Georgetown to Hamburg

Even as Rodney became a full-time activist of the Working People's Alliance, its principal organizer and intellectual, he was compelled to travel to teach and work. One trip he took to Germany, from April to July 1978, provides us with particularly rich insight into his political development and thought. Leaving the close, hot embrace of Georgetown in early April for the artificial blast of air-conditioning on a British Airways flight, he carried a stack of reading for the eleven-hour flight to London, from where he would take a short hop to Hamburg.

Walter was familiar enough with the protocols of flying—a necessary evil to cross the globe. In the 1970s, travel on a transatlantic flight was a formal affair, calling for smart clothes—collared shirts and ties for men, and skirts and blouses for women. The flights, frequented by wealthy members of Guyana's elite, were nevertheless noisy and frequently filled with cigarette smoke.

The weather is still cold in Hamburg in April; early in the month there are rare highs of 53 degrees Fahrenheit, while nights can plunge to 37 degrees. What warm clothes Walter had, he packed; others he purchased when he arrived. Like all writers and scholars packing for a long trip, luggage limits meant Walter had to contend with a fierce competition between his books and papers and other necessities, such as clothes and toiletries. At the time, he was still working on his manuscript on the Guyanese working class in the former British slave colony; he packed some of the relevant material, including photocopied documents. He also brought along prescribed readings for the course he was going to teach, and notebooks to flesh out his lectures. Anxious to keep abreast of political events in Guyana, he would also have taken party work with him—pamphlets to write and internal perspective documents to draft. Meanwhile, he left clear instructions to his fellow WPA activists.

When he arrived on April 6, almost a full day after his departure, he would have been stiff from the flight and tired; sleep would have been a necessity before he could think of the teaching at the university that was due to start shortly. Walter was an outspoken revolutionary and the celebrated author of *How Europe Underdeveloped Africa*, and expectation of his arrival was intense. He had been invited by two radical German scholars, Rainer Tetzlaff and Peter Lock, to teach a course on the history of African development, which would take place between April and June at the University of Hamburg. The lectures were recorded, of which full transcripts were later prepared, including the question-and-answer sessions with the students.

Once more, Walter had to be cautious when it came to money. Generous though the university had been with the salary for the three-month teaching post, after accounting for expenses and travel, he would hardly be living the life of a wealthy man. Writing to his close friend in Hamburg, Albert "Al" Parkes, on January 22, 1978, he remarked that "things seem firm enough to ask you to make definite arrangements for housing on my behalf." Rodney then explained: "I would obviously prefer to stay with you. . . . I will be staying for three months, and I will need to save as much as possible on expenses. If you have to check out another place for me, please bear that in mind."[1] Patricia explains: "It was entirely logical for him to stay with Al, since they were close friends and the only person that he knew in Germany. Walter was not on vacation but working, and he was always careful with money. His only 'extravagance' were books."[2]

The lecture course was titled "African Development, 1878–1978" and comprised, according to the one-page program, "(i) a brief introduction to development concepts; (ii) a survey of African colonial economies with special reference to East and West Africa; and (iii) an examination of post-colonial developments in Kenya and Tanzania." According to the brief plan, there were going to be twelve lectures, comprising "The Debate on Development Concepts in Africa" and "Post-colonial Development Strategies." Included in the program's "essential reading" was Samir Amin's 1972 article "Underdevelopment and Dependence in Black Africa: Their Historical Origins and Contemporary Forms," Rodney's own *HEUA*, and Issa Shivji's 1976 *Class Struggles in Tanzania*.[3]

Some of the most interesting aspects of this astonishing course concerned Rodney's contemporary reflections on Africa's political economy, and, specifically, Tanzania's apparently radical trajectory. For some of this analysis, Rodney leaned heavily on Shivji's recently published book. Rodney also advanced criticism of Africa's various experiments in socialist change, in Tanzania *and* across the continent; he had become more critical—scathing, in fact—about these projects, which he now argued were scams that offered nothing to the poor. As we have seen, Syl Lowhar reported in 1975 on Rodney's "lavish" praise of socialist revolutions of the world, but also his equally fulsome attack on the "pseudo-socialists who are to be found everywhere in the Third World." In particular, Rodney singled out Nyerere's African socialism as "petty bourgeois nationalism" that was neither socialist nor African. His experience in Guyana under Burnham's murderous and dictatorial "socialism" had deepened his critical opinion of all self-declared socialist governments. Burnham paraded himself, internationally and nationally, as a socialist who supported progressive causes—despite receiving covert funds from the CIA and crushing any serious opposition. Under Burnham, all independent political groups were suppressed, and activists targeted. Socialism in Guyana was a cruel, violent charade. Yet it was in Tanzania where Rodney learned some of his most important lessons.

Dar es Salaam was the place where Rodney had once nurtured hope in state-led projects of radical changes. Tanzania had been a place of incredible optimism; the government of Julius Nyerere had boldly declared its intention to construct socialism in the East African country and reverse the country's poverty and marginalization. As we have seen, Rodney threw himself into debates at the university, as it began to transform itself from a colonial institution, and on the country's national political scene, as it sought to address decades—indeed generations—of enforced underdevelopment. Though he had always been critical of state-led initiatives—these "briefcase revolutions," as he had quipped in Dar in 1969—he had given Tanzania and Nyerere his full support.

Omissions and Inclusions

During the late 1970s—which, tragically, would be the last years of his life—Rodney was at the height of his powers. He had an extraordinary capacity for work, as we have seen in the combination of intense activism, travel, and research he undertook. His efforts, including his political involvement in the WPA, were focused resolutely on struggles from below.

There are invaluable signs of this shift, this new orientation, in the lecture course he presented in Hamburg.

When I first laid eyes on the original transcripts of these lectures during a 2018 visit to the Atlanta University Center archive, the excitement was intense. In the silence of the reading room at the Robert W. Woodruff Library, the skin on the back of my neck puckered and my heartbeat quickened. With the low hum of the library's air-conditioning in the background, punctuated only by the slight rustle of the papers from other readers, I read on breathlessly, my mind focused entirely on the papers.

The lectures give a powerful impression of an activist and thinker on astonishing form. Rodney engages with challenging and wide-ranging issues, including the continent's past, slavery, independence, and projects of radical socialist development. Frequently interrupted by students asking him to clarify a point or justify a statement, Rodney deals with complex questions of history, political economy, and Marxist theory with sophistication and clarity, never losing patience or his narrative thread. The transcripts and recordings of the lectures in the archive in Atlanta also give a sense of Rodney's own political development, reflecting on his activism and his current work with the working class in Guyana.

The entire course was recorded on cassette, with some expectation that the transcripts would be typed up after Rodney had left the country. In the end, the recordings were transcribed only after Rodney's 1980 murder. In 1984, they were assembled into a small, photocopied booklet, which was placed in the library of the University of Hamburg and distributed to a number of comrades and students; copies also ended up in a private collection put together by Peter Lock and Rainer Tetzlaff, the organizers of Rodney's visit.

It was during my research at the archive in Atlanta that I became aware of the existence of this booklet. Soon after, in December 2018, I contacted Peter Lock; within a few hours I had received a reply: "[I]t was indeed Rainer Tetzlaff who brought Walter Rodney to Hamburg where he taught courses and attracted a large group of students. I had many conversations with him." According to Tetzlaff, it was for reasons of "loss and guilt" (which will be explained in the conclusion) that he coordinated the publication of the lecture series into an "occasional publication"—the photocopied "tribute to Walter Rodney," which was distributed to friends and comrades. On December 18, 2018, Lock was confident in his emails to me that he would be able to find his private copy among his papers in the basement: "I should find somewhere in the basement this publication and can send you my copy, if it would be of any use for your investigation." After an extensive search, he was in the end unable to locate the document and instead asked for the one copy in the library at the university to be scanned. On January 10, 2019, I received it, in two scans.

One of the impressive aspects of the course is Rodney's staggering criticism of Tanzania's socialist efforts. He is uncompromising: there was, he said to the "large group of students," simply nothing socialist about the reforms. In fact, he points to the strikes and working-class activity in a wave of action from 1973 as the center of a genuine movement for socialist change—one that saw a shift in the consciousness of those involved in struggle, Rodney explains. It is here that we need to look for change, Rodney asserts. As I sat in the windowless reading room of the Atlanta University Center in November 2018, it was clear to me that his critical reappraisal, made in public, in front of his class, remains a tremendously exciting and original analysis.

Understanding this wave of working-class action required that Rodney undertake a detailed reading of what had taken place in Tanzania. According to Rodney, Nyerere was no socialist; when workers had dared to take matters into their own hands, he had crushed their strikes and occupations. Yet as I scanned the book that Peter Lock had sent me, I realized that the most significant part of the course, Rodney's account of the strikes and the wildcat action, had been excluded; this important story had simply disappeared from this 1984 account of the lectures. What on earth could be the reason for leaving out this still-scintillating account of Nyerere's and Tanzania's socialist failings? I can only imagine that even in 1984—when Nyerere had finally resigned as president—it was considered too critical. But by whom? By Lock and Tetzlaff? Or the university administration in Hamburg? Surely it could not have been due to an editorial decision, the limits of space, or mere oversight. Whatever the reason, in this chapter I focus on Rodney's account of working-class struggle in Tanzania—the principal source that he used to understand what had happened. For this, I have had to use the account of the lectures taken from the archive, rather than the booklet. However, to start, I need to briefly present the entire course Rodney was invited to teach in the spring and summer of 1978 in Hamburg.

The Course

Rodney's lectures were fresh, lively, and original. Indeed, they are perhaps the best example of the dizzying breadth of Rodney's scholarship, reading, and activism, synthesized into a single course. The course also display's Rodney's astonishing capacity for clarity and description—a rare ability among scholars and activists—which he had developed during long years working as a teacher and activist. In their introduction to the 1984 booklet, Rainer Tetzlaff and Peter Lock explained that the course was "an entirely new enriching experience when the students of the Institute for Political Science and the Seminar of History at the University of Hamburg were offered an intellectual discourse with an authentic representative of the Third World."[4]

Rodney starts the lectures by challenging two views of African history. One is represented by Hugh Trevor-Roper—a British historian and racist of the establishment, who saw pre-colonial African history as primitive and basic. The second view, Rodney explained, sees the colonial period as "insignificant, almost irrelevant." These historians arrive at this position by "saying that African history and African development must be seen in a totality, that African history is almost ageless."[5]

Unsurprisingly, Rodney rejects both positions, including the second view, which sees colonialism as insignificant, a "flea-bite," and holds that already (in 1978) "Africa had . . . moved away from the colonial heritage." These were arguments made by both academics and politicians, who saw Europeans as simply "visitors"; now that they had formerly left the continent, they believed, Africa could reestablish its authenticity.

The idea of "authenticity"—the return to a "real" and "proper" African culture and history—had been taken up and established as official government discourse in different parts of the continent, justifying policies that were often draconian and dictatorial. For instance, Congolese president Mobutu Sese Seko had used to his own advantage the so-called "recourse to authenticity" in 1971, renaming the former Zaire as Democratic Republic of the Congo that year. His own change of name and title, and the names of towns and streets, reflected this "authenticity." On the other hand, the official proclamation of Patrice Lumumba as a national hero—a man Mobutu had been key in murdering—was all part of an attempt to forge a new African national identity true to its glorious historical past. These efforts were part of an endeavor to increase the resources available to the state and drive out "foreigners" through use of "nationalist" slogans. The class of state bureaucrats and businessmen was the chief beneficiary of this policy—a process Rodney discusses.[6]

The second stage of these state-led reforms in the Congo was the institutional and economic consolidation of "Zaireanization," which was initiated with the "takeover" of the bureaucracy and the "nationalization" of sectors of the economy previously in private or corporate (Belgian) hands into either private Zairean ownership or state ownership. This change tended to encourage the development of two different, and conflicting, social formations. The process saw the transfer of small and medium businesses, mainly in the transport and service sectors, from expatriate private ownership to Zairean private ownership. One of the major forces behind this process was a concern to gain greater control for the political elite over the resources of the Zairean economy, so that the profits generated could more easily be appropriated; another was to extend the range of resources under nominal state control, and to increase the profits available to a "bureaucratic elite."

This was the reality of the second type of history Rodney had identified: the "return to an ageless African history." As he explained explicitly: "I feel that the talk of authenticity has generally been associated with this desire to suggest . . . colonialism really did not make much of an impact." Rodney then moves onto his "third framework of analysis," which sees colonialism not as a minor moment in the continent's history but as a "major intervention" in Africa's politics and societies. This third position is aligned to Rodney's own perspective. As he describes to the students, "Colonialism in spite of being in Africa for a mere 70, 80 or 100 years, made a tremendous impact and that impact is visible and will continue to be visible on the African continent." He observes: "Colonialism reinforced tendencies that had already begun with the trade in slaves . . . for those sections of the African continent which were involved in the trading of slaves, it represented their first major involvement in the world economy and that with the coming of colonialism that involvement was going to be intensified in very many ways."

One thing that is astonishing about the course—and the "special anniversary book" produced in 1984 by Tetzlaff and Lock—is the scope of the lectures. The effect for the students, activists, and academics present must have been intoxicating. Early on in the course, Rodney takes the audience to the "start" of modern African history, which he places in context: "If we start in the 15th century with the first slave traders and we say it was a mere four [or] five centuries with the 1000s of years of African history," Rodney explains, then this might suggest that the European experience was relatively insignificant. But this would be a fatal mistake because these "modern centuries" in recent African history, Rodney argues, "have been so dynamic that it is necessary to see the involvement of Africa with Europe and with America as the really decisive phase in the development of modern Africa."

Rodney's complete confidence, mastery, and ease when surveying the five-century-long history of Africa in these lectures is remarkable. He provides historical detail, though he is never lost in the details; this is seen, for example, in his examination of the movements of resistance to imperial competition for African territory (including to the Portuguese colonies in Guinea) that led to the Berlin Conference in 1884 and the colonial scramble on the continent. He does this all within a Marxist framework that is never imposed or forced on the material.

He rapidly moves on to examine the solidarity between colonial liberation movements and the "labor movements and left-wing movements of the colonializing powers themselves." While this solidarity did exist, it was highly uneven; thus, "one notes . . . that the French communist party was the largest communist party in Western Europe . . . [and] was itself ideologically tied to its own bourgeois state apparatus with regard to colonial rule."[7] Rodney is quite right on the appalling role of the French Communist Party (PCF) over Algeria. But he is wrong that the PCF was the biggest communist party in Western Europe; in fact, the Italian party was bigger. Nevertheless, Rodney had studied the history of the Algerian struggle against the French in the 1950s in some detail. The French Left had equivocated, failing to support the Front de Libération Nationale (FLN) and the war. Though individual members supported the war for liberation, the PCF's official pronouncements were dreadful. They argued that the revolution would take place in France, not in Algeria, and that Algerian nationalists must follow the political lead of the French proletariat. Algeria was not ready for independence, let alone revolution. The greatest threat, the PCF stated, was that an independent Algeria could fall into the clutches of American imperialism.

What gives Rodney's lectures such a dynamic and living energy is that he was often interrupted by the audience with questions and queries. On Algeria, for example, one student asserts, "There are opinions many of which go back to the writings of Frantz Fanon which say that the use of violence or the armed struggle is a necessary pre-condition for a real independence, and you have already indicated that there are other ways of struggle."

Rodney responds: "I think Fanon himself of course was aware of the different possibilities of access to Independence. . . . But what we have to take as the premise is this: African people, as such, did not make the decision about armed struggle or no armed struggle; that decision was really dictated by the character of colonial rule." Rodney was not simply a teacher in Hamburg but a militant whose own activism in Guyana at the time would raise the possibility of armed struggle. He was responding—and lecturing—as a scholar and militant involved in the *ongoing* post-independence struggle for liberation in the Caribbean.

While the lectures were incredibly well prepared, based on intense scholarship and reading, Rodney also made detours, such as to recommend other books and writers. As with all aspects of Rodney's life, the course was an effort to educate and politicize students and activists. Despite his serious clash with John Saul years before at the University of Dar es Salaam, he praised the latter's "writings," explaining that Saul "developed a clear position on liberation."[8] Returning to Fanon, he says "that there is a quality to the armed struggle that is really absent from other forms of struggle, in that this armed struggle must develop the aspect of social consciousness."[9]

Fanon celebrated the armed struggle in his last book, *The Wretched of the Earth*, in which he seemed to argue that only a liberation movement that takes up arms can achieve the "real freedom" required for liberation. According to Rodney, Fanon in this respect was making a virtue of the FLN's obsession with a "war" for independence, turning what were strategic decisions into the "real struggle." In fact, he notes, it was the popular uprisings—the urban-based engagement, after independence, in the strikes in support for the war against the French—that achieved the greatest shift in the social consciousness.[10]

To Tanzania

Among the most significant parts of Rodney's Hamburg course were his lectures on Tanzania. Partly autobiographical, he starts by telling his students: "My own experience with those who have really loved Nyerere's words or read descriptions or discussions of Tanzanian socialism is normally when they come to Tanzania . . . . they experienced a certain amount of shock." Here, he is speaking about a large community of fraternal scholars, and fellow travelers who came to the country with a romantic notion of "Nyerere's words . . . [and] Tanzanian socialism." Rodney continues, "They had already begun to imagine the society transforming itself into a socialist society of plenty, when in fact we are dealing with an underdeveloped society where poverty and destitution is as much the common run as you would find in any one of the African territories which may not necessarily be claiming to be moving towards socialism." Quickly moving on to consider Tanzania's history and political economy, Rodney explains to his listeners that the real explanation of this "underdevelopment" was caused by the fact that Tanzania "began at the rear."

While Kenya was the regional hub, the economic "sub-imperialist center," the low level of productive forces in Tanzania earned the country the dubious honor of being the "Cinderella of East Africa." Yet there was nothing mythical or preordained about Tanzanian socialism; on the contrary, the country had approached development at independence in the conventional way. When the existing patterns of dependency in the country continued and failed to yield anything approximating pro-poor development, there was a radical reorientation in the country, Rodney told the class.

Rodney then proceeds to provide a detailed analysis of independence and dependency in the country—while maintaining his engaging and direct speaking style with the audience:

> That is another thing you have to learn when you are looking at third world countries, when you see companies and firms that begin with Tanganyika this, or Sudan this or Nigeria this, don't entertain any illusions that they belong to Tanzania or Sudan or Nigeria, in fact that is precisely the moment when you have to become suspicious because foreign firms like to decorate their companies with the names of these national countries.

He illustrates his point with a vivid example: the Tanganyika Development Finance Company, which sounds "home grown," a national example, but it is in fact "partly owned by the Netherlands Government."

With his exceptional power of explanation, Rodney provides the simplest description of what actually happened to a newly independent African country as it reached for economic development. Foreign governments and companies, he explains,

> simply said to African governments and other third world countries "we are going to set up a manufacturing center in your country. This is in line with your development strategy, you are becoming industrialized. Now if we are going to help you to be industrialized then obviously you must include the conditions under which this industry would succeed. You must provide tariff protection against other exports from Europe and Asia." . . . Never mind that the domestic industry is owned lock, stock, and barrel in many instances by foreign firms, it's still called domestic, it is still seen as local industry.

Though a trained historian, Rodney shows himself here as a master of contemporary political economy. As an activist and revolutionary, he had to be on top of current events, trends, and economics. Focusing intensely on his Tanzanian case study in the course, Rodney continues to detail the predicament the country faced. He describes a Japanese radio assembly line that wanted to produce in Tanzania. Philips, an Anglo-Dutch firm, insisted on tariffs of 37.5 percent, then 50 percent, "and really this was part of their struggle to keep Matsushita [the Japanese electronics firm] out of Tanzania." The solution was part of the standard rule book for multinationals operating in the region: an incorporation with the domestic economy in order to secure protection as if it was a national industry.

From this low economic level—colonial-era dependence and the failure to build a genuine autonomous basis for independence—President Julius Nyerere had pioneered the Ujamaa program for socialist economic development. As we have seen, Ujamaa was celebrated widely around the world by left-wing radicals. But by 1978, Rodney was extraordinarily sober in his analysis. He explains to the class:

> [U]jamaa has not increased production in Tanzania. It has not transformed technology. . . . It has not transformed social relations in the countryside as it aimed at. . . . It has strengthened the bureaucracy. It has failed to cut the dependency links . . . And at the ideological level it has created confusion in so far as it has sought to negate the concept of class struggle and class responsibilities.

All of this is extremely important. Rodney is saying—a few years after he left Tanzania—that Ujamaa has failed at every level and that, fundamentally, it has "created confusion" at the level of class struggle and class responsibility.[11] In the context of a state policy of socialist development, class conflict was rendered "subversive" or reactionary—despite the fact, as Rodney has just explained, that this development strategy failed categorically in any of its stated "socialist" objectives.

Rodney ploughs deeper into his argument. He asks the class: "Is it that they fail to grow because of socialism? The argument on the left is that they failed to transform social structures. They did precisely what other capitalist intensive plans also failed to do." What counts, Rodney argues, is whether the wider "social structure is mastering the technology and using it for its own purposes or whether that technology appears as an imposition which could weaken peoples capacity to control their environment."

Ujamaa, Rodney argued in Hamburg, was frequently greeted as a nuisance, alien and foreign to the very people at whom it was officially aimed—delivered from above without a coordinated plan, imposed with state edicts, even if the intentions were well meaning. The reforms were greeted at best with bemusement, and at worst with open hostility among the poorest communities. Without a self-generated, popular engagement from below, Tanzanian state socialism felt like the blind and ignorant processes of a repressive overlord; it mattered little that the intentions were noble, Rodney said. It was unpopular in some areas where capitalist farmers were displaced or pastoralists were forced into villages, but not in others where poor farmers were mobilized and given resources.[12]

Rodney then turns his attention to Tanzania's international position during the period of Ujamaa. Did the policies of the "socialist" state, he asks, manage to cut the "external dependency links"? When these questions are posed of Tanzania's projects and policies, Rodney explains, there is much on the "negative side." Indeed, the period saw, in his words, a "high degree of integration of Tanzania into the same capitalist economy from which it was supposedly trying to expiate itself." Rarely, he says, did these projects allow "for the utilization of domestic resources in a way that would be consistent with the principle of self-reliance."

This scathing criticism of Tanzania's socialism is immensely significant. Rodney was not just any critic; he had been one of the country's most intelligent and thoughtful supporters. His criticism came from deep—and no doubt painful—analysis of the country's realities and its failed hopes. Rodney's position on the country was one he had arrived at both by direct and personal experience in Tanzania, and by deep scholarly engagement with the country's and continent's political economy since he had left in 1974.

From such failures to sever the links with the global economy, Rodney goes on to explain there was an even more disastrous reversal of self-reliance: the "penetration" of the Tanzanian economy by the World Bank. The "bureaucratic bourgeoisie" in the country, which had grown at an alarming rate, had fallen into the hands of the international financial institution. Rodney described to the class his own astonishment: "I still find it surprising; I still find it a little difficult to explain. Because even from their own mass perspectives at one time, it seemed as though they were interested in a more independent development, and there is just no way you can be independent when under the control and supervision of the World Bank." The World Bank, Rodney explains, was organized to maintain the international economy in exactly its current shape.

Extrapolating from circumstances in the UK, Rodney describes how the Labour government—under the pressure of a financial crisis in 1976—requested a loan of US$4 billion from the International Monetary Fund (IMF). In return, the government were obliged to slash public expenditure. The loan signaled the beginning of the end for social democracy in the UK. In Rodney's words, the IMF want to "make sure that you return your economy to a very solid foundation within the context of international capitalism. They say that to Britain, they say that to Portugal." Rodney was pointing to the devastating process of global restructuring that saw the economies of the global South forced into the hands of the IMF and World Bank in the 1970s. Both institutions made loans available on the condition that the flimsy edifice of state protection and provision was pulled away. The Third World was at the start of the process of structural adjustment, and Rodney was one of its first and most trenchant critics.

If the effects of these policies could be felt in the North—in the UK—it was in the Third World that the impact was most devastating, Rodney argues. He lists the first wave of adjustment, "from Egypt through to Peru, Jamaica and of course Tanzania." Commenting on the objectives of the IMF for Tanzania, he observes, "An institution of that magnitude with such clear objectives in reproducing the system of social relations of international capitalism could only represent a very disastrous trend within the Tanzanian political economy."

However, Rodney acknowledges that there were serious efforts by the government, or some of the leading left-wing figures of the ruling TANU party, to implement a more thoroughgoing transformation. On the president, he explains, "[I]n many speeches, Nyerere himself was very perceptive in admitting that TANU needed to change, needed to reaffirm and reassess itself as a liberation movement, and not just as the old nationalist party."

A year before Rodney delivered this course, TANU had merged with the ruling party in Zanzibar, the Afro-Shirazi Party—from the neighboring island, off the coast of Dar es Salaam—to form a new party, Chama Cha Mapinduzi, or the Revolutionary State Party. The newly named "revolutionary" party was intended to promote popular and democratic participation in the country. Even this gesture, which was welcomed by some as signaling the continued "struggle against exploitation, colonialism, neo-colonialism and imperialism,"[13] was categorically condemned by Rodney. "In spite of all the rhetoric," he argues, "TANU has not been transformed, . . . it remained and remains a nationalist party under the control of the petit bourgeoise . . . incapable of providing the basis for sustained socialist transformation."

Rodney argues that the party is thoroughly integrated into the state and reflects and represents the dominant classes. Rodney then throws his weight behind a renewed and radical project of liberation in Portugal's African colonies. He explains, "[W]hen we look at Guinea-Bissau and we look at Mozambique and Angola, we find that these liberation movements were the only ones who asked themselves: 'Can we build the party now, while fighting for independence which will have dynamism to continue after independence to transform society?'"[14]

The second wave of independence was going to avoid the pitfalls of national liberation and blossom, Rodney explained, into a fuller "dynamic . . . to transform society." However, the intense pressures of global capitalism upon states—of which Rodney was the foremost Marxist critic—meant they were largely powerless to bring about the transformation sought. Instead of drawing out possible challenges these new radical movements would face in government, Rodney expressed hope in the possibility of a renewed project of socialist change. He was in good company; many shared his cautious hope in the new liberation movements in Portuguese's ex-colonies. If Tanzania had failed, then maybe Mozambique could succeed.

Much of the Left was equally enthusiastic at the possibility of socialist success in this second wave of independence. Founded as a radical publication to provide fraternal intellectual support for radical politics on the continent, the *Review of African Political Economy* was first published in 1974. The project was initially conceived by Lionel Cliffe, who Rodney had known in Tanzania, and other activists and researchers, including many who had lived and worked in Tanzania and others exiles from apartheid South Africa. Many of these activists and researchers now looked to the new projects of radical liberation as enthusiastic and "critical supporters." Rodney was clearly aware of the *Review*, but he kept his distance.[15]

Though Rodney was skeptical of the second wave of independence, his instinct—like much of his generation, including those then running the *Review*—was to swing behind the "renewed" radical liberation projects in Portugal's ex-colonies. He expressed this cautious desire in his Hamburg lectures:

> [T]his is what Cabral asked of PAIGC [African Party for the Independence of Guinea and Cape Verde]. And this is what FRELIMO [Liberation Front of Mozambique] and the MPLA [People's Movement for the Liberation of Angola] said themselves. . . . Now we don't know yet whether they will succeed. . . . But at least they raised the question.

As brilliant as Rodney's analysis is on the failure of national liberation in Tanzania (and elsewhere), he continues to express hope for other radical projects. If the project of transformation in Tanzania had failed, there was no need to despair because, farther to the south, socialism had found a more fertile home in Mozambique and Angola (and also in Guinea-Bissau and Cape Verde in the west). Yet the same predicament of liberation and independence awaited the poor in these countries—and for largely the same reasons that Rodney had so brilliantly outlined in Hamburg.

Almost answering his own equivocal hope about the second wave of critical independence in Portugal's ex-colonies, Rodney concludes: "[I]t is of course a mistake to see Tanzania as unique and it is important to recognize that it fits within the general pattern which we have been discussing so far by which the colonisation process ended through an alliance of classes . . . *but within this alliance the workers and peasants never really had hegemony*" (my emphasis). From Tanzania, Rodney had learned an invaluable lesson. As the leading organizer of the WPA in Guyana, he was determined to give this "worker and peasant" constituency hegemony in the struggles that they were fighting in Corriverton, Georgetown, Linden, and New Amsterdam. This is not to say that Rodney's emphasis in his writing and activism had not *always* been with the poor and working class, but that there was now a shift in giving this agency hegemony, or leadership, over state-led projects of socialist transformation.

Yet even more tantalizing is Rodney's comment in the lectures about the absurdity of colonial borders: namely, their ability to slice through the continent's communities, generating nation-states that were hopelessly incapable of resolving the issues of development that beset them. Rodney refers to Gambia—the sliver of land in the middle of Senegal—as an example. What capacity was there within this contrived and artificial colonial state to create a functioning country? Yet surely the same question could be asked of Guyana and many other states in Africa and the Caribbean. As Rodney had already explained, if the UK's "dependence" on the international capitalist economy curtailed *its* ability to maneuver, what hope was there for poor, peripheral countries in the Third World?

What is necessary, Rodney tells his class in Hamburg, is to situate the analysis "within the context of a world economy and this is a world capitalist economy." Indeed, Rodney's very first intellectual quest was to capture the connections between history and contemporary developments. "My own work initially came about precisely through an awareness that somehow neither the historian nor the economist in the traditional schools . . . had really sought to try and understand why the present was the way it was . . . to find the analysis which explains the inequality that could only have been done with a dynamic historical context."

It is the interaction between historical elements that is key. As Rodney explains, he used historical work to examine the impact of European involvement on the continent, first in the slave trade and later with colonization, in order to glean the full meaning of the present. For Rodney, the project involved examining the "fabric" of African history and, in his words, "the way in which there were independent forms in which people lived their own lives and produced." At the same time, these "independent forms" became "interwoven . . . with the international economy during the period of slavery and the slave trade and this had its impact on African development."

This was Rodney's method. His application of historical research—as the prerequisite for any serious Marxist analysis—sets his work and writing apart from a generation of Marxist scholarship. To be a Marxist—to understand contemporary social and political forms, and then chart a path forward—requires a thorough historical understanding. Indeed, Marxism without history is stale grandstanding, an approach devoid of analytical power and insight.

However, it is when Rodney begins his analysis of agency and activism that the excitement becomes tangible.

A Fork in the Road

In the final section of his lectures in Hamburg, Rodney moves on to discuss class struggle in Tanzania. In this part of the course, Rodney's mature thinking is a giddying roller coaster, audacious and brilliant. He tells his class, "The idea of class struggle does not suit a bureaucratic bourgeoisie or any sector of the petit-bourgeois, because it's an idea that speaks about the negation of their own existence over time."

Here, Rodney dispenses with the widely held notion of the working class in Africa as an "aristocracy," in some ways privileged in the post-colonial state. As he explains, "In some parts of the ideological justification of Tanzanian socialism [they] come very close to saying that the worker is an exploiter of the peasantry, that the workers are part of the exploiting classes. Even though the workers earn a minimum wage, even though the workers in the towns and in the countryside were in the vanguard of the struggle against colonialism."[16]

In 1978, Rodney argued that this argument was now being advanced by the "petit bourgeoise . . . who were trying to disseminate this idea that workers exploit the countryside." This was a self-serving point that could be used against wage claims and demands "for a larger share of the surplus which they produce." These were not abstract arguments in an academic discussion, but justifications made in the organization of the Tanzanian state (and "socialist" and "capitalist" states across the continent). Nyerere, the radical president of Tanzania, was fond of making such claims himself; Rodney explained, "[I]f the workers ask for more, the bureaucratic bourgeoise would reply, 'You are getting that at the expense of the peasants.'"

On the role of the state in Tanzania, his attitude had become much more critical. In the strikes and occupations reported by Issa Shivji in his 1976 *Class Struggles in Tanzania*, and noted by Rodney, there was a new politics in formation.[17] Reporting on the "workerist" turn in the factory occupations in the early 1970s, Rodney tells his audience, "We as workers are capable of running this enterprise more efficiently than the economic bureaucracy." In posing a direct challenge to the management of companies, workers were "making arguments that went beyond their own immediate material interests. They were carrying the class . . . to even higher levels by in fact posing the question who should control production."

In these struggles from below, celebrated by Rodney, he saw a direct challenge to a state that had declared itself socialist, and the possibility of a new society based on that class challenge. However, there were serious obstacles. "Even though theoretically the Tanzanian revolution accepted a greater role for workers, when they made an important policy statement in 1971 called Mwongozo . . . the workers themselves tried to implement the rights that was supposedly safe-guarded by Mwongozo." Rodney records one of these cases:

> In one very important instance, workers actually took over a factory and they didn't take it over from the government, they took it over from a private owner. . . . And they said we can run this factory which was a rubber factory, [Mount] Carmel Rubber Factory. . . . They locked out the management and they were running the factory. And this caused the greatest excitement and fear on the part of the bureaucracy.

Rodney draws the vital and obvious conclusion, as did Tanzania's political elite: "[I]f workers were running one factory then maybe they will run another and another. And this doesn't look too good for the economic wing of the bureaucracy . . . their whole rationale of production as a class would disappear if there was workers' control . . . so they moved to crush those initiatives." In other words, it made no difference what the complexion of the government's rhetoric had been; the threat of these occupations, and the possibilities for real transformation that they contained, was the same. The strikes and occupations had to be stamped out.

Rejoicing at what the "bureaucratic bourgeoise" despised, Rodney goes on: "What in English we call wild-cat strikes, [are] not strikes which the union initiates but strikes which come from below. The workers themselves decide on direct action." The "unorganised" strike, not prearranged by trade union leaders, becomes the center of Rodney's focus in these reflections.[18] However, it was not simply the strike with which he was concerned, but rather what the strike encompasses. Emerging from such action, apart from the immediate material interests of the workers themselves, were the seeds of another society and power.

Rodney's own political transformation can be seen in these comments—in particular, his emphasis on working-class self-activity in wildcat strikes and occupations. Indeed, Rodney's own experiences since 1974—as one of the WPA's leading militants in Guyana—had drawn him closer than he had ever been to the politics of the working class. More than any manifesto, book, or declaration, this direct involvement in the struggle caused his thinking to shift. Working in the WPA, but also with partner groups, including the Organization of Working People, had convinced Rodney of the emancipatory "power" he spoke about in Germany—the power of unofficial action. All the same, a significant part of his analysis of Tanzania, and the dramatic spike in working-class struggle in the country, was indebted to the research of Shivji, his former comrade and student.

Class Struggles in Tanzania

Issa Shivji's book was an important influence on Rodney. In Rodney's Hamburg lectures, he highlights the text in a note to students as "essential reading" and then references it throughout the course. Since its publication in 1976, *Class Struggles* had been the most significant and rigorous Marxist critique of Nyerere's Tanzania and the efforts at socialist change. Even reading it today, when nothing of Nyerere's left-wing and socialist garb remains intact, the effect is still startling. Nyerere's projects, from the the nationalization of firms to the collectivization of farms, are exposed as "petty-bourgeois nationalist reforms" that have not challenged the underlying legacy of capitalism and underdevelopment in Tanzania. Drawing a comparison to the classic fairy tale *The Emperor's New Clothes*, Shivji declares fearlessly: "The emperor is not wearing anything at all!"

Rodney's activist work among the workers and the poor in Guyana had led him to reach similar conclusions—regarding not only the agency of the poor but also Burnham's claims to socialism. Likewise, Shivji exposed the lie of Tanzania's great socialist hope. Shivji shut down the idea of socialist change from above, with which a generation had flirted in Tanzania and elsewhere. But his immense gift to the Marxist Left in his 1976 book was to bring class struggle to the center of socialist transformation; throughout, he quotes Lenin's line: "[O]utside the class struggle, socialism is either a hollow phrase or a naïve dream."

This was the basis of Shivji's critique of Nyerere.[19] It may seem odd to the chronology of a book on Rodney that we make a detour to Tanzania, but a critical "return to Tanzania" and everything it represented—its dizzying heights of political hope—is exactly what Rodney was doing in Hamburg, furiously excavating the illusions of Nyerere's failure and recovering the indispensable core of emancipatory Marxism.

Essentially, the book describes the class nature of the project of transformation in Tanzania since independence; at the same time, however, the volume is a challenge to what was apparently a radical and fashionable thought across the continent at the time. In the preface, Shivji explains how the book came out of his *The Silent Class Struggle*, published in 1971: "I have tried to give an outline sketch of the class struggles in Tanzania since independence." Though not pretending to write a definitive account, he explains, "My aim has been simply to indicate the course of these struggles and hope that further historical research will fill in the many gaps that no doubt exists in the present work."[20] Predicting that the volume would upset those seeking "celebration" of Tanzania's "experiment," Shivji explains that his analysis is aimed not at celebration or criticism, but explanation.

Shivji then details Marx's method and theory of class struggle, challenging, first of all, the "alleged non-existence" of classes and class struggle in Africa and in the work and practice of African socialism. He writes: "The propagation of the non-existence of classes and its theoretical rationalisation in the elite theories attempt to exclude by definition the Marxist theoretical tools and therefore the possibility of genuine revolutionary movements." Among a group of African socialists, including Nyerere, the rejection of class struggle was a near-universal principle, or, as Shivji puts it, "The expounding of the revolutionary ideology as applied to concrete conditions in Africa is at once condemned as un-African."[21] Whether in the writing of Léopold Senghor, Kwame Nkrumah (before 1966), or Nyerere, Marxism was condemned as an alien ideology, imposed by the North, with little in common with African conditions.

Instead, Shivji develops a rigorous Marxist account of the country's trajectory. Indeed, his entire book is a sustained and creative application of Marxism to Tanzania's political economy—not as an aberrant or exceptional part of the world, but one tied into the whole fabric of global capitalism. Nor is the exercise an academic one; it is rooted in the practice and politics of the oppressed classes. On this, Shivji was categorical: "[P]otential revolutionaries must themselves fully appreciate the theoretical problems involved because they have immediate significance and relevance for guiding *revolutionary practice*." In fact, Shivji is scathing about "metropolitan academic Marxists"—an argument that Rodney would have shared—who, quite unlike an earlier generation of Marxists, have not been involved in revolutionary practice.[22]

Chapter 2 discusses the applicability of Marxism to Africa—or the predicament thereof. Shivji debunks certain important myths. As we have seen, one of the central arguments at the time saw "Marxist socialism" as a peculiar development of the global North, with exclusive relevance to the developed economies. In Africa, as Shivji writes, "there is no highly developed capitalism and, therefore, according to Marxism, we would first have to develop capitalism." However, this is impossible, he argues; therefore, the capitalist stage must be skipped: "[W]e must build socialism on the basis of African traditions—hence African Socialism."[23] Like Rodney in *How Europe Underdeveloped Africa*, Shivji argues that Tanzania and all parts of the continent are intimately connected to global capitalism: "[W]hen we talk about Africa today . . . we are talking about the countries which have had long historical relations with advanced capitalist countries and which now form part of the world capitalist system."[24]

Shivji concludes:

> [B]uilding of socialism is not skipping or jumping the capitalist stage for we are very much part of the capitalist relations. . . . Neither is the option of developing vigorous national capitalisms open to many African countries for, among other things, it would require disengagement from the international capitalist system, a period of primitive capital accumulation (without the slave trade or the colonies!), a vigorous national bourgeoisie to do this and the docile masses to endure a long period of sacrifice.[25]

Against this impossibility, Shivji suggests another route, centered on the struggle of classes—"a social-political struggle against existing relations of production, which are responsible for throttling the development of productive forces."[26] Given Tanzania and the continent's "underdevelopment," this struggle is, he argues, "going to be arduous and calls for new tactics and strategies." At the heart of this battle is "a struggle of classes. . . . The fight against the existing natural conditions is inseparably tied with the fight against existing socio-economic organisation."[27]

There is, Shivji is clear, no capitalist path. What there is of a national bourgeoisie in Africa is neither national nor bourgeois—where there was the development of such a class in the nineteenth century in Egypt or Madagascar, for example, it was snuffed out when it came into contact with advanced capitalism. Instead, a "petty bourgeois" elite, tied to metropolitan capitalism, does not have an economic base; it is, rather, the leading role this class played in independence that has bestowed on it the function of ruling.

Unlike many of his generation, Shivji does not abandon working-class agency, even if he makes certain important addendums to classical Marxism. "In many African countries" he argues,

large groups of wage-earners employed in large capitalist industry . . .
did not develop and could not have possibly developed in the conditions
of the colonial . . . economies. Nevertheless, in all these countries a class
of wage-earners did develop . . . employed mainly on plantations, in the
docks, in transport and commerce, and in construction, building, etc.

Despite evident "weaknesses" in the development of an African working class, they played a strategic role in the struggle for independence, conscious of their position and their economic importance, frequently launching
strikes and initiatives without any support. The key, Shivji argues, to the
development, or furtherment, of "this potential revolutionary strata" is that
they are "mobilised under the leadership of the *proletarian ideology.*"[28]

These arguments may seem self-evident, or unremarkable; however,
we must try to glimpse them in their context. Shivji was not writing a
monograph that would see him through to his next academic promotion
(in fact, a book that targeted Nyerere's very political foundations would
likely have had the opposite effect); while an assertion of the revolutionary role of the working class in Africa was an act of considerable daring,
placing this class and its struggles at the center of Marxism was a far
more radical undertaking—forcing a break with many narratives on the
Left that were fashionable at the time. Marxism with class struggle at its
heart, Shivji announced in 1976, was not a "foreign" or imposed theory, as
African socialists would have it. Rather, Shivji applied Marxist methods
to the history of class struggle in Tanzania.[29]

Shivji proceeds to pull up the foundation stones of Tanzania's socialist
achievements. The Arusha Declaration, he writes, marked the "end of one
phase of struggle between the petty bourgeoise and the commercial bourgeois and the beginning of the second."[30] The "commercial bourgeois,"
made up almost exclusively of Tanzania's Asian population had long mo-
nopolized the "import and export business"; therefore, with the nationalization of these sectors, the class was largely broken. The declaration
was an important "staging post," not in the dismantling of Tanzanian
capitalism but in the development of the "bureaucratic bourgeoisie." This
"bureaucratic" class used the rhetoric of socialism, which, while hollow,
did usher in a period of debates and discussion on the meaning of socialism and Marxism.[31] Shivji's own contributions were a direct expression of
this period of debate and learning.

Prior to this period, the government had already effectively banned
strikes, while moving the National Union of Tanganyika Workers (NUTA)

in 1964 under government control. In an effort to secure social acquiescence, it had implemented certain reforms, including a minimum wage, security of employment legislation, and the National Provident Fund; yet in exchange, the government wanted to see an increase in "productivity" in the name of "national development." Reinforcing a widespread notion of privilege, a 1967 report by Professor Turner, entitled "Wages, Incomes and Prices Policy" (written for the International Labour Organization), argued that workers had secured their increase in wages at the direct expense of peasants. The government concurred, going so far as to say that the report dovetailed with the socialist principles of the Arusha Declaration. Shivji explains, "[S]acrifices, rises in productivity, restraint in wage demands, etc., were asked of workers when the profits of the capitalists continued to increase." This apparent contradiction—austerity for workers, profits for the bosses—was resolved by the state becoming a majority shareholder in private enterprises.[32] Now that the businesses they worked for were officially "theirs," workers could be pressed even harder.

There was another element in the report that Shivji highlights: it drove a wedge between the working class and the peasantry. How could they possibly come together in united struggle if they were objective antagonists in the fight against capital? Shivji disagreed with this thesis, and he challenged much left-wing orthodoxy at the time—not least the writings of Fanon in *The Wretched of the Earth*. Fanon had seen the urban working class as a privileged colonial class whose interests stood in direct opposition to both the lumpenproletariat in shantytowns and slums, and the "revolutionary peasantry." Both groups were exalted for their selfless revolutionary activity. In this respect, Shivji argues, Fanon had been wrong.

The Arusha Declaration, therefore, was not a socialist project; instead it saw the deepening involvement of the state in trade, milling, export and import, and in light industries, substantially dislodging the commercial bourgeoisie. The resulting exodus of the Asian bourgeoise, Shivji noted, was almost universal, though "in a few cases, those without ready money took loans to get out of the country."[33] To see these celebrated reforms—which have continued, somehow, to glitter and dazzle through the intervening decades—subjected to such ruthless scrutiny, in a text written forty-five years ago, is impressive.

Along with the "bureaucratic bourgeoisie's" growing confidence and dominance, Shivji notes, had come the development of a panoply of class benefits. Its high income levels secured access to education and medical facilities; its urban base secured access to the best services. The class also had everything it needed for its own continued reproduction. Common social and income status meant that the class mixed together, in bars, clubs, hotels, and neighborhoods—even if this social reproduction was pathetic by the standards of the European or North American bourgeoisie, in its "age-old exclusive social and cultural class-institutions."[34]

As we have seen, although the Arusha Declaration did not launch a socialist transformation of the country, it did have one enduring legacy. For many years afterward, it raised a debate on socialism, and through the critique of its program and promises, it "put socialism on the agenda for the first time in a concrete way."[35]

Moving on, Shivji examines the vaunted programs of villagization and Ujamaa, which were efforts to integrate non-monetarized (or subsistence) sectors into the cash economy. This meant, in his words, deeper "integration within the world capitalist system." The task of a "real transformation" of agriculture, he writes, "is above everything else, [a] . . . political struggle—class struggle against the internal and external classes with vested interests in maintaining and perpetuating the existing relations of production."[36] Needless to say, the policy of Ujamaa did not quite see things in this way.

Having pulled away the veil of the Tanzanian socialist experiment, Shivji turns his attention to the actual class struggle. Specifically, he writes of the "transformation of the people themselves through struggle."[37] It is here that the book receives its fullest development in Rodney's hands in Hamburg.

As we have seen, Shivji dismantles the notion of the "labor aristocracy"—which lifted the peasantry to the status of revolutionary class. He argues that the working class and its political potential rest on its position in the process of production more than its numerical size. Though tiny compared to its Northern counterpart, it plays, he argues, "an important role in the process of production but a very strategic one too. . . . To be sure, even in the independence struggle the workers were in the forefront."[38] By contrast, Shivji remarks: "There has been no example in Africa where the peasants have played a leading revolutionary role while the workers have sided with the dominating classes. It is a complete confusion therefore to identify the whole working class (as [Giovanni] Arrighi does) as a labor aristocracy."

The most exciting parts of Shivji's book are when he turns his focus directly to a wave of working-class struggles in Tanzania. During the post-Mwongozo period that he examines—the high point of post-independence class struggle—numerous strikes and occupations took place. As we have seen, Mwongozo guidelines were a code of conduct for party members, written in the context of both the invasion of Guinea in November 1970 by Portuguese mercenaries (so-called Operation Green Sea, targeting fighters from Amílcar Cabral's PAIGC) and the coup that overthrew President Milton Obote in Uganda (Tanzania's neighbor) in January 1971. These joint operations, carried out against similarly radical regimes in Africa, had alarmed the Tanzanian government. Nyerere saw the two events as a direct challenge, in his words, to "progressive African countries."[39]

The Mwongozo guidelines, published in 1971, stated clearly that in the case of Uganda, "imperialism prefers to use local puppets to overthrow the legitimate government and replace it with a government of 'foremen,' and that "such a local government will allow the imperialists to exploit national wealth in partnership with the local bourgeoisie." The aim of the guidelines was to deepen the involvement of people in decision making, and to hold party leaders to account; thus, according to Shivji, this leadership must not be, "arrogant, extravagant, contemptuous, and oppressive."[40]

For Shivji—reading between the lines—the Mwongozo document was a broadside by a section of the "bureaucratic bourgeois" against rightwing members of the petty bourgeoisie who they regarded as posing "a potential threat, possibly even with the backing of colonial and racist powers like Portugal and South Africa,"[41] who might attempt an overthrow of the Tanzanian government.

The impact of the document calling for popular reengagement with Tanzania's anti-imperialist project was a series of workers' actions—"wildcats," as Rodney referred to them in his Hamburg lectures—including a series of strikes and occupations. Many of these actions were taken in the name of Mwongozo. None of these strikes were expected, or indeed welcomed, by the government. In May 1973, the *Monthly Bulletin* of the Federation of Tanganyika Employers complained that it was the "famous clause 15 of the TANU [Mwongozo] Guidelines"—the above-cited line on "arrogance, extravagance, contemptuous and oppressive" attitudes by party leaders—to which striking workers frequently referred as a motivation. The bulletin noted that, "[a] characteristic style is that workers stop working immediately when the unwanted Manager enters the compound of the firm, and the work resumes again when the victim steps out of the fence."[42]

The action was not sanctioned by the trade union movement. On the contrary, the NUTA had by then become the only officially sanctioned union, firmly under the control of the ruling party. Bureaucratic and state-sanctioned "workers committees," established as part of the Security of Employment Act of 1964, were seen as ways of controlling and disciplining workers; these committees, however, played an important role in the post-Mwongozo worker struggles. Shivji notes a curious fact: it is "the workers' committee which is closest to the workers . . . and . . . being wholly elected, the militant workers were able to get elected to the committees and thereby provide the necessary leadership in the post-Mwongozo period."[43]

Shivji also notes that working-class strikes were not marginal to the success of Tanzania's independence, but crucial to it: "[T]he workers strikes in the late 1950s played a crucial role in the struggle for independence. In the three years (1958–60) just before independence, there were 561 strikes involving 239,803 workers, 2,194,212 man-days lost, the greatest number to be recorded."[44] This number dropped to 613,778 days lost in the years between 1961 and 1964, and then, remarkably, to 26,518 from 1965 to 1970.[45] By 1971, Shivji writes, "having cleared all the ground, the fundamental contradiction between the 'bureaucratic bourgeoisie' and the workers came to the fore and asserted itself in a dramatic way in the post-Mwongozo 'downing of tools.'"[46] In the period of the post-Mwongozo strikes between February 1971 and September 1973, there were thirty-one "downings of tools," involving something like 28,708 workers and almost 64,000 days lost in strikes. This is twice the figure for the previous six years, from 1965 to 1970.[47]

However, these initiatives involved not just strike action, but also general militancy and class consciousness. In the later periods of this action, workers started to "lock out" officials who they could not tolerate; later, as workers' action intensified, there were direct factory "takeovers." These resulted, in some cases, in the sacking of the entire workforce.[48] In the great majority of these actions, NUTA was entirely absent.

The wave of working-class militancy was not only centered on remuneration; frequently, workers made "nonwage" demands, including for better treatment of workers by management—with workers enthusiastically citing the famous clause in the TANU's Mwongozo guidelines. In a strike at Tanganyika Motors in January 1974, workers locked out four of the company's top officials, who they claimed looked down on African workers. (Though there is no account of their specific grievances in the book, the abuse would have been intensely real.) Management responded by shutting down the entire enterprise. A NUTA official tried to get the workers back to work by explaining that the factory's contract with Peugeot was important because these cars were used by government institutions; therefore, for the sake of the country, workers should return to work. A worker representative replied to the official that "human dignity was more important than the economy of the country."[49]

Another strike reported by Shivji at the British American Tobacco Company of Tanzania—a subsidiary of the National Development Corporation—took place in 1973. On May 23, when Mr. Kashaija, the personnel manager, came into the factory, a fire alarm was sounded, and workers immediately stopped work. A delegation of workers went to his office and ordered him to leave the factory, or his office would be pulled down. Mr. Kashaija was accused by the workers of using resources "extravagantly," in breach of the TANU code—in particular, they cited his use of the company's Range Rover and of company money to throw a party for members of the elite. The demands escalated: not only did the workers want Kashaija dismissed, but they drew attention to the wider discrimination in the company. One worker, for instance, complained that while workers received "prison food," the senior management members were served "delicious dishes of tourist standards."[50] Only when the police arrived at the factory armed with guns and tear gas were workers forced to back down. Ultimately, a labor tribunal found that the allegations against the personnel manager were justified and suggested he be removed.

The apex of the militancy, however, was a series of takeovers of factories, which in one case succeeded in forcing the government to support the action. The Mount Carmel Rubber Factory was one example cited by Rodney in his Hamburg course. Conditions at the factory were regarded as deplorable. A workers' committee had been set up in 1971, and NUTA remained almost entirely moribund. Though an agreement was soon drafted by the new workers committee, it was never implemented. Shivji takes up the story: "It was under such circumstances that the workers finally decided to take over the factory . . . encouraged by the neighbouring factory [which had been taken over by the government]." In June 1973 when the personnel manager tried to enter the factory, he was greeted by booing and jeering workers. "He was told," Shivji reports, "by the Chairman of the TANU branch and the workers' committee that the workers did not want him or the Managing Director. . . . The workers had taken over the factory." The workers posted a guard on the gates, while the rest of the workforce continued work—the exterior of the factory was festooned with slogans and placards: "Long live Mwalimu and Mwongozo"; "We are ready to work night and day if allowed to take over the factory"; and "The factory belongs to the workers."[51]

The workers refused to have their dispute negotiated by NUTA or any other labor official. Instead, a regional commissioner came to the factory to negotiate, accompanied by an armed group of policemen. In the midst of these events, workers at Hotel Afrique were infected by the insurgent mood; they too readied themselves to take control of their workplace. Fearful of the example being established across the city, the following day the police arrived with trucks at the occupied factory, where "all workers who refused to accept their employer's leadership were ordered to enter packed vehicles."[52] Sixty-two were driven away to the central police station, leaving only on fifteen workers. Every member of the workers' committee and of the factory's TANU branch had been arrested.

Frightened by the wave of occupations and takeovers, the government warned workers against the "habit of unilaterally taking over factories," explaining that it would not tolerate "unruly behaviour on the part of the workers."[53] By June 21, 1973, the *Daily News* reported joyously that "early yesterday morning the Government re-instated the owner of the firm in his factory and opposed the workers' demands to take it over."[54] Mwalimu, it seemed, had spoken: order had been restored.

Shivji is relentless in his conclusions. "[T]he state," he writes, "thus asserted its class character regardless of the ideology. But in so doing it laid bare the fundamental contradiction between the exploited and the exploiter."[55] Yet there was still work to do. Shivji concludes that the vital exercise of converting class instinct into sustained class consciousness required "proletarian ideology." The astonishing wave of strikes, occupations, and workers' militancy marked the end of a period when workers could be used as "cannon fodder" in petty-bourgeois politics. Finishing the book, Shivji declares, optimistically: "This time it will be their own struggles—their own class war—and the struggle of their fellow exploited class, the poor peasants that they will fight, not to replace one exploiter with another but to begin to replace the very system of exploitation."[56]

The book is a brilliant takedown of the entire socialist pretense of the Nyerere government, which had inspired those who lived and worked in

Dar—Rodney included. While Rodney had reached many of these conclusions himself well before 1978, to see them worked out by a trusted comrade and former student made a lasting impression on him. It was for these reasons that he marked the book as vital reading for students of Africa's (flawed) radical experiments in Hamburg.

However, I am left with an awkward observation: during this immense and important wave of post-Mwongozo strikes and militancy, many prominent socialists were still in Tanzania, working, studying, and teaching. Why was this group of socialists and Marxists unable to relate to an unprecedented period of working-class action, or even to draw the militant leadership into the rich discussions about socialism taking place in the country? Rodney's comrade Karim Hirji makes a similar point, asking the same question of himself and others who were more critical than Rodney of the projects taking place in Tanzania in the early 1970s. He writes, "The irony is that those of us who theoretically critiqued him for having too much hope were not able to fully follow our own recipes for community mobilisation and struggle." By contrast, Rodney's actions were fully consistent with his thinking and, in Hirji's words, "evolved as the concrete conditions demanded."[57] In Hirji's view, Rodney moved into struggle and popular organizing in Guyana better than those around him who had been more advanced in their criticism of Tanzania and Nyerere.

Leaving Hamburg

Rodney concluded his lectures on Tanzania by posing serious questions about Tanzania's radical future. He argued that the apparent rehash of national liberation advocated at the time by TANU was not enough. Rather, "reassert[ing the] liberation movement" was likely to fail. Rodney was clear about this: "[M]y feeling is that in spite of all the rhetoric, TANU has not been transformed, that it remains a nationalist party under the control of the petit bourgeoise . . . incapable of providing the basis for sustained socialist transformation."[58]

In other words, socialist change required pressure from *outside* the ruling party and in opposition to it, much as Rodney's WPA was working against Burnham's regime in Guyana. The regimes were profoundly different, but the essential class component was not. If working-class struggle from below (in occupations and wildcat strikes) was necessary in Guyana, it was also indispensable for the construction of socialism in

Tanzania. To those who declared that there was something unique about Tanzania, Rodney was equally dismissive: "[I]t is important to recognise that it fits within the general pattern, which we have been discussing so far," he noted, "by which the colonisation process ended through an alliance of classes . . . but within this alliance the workers and the peasants never really had hegemony."

The Hamburg lectures confirmed the shift in Rodney's work toward an emphasis on the self-activity of the working class—through occupations and wildcat strikes—not as *one* of numerous players in the revolution, but as *the* central organizing force. A new state, he believed, would not come about by an enlightened leader or party, but through the frenzy of a class in the process of knowing itself, and through what it alone was capable of creating. This would require what Shivji described as a "proletarian ideology." In this scenario, the existing national bourgeoisie, in Rodney's words, and "their whole rational of production as a class would disappear."

While the full development of this politics would never be realized, Rodney's decisive turn to the working class, as recorded in his Hamburg lectures, was an important moment in an extraordinary life. However, there was still an equivocation: while Rodney looked to this self-organization as the real center of Marxism—and revolution—he still held on to the possibility of a new or better liberation movement that would avoid the pitfalls of Tanzania's failed socialism. In Hamburg, there was hope for the late radical liberation of Mozambique, Angola, and Guinea-Bissau, at the same time as a celebration of working-class self-organization.

Returning to Guyana via Barbados in early July, Walter wrote on July 10 to his friend Albert Parkes in Hamburg to explain he had arrived safely and to "please inform mutual friends that I returned home safely and that I have sent greetings." Walter was able, he explained, to meet up with Patricia in Barbados, and "the result is that we both got home on the same flight late on Tuesday night. The children were of course delighted." Writing again to Al on September 25, he explained that he was traveling once more to Germany for a conference of the World Council of Churches on "racism in children's and school textbooks"; he had recently written two children's books, *Kofi Baadu Out of Africa* and *Lakshmi Out of India*.[59]

The conference on racism in children's books was going to be held in Frankfurt from October 13 to 18—a roughly three-hundred-mile drive from Hamburg—so it was unlikely that a trip to see Al's family would be possible. However, Rodney hoped he would manage it somehow; moreover, he was traveling later in the year to the United States, and he would need some of the supplies he had left with his friend in Hamburg. "I'll definitely be going to the USA for a few weeks before the year is over," he explained to Al in the letter, "and it will have turned fairly cold by then. Therefore, if you select any serviceable warm clothing from the stuff I left behind, there might be a way of my collecting before leaving Germany. The shoes could also be in the same packet."

In the letter to Al, Walter described the political situation in veiled terms: "['T']hings are moving as well as one could expect in a difficult situation."[60]

CHAPTER 12

Those Heroic
Months of Revolt

In the last year of his life, Rodney organized, taught, and fought. Walter the labor militant and writer remained tightly platted with Walter the husband and father; he continued to pick his three children up from school, play with them, let them lie on his lap while he wrote, and involve them in the various elements of his work. These aspects of his life could not be separated, and the popular education classes he conducted at the family home were the clearest example of this. The couple was also remarkably collaborative, running the household and its chores equally. Patricia's work and education were given the space they needed to develop; for example, she traveled to Kingston in September 1978 to complete her degree. Amid the intense pace of political activity and repression, this is an overlooked and astonishing dimension of the Rodney family (and Walter's story).

Faced with a mass movement that almost toppled the cynical and brutal dictatorship of Forbes Burnham, Walter did not despair. After the great protests, the Civil Rebellion, had begun to ebb in September 1979, he fought hard to keep it afloat, frustrated that the movements led by the Working People's Alliance had come so close to removing the dictatorship—replacing it not simply with new elections but with its own power and popular assemblies of the poor and working class.

Rodney faced enormous challenges as an activist, father, and husband, but he tried hard to keep ahead of rapidly changing events in 1979 and to lend a coherent focus to the developing struggles. Through this tumultuous year, he maintained his breakneck schedule of international travel, lecturing, speaking, and fundraising—work he was forced to take in order to pay the bills.

During this period, Rodney maintained a remarkable momentum of scholarly work and activities. On January 8, Michael Craton—a scholar of slavery who was based in Canada—wrote to "supporters and funders" to request funding for Rodney. He explained that Rodney would be attending "the Slave Studies Conference at the University of Waterloo between March 14 and 17, 1979, to give a paper on 'Slavery and Underdevelopment.' . . . Beside taking part in the conference, Dr. Rodney is eager is talk in public." Detailing Rodney's circumstances to the "potential funders," Craton writes, "[T]hose who know Dr. Rodney will testify that he is a charismatic lecturer, who strikes responsive chords in all audiences, be they African, Afro-American or Canada. Though he is committed to spreading the word with or without fee, because of the sensitivity of his political role in Guyana he occupies no salaried post and must subsist by lecturing." He goes on to request a speaker's fee of five hundred dollars—a typical procedure in universities, when raising funds for speakers and research.[1]

Rodney had also been in touch with an organization called the Council of Interracial Books for Children, part of his own work in publishing for children. At the end of January 1979, they wrote to him from New York about "an operation 'Guyana Airlift' to get books for children in the area. . . . We are sending you the books mentioned below via boat mail." The titles included various picture books—*Jambo Means Hello, Shawn's Red Bike, Playtime in Africa* (for smaller children)—and profiles of prominent Black figures in US culture and politics, including Paul Robeson, Ray Charles, and Rosa Parks.[2]

At the end of April 1979, confirmation of Rodney's "round-trip to Los Angeles" was mailed to him by a research associate, Patti Iiyama, from the Center for Afro-American Studies in Los Angeles. He had been invited to speak at a symposium, "The Political Economy of the Black World," to be held between May 10 and 12, and to stay for the nights of the event in "a single room . . . at the Holiday Inn in Westwood." Rodney spoke on the "roots and consequences of African underdevelopment"—a talk that, on June 4, was commended in a letter from the organizers as "very stimulating . . . very much appreciated by the audience and contributed significantly to the success of the symposium."[3]

Rodney had also agreed to speak on May 5 at Hunter College—part of the City University of New York. Invited by Laura Randall, a political economist of Latin America, who asked Rodney in a letter on January 30,

1979, whether "Patterns of Influence in the Caribbean: Cuba, Venezuela and Trinidad" would be an appropriate title. Rodney delivered the talk as planned and soon after received a letter with Randall's words of gratitude: "[T]hank you for a magnificent talk, and your generosity with your time." She was clearly quite captivated by his speaking style: "I'm struck with the fact of how well you held an audience through a presentation that included so many helpful facts, that were adduced in ways that did not interfere with the clarity of presentations. It was a pleasure to watch." Tapes of the talk would be made available, she explained.[4]

I give these examples of Walter's continued international schedule to indicate a few things—first, that he kept up international speaking commitments, even as the struggle in Guyana intensified. We should remember that between these symposiums and talks in North America, he was being called on to speak to organized workers on sugar plantations and in mines across the country. Secondly, this visit—to New York and Los Angeles—would be his final international trip before his arrest in July on charges of arson during the great summer of discontent. Rodney would not leave the country again until May 1980, the following year.

In addition, throughout this period, Rodney maintained strong and close relationships with leading figures of the African liberation movement, those still fighting for the liberation of the continent from white settler rule. Many of these connections he had made while in Dar, but now, as a leading figure in the WPA, he regarded Guyana's liberation—its *real* liberation and independence—as part and parcel of Africa's late liberation, being fought for in Southern Africa. These were his comrades in arms.

No struggle on the continent interested him as much as Zimbabwe's, which was regarded widely as representing a fresh start for the continent's liberation—led by the socialist-inspired Zimbabwe African National Union and Robert Mugabe, who few at the time could fault. The radical journal *Review of African Political Economy* celebrated Mugabe and the fall of the white minority regime in Rhodesia in the following terms: "Of all the political movements in Zimbabwe, ZANU-PF stands out as the most progressive and patriotic organisation fighting for the true interests of the labouring masses."[5] Meanwhile on the radical left, theorist Alex Callinicos wrote in 1981 in a study of Zimbabwe and Southern Africa about "this remarkable man."[6]

Rodney was not alone; many figures and groups on the left at the time, across a broad spectrum, saw a new dawn for liberation in Zimbabwe's independence. When he eventually made his way to Zimbabwe for its independence in April 1980, he was returning to the bosom of militant pan-African liberation. At the end of 1978, the prominent nationalist Nathan Shamuyarira—then director of education and culture for the ZANU in the liberated zones controlled by the party—sent Walter a letter. Nathan, a talented journalist and writer, had been Walter's friend and comrade in Dar, when the two men were teaching at the university.

He wrote: "Your letter of 6th June said we should consider you available for 6 weeks in March/April. While this is good news for us, I regret that I am not able to confirm your visit to us because of the deteriorating security situation in our war zones." Shamuyarira explained that while it would not be possible for Rodney to travel as part of ZANU's "general education program" for these months, they wanted "to see you here as soon as it is possible." He then goes on to explain the situation in the country in 1978: "[W]e were able to establish liberated areas in three rural areas where 1.3 million now live, and look to us for providing basic social and security services; and in 1979 we intend to consolidate our hold in these areas; as well as start work in the urban areas to which the settler system and its agents have retreated."

Explaining that the ZANU's president, Mugabe, had established good relations with Cuba in 1978, Shamuyarira nevertheless appealed to Rodney: "[W]e would be grateful for any assistance you are able and willing to give to enhance that relationship." Referring to the progress of the war and support from neighboring states, he explained: "Mozambique has continued to form our strongest and most reliable rear base. . . . Although the casualty rate has climbed to about 20 a day, our people are coming out in ever-increasing numbers to support the war and to make heroic sacrifices all along the line." The tone of the letter changes when he signs off, in pen: "Warm greetings and regards to the family. Pamberi ne Chimurenga! [Forward with the Revolution!], Nathan."[7]

The letters came and went between the two men, with news and information about their respective struggles, suggestions, requests, and expressions of heartfelt solidarity. Nathan wrote again on January 10, 1980, from the ZANU postal address in Maputo, starting his typed letter: "Dear Walter, All the comrades here wish you a successful 1980, and happier days than in 1979. Since July '79 when news reached us here through the British press of the suppression of your movement, and the ill-treatment of yourself personally, by the Burnham regime, Comrade President Mugabe has not spent as much as 3 weeks in Maputo." Mugabe, he reported, had been on a tour of Eastern Europe, in Havana in September 1979, and then in London for a three-month conference at Lancaster House in London that would lead to elections and independence for Zimbabwe soon after. The "Comrade President" had been busy, Shamuyarira explained: "I am recounting this programme to show that we have not had time to brief him on the Guyanese situation, and for a serious in-depth analysis of the trends emerging there so we could take our progressive position."

Preparations were busily being made for elections and Mugabe's return home, he explained, but Nathan's reference to a "progressive position" is fascinating. Presumably, this meant a nuanced stand on the struggle against Burnham's People's National Conference. Among nationalist governments on the left, the PNC government in Guyana might have been an outlier, but with its socialist camouflage it was still regarded by many as a family member. Rodney—and his allies in ZANU—had to intervene to ensure a full picture of the regime's true politics was received; indeed, Nathan is almost apologetic that he had been unable to discuss the "Guyana matter" with Mugabe.

Shamuyarira continued with the timetable of 1980: "We are supposed to be flying to Salisbury the day after tomorrow in an advance party of 120 people to set up our election campaign for next month." Doubtful about whether the election would be fair and people could vote "freely," he explained: "The press and radio in Salisbury continues to carry out a vendetta against us, and our partners in the PF [Patriot Front]. The whole exercise has been a big imperialist conspiracy to cheat us out of our hard won politico-military struggle; but, unfortunately, the struggle had advanced to a stage where it cannot be diverted or defeated completely."

This was indeed a period of intense political consummation for the struggle to liberate Zimbabwe, and it seemed that efforts to speak to the leader about Guyana could not be guaranteed. Shamuyarira closed his letter: "Let's keep in touch through our Maputo address. If there comes a time when we have the energy to turn to other issues Guyana will be high on our list; in the meantime, you and your family, and the safety of your colleagues is very much in our minds. . . . Yours in arms, Nathan."[8]

For a revolutionary—and presumably internationalist—organization on the verge of taking power, how could the relationship with other revolutionaries fighting against repression not be an issue of immediate concern? Reading the sentence that begins, "If there comes a time . . . " must have—at some level—been a blow to Rodney's hope of isolating Burnham or receiving practical support from a new socialist government in Zimbabwe, which was much celebrated around the world. As we will see, Rodney went to great lengths in April to appeal to the internationalism of the new ZANU-led government.

In radical circles in early 1980, the political mood was dominated by Zimbabwe and the prospects for a radical turn in the Third World. From London, Sule Mombara, a comrade who knew the family from Tanzania, wrote to Rodney on March 21: "Ndunga Baba Shaka [Dear Father of Shaka] . . . As you see in Southern Africa there was a tremendous victory for the people. They tried everything. Believe me everything. They locked up 10,000—killed so many and yet they lost." This was a message to Rodney to remain steadfast; liberation would be difficult, but it would come. Yet for now, all eyes were fixed on Zimbabwe. "I want to make a trip there," Mombara wrote, "for the celebrations in April 17/1980. It would be good for my work and get me out of Babylon."[9]

Burnham had thrown sand in the eyes of radical movements and governments around the world, and even an elementary investigation would have revealed the true character of the government in Guyana. Yet these nominally socialist regimes had little interest in carrying out this work and making a principled judgment of the situation based on the facts. Cuba led the pack. In early May 1980, Rodney received a letter from a Tanzanian friend—working in the country's embassy in Mozambique—that expressed the "confusion" even in "Revolutionary Mozambique": "There is great ignorance here about the reactionary reality that hides behind Guyana's 'progressive manifestations' in the international arena, which partly explains the man's [Forbes'] visit here. Partly it is ignorance and partly it is Fidel's endorsement of the man on account of his supposed 'progressive credentials' as an architect of 'a non-capitalist way of development' for Guyana."[10]

There were few revolutionaries in the world who would have understood the pitfalls of these revolutionary nationalist regimes, once in power, better than Rodney. Yet by the end of 1979, he felt he had few choices; therefore, he fought hard against the cynicism and insularity of activists, friends, and comrades now in government.

The "Rodney Airport" to Zimbabwe, Tanzania, and Germany

In 1979 and 1980, the noose was tightening around the neck of Guyanese activists; the government felt itself backed against a wall, and it fought viciously. The regime was extremely worried about the work of Rodney and his comrades in the WPA, challenging them openly through several legal cases and leading a campaign of terror through a "death squad" that terrorized opponents of the regime. For an organization still extremely young, the government's response was surprisingly deadly and ultimately devastating. The PNC government made every effort to discredit the WPA, including by spreading a rumor that the party specialized in the recruitment of people with a dangerous criminal past; it accused members of the party of advocating armed violence. On November 18, 1979, Ohene Koama—one of the organizers of the WPA—was shot dead by the police in South Ruimveldt, Walter and Patricia's neighborhood in Georgetown. Bizarrely, a subsequent investigation reported that Rodney was seen in the area close to where Koama had been murdered. On February 24, 1980, Edward Dublin, another WPA activist, was murdered by the police in Mackenzie—near the bauxite-mining town of Linden.

To some extent, these targeted murders—always denied by the regime—were not new, but their escalation was. All manner of repression was attempted; among those the PNC government pursued was leading WPA member Moses Bhagwan, who was accused of having been the principal organizer of an illegal demonstration on August 22, 1979. Rodney's biographer Amzat Boukari-Yabara writes how in December 1978, the Guyanese ambassador in Washington invited the US authorities to listen closely to a recording of an interview with Rodney that he saw as a veiled threat to overturn the government. As resistance to the regime grew, so did the repression against Rodney and the WPA.

At the opening of the case against those accused of firebombing the PNC headquarters, fourteen members of the WPA were accused of organizing a demonstration in October and subsequently arrested. Wherever the activists stepped, they seemed to face the force of the state. Boukari-Yabara writes: "The multiple legal cases were a strategy of the state to gain time as the elections approached. The regime had the intention of occupying the time and energy of the leaders by involving them in legal cases." Rodney was acutely aware of what was happening and how this strategy made it difficult to organize the party under conditions increasingly determined by the state.[11]

There is no better account of the period and its exceptional challenges than Rodney's "circular letter," sent to groups and comrades in May 1980. It is worth citing at length:

> As you know, in August '79 the four progressive unions went out on strike in solidarity with striking bauxite workers. Given the unions involved—and the fact that they had come out in support of bauxite workers—the strike involved not simply a majority of the Guyanese workers, but of the most militant and progressive workers. There was therefore some basis for optimism as to its potential; but the strike ended with the workers being beaten back to work, and the leadership of the progressive unions was neither strong enough nor cohesive enough to withstand the pressure. In the end, more than 80 of the striking workers were dismissed from their jobs and replaced with scab.

The beating back of the strikes had consequences for the movement as a whole, which saw what Rodney described as a "lull in street activity." In the same letter he describes

> some sense of frustration . . . [in the] loss of momentum in the mass movement. There is a feeling of the moment not being seized. While this view overestimates the possibilities of that period, it is true the leadership—whether of . . . [the] left political party, the progressive trade unions or of the other anti-dictatorial parties and groups—did not see the possibilities that were present in the simultaneous explosion of mass militancy and worker action; they were, in fact, overwhelmed by their sense that in the face of all this, the power of the state nevertheless remained intact.

Despite militants' "overestimation" of the continued power of the state, Rodney explained that there was a "real weakening." The regime, lacking popular support, increasingly struggled to maintain its power, he argued. He writes, "The regime has reorganised the police force and the army under loyal leadership; but its inability to trust the official armed services is leading to a growth in the number and size of its private armies." There is, he notes, growing dissension in the ruling party about how to manage the crisis.

In the letter that was sent to allies internationally—who he credits as having been "crucially important in the months since July"—he refers to "talks" taking place with "political parties, the progressive trade unions, farmers organisations, professionals and businessmen" to find agreement on a possible "government of national unity." Unsurprisingly, it was on an "economic program" that there was currently no agreement.[12]

This frustration Rodney speaks about in his letter was also his own; Rodney's comrade Rupert Roopnaraine describes this brilliantly: "I think he was beginning to feel the civil rebellion had ebbed; the high points we had reached after August, September, November, those heroic months of revolt, had been beaten back. The revolution was at a very low ebb at that stage. I think he felt more impelled to get it going again."[13]

In late April 1980, this desire to deepen the divisions in the state drove Rodney to plan another trip to Africa—one that would turn out to be his last. Facing arson charges, along with his comrades, he was forbidden from traveling; he had therefore been unable to attend the anniversary of the "revolution" of Maurice Bishop's New Jewel Movement in March 1980. He had also received an invitation—a "personal" one from Mugabe, according to Boukari-Yabara—to attend the independence celebrations in Zimbabwe on April 18.[14] Once more Rodney was unable to travel; in fact, officials prevented him, at the last minute, from boarding a British Airways plane. This time, his passport was seized; as enforcement of his imprisonment, he was required to present himself in front of a judge on April 22. That decision, Boukari-Yabara argues, was made directly by Burnham, who was head of the official state delegation to Zimbabwe; indeed, it was inconceivable that Burnham would allow Rodney to meet his nemeses in Rufaro Stadium in Salisbury, where the official ceremony was taking place.

Rodney and his comrades in the WPA were determined that he would travel to Zimbabwe, whatever the obstacles. Getting him out of the country was—Roopnaraine reports—a "horrendous task." Leading members of the WPA, under surveillance day and night, were often forced to change addresses to dodge police raids. Rodney first had to travel from Georgetown to Courentyne River, on the border with Suriname. A small group smuggled Walter across the country to Rosignol, a village on the west bank of the Berbice River. From there, he needed to cross the river, and instead of using the ferry, the group took a "small fishing boat,"[15] which transported them to New Amsterdam, a port town on the east bank. From the town they had to travel—changing cars as they went—to Crabwood Creek, at which point they took another small boat at night to Nickerie. Later, the expression "Rodney airport" would be used locally to signify those who leave Guyana by "underground" routes.

Suriname—the first foreign destination—was undergoing its own "revolution," and the WPA were close to some of the revolutionaries. Earlier that year, on February 25, a radical coup led by a group of army sergeants, headed by Desi Bouterse, had overthrown the previous government; a friendly and multiethnic government had just come to power, and their instincts were pro-WPA. Once he had arrived in Nickerie, Rodney was in the care of the Suriname authorities, who would get him out of the country. Roopnaraine, who participated in the escape, takes up the story: "They gave him an entry stamp and from everything we know from the Zimbabwean episode, Burnham was in a state of shock to find Walter there. . . . Not only was he in Zimbabwe in the flesh, he was being treated as an African prince. This did not go down very well."[16]

The trip to Zimbabwe was a mixed event. It was an utter humiliation to Burnham; his arch-opponent had stolen his thunder, while Rodney was greeted by comrades he knew in Zimbabwe, Nathan Shamuyarira among them, with a warm welcome. He was also given, according to Shamuyarira's account (published in the press in Guyana), an audience with the new leader of the country, Robert Mugabe—apparently Rodney spent two hours with the new prime minister and members of his cabinet. Humiliation is a useful political weapon, but in this case it would prove a dangerous emotion. After all, Burnham had been working for years on his reputation as a leftist, and he had come away from his own visit to Zimbabwe with nothing—except perhaps the resolution to kill Rodney. In contrast, Mugabe had offered Rodney a job—to work in the country as a historian and researcher. ·

According to Patricia, Rodney returned to Guyana from his visit to Zimbabwe with a clear offer. Mugabe was inviting him and his family to stay for a year in the country. Walter shared the letter of invitation, signed by President Mugabe, which cited several reasons. In Patricia's words: "One, we needed a break, Walter needed a break, to assess the situation that was taking place in Guyana. The other reason, Walter had worked with the movement in Tanzania." Initially Mugabe had requested that Walter stay and send for his family, but Rodney was clear: "No, I cannot do that; I have to go back home first and tie up several things before I leave." This was what Rodney told his wife the morning before he was killed.[17]

The content of Rodney's May 1980 meeting with Mugabe remains unclear, but among the topics would have been the struggle in Guyana, which was lagging and needed international support from friendly states.

Roopnaraine believes Rodney had traveled to Zimbabwe, in his words, "with the hopes of getting some kind of assistance from Mugabe and from some of the African comrades. That did not happen . . . but the fact is he had been very disappointed . . . as far as assistance to the Guyana revolution."[18] However, Mugabe had made an offer of a temporary placement, or sanctuary for the family, until the situation in Guyana calmed down.

Boukari-Yabara reports that Rodney spent ten days in Africa and then secretly returned to Guyana after a short stop in Tanzania.[19] However, this account disagrees with others suggesting he made stops in Hamburg on the way to and from Zimbabwe. Walter did begin his return through Dar es Salaam—a stay remembered by his friend from his Dar days, Walter Bgoya. On a muggy afternoon in December 2018 in his office in downtown Dar, where he still publishes and runs a bookshop, Bgoya spoke to me about Rodney's last visit.

During Walter's stay, Bgoya explained, they spoke extensively on many topics. Foremost on Walter's mind at the time was "how far he could take the struggle in Guyana, through peaceful means." Bgoya thinks Rodney returned through Dar to practically consider these questions, as well as to seek advice and source support. Bgoya was disturbed—something was wrong. He sensed from these conversations that Walter, the movement, and the party were at serious risk. He feared that Walter was going to die and wrote to President Nyerere saying, "Unless you intervene, I think Burnham is going to have Walter Rodney assassinated." This was a meaningful effort, if a naive one. What would Nyerere really be prepared to do? At that time Guyana had good relations with Tanzania. The two countries operated "exchanges" from their respective national service programs, with Guyanese volunteers working in Ujamaa villages.[20]

In fact, Walter's plans seem to have been more advanced than he indicated to Bgoya. His stay was short in Tanzania, and he moved on quickly to Germany. His pressing desire was to get the struggle moving again—by any means. Once in Hamburg, he was in touch once more with his friends and comrades, staying with Al Parkes—who, as we have seen, had been the best man at Walter and Patricia's wedding in London in 1965, before he moved to Hamburg. Walter was also in touch with Peter Lock, who, together with Rainer Tetzlaff, had been one of the cohosts of the lecture course Rodney had taught in the spring and summer of 1978. Lock was a trusted comrade who followed events in Guyana closely and had contacts that could be useful.

During Rodney's months in Hamburg in 1978, the two men had grown close, and they had many "long conversations—about politics and life. At that time," Lock recalls, "my subject . . . was the militarization of the Third World and the arms industry"—a fact that Rodney had remembered. The trip to Germany carried its own risks: Rodney was not traveling under his own name but using a false passport. Rodney explained to his friend that the struggle in Guyana was, in Lock's words, "inevitably becoming violent."[21]

After Germany, Rodney made his way back to Georgetown. His trip was already in the public domain, and Burnham's anger and humiliation were intense. Rodney had done it to him again. Paranoid and furious, the regime had been intensifying repression against the movement and the WPA since 1978. The party's leading activists were in the crosshairs of the PNC, and the WPA knew it. In 1979, the WPA had issued a warning: it "wished to alert the Caribbean and world opinion to the fact that there is a real possibility of attempts at assassination." The party was well informed; their statement quoted the PNC publication *The New Nation*, which they said "carries staff written letters under the caption, 'Exterminate the rats from our society,' 'Our Steel is Sharper Now.'" The threats were not idle rhetoric, but serious statements of intent. Burnham, as ever, led the charge, proclaiming, at a conference of the Young Socialist Movement on June 29, 1979, the urgent need to "exterminate the enemies of the party."[22]

Murders, arrests, and intimidation of WPA supporters and members were rapidly escalating, and the PNC and Burnham routinely issued direct threats to the party, describing the WPA as the "Worst Possible Alternative" and instructing members to "make their wills."[23] The police and state-funded militias had been issued with a *Recognition Handbook— Working Peoples Alliance*, essentially a hit list to identify leading WPA militants. The booklet explained its intention: "These notes are designed to provide a guide to the easy recognition of personnel of the Working People's Alliance and vehicles that are associated with the organisation's activities." The information provided in the "handbook" was detailed and chilling, including photographs of prominent members of the WPA, biographical details, and passport numbers. These activities were not limited to Guyana; a 2016 Commission of Inquiry reported on documentation on the WPA "by consular and diplomatic personnel abroad as well."[24]

The Murder

Following his return to Georgetown, Rodney's days were frenetic. He quickly moved to coordinate new actions while dodging the secret police and speaking to activists in secret. In the effort to get things moving again, he strained every muscle.

The details of the evening of Friday, June 13, have long been poured over, in different accounts. At about 7:30 p.m. on Church Street—a major road in the center of Georgetown that runs past the Botanical Gardens to the Demerara River—Walter got into the passenger side of the Mazda car owned by his brother Donald. The two men then drove toward Broad Street, several blocks away. They parked the car at the southeast end of Russell Street. Donald got out of the car and walked to the house of Gregory Smith—an undercover agent of the state—with the aim of picking up a walkie-talkie. Smith opened the door and asked him where Walter was.

"In the car," Donald replied.

In response, Smith asked if he planned to test the equipment while walking or driving at the wheel. Donald replied that the decision would be Walter's to make. Smith showed him the device and asked him to do two tests in order to establish that they worked. The first of the tests was carried out on Princess Street near the city's cemetery, and the second near Camp Street behind the prison—to test whether the transmission between the walkie-talkies would be able to penetrate the metal-reinforced walls of the prison.

Donald returned to Walter, who decided to test the equipment while driving, rather than walking. Donald started the car, drove some distance and then stopped on John Street. Smith sent the first transmission, which came through the device as a lit indicator. The two men were very pleased. The Mazda continued and crossed Durban Street, heading toward the prison—Donald then pulled the car up, cut the engine, raised the handbrake, and turned off the headlights.

Abruptly, at about 8:30 p.m., an explosion ripped through the passenger's side of the vehicle, blowing a hole in the roof. Hurt by flying splinters, Donald could see that his brother was bleeding profusely and could not possibly survive. Donald recalled: "Suddenly, I heard a loud noise and at the same time I felt my body being twisted against the driver's door which flew open. . . . I realised then that there had been an explosion on Walter's side of the car and that he was seriously injured."[25] Donald staggered out of the vehicle and rushed toward the house of their comrade, Omowale, on Croal Street—two blocks away—to seek help. He climbed the stairs and breathlessly told two members of the WPA, Andaiye (Sandra Williams) and Karen De Souza what had happened. He was finally taken to the home of a medical doctor, Horace Taitt—bleeding and injured and accompanied by the WPA activist Kathy Wills.

Abyssinian Carto, a young comrade who was also staying on Croal Street, recalled years later:

> I came back in the evening, it might have been about seven or eight . . . when I came to the front door, I saw fresh blood on it . . . I saw Donald. He was standing there. He had just come out of the toilet and he had his shirt off and I said, "Donald, what happened?" And he didn't answer me. He stared like in a shock, and I noticed there was some blood on the side of his face. I said, "What happened?" And then he was sort of stunned and then I came up to him and he just said, "They killed Walter." And I said, "What?" And he said, "Yes" And I said, "Where?" And he said, "It happened around the corner." I said, "Around where?" And he said, "Around John Street."[26]

About ten minutes later, Andaiye, De Souza, and Carto made their way to the place of the explosion, only to see a crowd and security services personnel already assembled. De Souza immediately saw that the top of the car had been blown off. She moved through the crowd, pushing past bystanders and a policeman. De Souza recalls: "I moved closer and saw a smooth dark expanse of flesh. I saw that the body was on the floor almost pasted on. The head was pressed up against the dashboard. I thought I recognised the back of the head which was the part visible." She could tell that it was Rodney.[27]

The night her husband was killed, Patricia and the couple's youngest daughter, Asha, were attending a fundraising event at her school, Saint Agnes Primary School. It was here that Donald had picked up Walter for his last mission. Carto, with Malcolm Rodrigues, a Jesuit priest active in the WPA, searched the city for Patricia—eventually finding her and Asha at the school. Malcom broke the news to Patricia before they proceeded to pick up Shaka and Kanini, who were attending a farewell party. The same night, the police raided the family home. Patricia remembers how the armed plainclothes police ransacked their house and, on entering Shaka's room and seeing a poster of Che Guevara, commented, "Even the child has a picture of 'Che' on the wall."[28]

The authorities claimed that because the bomb had exploded in Rodney's face, it was impossible to identify the victim. On the evening of the murder, Rodney's mother's home was also searched by the authorities for arms and ammunition. Meanwhile, Walter's older brother, Edward, was taken in for questioning. He was unable to identify the body, unclear if it was Walter or Donald. Patricia was unable to see the remains of her husband before Monday because the government claimed it was urgent to first identify the victim.

As hard as the government tried to cover up the news, by early Saturday, the BBC and Radio Suriname announced the death of Rodney; the local news said nothing. Within a few hours, the news spread across the Caribbean, to the United States, Canada, Great Britain, and Africa. Supporters quickly organized demonstrations against the government.[29]

On the morning of June 14, the first autopsy was carried out and concluded, unremarkably, that Rodney had died from the explosion. Despite the media's lie that the victim's face was destroyed, positive identification was simple—Rodney was clearly recognizable. Father Malcolm Rodrigues, a close family friend, positively identified the body on behalf of Patricia Rodney. During the Commission of Inquiry on the Death of Walter Rodney in 2016, he testified: "I walked around to the side and look in, and Walter's face was perfect. . . . The beard was too perfect also, not one of those scraggly beards he normally had. It looks as though somebody took a torch and went and singed it nicely. So, I looked at it and thought, 'What an extraordinary thing.'"[30]

Quickly, the WPA wrote, printed, and distributed leaflets accusing the PNC regime of the murder. As students and WPA members protested in Georgetown in their thousands, the government quickly outlined their version of events. Rodney, the government announced, had been killed by the explosion of a bomb of his own crafting, which was intended to blow up the prison.

Unable to access the local media, which was under Burnham's control, the WPA made use of its own international networks (which had long been cultivated by Rodney himself) to launch an international "mobilization" campaign. There was outrage among "high ranking" radical Caribbean politicians, and the initially shock and anger was tangible. For example, George Weekes, leader of the Oilfields Workers' Trade Union in Trinidad—who had been in direct contact with Rodney the previous year—threatened Guyana with a petrol embargo. Irritated by the international reaction to the murder, the regime nevertheless agreed to give overseas officials a forty-eight-hour visa to attend the funeral. Maurice Bishop—the prime minister of the radical government in Grenada that had come to power in 1979—expressed his support for Rodney, as did Prime Minister Michael Manley in Jamaica.

Only on June 17 was Patricia allowed to see her husband's body. Like Father Rodrigues, she immediately recognized him—even if the experience was profoundly traumatizing. Patricia reports: "Father Rodrigues and I returned to the Newburg Funeral Parlour, where . . . some policemen were present. The funeral parlour was very depressing and not kept in a sanitary state. We all went in to see the body. It was a huge poorly working refrigerator with about eight other bodies, some naked, some half naked. . . . Walter's body was at the bottom of the pile. It was a dreadful experience."[31]

A memorial service was held at the Brickham cathedral on June 21. As WPA comrade and friend Clive Thomas recalled in the 2000s: "I can remember the funeral ceremony and . . . the funeral service. . . . I nearly broke down; it was quite a moving experience because it was an ecumenical service, and it was in a Catholic cathedral."[32] Members of the Catholic Church in Guyana were close to the WPA and sympathetic to its objectives.

Finally, on June 23—ten days after the murder—Rodney's body was buried. When the body was returned to the family, it was transported on a carriage pulled by a horse, with a large crowd following. Walter's younger brother Hubert—then a student in law in Barbados—spoke, comparing the murder of his brother to the manner in which slave masters publicly tortured and mutilated rebel slave leaders in order to break the popular will for a general uprising.[33]

Rodney's body was taken to Buxton, about nine miles from the capital, behind an enormous banner with a picture of Rodney holding a microphone, and the words "This act in itself will not delay their day of judgement." Boukari-Yabara estimates that between thirty and fifty thousand people participated in the procession. This was the largest demonstration seen in the country since 1948, when five workers, the Enmore Martyrs, were killed by the police while fighting for better working and living conditions. It was a similarly pivotal event in the country's political struggles.

Songs against the regime rang out as the march made its way slowly back to Georgetown. Boukari-Yabara writes: "Speeches were made, then, under sporadic showers, the procession resumed . . . to the sound of drums, and with a brisk step. Finally, at about seven o'clock the coffin containing the remains of Rodney entered the alley of tall palm trees in the cemetery, Repentir."[34]

Karen De Souza recalled that the funeral of Rodney showed an "astonishing display of racial solidarity and defiance." The "defiance," she argued, was due to the fact that attending the funeral meant one risked losing their work. The funeral procession was, in her words, "the most massive display of racial solidarity in the recent history of Guyana with over 30,000 in attendance."[35]

The pain and suffering Patricia and the children experienced is hard to imagine. During the days immediately following the murder, the agony of loss would have been slightly blunted by the sheer pace of events, and then by arrangements for the funeral, the memorial service, the precession from Buxton, and endless discussions about what to do next. The real pain would have come after these events, when the loss was no longer shielded by friends. Many have experienced such loss, but Patricia and the children had something else to contend with: they had to share their grief with thousands of people, everywhere they went, who were also in mourning. Comrades, friends, and colleagues all made a claim to the man who was Patricia's husband, and Asha, Kanini, and Shaka's father. How could this not have felt like an intrusion?

Shortly after Walter was assassinated, family friends George Lamming and Margaret Hope—who was the assistant information officer for the Barbados Government Information Service—arrived in Georgetown, bringing airplane tickets for Bridgetown for Patricia and the three children. Patricia received an offer of "refugee status" from then–prime minister Tom Adams—who led a government of the Barbados Labour Party. However, she refused—a significant decision and an indication of Patricia's deeply held political convictions. Years later, she explained: "I refused because I could not envision any Caribbean person being designated a refugee. As a result, I was granted residence status, which allowed me to work. I have been a citizen of Barbados for many years."[36]

Over the next eight years, Barbados provided the family with safety, space, and an environment that was necessary to begin the long healing process. In many ways, it meant starting over. As Patricia explains:

It was important to both Walter and I that the children spend their formative years in the Caribbean. This gave them a real sense of their Caribbean identity and heritage. The family lived and progressed in Barbados, which is still considered home. I was able to use my professional skills working in Barbados, an opportunity that was denied to me in my homeland Guyana.

In 1989, the family emigrated to Canada to begin a new chapter. My two daughters and I were all working and studying. Asha completed her first degree at the University of Toronto, Kanini completed graduate studies at Emory University in Atlanta and I completed a PhD at OISE, University of Toronto.

In 1995, I moved to Atlanta, Georgia, to take up an academic position at Morehouse School of Medicine. Kanini and Asha joined me in Atlanta, while Shaka remained in Barbados and built a very successful Custom Framing Company. Kanini and Asha are graduates of Morehouse School of Medicine and Georgia State Faculty of Law, respectively.[37]

Refusing to be defined by the tragedy, Patricia forged her own career—as she had done while she was married to Walter—and brought up the children in the same spirit: proud of their legacy while building their own lives. The family continues to honor Rodney's legacy through the creation of the Walter Rodney Foundation.

The campaign for justice for Rodney continues unabated and has been an endless battle for the family. Scandalously, his death certificate still states the cause of Walter Rodney's death as "death by misadventure"; until recently, Donald was judged responsible for his brother's death—an insulting farce connected to the broader injustice. The *Commission of Inquiry Report* in 2016 in Guyana concluded that "Dr. Walter Anthony Rodney, 38 years old, had been assassinated by the state on June 13, 1980." What was clear at the time was now stated categorically: the Guyanese government at the highest levels, including the army and police, appointed a killer to murder Walter Rodney.

However, the commission was prematurely shut down by President David A. Granger's administration. Arguing that enough time and money had been spent on the inquiry, they brought it to a close. Citing an "intense programme of public activities during the first half of 2016," they insisted that the "Report of the Commission cannot be extended beyond the 15th December 2015."[38] After the report was completed the government repeatedly scuppered efforts to adopt the findings of the *Inquiry Report*.

The government—made up of a coalition led by the PNC—described the findings as "dubious and questionable."[39]

In an important development in the ongoing battle for justice by the Rodney family, on April 13, 2021, a Court of Appeal "set aside" Donald's 1982 conviction. In the grotesque hall of mirrors of PNC-run Guyana, Donald had been convicted for possession of explosives and sentenced. The explicit message was that the Rodneys—both Walter and his brother—were responsible for the "misadventure" on June 13. Donald had to live with this outrage for more than forty years. The decision to "set aside" the conviction was a result of years of campaigning and activism.[40] It is important to state that the PNC, as the perpetrating regime, has never acknowledged the assassination of Walter. In March 2015, for example, the PNC leader at the time, David Granger said that the party should not accept blame for Rodney's death.[41]

In spite of the relentless pace of Rodney's writing and organizing at the time he was killed, he remained remarkably decent, thoughtful, and reflective. The Atlanta-based scholar-activist Jesse Benjamin describes some of this loss:

> Rodney's . . . transnationalism was off putting to nationalist party leaders, as were his withering but essential critiques of comprador petty-bourgeois elites and neo-colonialism, and he knew that his groundings would be deeper in Guyana than anywhere because it was his home society. . . . He produced his definitive, A *History of the Guyanese Working People*, and the subsequent two volumes intended to follow it were done or nearly completely when they were stolen from his house [in the police raid following his murder]. He produced the beginnings of an ambitious children's book series which was to cover the true historical stories of all the major groups in the country, to undermine the divide and conquer legacies that separated Guyanese communities. And his speeches to the Guyanese people, including "Peoples Power, No Dictator," are another set of documents altogether, some of his least known and most important, though his comrades have maintained a steady literature and engagement with this and all the literature in *Dayclean*, and more than a few other venues.[42]

Meanwhile, Rodney's assassin went free. Shortly after the murder, Gregory Smith fled to Suriname, then to Trinidad (receiving the official papers he needed to travel); he finally settled in Cayenne in French Guiana—an overseas département of France. In a 1987 interview, Smith revealed no details of interest; Walter's death, he claimed, was an accident, a misadventure, while obliquely referring to WPA involvement. In June 1980 the first response of the Guyana police, army and government was to deny that Smith existed at all.[43] Half-hearted efforts were made by the Guyanese authorities to extradite Smith to Guyana in the early 1990s, but the French authorities refused the request. Smith died in 2002 in the French colony.

There are many obscenities in this story: murder committed with impunity, justice unanswered, and still-rampant poverty and inequality (the cause of Rodney's lifelong crusade). But perhaps the most audacious of these crimes and obscenities is the manner of Burnham's own death and commemoration. The dictator died on August 6, 1985, while in hospital in Georgetown—Cuban doctors had flown in to try and treat his cancer. He was then buried to much fanfare as the "father of the nation." Soon afterward, his body was disinterred and transported for embalming in the Soviet Union, and then returned and reburied. This chieftain of the people—a butcher of his opponents, who Rodney had relentlessly exposed in his life—is commemorated in a mausoleum constructed in the city's Botanical Gardens for fallen presidents.

By contrast, Rodney is buried in a modest grave surrounded by a mass of others that are sinking into the ground. Gravestones in the Le Repentir Cemetery are broken and collapsed, bones of the dead protrude from the earth, and the bodies of dead animals are thrown onto what amounts to a city dump for the dead. In a world that remains unchanged—its poverty and misery constant, its wealth amassed and stolen—perhaps it is fitting that Rodney is buried among the poor. He spent his entire life with them, searching them out, talking to the impoverished of Trench Town in 1968, and listening to the bauxite and plantation workers throughout the 1970s. In every case he argued, with great modesty and brilliance, for unity and action. Rodney does not belong in a mausoleum of the "great and good"; indeed, he would have seen such a display as merely another means by which the present destroys the life and memory of the past.

CHAPTER 13

The Enemies of the State

The politics of the Working People's Alliance was radically and dramatically different from that of mainstream "socialist" parties, both in Guyana and elsewhere. As one of its leading militants, Clive Thomas, recalled: "We were really, if you look at the mechanics of the party, a party that was 90 percent financed by the contributions of the activist group. You're talking about tens of dollars and twenties. You're not talking about any million-dollar effort."[1] Other funding came from donations made by Guyana's diaspora and fellow militants around the world.

The day-to-day politics of the organization—following the inspiration of Rodney specifically, but many others as well—was a focus on the rights of women, popular education, the battle against racial division, and working-class struggle and unity. The WPA advocated revolution, not reform, and its leaders saw the revolutionary road paved by the self-activity of the poor and working class themselves; no enlightened leader or soapbox speaker could substitutee for the activism of the poor themselves. Though Rodney was a prominent member of the WPA, he was also influenced by many others in the organization, in particular Eusi Kwayana. In his final interview, Rodney described Kwayana in glowing terms: "He is a tremendous example to those of us who are younger than he is because if he could have moved through the various epochs of struggle, against first colonialism and then against one or other form of racist distortion in our history, and is still as young, as fresh as ever."[2] These affectionate terms closely resembled those he had used before to describe C. L. R. James.

The party was led by a fifteen-member committee, which included Thomas, Kwayana, Diana Matthews, Andaiye, Bonita Harris, Karen De Souza, Vanda Radzig, Jocelyn Dow, Rupert Roopnaraine, and Moses Bhagwan. Each had their responsibilities and their specific areas of competence; yet, according Amzat Boukari-Yabara, the WPA refused the typical "approach of the Messiah specific to the political parties of Guyana." The party sought mass mobilization, politicization, and self-activity. As he writes, "The multiracial Alliance showed that the need among the people to seek out a prominent political leader who would solve problems for them was a weakness threatening democratic freedoms."[3]

Few radical organizations of the Left have placed such emphasis on political education and the founding of a new political culture. The WPA was not based on the specific allegiance to a particular Marxist state. The organization—like the early Bolshevik Party—had as its objective a different vision of politics: one that would not focus exclusively on elections but on developing a critical habit of thinking. Boukari-Yabara summarizes this spirit in the WPA as "like a laboratory of progressive ideas, aiming to transform society."[4]

After Rodney's murder there was an outpouring of grief—not least from his mentor and comrade C. L. R. James, who had invited Rodney into a Marxist study group in London years before. Addressing a crowd in London on January 30, 1981, James is almost chastising of Rodney—expressing, perhaps, his own deep feelings of loss and upset—for taking too many risks, for not realizing the extent of the regime's murderous intent. He contrasts Rodney's behavior, in carrying out the most dangerous work himself, with that of Vladimir Lenin, who at a moment of great danger during the revolutionary turmoil of 1917 disguised himself and went underground. Like a schoolmaster, he explained: "I am going to deal with what Walter did not know and what he should have known, and what you will have to know; if you do not pay the proper attention, you will pay the consequences for it." Walter did not study, he argued, the important task of taking power.

James's pain is palpable in the speech in January 1981, which marks the loss of a remarkable son; nevertheless, he is strict, clear on the lessons that must be drawn, insisting on a process of learning:

> It is a knowledge that there is somebody waiting to destroy you. But Walter did not do that. Instead, he took on all sorts of activities, on the conception that he had to show them that he was not asking anybody to do anything that he would not do himself.
>
> That is why Walter found himself in a car with . . . some gadget that turned out to be an explosive. *He should never have been there.* No political leader had any right to be there. Not only should he have never been there, the people around him should have seen to it that he was

not in any such position. That was a fundamental mistake, and it was a political mistake. It was not a mistake in personal judgment.[5]

C. L. R. James was clear that the mistake had been a failure—one shared by the entire Left in the Caribbean—to grapple with the real challenges of taking power. Still, Rodney had also made the mistake of carrying out the "dirty work" of dangerous party activities. Presumably, someone else should have been charged with the collection of walkie-talkies on June 13, 1980.

This may be true, and James's peculiar eulogy to Rodney is full of insight and revolutionary history. However, what he did not understand was that Walter was no more willing to delegate "manual work" to other comrades than to betray the movement. The meaning of his activism *was* direct involvement—whether it was sitting on an oil drum as he spoke to the poor in Kingston, or addressing striking workers and the landless poor in Guyana. To remove Rodney from that car on the night of June 13 would be to remove him from the revolutionary scene altogether. Put simply, Rodney would not have been Rodney.

Rodney's very strength as a leader and activist was his willingness to do things himself. The same point was made by the Guyanese activist and scholar David Hinds, who spoke about whether Rodney should have picked up the walkie-talkies himself: "[H]ad he delegated it to me then you're saying that my life is not worth as much as Rodney's life. That was not the Rodney way. Rodney was what the Rastafarians call a 'forwarder.' When you were out there, he was there with you."[6]

When it came to the question of seizing power, Rodney was clear on this point. But again, James misread the situation. Rodney had been aware of the enormous power of the mass movement in the extraordinary political movement of 1979—the Civil Rebellion. Yet there were weaknesses, some of which James knew of:

> As Burnham watched the working class getting together and taking part in demonstrations against the government, he threatened to disallow the funds that the labour leaders were receiving from the employers and by which they lived. Whereupon these fellows, faced with what was a difficult situation, drew back; and for the moment the working class was being led by leaders who were not at any time very revolutionary, though they were on the way to becoming so.
>
> In any case, they faced the breakup of their organizations. The temper of the working class went down. That was number one: they were

> not ready. . . . But they were not really ready in Guyana when Walter was there to lead them. It can come with sudden speed; but you must wait for it.

This much is true. There were serious challenges, and by late 1979 the enormous flow of the mass movement had ebbed. Rodney was acutely aware of this, and according to his comrade Roopnaraine, in 1980 he was impatient to get it going again—to return to the giddy heights of struggle. Yet, as James explained, there can be no serious question of "taking of power" if the state (and its army and police) are not taken into account:

> He recognized that Burnham meant mischief and that he was prepared to use all power, the armed power of the state, to destroy the opposition. Rodney knew that and he tried to organize against it. And he organized wrong. A key problem in the face of overwhelming state power is how to arm oneself against it. In fact, the arms for a revolution are there: the police and the army have them. What you have to do is win over a section of the army, and you have arms. And you could also take away arms from the government.
>
> A revolution is not made with arms, but a revolution is made by the revolutionary spirit of the great mass of the population. And you have to wait for that.[7]

These were enormous challenges; in James's formulation, to face them required wedding the mass movement, as the true engine of a revolution, with a close and careful attention to "seizing power" in the "face of overwhelming state power." When Burnham had used the phrase "prepare your wills" and had ordered his followers to "exterminate the enemies of the party," he had done so not only as an oratorical device but as a concrete statement of action. Thus, what James was urging was correct, but to a large extent it also reflected the very thing the WPA had been trying to do. Rodney was aware of the essential work of winning over members of Burnham's security services, the army, and the police; indeed, it was a weakness that he was trying to address in 1980.

Rodney was also aware of something that James was not: there were already important divisions in the military (that "armed body of men" that helped keep Burnham in power). Opposition had spread in the late 1970s; Colonel Ulric Pilgrim, for example, a leading figure in the military charged with running the Guyana Defence Force, had voiced his own misgivings to military cadets in 1979: "There are a number of powerful forces working against the professional skills of the military . . . when society goes into a state of confusion and disorder the military then becomes the hope of salvation."[8] The same year, twenty-three officers in the army decided they could no longer work under a PNC government, and they resigned—resignations which were refused.

The expansion of the regime's military and paramilitary forces bears emphasis. From 1974, military forces underwent significant expansion with the creation of the Guyana National Service, followed in 1976 with the establishment of a National Militia (which existed for over twenty years). Other armed groups were also formed, including the Young Socialist Movement and the Women's Revolutionary Socialist Movement. In addition, there was a tenfold expansion in the size of the armed forces between 1964—when the British relinquished security control to the Guyanese government—and 1977. In this period, military personnel expanded from 2,135 to 27,751, and spending rose to $48.72 million by 1976.[9]

Rodney knew that the key to revolutionary transformation was the mass movement and also that it would reach a point at which the question of the seizure of power would be posed. Rodney saw the armed struggle as an element in this revolutionary conundrum; this is no secret. As Roopnaraine explains, "[W]e were accumulating equipment of various kinds, and a certain amount of that was coming from the military."[10] In this respect, James was completely wrong: there was a fully conscious effort, in Roopnaraine's words, to "put ourselves in a state of readiness to make an assault on the state." Readying the masses for an insurrectionary assault on the state was precisely what the WPA was trying to do. Yet the task of "amassing weapons" was distributed unevenly and not, according to testimony in the 2016 *Commission of Inquiry Report*, an initiative of the general party. Some cells were acquiring weapons, while others were not.[11]

However, even the limited acquisition of arms was for self-defense, as then–executive member of the WPA Tacuma Ogunseye explained to the commission:

> We felt that the WPA would have to acquire some amount of arms for self-defence purposes and we took steps to do that . . . not only against the state machine. You see in Guyana, we faced the House of Israel, we faced PNC private people with weapons . . . far more and our weapons were so minimal; it was more of a psychological boosting for our comrades so that they could perform knowing that they are not totally exposed.

Importantly, as the commission's report states, neither Walter nor the WPA were committed to a "policy of violence even though some individuals in a limited number of cells in the WPA were arming themselves."[12]

Though a "singular and remarkable" man, as James described him, Rodney also combined elements of the revolutionary Left's eclectic influences. As we have seen, in his 1978 Hamburg lectures Rodney celebrates the power of working-class "wildcat" strikes and occupation in Tanzania as a force for transformation. However, echoing arguments made by Frantz Fanon, he says, "[T]here is a quality to the armed struggle that is really absent from other forms of struggle, in that this armed struggle must develop the aspect of social consciousness."

Fanon celebrated the armed struggle and, in his last book, *The Wretched of the Earth*, appeared to argue that only a liberation movement that takes up arms can achieve the *proper* freedom required by liberation. Indeed, Fanon saw this as the "real struggle." His influence on Rodney was clear: in both of their writing, there was a blurring of perspective, reflecting both a celebration of mass struggle as the primary engine of social change, and a role for "armed struggle." Rodney, for his part, sought to wed the two aspects of liberation—the mass movement and the armed struggle—which would achieve the crucial mutation in consciousness necessary for revolutionary change, in Fanon's words.

It was on good authority that Rodney embraced a turn to armed struggle: he did so on the basis of revolutionary theory and history, and his experience of the dramatic turn of events in the stalled struggle in Guyana. There was an exciting eclecticism in Rodney's approach; he innovated, thought rigorously on key questions of the movement and organization, and depended always on his own reading and study rather than hand-me-down shibboleths from Marxist grandmasters. Yet the "armed struggle" in Algeria was not the "real struggle" guaranteeing liberation. Rather, it had become a substitute to a mass movement in the cities and towns. These were different projects, and the Front de Libération Nationale's celebration of the armed confrontation with the French had serious consequences to post-independence Algeria—crucially taking power away from the street, the factories, and the people.[13]

When Rodney looked at revolutionary action taking place around the world in 1980, he saw a range of experiences and lessons. A new radical government had come to power in Grenada in 1979, and though it had been challenged by repeated coup attempts, it had managed to instigate some progressive reforms. Nevertheless, this was not the model of change Rodney envisaged for Guyana. In Mozambique, a new Marxist-Leninist state had been declared after a long battle against the Portuguese. The ruling party of the Mozambique Liberation Front (FRELIMO), led by Samora Machel, was largely directing change from above, with popular involvement when possible, but normally through state-ordered programs and policies. Cuba too remained a source of inspiration in the Caribbean; an avowedly anti-capitalist country, it had managed to hold the United States at bay while making progress on the country's underdevelopment.

The mass of largely state-led projects around the world offered the WPA a model and inspiration. At the same time, such models could not be embraced uncritically; Rodney, better than any of his contemporaries, knew that militant national liberation frequently decayed into political chaos that served a "bureaucratic petty bourgeoise." Rodney had witnessed this directly in Tanzania and seen the crushing embrace of this class in Guyana (and elsewhere in the region). Wherever Rodney turned, he was confronted with the cynicism of global power, even among apparent allies; moreover, Forbes Burnham knew how to play the international game, in which he tried to insert himself as a radical. Nevertheless, there was always somewhere else to pin one's hope, and in 1980, Zimbabwe was that hope.

But what did the WPA get from this mass of "radical governments"? Clive Thomas is scathing: "The Cubans . . . never isolated [Burnham]. And they were a big part of the scene because the Russians were not very active in Guyana matters. Fidel . . . did not break ranks in any serious way with Burnham." Turning to Grenada—a few hundred miles from Georgetown—the WPA similarly received nothing: "Even Bishop in Grenada," Thomas explains, "never sanctioned any support for the WPA once he was in power." Despite a few statements and sympathetic gestures, the neighboring country's New Jewel Movement yielded little, at a time when the WPA desperately needed equipment and finances. The list goes on.

There might have been radical words from Robert Mugabe in Salisbury during Rodney's audience with him in 1980, but the Zimbabwe African National Union itself soon started to decay, bringing about the kind of radical movement in the 1990s that Rodney and his comrades were fighting in Guyana in the 1970s. Some claim that Mugabe, too, offered Rodney little—except a post in Zimbabwe. Roopnaraine describes the aftermath of the visit: "At the time he came back . . . I remember him coming to see me, and it occurred to me that I had never seen Walter more depressed. . . . He had gone to Zimbabwe with the hopes of getting some kind of assistance from Mugabe and from some of the African comrades. That did not happen."[14] However, Roopnaraine's words need to be contrasted with Patricia's recollection of Walter's return to Georgetown; in her recollection there was no sense of "depression." As she explains: "When Walter returned from Zimbabwe . . . he may have been disappointed but not depressed. He and I spoke about a lot of things that fateful Friday morning, and I was not speaking to a depressed person."[15]

The "Marxists" and "socialists" in Guyana itself were, largely speaking, an irritant to Rodney, fakers who mouthed "socialism" while dividing the working class—and worse, in the case of Burnham, who broke strikes and carried out targeted assassinations. But even the People's Progressive Party, the apparently radical "electoral" party that had emerged in the 1940 to such great fanfare and hope, was a disappointment. There is no better characterization of the party's leader, Cheddi Jagan, than in C. L. R. James's acerbic prose from 1981: "Jagan had insisted that he was a Marxist, entirely connected, and the man of Moscow. Jagan was revolutionary in London, he was terrific in Cuba, he was wonderful in Moscow. I must say, in the air he was, but the moment his place reached Guyana, that disappeared."

Rodney and the WPA were sandwiched between the dictatorial "socialism" of Burnham and the socialist pronouncements of the PPP, even though he knew the socialist charade, having seen it firsthand in Tanzania. James put it like this:

> [T]he Cooperative Socialist Society [as Burnham has christened the country], and 80 percent of the economy of Guyana [were] in the hands of Burnham. All it means is that, instead of being exploited by the foreign bureaucrat, the Guyanese are now exploited by the local bureaucrat, which in many cases is worse than the foreigner. 80 percent of the economy is in one hand. And on the other side, there is Jagan, who speaks about Marxism, as he has done for fifteen or twenty years, making periodic visits to Cuba and to Moscow.[16]

This was a farce and a dangerous one. In this sea of socialisms, the WPA, with Rodney as its leading thinker, was attempting to craft a genuine socialism led by the working class from the bottom up.

Nevertheless, the magnetic pull of regional "socialist" states, especially Cuba, was enormous. Rodney's approach—as in all aspects of his life—was to be critical. He knew what these societies were like from the inside, how they felt, what sort of real voice the poor had, and how the struggles of the working class were frequently suppressed. Yet the northern Caribbean island cast an important glow on all radical and socialist forces in the region. Cuba asserted—to Rodney and everyone else—that an island with a people of African descent could, even in the direct line of fire of the United States, build an alternative society based on certain progressive principles. Speaking on behalf of the WPA on August 30, 1979, Rodney expressed delight at Cuba hosting the Sixth Conference of Heads of State or Government of the Non-Aligned Countries in Havana from September 3 to 9, 1979. The presence at this conference of the new radical governments of Grenada and Nicaragua—coming to power in 1979 and 1980, respectively—demonstrated a singular capacity of radical states to emerge in a region dominated by the almighty power of the United States.

Boukari-Yabara puts Rodney's praise of the Cuba experience in 1979 in a compelling way: "Noting that one of the successes of the Cuban revolution was to declare war on racism, capitalism and imperialism united in the same structure of oppression, Rodney invited Caribbean politicians and intellectuals to study the whole of the Cuban system rather than to be satisfied with analysing or borrowing isolated parts, generally transmitted by Westerners."[17] Rodney's murder less than a year later, the invasion of Grenada in 1982, and the US-sponsored attacks on Nicaragua by Contra rebels in the same year seemed to demonstrate not radical possibilities but the persistent power of the United States and its regional backers.

The WPA was the greatest of the Caribbean radical projects and, largely under Rodney, emphasized mass struggles and working-class self-activity; in this respect, the organization stood in the inspiring tradition of the early Bolsheviks in Russia under Lenin's leadership. The history of the WPA in the 1970s is unique and largely unrecognized, and it still has much to teach us. However, the multiple paths it pursued toward socialism—guerrilla struggle, coup, progressive military action—were not distinct roads to the same goal but ultimately completely inimical goals altogether. Mass action, strikes, and working-class self-organization—the beating heart of Rodney's activism—could not be married with popular (though essentially elite-led) change through armed struggle. Rodney knew this and grappled with it, but it was a knot that he was not completely able to untie.

Organizing and Learning from Workers

As all revolutionaries must, Rodney learned from practice. It was his experience in working-class politics from the mid-1970s that laid bare his focus on militant self-activity. Much of this development took place amid the day-to-day struggles of the WPA, and Rodney's work with rank-and-file union members—who were frequently battling their own entrenched and corrupt officials—as well as the Organization of Working People. The OWP and the WPA came together and challenged the leadership of the Guyana Mine Workers Union (GMWU)—at the time, the most powerful trade union representing Guyana's mine workers. The battles were conducted in strikes, in court, and on the street. Through the 1970s, the working class, who had been shepherded to a large extent into the government's hands, started to break away from the ruling party. As former mine worker Odida Quamina writes, "[T]he OWP and WPA's confrontation with the Union's leadership had brought them directly into confrontation with the PNC and the whole government machinery."[18] The old politics of ethnic divide-and-rule was beginning to break down.

With the foundation of the OWP and WPA in 1974, as well as the break between the African Society for Cultural Relations with Independent Africa (ASCRIA) and the PNC, the old politics had begun to fracture. This was not simply a "shift" from progovernment accommodation to confrontation, but a radical break of ethnic politics toward a revolutionary perspective of change.

The nationalization of the private Demerara Bauxite Company (DEMBA) on July 15, 1971, renamed the Guyana Bauxite Company (GUYBAU), pushed militant working-class action across party lines and into a direct challenge of the ruling party. Immediately, the stakes became higher, and every strike a direct skirmish with the economic heart of the state. The OWP emerged to deal with the mass disgruntlement of workers who felt betrayed by their union, the GMWU. However, unlike every previous initiative, the OWP took on the union leadership directly. Quamina explained, "The workers, unlike the PNC's leadership, understood who their real leaders were, and refused any compromises."[19] New branches of the OWP were set up, which often paved the way for the

WPA to grow in working-class areas, in Linden and elsewhere. Quamina describes the focus of the WPA from 1974: "At the outset, the WPA concentrated its efforts . . . on educating the workers and other members of the community."[20] In this work, it was naturally a larger threat than the OWP, which tended to limit itself to workplace issues and questions of trade union leadership. The WPA enlarged the field of vision, audaciously including the entire horizon of society, politics, and life. For an organization that had just been formed—though from rich and fertile terrain—it was a remarkable undertaking.

Writing in the late 1980s, Quamina, in an otherwise sober and cool-headed study, manages to distill the impact of the WPA on the PNC with considerable concision:

> In time the WPA would pose the first real political challenge to what was traditionally regarded by many as the PNC's private property. The fact that the organising efforts were all-embracing (industry and community alike) raised the level of politicisation and consciousness. The fact, also, that the industry became the target and battle ground for both the WPA and the PNC, gave the Party the much need opportunity to unleash the whole State machinery against the "enemies of the State."[21]

This is exactly what happened: the "whole State machinery" was hurled at the WPA, and irreplaceable comrades fell. However, it was the success of the WPA's "industry and community" organizing, its rapid politicization of Indian and African workers, that led to the hurricane of repression after 1978.

The challenge was not just from state repression but also from within the workers' trade unions themselves. As we have seen, the bauxite workers in Linden took strike action in July 1979, part of a struggle that had started in 1977 for a minimum wage for all workers to which the government had agreed with the Guyana Trades Union Congress (TUC), but had not implemented. While the bauxite workers were on strike, four other unions came out, including the Clerical Commercial and Industrial Workers Union (CCWU). They also demanded that the government honor its commitment to the TUC. They fought with a deadline—an ultimatum for the government to implement its agreement—which expired on August 14. On the same day as the expiration of the deadline, sugar workers struck in solidarity with the bauxite workers. Never, in the country's history, had there been such unity: a largely Indian group of workers had come out in solidarity with strikers from the African-dominated bauxite industry. There were astounding waves of working-class action, each one overlapping the other in a rising tide of militancy; the WPA was rushing to keep up, and Rodney was in a frenzy of almost-permanent speaking and organizing as he crisscrossed the country.

Yet as the strike developed, so did the regime's efforts to undermine it. Strike leaders in workplaces were targeted and threatened by managers and the police. The PNC tried to get workers in the CCWU to leave the union and join Burnham's front organization, the Guyana Labour Union. The president of the CCWU, Gordon Todd, was arrested and interrogated by the Guyana Defence Force on August 17. In the end, the CCWU was told that if the strike was not suspended then the "check-off system" would be ended—the system in which union dues where deducted from wages by employers. This challenge to the union bureaucracy's very ability to survive spurred them to call off the strike. Sixty workers were immediately sacked, and the WPA launched a call for donations to support the dismissed strikers and their families. Strikes began to collapse, and after a month, the bauxite strike was also called off by the union leaders. In Berbice—an important base of bauxite workers—workers expressed disgust at their leaders' orders for members to return to work, heckling and shouting angrily at their representatives. A shoddy compromise was made to implement a "merit increase" within four weeks. Ultimately, the rank-and-file bodies—the OWP with the support of the WPA—proved too weak to maintain the pressure. The wave of militant strike action crumbled.

James and Rodney were right that there needed to be a defense against this "hurricane"; both thinkers knew that it could come from a radicalizing army, willing to break with the regime and join the mass social resistance—under the direction of the working class and poor themselves. Rodney was clear that there could not be a radical, armed solution over the head of, and in the name of, the mass struggle. It is important to add that Rodney's approach to the working class, while seeing them as a key, indeed central, part of the struggle for a new society, was also highly nuanced. He recognized that the nature of the working class in Guyana and across the Caribbean—small, and concentrated in farming and mining work—required the mobilization of other elements who were not central to production. African American studies scholar Horace Campbell, in his widely read 1985 study on the Rastafarians, makes this point, writing: "Underdevelopment had rendered more than 40% of the population unemployed, cosmetic measures . . . could not deal with this fundamental problem of failure to fully mobilize the productive capacity of the working people."[22]

Today, the WPA is a fallen giant. Although there is no space here to chart the party's degeneration, a few words are in order. Shockingly, the organization joined the PNC-led APNU (A Partnership for African Unity) government when the coalition won elections in 2015. For a party that had fought valiantly against the PNC dictatorship in the 1970s and had suffered a terrible toll, the decision to combine forces was baffling in the extreme. Yet the WPA was able to provide important left cover for the PNC's efforts to win power in the elections. Although no longer a militant socialist organization, its leading members still managed to play a particularly sordid role. Rupert Roopnaraine, a comrade of Rodney's in the 1970s, was appointed minister of education of Guyana in the coalition government in 2015 and was then promoted to the Ministry of the Presidency in 2017. He served directly under the PNC president David A. Granger. Granger, it should be noted, had been a commander of the Guyana Defence Force in 1979, working intimately with Burnham and the entire brutal apparatus of the party-state before, during, and after Rodney's assassination. If Roopnaraine's ambitions for political office were not depressing enough, he refused to testify before the Commission of Inquiry into Rodney's assassination, and then refused to accept the COI report. Another luminary of the WPA, Clive Thomas, also joined the 2015 PNC-led government as a presidential advisor on sustainable development. Commentators, former comrades, and newspapers gasped in shock at the rush to high office by two long-standing militants of Guyana's working people.[23]

A Singular and Remarkable Man

Patricia Rodney, for one, warns us not to trust histories of great men, and not to ignore the vital context that draws out "greatness." Her husband had the same hostility to the "great man" version of history, and every word he wrote was a challenge to it. It was Patricia and the children who were in the eye of the storm, and suffered for it—even as they were shored up, following Walter's June 1980 murder, by a mass of solidarity, the arms of friends and comrades drawn tightly around them.

On December 10, 1980, James Turner, then an "associate professor" at the Africana Studies and Research Center at Cornell University, wrote to "Mr. Ricky Singh," editor of *Caribbean Contact* in Bridgetown,

Barbados—where Patricia, Asha, Kanini, and Shaka were now residents. He wrote:

> The enclosed money order is sent to you with the hope that you will be able to assure us that Dr. Walter Rodney's widow, Pat, and their children will receive it. . . .
>
> This money was raised at a meeting organized by our academic program and represents the contribution of many people. However, Minister Louis Farrakhan of the Nation of Islam contributed one third of the sum.
>
> Please convey to Pat our deepest concern for her and the welfare of the children.
>
> Please convey our fond regards to her and the children.[24]

Solidarity and support in the form of financial help was vital. The family had arrived in Barbados with limited resources and had to survive, ripped away from the support of not only Walter but also that of friends and family in Guyana. The remarkable feat of the last forty years has been the astonishing efforts of Patricia and the children to maintain the campaign for justice while sustaining Rodney's work through the Walter Rodney Foundation, based in Atlanta.

One element of this work was the Rodney family's decision to donate the Walter Rodney Papers to the Atlanta University Center's Robert W. Woodruff Library—where they comprise an astonishing resource on Rodney's work and life. What we see in the archive—and what I have tried to capture in this book—is Rodney's exhaustive historical work and scholarship. In each box and folder is evidence of an entirely unsectarian approach to his work and life. His writing is ruthlessly critical and free of left prejudices, and he never accepted secondhand opinions, while reading everything himself; his praise and careful study of Trotsky's work are exemplary in this respect. A new volume, published in 2018 from Rodney's notes on the Russian Revolution, demonstrates his approach. In the book, Rodney works out concepts and positions for himself—an attitude toward learning on which he insisted in his teaching and popular education.[25] Writing in 1981, Horace Campbell drew similar conclusions, noting that Rodney had left a legacy of hard work and a commitment to critical inquiry.[26]

Perhaps the most accurate tribute to Walter Rodney—of the many that were written after his murder—came from the extraordinary pen of Wole Soyinka. He had never met Rodney but knew his work and respected him enormously. In 1974, he had hoped to see him in Tanzania at the Pan-African Congress, an event that he brilliantly lampooned in "The Man Who Was Absent," his tribute to Rodney:

> And so, Walter Rodney remained in Tanzania, but did not appear at the Congress. Needless to say . . . Walter Rodney was someone with whom many of those present had hoped, as a matter of course, to make contact. . . . Yet the "progressive" government of Tanzania had succumbed to the blackmail of reactionary Caribbean governments to keep out this radical scholar from such a gathering.[27]

As we have seen, Rodney was in fact well aware of what the congress had become and had condemned it before it began. Following his militant lead, others, including C. L. R. James, had decided that they too could not attend—refusing to give the congress the blessing of their presence. Soyinka goes on: "The Congress of course failed before it even started. It ended up as yet another play of opportunistic interests, opening with a three-hour recorded speech by Ahmed Sekou Touré re-hashing old, private quarrels, to which the gathering eventually reacted as if to a revelation." Indeed, the Sixth Pan-African Congress was a wretched affair full of officially sanctioned "pan-African" organizations and parties, many already in power but now facing their own oppositions—frequently radical and socialist ones. Soyinka tells us that the event was a "takeover," a victory for governments in Guinea, in Tanzania, and in the Caribbean: "And those of you who know the history of the Pan-African movements will agree with me indeed that this is the seal of doom on a forum," while, he writes, "movements were simply snuffed out through protocol."

Better than many who actually knew Rodney directly, Soyinka could immediately see what he was, pointing out the aspects of his writing and politics which were almost entirely unique. While he had not managed to meet Rodney in Dar, he wrote:

> I had read . . . HEUA. . . . In an intellectual world rendered increasingly turgid by ideological mouthers and phrasemongers, Walter Rodney stood out for lucidity, relevance, for a preference for actuality, its analysis and prescription over and above slavish cant. He proceeded from attested facts to analysis not, like many others, commencing with worn and untested frameworks—usually made up of someone else's summary, thesis, or even a bare out-of-context quotation—onto which existing facts are then stretched, pruned, tortured and distorted to obtain a purely theoretical semi-fit. Walter Rodney was not of the latter kind.

Rodney pulled this approach to his "literary" work into his political action. His approach to Guyana was not as a terrain on which to impose preexisting models and formulas, or in which to stretch facts, as Soyinka writes, in a theoretical semi-fit. Rodney's attitude to activism was based on a profoundly grounded and analyzed context, and it was within this context that he worked as a revolutionary—formulating and reformulating radical propositions against the severe and blustery headwinds of real life. As Soyinka observed, "He was clearly one of the most solidly ideologically *situated* intellectuals ever to look colonialism and its contemporary heir—black opportunism and exploitation—in the eye, and where necessary, spit in it."[28]

A year or so before he was murdered, Rodney spoke about the mortal perils historically faced by those struggling for liberation. Addressing a group of Guyanese supporters about the country's history of slavery, he explained:

> Few individuals want willingly to invite their own death. Yet many will be found who are prepared to fight fearlessly for their rights even if their lives are threatened. The human spirit has a remarkable capacity to rise above oppression, and only the fools who now misrule Guyana can image that our population alone lacks such capacity. During the famous 1763 slave rebellion in Berbice, there were numerous examples of the undying courage of our fore parents. The Dutch slave masters captured Accabre, one of the leaders of the rebellion, and he simply laughed scornfully when they tormented him. Soon after, Accabre and eight other freedom fighters were put to death by roasting over a slow fire. Even their enemies were impressed by the fact that Accabre's men were firm to the end and did not flinch.[29]

Rodney was one of these men. He did not invite death, but he laughed in the face of his tormenters, refusing to flinch when faced with their threats and brutality. A return to his life and work is vital if we wish to understand a world that must be transformed today.

CHAPTER 14

Walter Rodney's Legacy Today

In a powerful 2021 short film, *Two Distant Strangers*, by Travon Free and Martin Desmond Roe, a Black graphic artist gets caught in a time loop that always ends with his murder by a white police officer. Behind this dramatic device resides a fundamental and troubling truth. The bulk of our struggles, our campaigns for justice, and our exertions to change society are on constant replay; while they do not comprise exactly the same events, they share many of the same features of similar struggles in the past.

The anti-racist struggles today—epitomized in the Black Lives Matter movement that broke out after the murder of George Floyd on May 25, 2020—look to a recovery of history, of previous struggles for Black Liberation, and of the Black Power movement of the 1960s and 1970s. At the core of this movement is an urge to understand the history of slavery, the resistance to colonial occupation in Africa, and the efforts of people to understand the complex richness of the continent's pre-colonial history.

For a generation today who are fighting on many battlefronts, against deep and seemingly immoveable misogyny, racism, and ethnic divide and rule, there is—once more—the need to return to the work, writing, and activism of the past. This is where Rodney's legacy lies. His struggles, his forensic research and work, and his revolutionary activism took place in a time that bares many of the same challenges and demands as our own. Rodney's writings—as I hope this book has shown—remain vital to understanding our world, and the pressing need to revolutionize it. If Rodney had lived, he would not have been surprised by the unending destructive capacity of global capitalism and its ability—about which he had written in terms of the colonial destruction of African ecosystems in the eighteenth and nineteenth centuries—to destroy the very source of human life, the earth itself. Rodney understood that the avaricious, insatiable hunger for profit in capitalism generates the devastation we see today, and that the economic system cannot be reformed.

This last fact is at the core of Rodney's revolutionary practice. He was both a historian with a ferocious capacity to read, synthesize, and learn, and an activist who sought to understand and revolutionize our contemporary conundrum. The celebrated writer and activist Angela Davis identifies the heart of Rodney's contribution along these lines. Writing in 2018, she explains, "[W]e . . . need such brilliant examples of what it means to be a resolute intellectual who recognises that the ultimate significance of knowledge is its capacity to transform our social worlds."[1]

Rodney's political work and writing were constantly in a process of dialectical development. His understanding of the world was not written on biblical tablets but evolved on the basis of research and informed by political action. When evidence demanded it, his conclusions could and had to be revised. Indeed, dogmatism or sectarianism was antithetical to Rodney's approach to Marxism.

Rodney critically engaged with Marxism, while understanding that revolutionary theory needed to be historically grounded and adapted to concrete experience. In this regard, Davis, summarized his approach as reflecting "both a sober, well-reasoned historical investigation, shaped by Marxist categories and critiques, and a deep sense of the historical conjuncture defined by global revolutionary upheavals."[2]

In *How Europe Underdeveloped Africa*, Rodney undertook to challenge capitalism's assumptions about what was normal. Davis explains, "In refuting the argument that Africa's subordination to Europe emanates from a natural propensity toward stagnation, Rodney also repudiates the ideological assumption that external intervention alone would be capable of provoking progress on the continent." Imperialism and colonialism, the emissaries of early European capitalism, created structural obstacles to economic and political progress on the continent. This was one of Rodney's main arguments in his 1972 classic.[3]

The effort to forge unity in the struggle of the oppressed was at the center of Rodney's work. If there was any hope of revolutionary transformation, he consistently argued, then this was predicated on the unity of working people. Indeed, capitalism's survival depends on its ability to drive communities and people apart—the poor against the poor, Black against white, Indian against African workers, man against woman.

Although Rodney did not employ the feminist vocabulary that is now in common usage, he was acutely aware of gender issues in his writing and activism. Davis writes how in 1972 Rodney "addresses the role of gender, and he is careful to point out that under colonialism, African women's 'social, religious, constitutional, and political privileges and rights disappeared while the economic exploitation continued and was often intensified.' He emphasizes that the impact of colonialism on labor in Africa redefined men's work as 'modern' while constituting women's work as 'traditional' or 'backward.'"

Davis also explains that when *HEUA* was published, Black activism (in the United State in particular) was heavily impregnated with cultural nationalist ideas of female inferiority. The book, she argues, was a vital instrument to activists seeking to challenge these "essentialist notions of gender within Black radical movements of that era."[4] The book continues to resonate in these ways today.

Rodney was also an *organized* revolutionary. Movements were vital, the indispensable steam pushing the pistonheads of change, but they were not sufficient. History had taught him that great social movements—whether for justice, anti-racism, equal rights, or freedom from colonialism—would rise and fall. A principal concern of his was that these movements might not be able to sustain and develop into a deeper and more profound struggle for global transformation and revolution.

Under capitalism, all life and injustice seem to repeat on an unending cycle. Rodney understood this feature of capitalism: racism, ethnic violence, environmental destruction, and sexism were the natural outgrowths of a system that needed to divide working people in order to survive. In any serious project of radical transformation, capitalism had to be overthrown—this Rodney taught us.

Capitalism is the force that underpins the complex and intersecting inequalities that generate the struggles we see today. The struggle against this system was central to Rodney's life and practice. At the same time, he recognized that this does not mean we should sublimate or minimize racism, for example, as a simple consequence of capitalism. Once more, Davis illuminates this fundamental point with a question: "[H]ow can we encourage radical critiques of capitalism as integral to struggles against racism as we also advance the recognition that we cannot envision the dismantling of capitalism as long as the structures of racism remains intact?"[5] Rodney understood how vital it was to pull together a variety of social movements, groups, and campaigns. As we have seen, in Guyana in the 1970s, Rodney became the leading member of an astonishing anti-capitalist organization, the Working People's Alliance. The gathering steam of protest and social movements had to be combined, focused, and channeled in a democratic, socialist organization.

If we want a world free of the scourge of sexism, racism, and environmental destruction, Rodney reminds us today, it is to an anti-capitalist and socialist revolution that we must add our labors. But something else he said was of equal importance. According to Rodney, the radical power of social movements can only be fully realized if we capture its force before it disperses and the loop of history is allowed, once more, to repeat—each time reoccurring with more destructive energy. The vessel that can capture this energy is an organization: one committed to the unity of the poor and working people. The WPA, for a brief time, was an attempt to forge such an organization, and Rodney was its most brilliant organizer and thinker.

Revolutionary struggle *and* organization, in Rodney's hands, can be seen as an effort to break humanity from its destructive and seemingly unending cycle. History was the tool he used to help us see the repetitive and ruinous pattern of global capitalism: the millions of lives it had destroyed, and the devastation it had wrought upon the earth, in its brief five centuries of existence.

Today, more than ever, we need to improve the manner in which we capture the immense, animating power of social movements. We confront a vast and organized apparatus of states, and an international ruling class, who use global clubs and institutions to fix the rules in a deadly game of capitalist accumulation and profit.

◊

Rodney was murdered when he was thirty-eight years old. However, a life cannot be measured by the number of years we live, and his contribution to activism, history, antiracism, and socialism is equal, in any proper system of accounting, to many lifetimes. Rodney's work was a constant effort to sharpen the arrowhead of our popular struggles with learning, history, and organization. His was a clarion call to end the loop that our lives and struggles seem doomed to repeat in an ever-deepening crisis of destruction, unless, as Rodney wrote in 1972, we can finally unite our intersecting struggles to destroy capitalism. As Rodney put it, "That is the element of *conscious activity* that signifies the ability to make history by grappling with the heritage of objective material conditions and social relations."[6] This does not mean, as Rodney would have told us, that all efforts for reform are futile. One of the significant achievements of the Walter Rodney Foundation, and the family's relentless campaigning, was the Commission of Inquiry that published its findings in 2016 in Guyana. At the end of an arduous period of investigation into the circumstances surrounding Rodney's murder, the report made a series of recommendations.

Many of these were fundamental, baseline suggestions about how Guyana could reform its legal and policing procedures. For instance, they called for ensuring a "well-trained and highly professional Police Force" that would be loyal to the country and not to ethnicity and party affiliation. The report recommended that there should not be an eight-year delay, as there was in Rodney's case, before there is a coroner's inquest into a "death in unnatural circumstances or in any circumstances"—indispensable for maintaining trust and confidence in a country's justice system. The report stated that the police force should be tasked with responsibility to investigate serious crimes like murder "and strive to do so with thoroughness and urgency."

When the Commission of Inquiry had requested to see files and records related to the Walter Rodney case, they were told they were not available—that they could not be found. The commission thus recommended "thoroughness, efficiency and security in record keeping." The report also spoke of elections and how these are conducted in the country—recommending that they should be properly monitored, and that every effort should be made to maintain "ethnic harmony": "Every government has a continuing responsibility to work in close consultation with national associations and diverse interest groups to design and implement a programme to strengthen . . . a sense of national unity."[7] These recommendations are a necessary part of the reform of Guyana's society.

However, when it comes to the deeper structural changes that will undermine how our global economy and society is run, it is to revolutionary change that we must turn. To this end, we must learn from, develop, and deepen Rodney's legacy.

The Black Lives Matter movement and the ideas around it are reframing politics, as did the political movements of the period that Rodney lived through. Correspondingly, the connected political, ecological, and ideological crises of today call forth Rodney's work and revolutionary activism. Our times are radical, and we need to radicalize with them in theory and practice. Walter Rodney remains a revolutionary for our time.

Selected Bibliography

Books

Adi, Hakim. *Pan-Africanism: A History*. London: Bloomsbury Publishing, 2018.

Barker, Colin, ed. *Revolutionary Rehearsals*. Chicago: Haymarket Books, 2008.

Bornstein, Sam, and Al Richardson. *Against the Stream: History of the Trotskyist Movement in Britain, 1924–38*. London: Merlin, 1986.

Chung, Clairmont, ed. *Walter A. Rodney: A Promise of Revolution*. New York: Monthly Review Press, 2012.

Curtis, Mark. *Unpeople: Britain's Secret Human Rights Abuses*. London: Vintage, 2004.

Cushion, Steve, and Dennis Bartholomew. *By Our Own Hands: A People's History of the Grenadian Revolution*. Boston: Cutlass, 2018.

Davidson, Basil. *Africa in History*. London: Weidenfeld & Nicolson, 1968.

Davis, Mike. *Late Victorian Holocausts: El Niño Famines and the Making of the Third World*. London and New York: Verso, 2000.

Fanon, Frantz. *Towards the African Revolution*. New York: Grove, 1994.

First, Ruth. *The Barrel of a Gun: Political Power in Africa and the Coup d'Etat*. London: The Penguin Press, 1970.

Fryer, Peter. *Staying Power: The History of Black People in Britain*. Edmonton: University of Alberta Press, 1984.

Grady-Willis, Winston A. *Challenging U.S. Apartheid: Atlanta and Black Struggles for Human Rights, 1960–1977*. Durham: Duke University Press, 2006.

Gray, Obika. *Radicalism and Social Change in Jamaica, 1960–1972*. Knoxville: University of Tennessee Press, 1991.

Harris, Nigel. *The End of the Third World: Newly Industrializing Countries and the Decline of an Ideology*. New York: New Amsterdam Books, 1987.

Hirji, Karim F., ed. *Cheche: Reminiscences of a Radical Magazine*. Dar es Salaam: Mkuki na Nyota Publishers, 2010.

———. *The Enduring Relevance of "How Europe Underdeveloped Africa."* Ottawa: Daraja Press, 2017.

———. *Growing Up with Tanzania: Memories, Musings, and Maths*. Dar es Salaam: Mkuki na Nyota Publishers, 2014.

———. *The Travails of a Tanzanian Teacher*. Ottawa: Daraja Press, 2018.

Hochschild, Adam. *King Leopold's Ghost: A Story of Greed, Terror, and Heroism in Colonial Africa*. New York: Mariner, 1998.

Ibbott, Ralph. *Ujamaa: The Hidden Story of Tanzania's Socialist Cillages*. London: Crossroads, 2014.

Naomi Klein, *On Fire: The (Burning) Case for a Green New Deal* (New York: Penguin, 2020).

Legum, Colin. *Republic in Trouble: South Africa, 1972–73.* London: Rex Collins Ltd., 1973.

Lewis, Rupert C. *Walter Rodney's Intellectual and Political Thought.* Barbados, Jamaica, and Trinidad and Tobago: University of the West Indies Press, 1998.

Mars, Perry. *Ideology and Change: The Transformation of the Caribbean Left.* Kingston, Jamaica: University of the West Indies Press, 1998.

Mboya, Tom. *Freedom and After.* London: Andre Deutsch, 1963.

Nyerere, Julius. *Freedom and Unity: Uhuru Na Umoja; A Selection from Writings and Speeches, 1952–65.* Tanzania: Oxford University Press Tanzania, 1966.

Peter, Chris, and Sengondo Mvungi. "The State and Student Struggles." In *The State and the Working People*, edited by Issa G. Shivji. London: Marram, 1986.

Quaminda, Odida T. *Mineworkers of Guyana: The Making of a Working Class.* London and New Jersey: Zed, 1987.

Rodney, Walter. *The Groundings with My Brothers.* London and New York: Verso, 2018 [1969].

———. *A History of the Guyanese Working People, 1881–1905.* Baltimore: Johns Hopkins University Press, 1981.

———. *A History of the Upper Guinea Coast, 1545–1800.* New York: Oxford University Press, 1970.

———. *How Europe Underdeveloped Africa.* London and New York: Verso, 2018 [1972].

———. *The Russian Revolution: A View from the Third World.* Edited by Robin D. G. Kelley and Jesse Benjamin. London and New York: Verso, 2018.

———. *Walter Rodney Speaks: The Making of an African Intellectual.* Edited by Howard Dodson and Robert Hill. Trenton, NJ: Africa World Press, 1990.

Sagers, Thomas and Matthew Maraffa. "Soviet Air-Passenger Transportation Network." *Geographical Review* 80:3 (1990). 266–67.

Saul, John S. *Revolutionary Traveller: Freeze-Frames from a Life.* Winnipeg: Arbeiter Ring, 2009.

Shivji, Issa G. *Class Struggles in Tanzania.* London: Heinemann, 1976.

———. *The Silent Class Struggle.* Dar es Salaam: Tanzania Publishing House, 1974.

Thomas-Johnson, Amandla. "Chimurenganyana: Becoming Kwame Ture." *Chimurenga Magazine*, 2020.

Trevor-Roper, Hugh. *The Rise of Christian Europe.* London: Harcourt, Brace & World, 1965.

Wong, Dwayne (Omowale). *The Political and Intellectual Legacy of Walter Rodney.* Wroclaw: CreateSpace Publishing, 2016.

Boukari-Yabara, Amzat. *Walter Rodney: Un historien engagé (1942–1980).* Paris: Présence Africaine, 2018.

Zeilig, Leo, ed. *Class Struggle and Resistance in Africa.* Chicago: Haymarket Books, 2009.

———. *Voices of Liberation: Frantz Fanon.* Chicago: Haymarket Books, 2016.

Articles and Reports

Ahmed, Ali Jumale. "In Memory of Walter Rodney." *Ufahamu: A Journal of African Studies* 12:2 (1983). https://escholarship.org/uc/item/8pq310s6.

"Ahmed Gora Ebrahim." *South African History Online.* October 25, 2013. https://www.sahistory.org.za/people/ahmed-gora-ebrahim.

Ampofo, Akosua Adomako. "In Conversation with Professor Akilagpa Sawyerr." *Contemporary Journal of African Studies* 6:2 (November 2019). https://www.ajol.info/index.php/contjas/article/view/197352.

"The Arnold Rampersaud trials." N.p. May 31, 2006. http://www.guyana.org/features/postindependence/chapter12.html.

Bagree, Sunit. "The Money Drain: How Trade Misinvoicing and Unjust Debt Undermine Economic and Social Rights in Southern Africa." *Action for Southern Africa.* August 2019. https://actsa.org/campaigns/the-money-drain/.

Barongo, Yolamu R. "Walter Rodney and the Current Revolutionary Struggles in the Carribean." *Ufahamu: A Journal of African Studies* 12:1 (1982). https://escholarship.org/uc/item/3g2487d1.

Brown, Ruth. "Racism and Immigration in Britain." *International Socialism* 2:68 (Autumn 1995). https://www.marxists.org/history/etol/newspape/isj2/1995/isj2-068/brown.htm.

Campbell, Horace. "Remembering Walter Rodney." *Socialist Worker* 1955. June 11, 2005. https://socialistworker.co.uk/art/6543/Remembering+Walter+Rodney.

———. "Walter Rodney—People's Historian." *Ufahamu: A Journal of African Studies* 10:1–2 (1981). https://escholarship.org/uc/item/0gr9g3hs#author.

Campos, Lola. "In Honour of Maurice Bishop and the Revolutionary Caribbean." *Anticonquista,* March 13, 2018. https://anticonquista.com/2018/03/13/in-honor-of-maurice-bishop-and-the-revolutionary-caribbean/.

Chukwudinma, Chinedu. "Towards a Full Understanding of Walter Rodney." *Review of African Political Economy.* August 1, 2019. https://roape.net/2019/08/01/towards-a-full-understanding-of-walter-rodney/.

Daum, Walter. "In Defence of Walter Rodney: Workers, Imperialism, & Exploitation." *Review of African Political Economy.* June 11, 2020. https://roape.net/2020/06/11/in-defence-of-walter-rodney-workers-imperialism-exploitation/.

Elsby, Angus. "Stealing Africa's Commodities." *Review of African Political Economy.* August 7, 2019. https://roape.net/2019/08/07/stealing-africas-commodities/.

Empson, Martin. "Rodney's Russian Revolution." *Review of African Political Economy.* December 13, 2018. https://roape.net/2018/12/13/rodneys-russian-revolution/.

"Foreign Relations, 1964–1968, Volume XXXII, Dominican Republic; Cuba; Haiti; Guyana." *Guyana News and Information.* April 2005. http://www.guyana.org/govt/US-declassified-documents-1964-1968.html.

Gutzmore, Cecil. "Misunderstanding and Misrepresenting Walter Rodney." *Review of African Political Economy.* October 10, 2019. https://roape.net/2019/10/10/misunderstanding-and-misrepresenting-walter-rodney/.

Harisch, Immanuel R. "Walter Rodney's Dar es Salaam Years, 1966-1974: *How Europe Underdeveloped Africa,* Tanzania's *ujamaa,* and Student Radicalism at 'the Hill.'" MA thesis, University of Vienna, 2018. https://www.academia.edu/37927700/Walter_

Rodney_s_Dar_es_Salaam_Years_1966_1974_How_Europe_Underdeveloped_Africa_Tanzania_s_ujamaa_and_Student_Radicalism_at_the_Hill_n.

Hart, Richard. "Labour Rebellions of the 1930s in the British Caribbean Region Colonies." Caribbean Labour Solidarity and the Socialist History Society, 2002. https://libcom.org/library/labour-rebellions-1930s-british-caribbean-region -colonies-richard-hart.

Higginbottom, Andy. "The Revolutionary Legacy of Walter Rodney." *Review of African Political Economy.* January 8, 2019. https://roape.net/2019/01/08/the-revolutio nary-legacy-of-walter-rodney/.

Hill, Robert A. "Walter Rodney and the Restatement of Pan Africanism in Theory and Practice." *Ufahamu: A Journal of African Studies* 38:3 (2015). https://escholarship. org/uc/item/94h9q4h3.

———. "Walter Rodney on Pan-Africanism." *Ufahamu: A Journal of African Studies* 12:3 (1983). https://escholarship.org/uc/item/6b5507c6#author.

James, C. L. R. *Walter Rodney and the Question of Power.* Montreal: Black Rose, 1982. https://www.marxists.org/archive/james-clr/works/1981/01/rodney.htm.

Kwayana, Eusi. "39 Years Since Walter Rodney Fell; Andaiye, Walter Rodney's Colleague Has Re-joined the Ancestors." *Pambazuka News.* June 15, 2019. https://www. pambazuka.org/pan-africanism/39-years-walter-rodney-fell-andaiye-walter-rod-ney%E2%80%99s-colleague-has-rejoined-ancestors?utm_campaign=shareahol-ic&utm_medium=facebook&utm_source=socialnetwork&fbclid=IwAR3DrSY-WiE1F1_fUuLvMiOQr--paArJmbSmW7oIZfdpL7J6s2to5zXMzzx4.

———. "Walter Rodney." *Guyana Under Siege.* n.d. http://www.guyanaundersiege.com /Leaders/Rodney1.htm.

Legassick, Martin. "Perspectives on African 'Underdevelopment.'" *Journal of African History* 17:3 (1976).

Lewis, Rupert C. Interview with Patricia Rodney. April 5–6, 1989. "Walter Rodney: 1968 Revisited." *Social and Economic Studies* 43:3 (September 1994).

Lowhar, Syl. "On Black Power." *Tapia.* August 4, 1974. https://ufdc.ufl.edu /UF00072147/00121/1x.

Magubane, Bernard. "On Walter Rodney's *How Europe Underdeveloped Africa.*" *Ufahamu: A Journal of African Studies* 3:3 (1973). Available at https://escholarship.org /uc/item/1w99x2h9.

Martin, Guy. "*How Europe Undeveloped Africa,* by Walter Rodney." *Ufahamu: A Journal of African Studies* 6:1 (1975). https://escholarship.org/uc/item/9vc6w3dv.

McDowell, Linda. "How Caribbean Migrants Helped to Rebuild Britain." *British Library.* October 4, 2018. https://www.bl.uk/windrush/articles/how-caribbean-migrants-rebuilt-britain.

Mora, Esteban. "Mutual Profiting: Unpicking the Harvey-Smith Debate." *Review of African Political Economy.* June 21, 2018. https://roape.net/2018/06/21/mutu-al-profiting-unpicking-the-harvey-smith-debate/.

Murray, Roger, and Tom Wengraf. "The Algerian Revolution: Part I," *New Left Review* 22 (1963). https://www.newleftreview.org/issues/i22/articles/roger-mur-ray-tom-wengraf-the-algerian-revolution-part-i.

Nehusi, Kimani, and Nigel Westmaas. "How Europe Underdeveloped Africa: A Tribute to Walter Rodney." *Africa Update* 26:3 (Summer 2019). https://www2.ccsu.edu/africaupdate/?article=414.

Nyerere, Julius. "The Arusha Declaration." February 5, 1967. https://www.marxists.org/subject/africa/nyerere/1967/arusha-declaration.htm.

Rampertab, Rakesh. "House of Israel." *Guyana under Siege*. N.d. http://www.guyanaundersiege.com/Historical/House%20of%20Israel.htm.

Rodney, Walter. "Aspects of the International Class Struggle in Africa, the Caribbean, and America." In *Pan-Africanism: Struggle against Neo-colonialism and Imperialism—Documents of the Sixth Pan-African Congress*. Toronto: Afro-Carib Publications, 1975. 18–41. https://www.marxists.org/subject/africa/rodney-walter/works/internationalclassstruggle.htm.

———. "Problems of Third World Development." *Ufahamu: A Journal of African Studies*. Vol. 3, no. 2 (1972): 27–47. https://escholarship.org/uc/item/2th7j61n.

———. "Tanzanian Ujamaa and Scientific Socialism." *African Review* 1:4 (1972): 61–76. Available at https://www.marxists.org/subject/africa/.

Seeram, Ralph. "From the Diaspora . . . Kaldor Budget and Black Friday February 16, 1962." *Guyanese Online*. March 30, 2014. https://guyaneseonline.net/2014/03/30/kaldor-budget-and-black-friday-february-16-1962-commentary/#more-31812.

Shivji, Issa G. "Lionel Cliffe, 1936–2013: A Comradely Scholar in Nyerere's Nationalist Tanzania." *Review of African Political Economy* 41:140 (April 2014): 284–87. https://www.tandfonline.com/doi/full/10.1080/03056244.2014.873162.

———. "Walter Rodney in Tanzania: A Tribute." *Pambazuka News*, June 27, 2013. https://www.pambazuka.org/governance/walter-rodney-tanzania-tribute.

Singh, Europe. "The Black Worker in Britain." *International Socialism* no. 73 (1974):29. https://www.marxists.org/history/etol/newspape/isj/1974/no073/singh.htm.

Sookhdeo, Ronnie. "For a Socialist Caribbean." *The Militant* 543 (March 13, 1981): 10. https://www.marxists.org/history/etol/writers/sookhdeo/1981/03/soccarib.html.

Student Nonviolent Coordinating Committee (SNCC). "6th Pan-African Congress." accessed January 27, 2022. https://snccdigital.org/events/6th-pan-african-congress/.

Szentes, Tamás. Interview by Tamás Gerőcs. "To Be Bravely Critical of Reality." *Review of African Political Economy*. November 8, 2018. https://roape.net/2018/11/08/to-be-bravely-critical-to-reality-an-interview-with-tamas-szentes/.

Treaster, Joseph B. "Guyana's President Facing Biggest Challenge in 15 years." *New York Times*. October 13, 1979. https://www.nytimes.com/1979/10/13/archives/guyanas-president-facing-biggest-challenge-in-15-years-it-will-stay.html.

Walter Rodney Foundation. "Sharing the Life and Works of Dr. Walter Rodney." N.d.

Wengraf, Lee. "U.S.-China Inter-Imperial Rivalry in Africa." *Review of African Political Economy*. November 16, 2018. https://roape.net/2018/11/16/u-s-china-inter-imperial-rivalry-in-africa/.

West, Michael O., "The Targeting of Walter Rodney." *Against the Current* no. 120 (January–February 2006). Available at https://www.marxists.org/history/etol/newspape/atc/136.html.

Westmaas, Nigel. "'A Field of Ideas'. The New World Group, the Caribbean and Guyana of the 1960s." *Stabroek News.* June 26, 2011. https://www.stabroeknews.com/2011/06/26/features/%E2%80%98a-field-of-ideas%E2%80%99-the-new-world-group-the-caribbean-and-guyana-of-the-1960s/.

———. "1968 and the Social and Political Foundations and Impact of the 'New Politics' in Guyana." *Caribbean Studies* 37:2 (January 2009): 105–32.

———. "Resisting Orthodoxy: Notes on the Origins and Ideology of the Working People's Alliance." *Small Axe* 8:1 (March 2004): 42–44. https://read.dukeupress.edu/small-axe/article-abstract/8/1%20(15)/63/89500/Resisting-Ortho-doxy-Notes-on-the-Origins-and?redirectedFrom=fulltext.

Working People's Alliance. "Toward a Revolutionary Socialist Guyana." *The Black Scholar* 11:3 (1980).

Zeilig, Leo. "Walter Rodney's Journal to Hamburg." *Review of African Political Economy.* February 14, 2019. https://roape.net/2019/02/14/walter-rodneys-journey-to-hamburg/.

Online Media

Chung, Clairmont Mali. "Amiri Baraka on Walter Rodney, Black Power and Obama." YouTube video, 17:17. January 18, 2014. https://www.youtube.com/watch?v=rwfAczX5--0.

Cox, Juanita. "Dr. Patricia Rodney Speaking at Guyana SPEAKS about Dr. Walter Anthony Rodney" (October 27, 2019). YouTube video, 29:50. October 29, 2019. https://www.youtube.com/watch?v=o5dLjDT7A2E.

Hinds'Sight: Dr. David Hinds' Guyana-Caribbean Politics. "Dr. David Hinds and Dr. Rupert Roopnarine Discuss Dr. Walter Rodney's Life and Work." YouTube video, 1:00:21. November 26, 2014. https://www.youtube.com/watch?v=I7416IIrlQ4&t=1205s.

———. "In the Sky's Wild Noise: A Documentary on Dr. Walter Rodney." YouTube video, 28:58. December 17, 2014. https://www.youtube.com/watch?v=YqfcbmncFI0&t=336s.

KONNECTIONS NC. "Walter Rodney—Crisis in the Periphery: Africa and the Caribbean." YouTube video, 1:15:39. March 9, 2020. https://www.youtube.com/watch?v=xxTBujB8xhU&t=550s 9:10

Newguymedia. "The Trail of the Vanishing Voters: A Look at How PNC Rigged Elections in Guyana." YouTube video, 25:32. March 17, 2015. https://www.youtube.com/watch?v=X4edAtrKfaE.

Stephens, Devon. "Walter Rodney Groundings: Dr. Clive Thomas." YouTube video, 1:03:05. July 24, 2013. https://www.youtube.com/watch?v=Wumat-IITHk.

UCLAmericas. "Walter Rodney's 1978 Visit to Hamburg." YouTube video, 1:30:05. December 15, 2020.

Vanderbilt University. "Reconsidering a Classic: Walter Rodney's 'How Europe Underdeveloped Africa.'" YouTube video, 1:47:27. March 22, 2012. https://www.youtube.com/watch?v=SCiuFRiOW28&t=29s.

Vientianegirl. "Nicolas Sarkozy and the African Man." YouTube video, 1:24. February 26, 2012. https://www.youtube.com/watch?v=s32eInxqubw.

Archival Material

Walter Rodney Papers. Boxes 1–37. Identifier: 0000-0000-0000-0074. Archives Research Center. Atlanta University Center, Robert W. Woodruff Library, Atlanta, Georgia.

Notes

Preface

1. KONNECTIONS NC, "Walter Rodney—Crisis in the Periphery: Africa and the Caribbean (1978)," YouTube video, 1:15:39, March 9, 2020, https://www.youtube.com/watch?v=xx'l'BujB8xhU&t=550s.
2. Walter Rodney, *How Europe Underdeveloped Africa* (London and New York: Bogle-L'Ouverture, 1972), p. 44.
3. Rodney, *HEUA*, p. 45.
4. Robert Wallace, *Big Farms Make Big Flu* (New York: Monthly Review Press, 2016).
5. Naomi Klein, *On Fire: The (Burning) Case for a Green New Deal* (New York: Penguin, 2020).
6. Walter Rodney, *The Russian Revolution: A View from the Third World* (London and New York: Verso, 2018).
7. Cliff's work remains a guide to my own work and study. See Tony Cliff, *Permanent Revolution* (pamphlet), *International Socialism*, 1st ser., no. 12 (Spring 1963).
8. See Verso's three volumes of Walter Rodney's work: https://www.versobooks.com/authors/2268-walter-rodney.
9. Amzat Boukari-Yabara, *Walter Rodney: Un historien engagé* (Paris: Présence Africaine, 2018), my translation; Rupert Lewis, *Walter Rodney's Intellectual and Political Thought* (Barbados, Jamaica, and Trinidad and Tobago: University of the West Indies Press, 1998); Karim Hirji, *The Enduring Relevance of How Europe Underdeveloped Africa* (Tanzania: Daraja Press, 2017); Chinedu Chukwudinma, *A Rebel's Guide to Rodney* (London: Bookmarks, 2021). See also Clairmont Chung, ed., *Walter A. Rodney: A Promise of Revolution* (New York: Monthly Review Press, 2012).
10. Juanita Cox, "Patricia Rodney Speaking at Guyana SPEAKS about Dr. Walter Anthony Rodney," YouTube video, 29:50, October 29, 2019, https://www.youtube.com/watch?v=o5dLjDT7A2E.

Chapter 1: Beginnings

1. In this sense, he could be considered part of an artisan class, or a petty commodity trader. However, this "very academic" classification was rejected years later by Rodney in describing his family: "The very term 'working class' . . . has to be liberally or creatively interpreted in our own situation." Walter Rodney, *Walter Rodney Speaks: The Making of an African Intellectual*, Howard Dodson and Robert Hill, eds. (Trenton, NJ: Africa World Press, 1990), p. 1.

2. Rodney, *Rodney Speaks*, p. 2.
3. Clive Thomas, "Clive Yolande Thomas," in *Walter A. Rodney: A Promise of Revolution*, ed., Clairmont Chung (New York: Monthly Review Press, 2012), p. 98.
4. Eduardo Galeano, *Open Veins of Latin America: Five Centuries of the Pillage of a Continent* (New York: Monthly Review Press, 1971), p. 136.
5. Galeano, *Open Veins*, p. 136. In some respects, *Open Veins* might be regarded as a companion volume to Rodney's *HEUA*.
6. Rupert Roopnaraine, "Rupert Roopnaraine," in Chung, *A Promise of Revolution*, p. 114.
7. Rodney, *Rodney Speaks*, p. 6.
8. Rodney, *Rodney Speaks*, p. 7.
9. Roopnaraine, *A Promise of Revolution*, p. 121.
10. Rodney, *Rodney Speaks*, p. 8.
11. University College of the West Indies Student Record, 1963, Series B, Box 1, Folder 20, Walter Rodney Papers, Archives Research Center, Atlanta University Center.
12. Robert Moore, "Robert 'Bobby' Moore," in Chung, *A Promise of Revolution*, p. 30.
13. Moore, "Robert 'Bobby' Moore," p. 31.
14. Moore, "Robert 'Bobby' Moore," p. 32.
15. Moore, "Robert 'Bobby' Moore," p. 32.
16. Moore, "Robert 'Bobby' Moore," p. 33.
17. Rodney, *Rodney Speaks*, p. 9.
18. Formerly known as McKenzie, the town was renamed after Linden Forbes Burnham, the full of name of the country's president.
19. Odida T. Quamina, *Mineworkers of Guyana: The Making of a Working Class* (London and New Jersey: Zed, 1987), p. 87.
20. Quamina, *Mineworkers of Guyana*, p. 61.
21. Quamina, *Mineworkers of Guyana*, p. 62.
22. Mark Curtis, *Unpeople: Britain's Secret Human Rights Abuses* (London: Vintage, 2004).
23. Amzat Boukari-Yabara, *Walter Rodney: Un historien engagé* (Paris: Présence Africaine, 2018), p. 33, my translation.
24. Rodney, *Rodney Speaks*, p. 13.
25. Rodney, *Rodney Speaks*, p. 13.
26. Rodney, *Rodney Speaks*, pp. 10–11.
27. Rodney, *Rodney Speaks*, p. 11.
28. Rodney, *Rodney Speaks*, p. 12.
29. Rodney, *Rodney Speaks*, p. 12.
30. Michael O. West, "The Targeting of Walter Rodney," *Against the Current*, no. 120 (January 2006), pp. 5–8.
31. West, "The Targeting of Walter Rodney," pp. 5–8.
32. West, "The Targeting of Walter Rodney," pp. 5–8.
33. Rodney, *Rodney Speaks*, p. 17.
34. Matthew Sagers and Thomas Maraffa, "Soviet Air-Passenger Transportation Network," *Geographical Review* 80:3 (1990), pp. 266–67.
35. Sagers and Maraffa, "Soviet Air-Passenger Transportation Network," p. 267.

36. Rodney, *Rodney Speaks*, p. 18.
37. Rodney, *Rodney Speaks*, p. 19.
38. Thomas, "Clive Yolande Thomas," p. 97.
39. West, "The Targeting of Walter Rodney," pp. 5–8.
40. University College of the West Indies Student Record, 1963.
41. Linda McDowell, "How Caribbean Migrants Helped to Rebuild Britain," *British Library*, October 4, 2018, https://www.bl.uk/windrush/articles/how-caribbean-migrants-rebuilt-britain.
42. McDowell, "How Caribbean Migrants Helped to Rebuild Britain."
43. Peter Fryer, *Staying Power: The History of Black People in Britain* (Alberta: University of Alberta Press, 1984), p. 373.
44. McDowell, "How Caribbean Migrants Helped to Rebuild Britain."
45. Ruth Brown, "Racism and Immigration in Britain," *International Socialism* 2:68 (Autumn 1995).
46. Brown, "Racism and Immigration in Britain," 1995.
47. The Notting Hill riots led to the foundation of the annual Caribbean Festival, which later became known as the Notting Hill festival.
48. Rodney, *Rodney Speaks*, p. 20.
49. Rupert Lewis, *Walter Rodney's Intellectual and Political Thought* (Barbados, Jamaica, and Trinidad and Tobago: University of the West Indies Press, 1998), p. 32.
50. Leo Zeilig, ed. *Class Struggle and Resistance in Africa* (Chicago: Haymarket Books, 2009), pp. 24–25.
51. Rodney, *Rodney Speaks*, p. 21.
52. Rodney, *Rodney Speaks*, p. 21.
53. Lewis, *Intellectual and Political Thought*, p. 32.
54. Lewis, *Intellectual and Political Thought*, p. 33.
55. Rodney, *Rodney Speaks*, p. 20.
56. Rodney, *Rodney Speaks*, p. 21.
57. Patricia Rodney, personal communication with author, April 8, 2021.
58. Rodney, *Rodney Speaks*, p. 22.
59. Student Record, 1963.
60. Rodney, *Rodney Speaks*, p. 23.
61. Rodney, *Rodney Speaks*, p. 23.
62. Rodney, *Rodney Speaks*, p. 24.
63. Rodney, *Rodney Speaks*, p. 24.
64. Rodney, *Rodney Speaks*, p. 24.
65. Missenden Abbey, 1966, Series F, Box 5, Folder 7, Walter Rodney Papers, Archives Research Center.
66. Richard Gray to Walter Rodney, January 27, 1964, Series E, Box 3, Folder 17, Walter Rodney Papers.
67. Richard Gray to Walter Rodney, February 4, 1964, Series E, Box 3, Folder 17, Walter Rodney Papers.
68. University of London, 1964–1966, Series B, Box 1, Folder 21, Walter Rodney Papers, Archives Research Center.

69. Rodney, *Rodney Speaks*, p. 25.
70. Rodney, *Rodney Speaks*, p. 25.
71. Rodney, *Rodney Speaks*, p. 26.
72. Walter Rodney to Terrence O. Ranger, November 1965, Employment Papers, 1965–1968, Series G, Box 7, Folder 1, Walter Rodney Papers.
73. Rodney, *Rodney Speaks*, p. 27.
74. Walter Rodney, *History of Upper Guinea: 1545–1800* (New York: Oxford University Press, 1970), p. 259.
75. Nigel Westmaas, "*How Europe Underdeveloped Africa* and the Contemporary Relevance of Walter Rodney," *Africa Update* 16:3 (2019).
76. Rodney, *Rodney Speaks*, p. 28.
77. Rodney, *Rodney Speaks*, p. 30.
78. Rodney, *Rodney Speaks*, p. 30. Perhaps a little caution is in order here. Rodney kept his distance from Trotskyists, so how did he get to attend "conferences"? He certainly would not have been let in to most conferences as an observer. He also refers to factions lasting thirty years, but none of the British Trotskyist organizations had existed for thirty years. I suspect that this attitude did not exactly reflect his own experience, but was a quasi-satirical account based on what he had heard—perhaps from James, who did have inside knowledge of the Trotskyist movement, especially in the United States.
79. When the socialist historian Ian Birchall, for example, joined the Tottenham branch of the International Socialists in 1964, it contained no students, and he was the only graduate.
80. Rodney, *Rodney Speaks*, p. 31.
81. Rodney, *Rodney Speaks*, p. 31. Rodney's response to the "Trotskyist" Left was negative. But who exactly did he meet? It was probably the Socialist Labour League (later Workers Revolutionary Party), who certainly were an unpleasant bunch, possibly the Revolutionary Socialist League (Militant) or the International Marxist Group. However, before 1968 most members of the International Socialists (if Rodney met any) would not have called themselves Trotskyists.
82. Sam Bornstein and Al Richardson, *Against the Stream: History of the Trotskyist Movement in Britain, 1924–38* (London: Merlin, 1986), p. 263.
83. Rodney, *Rodney Speaks*, p. 15.
84. Rodney, *Rodney Speaks*, p. 15.
85. Rodney, *Rodney Speaks*, p. 28.
86. Rodney, *Rodney Speaks*, p. 28.
87. Ian Birchall, personal communication with author, November 27, 2020.
88. Rodney, *Rodney Speaks*, p. 29.
89. C. L. R. James, *Walter Rodney and the Question of Power* (Montreal: Black Rose, 1982).
90. James, *Walter Rodney and the Question of Power*.
91. Rodney, *Rodney Speaks*, p 29.
92. C. L. R. and Selma James were also leading members of the Campaign against Racial Discrimination (CARD), founded in 1964. The International Socialists were also involved in the organisation.

93. Rodney, *Rodney Speaks*, p. 16.

94. Rodney, *Rodney Speaks*, p. 33.

95. Rodney to Ranger, November 1965.

96. Terrence O. Ranger to Walter Rodney, March 14, 1966, Employment Papers, 1965–1968, Series G, Box 7, Folder 1, Walter Rodney Papers.

Chapter 2: Socialist Africa or African Socialism?

1. Patricia Rodney, personal communication with author, October 1, 2020.

2. Sisal was Tanzania's major export crop at the time. Sisal is a flowering plant native to Mexico but cultivated in many other countries, including Tanzania. It grows a stiff fiber and can be used to make numerous products.

3. Tom Mboya, *Freedom and After* (London: Andre Deutsch, 1963), p. 167.

4. Cited in Leo Zeilig and David Seddon, "Marxism, Class, and Resistance in Africa," in *Class Struggle and Resistance in Africa*, ed., Leo Zeilig (Cheltenham: New Clarion Press, 2002), p. 8.

5. Ruth First, *The Barrel of a Gun: Political Power in Africa and the Coup d'Etat* (London: Penguin, 1970), pp. 57–58.

6. Frantz Fanon, *Towards the African Revolution* (New York: Grove, 1994), pp. 195–96.

7. However, during the few years he lived in exile before he died, Nkrumah plunged himself into a period of political refection—revisiting the ideas of socialism and class struggle.

8. Peter Lawrence, personal communication with the author, October 31, 2018.

9. Akosua Adomako Ampofo, "In Conversation with Professor Akilagpa Sawyerr," *Contemporary Journal of African Studies* 6:2 (November 2019), https://www.ajol.info/index.php/contjas/article/view/197352, p. 130.

10. Richard Gott, "Expatriates Control Fate of Africa's 'Center of Subversion,'" *Guardian*, 1970, 1942–1980, Series A, Box 1, Folder 5, Walter Rodney Papers, Archives Research Center, Atlanta University Center.

11. Julius Nyerere, *Freedom and Socialism* (London: Oxford University Press, 1968), pp. 179–84.

12. Cited in William J. Hanna, "Students, Universities, and Political Outcomes," in *University Students and African Politics*, William J. Hanna and Judith L. Hanna, eds. (London: Africana Publishing Company, 1975), pp. 12–13.

13. Issa G. Shivji, "Lionel Cliffe, 1936–2013: A Comradely Scholar in Nyerere's Nationalist Tanzania," *Review of African Political Economy* 41:140 (2014).

14. Chris Peter and Sengondo Mvungi, "The State and Student Struggles," in *The State and the Working People*, Issa G. Shivji, ed. (Dakar: CODESRIA, 1986) p. 165.

15. Josaphat Kanywanyi, interview by author, December 4, 2018.

16. Patrick Norberg, "The Role of Marxism-Leninism in the University Students' African Revolutionary Front's Opposition to Ujamaa," paper presented at the conference "The Revolutionary Left in Sub-Saharan Africa," October 30–November 1, 2019, University Cheikh Anta Diop, Dakar.

17. University College, Dar es Salaam to Walter Rodney, January 1967, Employment Papers, 1965–1968, Series G, Box 7, Folder 1, Walter Rodney Papers.

18. Colin Legum, *Republic in Trouble: South Africa, 1972–73* (London: Rex Collins, Ltd., 1973), p. 12.

19. Shivji, "Lionel Cliffe."

20. Shivji, "Lionel Cliffe."

21. Norberg, "Role of Marxism-Leninism."

22. Norberg, "Role of Marxism-Leninism."

23. Shivji, "Walter Rodney in Tanzania: A Tribute," *Pambazuka News*, June 27, 2013, https://www.pambazuka.org/governance/walter-rodney-tanzania-tribute.

24. Frantz Fanon, *The Wretched of the Earth* (New York: Grove, 1963).

25. Lawrence, personal communication.

26. Cited in Samwilu Mwaffis, "Restoring Mwalimu Nyerere's Fundamental Pillars," *Daily News* (Tanzania), October 15, 2018, https://dailynews.co.tz/news/2018-10-155bc43652d0be6.aspx#.

27. Walter Rodney and J. K. McCraken, course materials, 1966, Series G, Box 7, Folder 3, Walter Rodney Papers.

28. Rodney and McCraken, course materials, 1966.

29. Rodney and McCraken, course materials, 1966.

30. Walter Rodney, *Walter Rodney Speaks: The Making of an African Intellectual*, Howard Dodson and Robert Hill, eds. (Trenton, NJ: Africa World Press, 1990), p. 34.

31. Rodney, *Rodney Speaks*, p. 34.

32. Amandla Thomas-Johnson, "Becoming Kwame Ture," *Chimurenga*, October 21, 2020, https://chimurengachronic.co.za/book_series/chimurenganyana-becoming-kwame-ture-by-amandla-thomas-johnson-oct-2020/.

33. Marjorie Mbilinyi, interview by author, December 3, 2018.

34. Mbilinyi, interview.

35. Akosua Adomako Ampofo, "In Conversation with Professor Akilagpa Sawyerr," *Contemporary Journal of African Studies* 6:2 (November 2019), https://www.ajol.info/index.php/contjas/article/view/197352, p. 131.

36. Mbilinyi, interview.

37. Kanywanyi, interview.

38. Kanywanyi, interview.

39. Ampofo, "In Conversation with Professor Akilagpa Sawyerr," p. 131.

40. Richard Small, "Introduction," in Walter Rodney, *The Groundings with My Brothers* (London: Bogle-L'Ouverture, 1983), p. 7.

Chapter 3: On an Oil Drum

1. Rupert Lewis, *Walter Rodney's Intellectual and Political Thought* (Barbados, Jamaica, Trinidad and Tobago: University of the West Indies Press, 1998), p. 86.

2. Cited in Rupert Lewis, "Walter Rodney: 1968 Revisited," *Social and Economic Studies* 43:3 (September 1994), p. 10, https://www.jstor.org/stable/pdf/27865974.pdf?refreqid=excelsior%3Adababa3e54f9a80594fb39854d7ecc56.

3. Hakim Adi, *Pan-Africanism: A History* (London: Bloomsbury, 2018), p. 169.

4. Hakim, *Pan-Africanism*, p. 170.

5. Robert Hill, "Robert Hill," in *Walter A. Rodney: A Promise of Revolution*, Clairmont

Chung, ed. (New York: Monthly Review Press, 2012), p. 65.

6. For a summary of recent demography, see "Jamaica Population," *World Population Review*, https://worldpopulationreview.com/countries/jamaica-population.

7. Horace Campbell, *Rasta and Resistance: From Marcus Garvey to Walter Rodney* (London: Hansib, 1985), pp. 1–11.

8. Lewis, "1968 Revisited," p. 21.

9. Robert Hill, *A Promise of Revolution*, p. 65.

10. Richard Small, "Introduction," in Walter Rodney, *The Groundings with My Brothers* (London: Bogle-L'Ouverture Publications, 1969), p. 11.

11. Lewis, "1968 Revisited," p. 24.

12. Lewis, "1968 Revisited," p. 24.

13. Lewis, "1968 Revisited," p. 25.

14. Michael O. West, "The Targeting of Walter Rodney," *Against the Current* 120 (January 2006), pp. 5–8.

15. West, "The Targeting of Walter Rodney."

16. Cited in Colin Palmer, "Identity, Race, and Black Power in Independent Jamaica," in *The Modern Caribbean*, eds., Colin Palmer and Franklin W. Knight (Chapel Hill: University of North Carolina Press, 1989), p. 120.

17. Cited in Palmer, "Identity, Race and Black Power," pp. 119–20.

18. West, "The Targeting of Walter Rodney."

19. Rodney, *Groundings*, p. 66.

20. "A Life of Praxis with Walter Rodney: Interview with Jesse Benjamin," by Leo Zeilig, *Review of African Political Economy*, June 9, 2020, https://roape.net/2020/06/09/a-life-of-praxis-with-walter-rodney-interview-with-jesse-benjamin/.

21. Hill, *A Promise of Revolution*, p. 66.

22. West, "The Targeting of Walter Rodney."

23. Hill, *A Promise of Revolution*, p. 67.

24. Patricia Rodney, personal communication with author, April 8, 2021.

25. Rodney, *Groundings*, pp. iv–vi.

26. "Interview with Jesse Benjamin."

27. Robert Hill, "Walter Rodney and the Restatement of Pan-Africanism in Theory and Practice," *Ufahamu: A Journal of African Studies* 38: 3 (2015), p. 153.

28. W. E. Gocking to Walter Rodney, March 20, 1970, University of the West Indies, 1960–1987, Series E, Box 4, Folder 54, Walter Rodney Papers, Archives Research Center.

Chapter 4: African History and Black Power

1. Ewart Thomas, "Editor's Preface," in Walter Rodney, *The Groundings with My Brothers* (London: Bogle-L'Ouverture Publications, 1969), p. 6.

2. Richard Small, "Introduction," in Rodney, *Groundings*, p. 9.

3. Small, "Introduction," p. 10.

4. Small, "Introduction," p. 11.

5. Walter Rodney, *The Groundings with My Brothers* (London and New York: Verso, 2018 [1969]), p. 12. Subsequent citations in this chapter are to the 2018 edition.

6. Rodney, *Groundings*, p. 13.

7. Rodney, *Groundings*, p. 14.

8. Rodney, *Groundings*, p. 15.

9. Rodney, *Groundings*, p. 16.

10. Rodney, *Groundings*, p. 16.

11. Rodney, *Groundings*, p. 17.

12. Rodney, *Groundings*, p. 18.

13. Rodney, *Groundings*, p. 19.

14. Rodney, *Groundings*, p. 20.

15. Rodney, *Groundings*, p. 21.

16. Rodney, *Groundings*, p. 22.

17. Rodney, *Groundings*, p. 25.

18. Rodney, *Groundings*, p. 25.

19. Rodney, *Groundings*, p. 26.

20. Rodney, *Groundings*, p. 26.

21. Rodney, *Groundings*, p. 27.

22. Richard Hart, "Labour Rebellions of the 1930s in the British Caribbean Region Colonies," 2002, Caribbean Labour Solidarity and Socialist History Society, Occasional Papers Series, no. 15.

23. Rodney, *Groundings*, p. 27.

24. Walter Rodney, *Walter Rodney Speaks: The Making of an African Intellectual*, Howard Dodson and Robert Hill, eds. (Trenton, NJ: Africa World Press, 1990), p. 76.

25. Rodney, *Groundings*, p. 28.

26. Rodney, *Groundings*, p. 29.

27. Rodney, *Groundings*, p. 29.

28. Rodney, *Groundings*, p. 31.

29. Rodney, *Groundings*, p. 32.

30. Rodney, *Groundings*, p. 32.

31. Rodney, *Groundings*, p. 33.

32. Rodney, *Groundings*, pp. 32–33.

33. Rodney, *Groundings*, p. 34.

34. Rodney, *Groundings*, p. 35.

35. Rodney, *Groundings*, p. 36.

36. Rodney, *Groundings*, p. 36. Rodney was not the only radical writer on African history. Basil Davidson, whose book *Africa in History* (London: Weidenfeld & Nicolson, 1968) had just come out, wrote about Africa having a long, rich, and varied history before colonialism. Rodney's PhD book makes favorable references to Davidson's work, and clearly the two authors shared a great deal.

37. Rodney, *Groundings*, p. 39.

38. Rodney, *Groundings*, p. 37.

39. Rodney, *Groundings*, p. 39.

40. Rodney, *Groundings*, p. 41.

41. Rodney, *Groundings*, p. 51.

42. Rodney, *Groundings*, p. 52.

43. Rodney, *Groundings*, p. 51.
44. Rodney, *Groundings*, p. 52.
45. Rodney, *Groundings*, p. 56.
46. Rodney, *Groundings*, p. 56.
47. Rodney, *Groundings*, p. 57.
48. Rodney, *Groundings*, p. 58.
49. Rodney, *Groundings*, p. 58.
50. Rodney, *Groundings*, p. 59.
51. Rodney, *Groundings*, p. 64.
52. Rodney, *Groundings*, p. 68.

Chapter 5: Revolution and History

1. Terence O. Ranger to Walter Rodney, November 4, 1968, Committee for Anti-Imperialist Solidarity with the People of Chile, 1978, Series F, Box 6, Folder 3, Walter Rodney Papers, Archives Research Center, Atlanta University Center.
2. Marcia Wright to Walter Rodney, November 12, 1968, Latin American Association for Afroasian Studies, 1978, Series F, Box 6, Folder 6, Walter Rodney Papers.
3. Alfred Rieber to Walter Rodney, January 1969, Latin American Association for Afroasian Studies, 1978.
4. University College, Dar es Salaam, to Walter Rodney, July 1, 1969, Employment Papers, 1969, Series G, Box 7, Folder 6, Walter Rodney Papers.
5. University College, Dar es Salaam, to Walter Rodney, July 1969, Employment Papers, 1969. At that time, it was seventeen shillings to the pound sterling. It had been twenty shillings to the East African pound until the pound sterling devalued in 1967.
6. Julius Nyerere, *Freedom and Unity: Uhuru Na Umoja; A Selection from Writings and Speeches, 1952–65* (London: Oxford University Press, 1966), p. 170.
7. Julius Nyerere, *Freedom and Socialism* (London: Oxford University Press, 1968), p. 324.
8. Kwame Nkrumah, *Consciencism* (London: Heinemann, 1964), p. 19.
9. Karim F. Hirji, *Cheche: Reminiscences of a Radical Magazine* (Dar es Salaam: Mukuki na Nyota Publishers, 2010), pp. 5–6.
10. Hirji, *Cheche*, p. 8.
11. Hirji, *Cheche*, pp. 55–56.
12. Such behavior was a reaction to the astonishing wave of student revolts in the 1980s and 1990s across Africa. See Leo Zeilig, *Revolt and Protest: Student Politics and Activism in Sub-Saharan Africa* (London: I. B Tauris, 2013).
13. Shivji's essay was first published in *Cheche*, then subsequently issued as a standalone pamphlet.
14. Shivji, *The Silent Class Struggle* (Dar es Salaam: Tanzania Publishing House, 1974), p. 11.
15. Shivji, *Class Struggle*, p. 13.
16. The nationalized British banks were amalgamated into one state bank, which did not have a management agreement with foreign banks. Management agreements were made in the case of new state-owned enterprises using foreign capital ma-

chinery and set up from scratch. Shivji was right in the case of new investments but not the nationalized ones.

17. Shivji, *Class Struggle*, p. 23.
18. Shivji, *Class Struggle*, p. 39.
19. Hirji, *Cheche*, p. 57.
20. Shivji, *Class Struggle*, p. 61.
21. Shivji, *Class Struggle*, p. 62.
22. Shivji, *Class Struggle*, p. 76.
23. Walter Rodney, "Tanzanian Ujamaa and Scientific Socialism," *African Review* 1:4 (1972), available at https://www.marxists.org/subject/africa/.
24. Shivji, *Class Struggle*, p. 17.
25. Shivji, *Class Struggle*, p. 18.
26. Shivji, *Class Struggle*, p. 19.
27. Shivji, *Class Struggle*, p. 19.
28. Shivji, *Class Struggle*, p. 20.
29. John Saul, *Revolutionary Traveller: Freeze-Frames from a Life* (Winnipeg: Arbeiter Ring, 2009), p. 22.
30. There were also moves around this time in the UK to develop "interdisciplinary" courses, especially in the "new" universities and the emerging polytechnics.
31. Saul, *Revolutionary Traveller*, p. 67. Saul's contract with the university had not been renewed, and he was returning to Canada.
32. Saul, *Revolutionary Traveller*, p. 69.
33. Julius Nyerere, "The Arusha Declaration," February 5, 1967, available at https://www.marxists.org/subject/africa/nyerere/1967/arusha-declaration.htm.
34. Tamás Szentes, "To Be Bravely Critical of Reality," interview by Tamás Gerőcs, *Review of African Political Economy*, November 8, 2018, https://roape.net/2018/11/08/to-be-bravely-critical-to-reality-an-interview-with-tamas-szentes/.
35. Peter Lawrence, personal communication with author, October 31, 2018.
36. Lawrence, personal communication.
37. Mbilinyi, interview by author, December 3, 2018.
38. Abdul Sheriff, interview by author, December 1, 2018.
39. Patricia Rodney, personal correspondence with author, October 1, 2020.
40. Walter Bgoya, interview by author, December 4, 2018.
41. Mbilinyi, interview.
42. Sheriff, interview.
43. *The Nationalist* was the party newspaper and *The Standard* the government one. They were merged in March 1972 to form the *Daily News*.
44. Bgoya, interview.
45. Abdalla Bujra, personal communication with author, November 28, 2019.
46. Issa Shivji, interview with author, November 30, 2018.
47. Leith Mullings, "Leith Mullings," in *Walter Rodney: A Promise of Revolution*, ed., Clairmont Chung (New York: Monthly Review Press, 2012), p. 79.
48. Mullings, "Leith Mullings," p. 80.
49. Mullings, "Leith Mullings," p. 80.

50. Hassan Waziri to Walter Rodney, February 4, 1973, 1960–1987, Series E, Box 4, Folder 62, Walter Rodney Papers.

51. Ted Mlay to Walter Rodney, July 20, 1971, 1960–1987, Series E, Box 3, Folder 68, Walter Rodney Papers.

52. Makerere Students' Guild (Uganda) to Walter Rodney, December 29, 1969; 1970, Series F, Box 5, Folder 14, Walter Rodney Papers.

53. Makerere Students' Guild to Rodney.

54. Department Memoranda, Employment Papers, 1970, Series G, Box 7, Folder 9, Walter Rodney Papers.

55. Karim Hirji, *The Enduring Relevance of How Europe Underdeveloped Africa* (Tanzania: Daraja Press, 2017), p. 93–94.

56. Hirji, *Enduring Relevance*, p. 94.

57. Shivji, "Issa Shivji," in Chung, *A Promise of Revolution*.

58. George G. Hadjivayanis, "Night-Shift Comrades," in Hirji, *Cheche*.

59. "Revolutionary Hot Air," editorial, *The Nationalist*, December 13, 1969.

60. Hadjivayanis, "Night-Shift Comrades."

61. Walter Rodney, "Dr. Rodney Clarifies," letter to *The Nationalist*, December 15, 1969.

62. Shivji, interview.

63. A good account of the lively intellectual discussions and debates at the university on tourism, development, and socialism can be found in a lecture Rodney gave in 1975 at Northwestern University in the United States, published as "Class Contradictions in Tanzania" in *The State in Tanzania: A Selection of Articles*, Haroub Othman, ed. (Dar es Salaam: Dar es Salaam University Press, 1980), available at https://www. marxists.org/subject/africa/rodney-walter/works/classcontradictions.htm.

64. Paul Sweezy and Harry Magdoff to Walter Rodney, November 5, 1969; Sweezy to Rodney, February 2, 1970; Tetteh A. Kofi, 1960–1987, Series E, Box 3, Folder 49, Walter Rodney Papers. See Rodney's paper "The Imperialist Partition of Africa," *Monthly Review* 21:11 (April 1970), pp. 103–14, available at https://www.marxists. org/subject/africa/rodney-walter/works/partition.htm.

65. Hirji, *Enduring Relevance*, p. 95.

66. Rodney, *How Europe Underdeveloped Africa* (Nairobi and Oxford: Pambazuka Press, 2012 [1972]), pp. xi–xii.

Chapter 6: How Europe Underdeveloped Africa

1. Walter Rodney, *How Europe Underdeveloped Africa* (Nairobi and Oxford: Pambazuka Press, 2012 [1972]), p. 26.

2. Rodney, *HEUA*, p. 201.

3. Issa Shivui, interview by author, November 30, 2018.

4. Cited by Shivji, interview.

5. Cited in Rupert Lewis, *Walter Rodney's Intellectual and Political Thought* (Kingston: University of the West Indies Press; Detroit: Wayne State University, 1998), p. 70.

6. Rodney, *HEUA*, p. 6.

7. Rodney, *HEUA*, p. 7. Much of this attitude still exists today. For example, Doreen Massey, who, despite being regarded as a sort of postmodernist Marxist, repeatedly

criticized Marxism as a stagist interpretation of space and history. Indeed, it is rare to read a postmodernist critique of Marxism that does not bring up stagism.

8. Rodney, *HEUA*, p. 9.
9. Rodney, *HEUA*, p. 8.
10. Rodney, *HEUA*, p. 11.
11. Walter Rodney, *The Russian Revolution: A View from the Third World* (London and New York: Verso, 2018), pp. 81–84.
12. Karim Hirji, *The Enduring Relevance of How Europe Underdeveloped Europe* (Tanzania: Daraja Press, 2017), p. 95.
13. Hugh Trevor-Roper, *The Rise of Christian Europe* (New York: Brace & World, 1965), p. 9.
14. Roper, *Christian Europe*, p. 9.
15. Vientianegirl, "Nicolas Sarkozy and the African Man," YouTube video, 1:24, February 26, 2012, https://www.youtube.com/watch?v=s32eInxqubw.
16. See Chris Harman, "The African Civilisations," in *A People's History of the World* (London and New York: Verso, 1999), Chapter 5, pp. 136–40.
17. Rodney, *HEUA*, p. 33.
18. Rodney, *HEUA*, p. 68.
19. Rodney, *HEUA*, p. 40.
20. Rodney, *HEUA*, pp. 42–43.
21. Rodney, *HEUA*, p. 44.
22. Rodney, *HEUA*, p. 47.
23. Rodney, *HEUA*, p. 56.
24. Rodney, *HEUA*, p. 58.
25. Rodney, *HEUA*, p. 58.
26. Rodney, *HEUA*, p. 65.
27. Rodney, *HEUA*, p. 66.
28. Rodney, *HEUA*, p. 66.
29. Rodney, *HEUA*, p. 69.
30. Rodney, *HEUA*, p. 70.
31. Rodney, *HEUA*, p. 113.
32. It is important to distinguish Rodney's analysis from that of Gunder-Frank, whose "development of underdevelopment" thesis was dominant on the Left at the time.
33. Rodney, *HEUA*, p. 114.
34. Rodney, *HEUA*, p. 135.
35. Rodney, *HEUA*, pp. 80–81.
36. Rodney, *HEUA*, p. 84.
37. Rodney, *HEUA*, p. 85.
38. Rodney, *HEUA*, p. 85.
39. Rodney, *HEUA*, p. 86.
40. Rodney, *HEUA*, p. 86.
41. Rodney, *HEUA*, p. 107.
42. Rodney, *HEUA*, p. 108.
43. Rodney, *HEUA*, p. 108.

44. Rodney, *HEUA*, p. 131.

45. Rodney, *HEUA*, p. 135.

46. Rodney, *HEUA*, p. 136.

47. Rodney, *HEUA*, p. 137.

48. Rodney, *HEUA*, p. 139.

49. Rodney, *HEUA*, p. 141.

50. Rodney, *HEUA*, p. 143.

51. Roger Murray and Tom Wengraf, "The Algerian Revolution: Part I," *New Left Review*, no. 22 (1963), pp. 22–23.

52. Francis Jeanson, *La Révolution Algérienne* (Paris: Feltrinelli, 1962), p. 29.

53. Mike Davis, *Late Victorian Holocausts: El Nino Famines and the Making of the Third World* (London and New York: Verso, 2000).

54. Rodney, *HEUA*, p. 171.

55. Rodney, *HEUA*, p. 172.

56. Rodney, *HEUA*, p. 195.

57. Rodney, *HEUA*, pp. 190–91.

58. Rodney, *HEUA*, p. 190.

59. Rodney, *HEUA*, pp. 180–85.

60. Rodney, *HEUA*, pp. 190–201.

61. Chinedu Chukwudinma, "Towards a Full Understanding of Walter Rodney," *Review of African Political Economy*, August 1, 2019, https://roape.net/2019/08/01/towards-a-full-understanding-of-walter-rodney/.

62. Angus Elsby, "Stealing Africa's Commodities," *Review of African Political Economy*, August 7, 2019, https://roape.net/2019/08/07/stealing-africas-commodities/. In an investigation into the continued European control of the global commodity trade, Angus Elsby examined the import and reexport of raw commodities from Africa by European countries. Elsby's case study was the international coffee market; he showed the impact of Europe's commodity "theft" on Africa's development. In addition to the concentration of Africa commodity export profits in Europe, there are also massive financial outflows from the continent to Europe. According to a 2019 report by Action for Southern Africa, countries in Southern Africa lose approximately US$8.8 billion in trade-related illicit outflows, and at least US$21.1 billion in external government debt payments annually—processes that can be seen as the continued and deepening of the continent's "underdevelopment." Sunit Bagree, *The Money Drain: How Trade Misinvoicing and Unjust Debt Undermine Economic and Social Rights in Southern Africa*, Action for Southern Africa, August 2019, https://actsa.org/campaigns/the-money-drain.

63. Nigel Harris, *The End of the Third World: Newly Industrializing Countries and the Decline of an Ideology* (New York: New Amsterdam Books, 1987), p. 200.

64. Esteban Mora, "Mutual Profiting: Unpicking the Harvey-Smith Debate," *Review of African Political Economy*, June 21, 2018, https://roape.net/2018/06/21/mutual-profiting-unpicking-the-harvey-smith-debate/.

65. Lee Wengraf, "U.S.-China Inter-Imperial Rivalry in Africa," *Review of African Political Economy*, November 16, 2018, https://roape.net/2018/11/16/u-s-china-in-

ter-imperial-rivalry-in-africa/.

66. Martin Legassick, "Perspectives on African 'Underdevelopment,'" *Journal of African History* 17:3 (1976), p. 347.

67. Rodney, *HEUA*, p. 263.

68. Rodney was critical of the Stalinist system and recognized its failings but, at this stage, thought it was moving in broadly the right direction.

69. Rodney, *HEUA*, p. 280.

Chapter 7: A Book to Change the World

1. Walter Bgoya, interview by author, December 4, 2018.

2. Anthony Ferguson to Walter Rodney, November 17, 1972, Caribbean Unity Conference, 1972, Series F, Box 5, Folder 28, Walter Rodney Papers, Archives Research Center, Atlanta University Center.

3. Wole Soyinka to Walter Rodney, April 3, 1974, 1960–1987, Series E, Box 4, Folder 46, Walter Rodney Papers.

4. Teshome Gabriel to Walter Rodney, 1973, Series E, Box 4, Folder 46, Walter Rodney Papers.

5. The book has continued to be debated and read widely. In 2019, for example, a special issue of *Africa Update* was devoted to the volume. See Biko Agozino, ed., "How Europe Underdeveloped Africa: A Tribute to Walter Rodney," *Africa Update* 26:3 (2019).

6. These are still influential ideas today, even among heterodox economists like Christopher Cramer or John Sender, although they argue this in terms of building foreign-exchange surpluses for importing industrializing capital goods.

7. These terms were first coined by the Argentinian economist Raúl Prebisch, then taken up by Frank, Amin, and others.

8. Katu Wambadia-Wamba to Walter Rodney, 1960–187, Series E, Box 4, Folder 59, Walter Rodney Papers.

9. L. L. Lawson to Walter Rodney, February 1976, 1960–1987, Series E, Box 3, Folder 52, Walter Rodney Papers.

10. Emmanuel T. Olarewaju to Walter Rodney, August 1973, 1960–1987, Series E, Box 3, Folder 85, Walter Rodney Papers.

11. José Dominguez to Walter Rodney, March 17, 1973, 1960–1987, Series E, Box 2, Folder 93, Walter Rodney Papers.

12. Jacques Depelchin to Walter Rodney, November 14, 1976;1976, Series E, Box 2, Folder 90, Walter Rodney Papers.

13. Name illegible (London, England) 1973, Series E, Box 2, Folder 14, Walter Rodney Papers.

14. S. K. Aboagye, 1976, Series E, Box 2, Folder 35, Walter Rodney Papers.

15. Letter to Walter Rodney, December 5, 1973, Race and Class, 1973, Series E, Box 4, Folder 11, Walter Rodney Papers.

16. Ferguson to Rodney.

17. Leo Neuwens, 1972; 1960–1987, Series E, Box 3, Folder 74, Walter Rodney Papers.

18. Walter Rodney to Leo Neuwens, 1972; 1960–1987, Series E, Box 3, Folder 74,

Walter Rodney Papers. For a more sympathetic review, see Bernard Magubane, "On Walter Rodney's *How Europe Underdeveloped Africa*," in *Ufahamu: A Journal of African Studies* 3:3 (1973), pp. 131–44.

Chapter 8: Class, Race, and Politics in Tanzania

1. Cited by Issa Shivji, interview by author, November 30, 2018.

2. Peter Lawrence, personal communication with author, October 31, 2018.

3. Rodney conducted this work in collaboration with Tanzanian historians who were sympathetic from a nationalist, anti-colonial position.

4. John Saul, *Revolutionary Traveller: Freeze-Frames from a Life* (Winnipeg: Arbeiter Ring, 2009), p. 54.

5. Saul, *Revolutionary Traveller*, p. 55.

6. University of Dar es Salaam Faculty Board meeting minutes, Employment Papers; Board of Faculty Papers, 1971, Series G, Box 7, Folder 12, Walter Rodney Papers, Archives Research Center, Atlanta University Center.

7. Kighoma Malima to J. F. Rweyemamu, November 25, 1971, Employment Papers; Board of Faculty Papers, 1971.

8. Peter Lawrence to J. F. Rweyemamu, November 29, 1971, Employment Papers; Board of Faculty Papers, 1971.

9. John Saul, letter, November 29, 1971, Employment Papers; Board of Faculty Papers, 1971.

10. Walter Rodney to J. F. Rweyemamu, November 30, 1971, Employment Papers; Board of Faculty Papers, 1971.

11. Peter Lawrence, personal communication.

12. Patricia Rodney, personal communication with author, October 1, 2020. Years later, Patricia recalled with sadness the end of her friendship with Pat, John's wife, as a direct consequence of the dispute.

13. Peter Lawrence notes, "We thought we were doing the right thing by Nyerere but didn't realise that we needed to find allies among the Tanzanians. I remember Lionel [Cliffe] saying that we should have made sure we had those allies. I also remember we used to criticize people like Arnold Kettle, the Marxist (and CP) academic from Leeds who came to Dar to head up English Department for not engaging politically. But I think people like him understood that they were guests, and their job was to enlighten students to different perspectives not mobilize them!" Lawrence, personal communication.

14. Lawrence, personal communication.

15. See Chapter 11 for a full discussion of Rodney's Hamburg lectures in 1978.

16. Walter Bgoya, interview by author, December 4, 2018.

17. "Ahmed Gora Ebrahim," *South African History Online*, October 25, 2013, https://www.sahistory.org.za/people/ahmed-gora-ebrahim.

18. Bgoya, interview.

19. Ray Tricomo to Walter Rodney, July 26, 1972; 1960–1987, Series E, Box 4, Folder 48, Walter Rodney Papers.

20. Abdul Sheriff, interview by author, December 1, 2018.

21. Claudia Lynn Thomas, "Takeover of Main Building, 1969" in *Vassar Encyclopedia*, http://vcencyclopedia.vassar.edu/interviews-reflections/claudia-lynn-thomas.html.
22. Urban Centre for Black Studies Tour (Milfred C. Fierce), 1970–1971, Series G, Box 7, Folder 11, Walter Rodney Papers.
23. Fred Brooks to Walter Rodney, April 25, 1972, Walter Rodney Papers.
24. Issa Shivji, interview by author, November 30, 2018.
25. Yoweri Museveni, "Activism on the Hill," in *Cheche: Reminiscences of a Radical Magazine*, Karim F. Hirji, ed. (Dar es Salaam: Mkuki na Nyota Publishers, 2010), p. 13.
26. Shivji, interview.
27. Chinedu Chukwudinma, "Towards a Full Understanding of Walter Rodney," *Review of African Political Economy*, August 1, 2019, https://roape.net/2019/08/01/towards-a-full-understanding-of-walter-rodney/.
28. History Department Newsletter, 1980, Series G, Box 6, Folder 41, Walter Rodney Papers. This amount is equivalent to approximately $47,000 today.
29. History Department Newsletter.
30. Patricia Rodney, personal communication, April 8, 2021. Mashaka was a woman the couple employed as a caregiver for their three children.
31. Tax forms (blank), Employment and Financial Papers, 1973–1975, Series G, Box 7, Folder 15, Walter Rodney Papers.
32. Elizabeth Allo Isichei, June 13, *1973, Series E,* Box 3, Folder 33, Walter Rodney Papers.
33. The congress was eventually held the following year. See "The Call," available at https://library.duke.edu/digitalcollections/snccdigitalgateway/6PAC_TheCall.pdf.
34. C. L. R. James to Walter Rodney, May 18, 1974, Series E, Box 3, Folder 36, Walter Rodney Papers.
35. Hakim Adi, *Pan-Africanism: A History* (London: Bloomsbury, 2018), p. 169.
36. Walter Rodney, "Aspects of the International Class Struggle in Africa, the Caribbean and America," in *Pan-Africanism: Struggle against Neo-colonialism and Imperialism—Documents of the Sixth Pan-African Congress*, Horace Campbell, ed. (Toronto: Afro-Carib Publications, 1975).
37. Robert Hill, "Walter Rodney and the Restatement of Pan-Africanism in Theory and Practice," *Ufahamu: A Journal of African Studies* 38:3 (2015), p. 151.
38. Rodney, "International Class Struggle in Africa."
39. Bgoya, interview.
40. Wole Soyinka, "In Memoriam," 1980–1981, Series A, Box 1, Folder 11, Walter Rodney Papers.
41. Robert Hill to Walter Rodney, May 19, 1974, 1960–1987, Series E, Box 3, Folder 24, Walter Rodney Papers.
42. Soyinka, "In Memoriam." Supposedly it was also a principle on noninterference in the internal affairs of another country—except of course when it involved the national interest, as in Tanzania's invasion of Uganda in 1979.
43. Saul, *Revolutionary Traveller*, p. 12.
44. Ralph Ibbott, *Ujamaa: The Hidden Story of Tanzania's Socialist Villages* (London: Crossroads, 2014).

45. Saul, *Revolutionary Traveller*, p. 50.

46. Saul, *Revolutionary Traveller*, p. 51.

47. Saul, *Revolutionary Traveller*, p. 52.

48. Ruth First, *The Barrel of a Gun: Political Power in Africa and the Coup d'Etat* (London: Penguin, 1970), pp. 57–58.

49. Ruth First to Joe Slovo, October 15, 1975, Ruth First Papers, Senate House Institute of Commonwealth Studies, London.

50. Karim Hirji, *The Enduring Relevance of How Europe Underdeveloped Europe* (Tanzania: Daraja Press, 2017), p. 100.

51. Walter Rodney, "Tanzanian Ujamaa and Scientific Socialism," *African Review* 1:4 (1972), available at https://www.marxists.org/subject/africa/rodney-walter/works/ujamaaandscientificsocialism.htm#_ednref32.

52. Hirji, *Enduring Relevance*, p. 101.

53. Walter Rodney, "Class Contradictions in Tanzania," in *The State in Tanzania: A Selection of Articles*, Haroub Othman, ed. (Dar es Salaam: Dar es Salaam University Press, 1980), available at https://www.marxists.org/subject/africa/rodney-walter/works/classcontradictions.htm.

54. Hirji, *Enduring Relevance*, 102–3. Rodney produced an interesting celebration of James's work and activism in a talk at the University of Michigan on March 31, 1972, where he explains his teacher's contribution to radical scholarship and Black history and nudges him on certain areas, correcting him on where world revolution will start: "Undoubtedly, a Revolution within the metropolitan centres would be of inordinate importance to the African Revolution, but it is no pre-condition. It may even be argued that the world revolution must continue to move from the 'periphery' to the 'centre' as far as the imperialist world is concerned." He also uses the article to once again restate the significance of the policy of Ujamaa and his (and James's) support for Nyerere's Tanzania. See Walter Rodney, "The African Revolution," *Urgent Tasks* 12 (1981), pp. 5–13, available at https://www.marxists.org/subject/africa/rodney-walter/works/africanrevolution.htm.

55. Hirji, *Enduring Relevance*, pp. 102–3.

56. Patrick Norberg, "The Role of Marxism-Leninism in the University Students' African Revolutionary Front's Opposition to Ujamaa," paper presented at the conference The Revolutionary Left in Sub-Saharan Africa, October 30–November 1, 2019, University Cheikh Anta Diop, Dakar.

57. Chris Peter and Sengondo Mvungi, "The State and the Student Struggles," in *The State and the Working People in Tanzania*, Issa Shivji, ed. (London: Marram, 1986), p. 180.

58. Issa G. Shivji, *The Silent Class Struggle* (Dar es Salaam: Tanzania Publishing House, 1974).

59. Walter Rodney, *Walter Rodney Speaks: The Making of an African Intellectual*, Howard Dodson and Robert Hill, eds. (Trenton, NJ: Africa World Press, 1990), p. 42.

Chapter 9: Returning Home

1. Walter Rodney to University of Guyana Registrar, October 31, 1972, Employment Applications, 1972–1977, Series G, Box 6, Folder 36, Walter Rodney Papers,

Archives Research Center, Atlanta University Center.

2. Walter Rodney to University of Guyana Registrar, May 14, 1974, Employment Applications, 1972–1977.

3. Clive Yolande Thomas, letter, Series E, Box 4, Folder 42, Walter Rodney Papers.

4. Amzat Boukari-Yabara, *Walter Rodney: Un historien engage* (Présence Africaine, 2018), p. 304, my translation.

5. Cited in Walter Rodney Commission of Inquiry, *Report of the Commission of Inquiry on the Circumstances Surrounding the Death in an Explosion of the Late Dr. Walter Rodney*, Volume 1, *Reports and Appendices*, February 2016, pp. 23–24.

6. Walter Rodney, "Statement," September 18, 1974, Employment Applications, 1972–1977.

7. Virgil "Mum" Duncan to Walter Rodney, September 4, 1974, 1960–1987, Series E, Box 2, Folder 97, Walter Rodney Papers.

8. Jemba Mwakalu to Walter Rodney, July 22, 1979, 1960–1987, Series E, Box 3, Folder 71, Walter Rodney Papers.

9. Jean Suret-Canale was a radical historian of Africa who had been denied teaching positions and forced into precarious employment.

10. Edward "Ned" Alpers to Walter Rodney, February 10, 1975, 1960–1987, Series E, Box 2, Folder 43, Walter Rodney Papers.

11. Navin Chandarpal to Walter Rodney, November 18, 1974, University of Guyana Students Society, Aspects of Capitalist and Socialist Development, 1975, Series F, Box 5, Folder 72, Walter Rodney Papers.

12. The article appeared in *The Student* 2:5 (January 1975), University of Guyana Students Society, Aspects of Capitalist and Socialist Development, 1975.

13. Walter Rodney to Navin Chandarpal, January 6, 1975, University of Guyana Students Society, Aspects of Capitalist and Socialist Development, 1975.

14. James Turner to Walter Rodney, October 1975, 1960–1987, Series E, Box 3, Folder 67, Walter Rodney Papers.

15. James Millette to Walter Rodney, November 1975, 1960–1987, Series E, Box 3, Folder 67, Walter Rodney Papers.

16. Cited in Rodney Commission, *Report of the Commission of Inquiry*, p. 27.

17. Robert Chrisman to Walter Rodney, February 4, 1975; May 1975; Series E, Box 2, Folder 76, Walter Rodney Papers.

18. Winston Grady-Willis, *Challenging U.S. Apartheid: Atalanta and Black Struggles for Human Rights, 1960–1977* (Durham: Duke University Press, 2006), p. 143.

19. Grady-Willis, *U.S. Apartheid*, p. 144.

20. Grady-Willis, *U.S. Apartheid*, p. 146.

21. Grady-Willis, *U.S. Apartheid*, p. 150.

22. Grady-Willis, *U.S. Apartheid*, p. 151.

23. Grady-Willis, *U.S. Apartheid*, p. 154.

24. Grady-Willis, *U.S. Apartheid*, p. 155.

25. Grady-Willis, *U.S. Apartheid*, p. 168.

26. Vincent Harding to Walter Rodney, July 29, 1976; Harding to Rodney, October 27, 1976; Institute of the Black World, 1960–1987, Series E, Box 3, Folder 30,

Walter Rodney Papers.

27. Syl Lowhar, "On Black Power," *Tapia*, August 4, 1974 https://ufdc.ufl.edu/UF00072147/00121/1x.

28. Walter Rodney, lecture at University of Waterloo, Ontario, Canada, November 1975, Institute of the Black World, 1960–1987.

29. The report appeard in *Stanford Daily*, November 11, 1976, Institute of the Black World, 1960–1987.

30. Walter Rodney to Hazel Campayne, November 13, 1975, Institute of the Black World, 1960–1987.

31. Job Offers/Search, 1969–1980, Series G, Box 6, Folder 32, Walter Rodney Papers, Archives Research Center.

32. Ernest "Kaza" Wamba dia Wamba to Walter Rodney, July 31, 1976, Series E, Box 4, Folder 60, Walter Rodney Papers.

33. Walter Rodney to George Jackson, September 23, 1976, Series E, Box 3, Folder 35, Walter Rodney Papers.

34. George Jackson to Walter Rodney, 1976, Series E, Box 3, Folder 35, Walter Rodney Papers.

35. Patricia Rodney, personal communication with author, April 8, 2021.

36. Idris Hamid to Walter Rodney, December 18, 1976; Hamid to Rodney, January 21, 1977; Hamid to Rodney, April 12, 1977, Caribbean Ecumenical Program, 1977, Series F, Box 5, Folder 89, Walter Rodney Papers.

37. W. H. Morris Jones to Walter Rodney, 1977, Institute of Commonwealth Studies, University of London, Series B, Box 1, Folder 26, Walter Rodney Papers.

38. Ikhenemho Okomilo to Walter Rodney, June 25, 1977, Pan African Association of Writers and Journalists in Britain, 1977, Series F, Box 5, Folder 93, Walter Rodney Papers.

39. Rainier Tetzlaff to Walter Rodney, February 18, 1978; Tetzlaff to Rodney, March 6, 1978, University of Hamburg (Germany), 1978, Series G, Box 6, Folder 45, Walter Rodney Papers.

40. Wilfred Röhrich to Walter Rodney, May 11, 1978, University of Hamburg (Germany), 1978.

41. Immanuel Wallerstein to Walter Rodney, May 25, 1978; Wallerstein to Rodney, August 1978, University of New York (Binghamton), 1978, Series G, Box 6, Folder 46, Walter Rodney Papers.

Chapter 10: Building the Party

1. Josh McClendon to Walter Rodney, July 1, 1976, Series E, Box 3, Folder 56, Walter Rodney Papers, Archives Research Center, Atlanta University Center.

2. Mark Curtis, *Unpeople: Britain's Secret Human Rights Abuses* (London: Vintage, 2004), p. 279.

3. Curtis, *Unpeople*, p. 282.

4. Curtis, *Unpeople*, pp. 283–84.

5. Curtis, *Unpeople*, p. 284.

6. Curtis, *Unpeople*, p. 285.

7. US State Department report, *Foreign Relations, 1964–1968, Volume XXXII, Dominican Republic; Cuba; Haiti; Guyana*, April 2005, http://www.guyana.org/govt/US-declassified-documents-1964-1968.html.

8. US government memorandum, July 14, 1964, Foreign Relations, 1964–68, Section 411.

9. Curtis, *Unpeople*, p. 286.

10. Rupert Roopnaraine, "Rupert Roopnaraine," in *Walter Rodney: A Promise of Revolution*, ed. Clairmont Chung (New York: Monthly Review Press), p. 115.

11. Roopnaraine, "Rupert Roopnaraine," p. 116.

12. Odida T. Quamina, *Mineworkers of Guyana: The Making of a Working Class* (London and New Jersey: Zed, 1987), p. 72.

13. Nigel Westmaas, "'A Field of Ideas': The New World group, the Caribbean and Guyana of the 1960s," *Stabroek News*, June 26, 2011.

14. Nigel Westmaas, "1968 and the Social and Political Foundations and Impact of the 'New Politics' in Guyana," *Caribbean Studies* 37:2 (July–December 2009), p. 109.

15. Westmaas, "'New Politics' in Guyana," p. 112.

16. "Certain Factors to be Considered in Dealing with the Present Ruling Class and the PNC," 1960–1987, Series C, Box 1, Folder 28, Walter Rodney Papers.

17. Westmaas, "'New Politics' in Guyana," p. 117.

18. Westmaas, "'New Politics' in Guyana," p. 118.

19. Quamina, *Mineworks of Guyana*, pp. 78–79.

20. Quamina, *Mineworkers of Guyana*, p. 70.

21. Quamina, *Mineworkers of Guyana*, pp. 70–71.

22. Quamina, *Mineworkers of Guyana*, p. 119.

23. Cited in Rodney Commission, *Report of the Commission of Inquiry*, pp. 36–37.

24. Quamina, *Mineworkers of Guyana*, p. 105.

25. Westmaas, "'New Politics' in Guyana," p. 120.

26. Westmaas, "'New Politics' in Guyana," p. 121.

27. "WPA on the Question of Elections," 1979, Series C, Box 1, Folder 36, Walter Rodney Papers.

28. WPA on the Questions of Elections, 1979.

29. WPA on the Questions of Elections, 1979.

30. WPA on the Questions of Elections, 1979.

31. See Walter Rodney, "People's Power, No Dictator" (Georgetown: Working People's Alliance, 1979). For criticism of the demand for a Government of National Unity, see Chinedu Chukwudinma, *A Rebel's Guide to Walter Rodney* (London: Bookmarks, 2021).

32. Amzat Boukari-Yabara, *Walter Rodney: Un historien engage* (Paris: Présence Africaine, 2018), p. 278, my translation.

33. WPA on the Question of Elections, 1979.

34. WPA on the Question of Elections, 1979.

35. Perry Mars, *Ideology and Change: The Transformation of the Caribbean Left* (Detroit: Wayne State University Press, 1998), p. 69.

36. Westmaas, "'New Politics' in Guyana," 2009, p. 123.

37. This is confirmed by women who were members of the WPA at the time, or of the organization's solidarity groups across the world. Patricia Rodney and Anne Braithwaite, personal communications with author, April 2021.

38. Lincoln Van Sluytman, "Guyana Background to a Murder," New York Working People's Alliance Support Committee, July/August 1980.

39. Roopnaraine, "Rupert Roopnaraine," p. 111.

40. Roopnaraine, "Rupert Roopnaraine," p. 27.

41. Roopnaraine, "Rupert Roopnaraine," p. 112.

42. Roopnaraine, "Rupert Roopnaraine," p. 115.

43. Roopnaraine, "Rupert Roopnaraine," p. 118.

44. Roopnaraine, "Rupert Roopnaraine," p. 116.

45. Clive Thomas, "Clive Yolande Thomas," in Chung, A Promise of Revolution, pp. 95–96.

46. Thomas, "Clive Yolande Thomas," p. 97.

47. Colin Barker, ed., Revolutionary Rehearsals (Chicago: Haymarket Books, 2008).

48. Thomas, "Clive Yolande Thomas," p. 97.

49. Thomas, "Clive Yolande Thomas," p. 106.

50. Cited in Lola Campos, "In Honour of Maurice Bishop and the Revolutionary Caribbean," Anticonquista, March 13, 2018, https://anticonquista.com/2018/03/13/in-honor-of-maurice-bishop-and-the-revolutionary-caribbean/.

51. Thomas, "Clive Yolande Thomas," p. 106.

52. Thomas, "Clive Yolande Thomas," p. 107.

53. This quote comes from the UK-based Palestinian revolutionary Tony Cliff, who I recall mentioning Desai's comment at meetings in the 1990s on the reality of trade union solidarity during the Grunwick strike in the UK in 1976.

54. Cited in Rodney Commission, Report of the Commission of Inquiry, pp. 45–46.

55. Abyssinian Carto, "Abyssinian Carto," in Chung, A Promise of Revolution, p. 39.

56. Perry Mars, Ideology and Change: The Transformation of the Caribbean Left (Kingston, Jamaica: University Press of the West Indies, 1998), p. 68.

57. Walter Rodney, People's Power, No Dictator (Guyana: Working People's Alliance, 1979), https://www.marxists.org/subject/africa/rodney-walter/works/peoplespowernodictator.htm.

58. Cited in Rodney Commission, Report of the Commission of Inquiry, pp. 69–70.

59. Guyana: The Terror and the Time (pamphlet, Victor Jara Collective, 1979). Box 1, Folder 8, Walter Rodney Papers.

60. Unfortunately, some of the radical Left remained ignorant of these developments in Guyana. Ian Birchall, an important member of the Socialist Workers Party (the successor of the International Socialists in the UK), recalled in 2020, "Again I am asking myself why I was unaware of these events in Guyana. In 1979–80 I was writing a regular column on international events for Socialist Worker. But as far as I recall I never considered writing about Guyana."

61. Carto, "Abyssinian Carto," p. 41.

62. Carto, "Abyssinian Carto," p. 42.

63. Carto, "Abyssinian Carto," p. 42.

64. Cited in Rodney Commission, Report of the Commission of Inquiry, p. 36.

65. Roopnaraine, "Rupert Roopnaraine," p. 111.

66. Quamina, *Mineworkers of Guyana*, p. 85.

67. Nigel Westmaas, "Resisting Orthodoxy: Notes on the Origins and Ideology of the Working People's Alliance," *Small Axe* 8:1 (March 1, 2004), p. 74.

68. Carto, "Abyssinian Carto," p. 44.

69. Carto, "Abyssinian Carto," p. 46.

70. Seeram Teemal to Walter Rodney, May 30, 1979, NAACIE, 1979, Series F, Box 6, Folder 21, Walter Rodney Papers.

71. Hinds' Sight: Dr. David Hinds' Guyana-Caribbean Politics, "Dr. David Hinds and Dr. Rupert Roopnaraine discuss Dr. Walter Rodney's Life and Work," YouTube video, 1:00:21, November 26, 2014, https://www.youtube.com/watch?v=I7416IIrlQ4.

72. Cited in Lewanne Roopnavaint-Jones, "Walter Rodney—In His Own Words," North American Congress on Latin America official website, https://nacla.org/article/walter-rodney-his-own-words. For a sense of Rodney's speeches to supporters and activists, see Walter Rodney, "Sign of the Times—Rodney's Last Speech," in *Sign of the Times: A Memorial Booklet to Commemorate Our Fallen Teacher* (Georgetown, Guyana: Working People's Alliance, 1981), https://www.marxists.org/subject/africa/rodney-walter/works/signofthetimes.htm.

73. *Guyana: The Terror and the Time.*

74. Quoted in Dwayne Wong (Omowale), *The Political and Intellectual Legacy of Walter Rodney* (Wroclaw: CreateSpace Publishing, 2016), p. 80.

75. Joseph B. Treaster, "Guyana's President Facing Biggest Challenge in 15 Years," *New York Times*, October 13, 1979, https://www.nytimes.com/1979/10/13/archives/guyanas-president-facing-biggest-challenge-in-15-years-it-will-stay.html.

76. Carto, "Abyssinian Carto," p. 47.

77. Ronnie Sookhedo, "For a Socialist Caribbean," March 13, 1981, available at https://www.marxists.org/history/etol. For more on what the WPA stood for, see Working People's Alliance, "Toward a Revolutionary Socialist Guyana," *The Black Scholar* 11:3 (1980), pp. 42–49, https://www.jstor.org/stable/41067878?seq=1.

78. George Lamming, "Preface," in Walter Rodney, *A History of the Guyanese Working People, 1881–1905* (Baltimore: John Hopkins University Press, 1981) p. xxiv.

79. Carto, "Abyssinian Carto," p. 47.

80. Lamming, "Preface," p. xv.

81. Lamming, "Preface," p. xvii.

82. Rodney, *Guyanese Working People*, p. 19.

83. Rodney, *Guyanese Working People*, p. 54.

84. Rodney, *Guyanese Working People*, pp. 1–2.

85. Rodney, *Guyanese Working People*, pp. 9–10.

86. Rodney, *Guyanese Working People*, p. 19.

87. Rodney, *Guyanese Working People*, p. 20.

88. Rodney, *Guyanese Working People*, p. 29.

89. Rodney, *Guyanese Working People*, p. 33.

90. Rodney, *Guyanese Working People*, p. 32.

91. Rodney, *Guyanese Working People*, p. 33.

92. Rodney, *Guyanese Working People*, p. 36.
93. Rodney, *Guyanese Working People*, p. 39.
94. Rodney, *Guyanese Working People*, p. 43.
95. Rodney, *Guyanese Working People*, pp. 44–45.
96. Rodney, *Guyanese Working People*, p. 87.
97. Rodney, *Guyanese Working People*, p. 84
98. Rodney, *Guyanese Working People*, p. 71.
99. Rodney, *Guyanese Working People*, pp. 90–91.
100. Rodney, *Guyanese Working People*, p. 96.
101. Rodney, *Guyanese Working People*, p. 98.
102. Rodney, *Guyanese Working People*, p. 101.
103. Rodney, *Guyanese Working People*, pp. 108–9.
104. Rodney, *Guyanese Working People*, p. 109.
105. Rodney, *Guyanese Working People*, p. 112.
106. Rodney, *Guyanese Working People*, p. 113.
107. Rodney, *Guyanese Working People*, p. 116.
108. Rodney, *Guyanese Working People*, p. 128.
109. Rodney, *Guyanese Working People*, p. 132.
110. Rodney, *Guyanese Working People*, p. 145.
111. Whether Rodney saw the Reform Club as an example in Guyanese history of a popular front that could be emulated in the modern period is a matter for debate.
112. Rodney, *Guyanese Working People*, p. 151.
113. Rodney, *Guyanese Working People*, p. 152.
114. Rodney, *Guyanese Working People*, p. 154.
115. Rodney, *Guyanese Working People*, p. 154.
116. Rodney, *Guyanese Working People*, pp. 155–56.
117. Rodney, *Guyanese Working People*, p. 156.
118. Rodney, *Guyanese Working People*, p. 160.
119. Rodney, *Guyanese Working People*, p. 160.
120. Rodney, *Guyanese Working People*, p. 161.
121. Rodney, *Guyanese Working People*, p. 162.
122. Rodney, *Guyanese Working People*, p. 163.
123. Rodney, *Guyanese Working People*, p. 164.
124. Rodney, *Guyanese Working People*, p. 165.
125. Rodney, *Guyanese Working People*, p. 165.
126. Rodney, *Guyanese Working People*, p. 168.
127. Rodney, *Guyanese Working People*, p. 169.
128. Rodney, *Guyanese Working People*, p. 171.
129. Rodney, *Guyanese Working People*, p. 172.
130. Rodney, *Guyanese Working People*, p. 173.
131. Rodney, *Guyanese Working People*, p. 188.
132. Rodney, *Guyanese Working People*, p. 192.
133. Rodney, *Guyanese Working People*, p. 193.
134. Rodney, *Guyanese Working People*, pp. 193–94.

135. Rodney, *Guyanese Working People*, p. 194.
136. Rodney, *Guyanese Working People*, p. 196.
137. Rodney, *Guyanese Working People*, p. 198.
138. Rodney, *Guyanese Working People*, p. 198.
139. Rodney, *Guyanese Working People*, p. 198.
140. Rodney, *Guyanese Working People*, p. 207.
141. Rodney, *Guyanese Working People*, p. 208.
142. Rodney, *Guyanese Working People*, p. 209.
143. Rodney, *Guyanese Working People*, p. 212.
144. Rodney, *Guyanese Working People*, p. 215.
145. Rodney, *Guyanese Working People*, p. 216.

Chapter 11: From Georgetown to Hamburg

1. Walter Rodney to Albert Parkes, Educational Resources Corporation, 1978, Series E, Box 3, Folder 3, Walter Rodney Papers, Archives Research Center, Atlanta University Center.
2. Patricia Rodney, personal communication with author, April 8, 2021.
3. Andrew Roberts, *TransAfrican Journal of History*, 1960–1987, Series E, Box 4, Folder 45, Walter Rodney Papers.
4. Walter Rodney, *A Tribute to Walter Rodney—One Hundred Years of Development in Africa*, eds. Rainer Tetzlaff and Peter Lock (Hamburg: Institut für Politische Wissenschaft der Universität Hamburg, 1984), p. 1.
5. Tape 2B, typescript, 1978, Series H, Box 19, Folder 1, Walter Rodney Papers.
6. Tape 4A and B, typescript, 1978, Series H, Box 19, Folder 5, Walter Rodney Papers.
7. Tape 5A and B, typescript, 1978, Series H, Box 19, Folder 7, Walter Rodney Papers.
8. Tape 7A and B, typescript, 1978, Series H, Box 19, Folder 9, Walter Rodney Papers.
9. Rodney's analysis of Nyerere and Tanzania was similar in some respects to that of John Saul in his *The State and Revolution in Eastern Africa: Essays* (New York: Monthly Review Press, 1979).
10. Frantz Fanon charted these changes in his brilliant 1959 book, *Dying Colonialism*. It seemed that Rodney saw one aspect of Fanon's argument, but not another.
11. In fact, far earlier than Rodney's critique was the experience described by Ralph Ibbott in his history of "Tanzania's socialist villages." Unpublished until 2014, it is an account of the "Ruvuma Development Association" that included seventeen self-governing villages working communally. The villages in the association were shut down and destroyed by the ruling party in 1969. In the end, Nyerere was unable *and* unwilling to defend a genuinely grassroots initiative toward Ujamaa and socialist farming. See Ralph Ibbott, *Ujamaa: The Hidden Story of Tanzania's Socialist Villages* (London: Crossroads, 2014), pp. 292–301.
12. Elisa Greco, in 2016, found there was still a legacy of Ujamaa in the country's rural areas. Elisa Greco, "Village Land Politics and the Legacy of *Ujamaa*," *Review of African Political Economy* 43 (August 2016), https://www.tandfonline.com/doi/abs/10.1080/03056244.2016.1219179.
13. Fred Halliday, "US Policy in the Horn of Africa: Aboulia or Proxy Intervention?,"

Review of African Political Economy 4:10 (September–December 1977), p. 102.

14. A generation of radical scholars and activists moved on to the next hopeful socialist candidate in Africa; in fact, many physically went to new states. The problem is that many did not really address the question of the internal political reasons why these countries ended up like they did. However, Rodney did address these failings in his Hamburg lectures. Leo Zeilig, "From Exile to the Thick of the Struggle: Ruth First and the Problems of National Liberation, International Sanctions Revolutionary Agency," *Review of African Political Economy* 41 (April 2014), https://www.tandfonline.com/doi/abs/10.1080/03056244.2014 .878085.

15. Rodney was clearly aware of *ROAPE*, but he kept his distance—though he had been encouraged by his friend, Ed Ferguson, who informed him on August 22, 1974, that "a new journal" is coming out, "which should be of great interest to you. It is called *Review of African Political Economy*. . . . It will be published three times a year. . . . Sounds like you should be a contributor—perhaps this is what you've been looking for." Ed Ferguson to Walter Rodney, August 22, 1974, 1874, Series E, Box 3, Folder 6, Walter Rodney Papers. The *Review* survived and became, for several generations, a beacon of left-wing and Marxist analysis of the continent. Indeed, it has been this for me—a school of research and study—and since I have worked on the editorial collective, a place of solidarity and comradeship.

16. Tape 8A and B, typescript, 1987, Series H, Box 19, Folder 11, Walter Rodney Papers.

17. Rodney was aware of the struggles of workers, specifically the reaction to Mwongozo, considerably earlier. In a lecture he delivered titled "Class Contradictions in Tanzania" in 1975 at Northwestern University, he discusses the contradictions and class tensions in the country after the implementation of the Mwongozo guidelines. He writes: "The workers used to move around with a very small version of the guidelines, a document printed up into a very tiny booklet, which could be stuffed into a top pocket or any pocket. Workers had a habit of moving around with the *Mwongozo* and taking it out . . . and opening it to the appropriate page, and confronting bureaucrats." "Class Contradictions in Tanzania" in in *The State in Tanzania: A Selection of Articles*, Haroub Othman, ed. (Dar es Salaam: Dar es Salaam University Press, 1980), available at https://www.marxists.org/subject/africa/ rodney-walter/works/classcontradictions.htm.

18. The term "wildcat strike" was an American one adopted in Britain.

19. I would not argue for a moment that Shivji's was the only critique—quite the contrary, there were other, stinging criticisms of Nyerere's socialism, many published at about the same period. However, Shivji's had an advantage; building on his 1971 essay, he wrote a comprehensive Marxist critique that challenged every left-wing shibboleth, with a focus on working class movements and struggles. His analysis stood out.

20. Issa Shivji, "Preface," *Class Struggles in Tanzania* (London: Heinemann Educational Books, 1976)

21. Shivji, *Class Struggles*, pp. 3–4.

22. Shivji, *Class Struggles*, p. 4.
23. Shivji, *Class Struggles*, p. 14.
24. Shivji, *Class Struggles*, p. 18.
25. Shivji, *Class Struggles*, p. 17.
26. Shivji, *Class Struggles*, pp. 17–18.
27. Shivji, *Class Struggles*, p. 18.
28. Shivji, *Class Struggles*, pp. 22–23.
29. Shivji, *Class Struggles*, p. 28.
30. Shivji, *Class Struggles*, pp. 76–77.
31. Shivji, *Class Struggles*, p. 77.
32. Shivji, *Class Struggles*, p. 78.
33. Shivji, *Class Struggles*, p. 82.
34. Shivji, *Class Struggles*, p. 96.
35. Shivji, *Class Struggles*, p. 98.
36. Shivji, *Class Struggles*, p. 107.
37. Shivji, *Class Struggles*, p. 97.
38. Shivji, *Class Struggles*, p. 116.
39. Shivji, *Class Struggles*, p. 124.
40. Shivji, *Class Struggles*, p. 125.
41. Shivji, *Class Struggles*, p. 125.
42. Shivji, *Class Struggles*, p. 127.
43. Shivji, *Class Struggles*, p. 130.
44. Shivji, *Class Struggles*, p. 134.
45. Shivji, *Class Struggles*, p. 134.
46. Shivji, *Class Struggles*, p. 136.
47. Shivji, *Class Struggles*, p. 136.
48. Shivji, *Class Struggles*, p. 137.
49. Shivji, *Class Struggles*, p. 138.
50. Shivji, *Class Struggles*, p. 142.
51. Shivji, *Class Struggles*, pp. 143–44.
52. Shivji, *Class Struggles*, p. 144.
53. Shivji, *Class Struggles*, pp. 144–45.
54. Shivji, *Class Struggles*, p. 145.
55. Shivji, *Class Struggles*, p. 145.
56. Shivji, *Class Struggles*, p. 145.
57. Karim Hirji, *The Enduring Relevance of How Europe Underdeveloped Africa* (Tanzania: Daraja Press, 2017), p. 103.
58. Tape 7A and B, typescript, 1978, Series H, Box 19, Folder 9, Walter Rodney Papers.
59. Rodney's children's books had been featured in a radio series in the 1970s in Guyana, though he had not been permitted to read them in the broadcast. Patricia, in 2011, explained that the reason Walter had written the books, planned as a series, was so "the children of Guyana could begin to understand their history and each other . . . to create not just tolerance but an understanding of people and their lives." "Walter Rodney: Writing a Proud Story," *Pambazuka News*, June 26, 2011,

https://www.pambazuka.org/governance/walter-rodney-writing-proud-story.

60. Walter Rodney to Albert Parkes, July 10, 1978; Rodney to Parkes, September 25, 1978; 1960–1987, Series E, Box 4, Folder 3, Walter Rodney Papers.

Chapter 12: Those Heroic Months of Revolt

1. Michael Craton, letter, Waterloo Slave Studies Conference, January 8, 1979, Series F, Box 6, Folder 26, Walter Rodney Papers, Archives Research Center, Atlanta University Center.

2. Beryle Banfield to Rodney, Council on Interracial Books for Children, January 1979, 1960–1987, Series E, Box 2, Folder 52, Walter Rodney Papers.

3. Patti Iiyama to Walter Rodney, Center for Afro American Studies, UCLA, April 1979, The Political Economy of the Black World, 1979, Series F, Box 6, Folder 23, Walter Rodney Papers.

4. Laura Randall to Walter Rodney, January 30, 1979; Randall to Rodney, May 9, 1979, Hunter College, 1979, Series F, Box 6, Folder 19, Walter Rodney Papers.

5. Cited in Leo Zeilig, "Mugabe Is Dead: Remember Chiadzwa," *RS21*, September 6, 2019, https://www.rs21.org.uk/2019/09/06/mugabe-is-dead-remember-chiadzwa/.

6. Alex Callinicos, *Southern Africa after Zimbabwe* (London: Pluto Press, 1981).

7. Nathan Shamuyarira to Walter Rodney, December 26, 1978, 1960–1987, Series E, Box 4, Folder 24, Walter Rodney Papers.

8. Nathan Shamuyarira to Walter Rodney, January 10, 1979, 1960–1987, Series E, Box 4, Folder 25, Walter Rodney Papers.

9. Sule Mombara to Walter Rodney, March 21, 1980, 1960–1987, Series E, Box 2, Folder 13, Walter Rodney Papers.

10. Charles (Tanzanian Embassy, Mozambique), May 9, 1980, Series E, Box 2, Folder 20, Walter Rodney Papers.

11. Amzat Boukari-Yabara, *Walter Rodney: Un historien engagé: 1942–1980* (Paris: Présence Africaine, 2018), p. 289, my translation.

12. Cited in Walter Rodney, *A Tribute to Walter Rodney—One Hundred Years of Development in Africa*, eds. Rainer Tetzlaff and Peter Lock (Hamburg: Institut für Politische Wissenschaft der Universität Hamburg, 1984), pp. 133–35.

13. Rupert Roopnaraine, "Rupert Roopnaraine," in *Walter Rodney: A Promise of Revolution*, Clairmont Chung, ed. (New York: Monthly Review Press), p. 111.

14. Boukari-Yabara, *Un historien engagé,*.

15. Roopnaraine, "Rupert Roopnaraine," p. 109.

16. Roopnaraine, "Rupert Roopnaraine," p. 110.

17. UCLAmericas, "Walter Rodney's 1978 Visit to Hamburg," YouTube video, 1:30:05, December 15, 2020, https://www.youtube.com/watch?v=n-H7jzZr-Klk&t=1945s.

18. Roopnaraine, "Rupert Roopnaraine," p. 111.

19. Boukari-Yabara, *Un Historien Engagé*, p. 291.

20. Walter Bgoya, interview by author, December 2018.

21. Peter Lock, personal communication with author, December 14, 2018.

22. Cited in *Guyana: The Terror and the Time* (pamphlet, Victor Jara Collective, 1979),

Box 1, Folder 8, Walter Rodney Papers.

23. Cited in Walter Rodney Commission of Inquiry, *Report of the Commission of Inquiry on the Circumstances Surrounding the Death in an Explosion of the Late Dr. Walter Rodney*, Volume 1, *Reports and Appendices*, February 2016, p. 73.

24. Cited in Rodney Commission, *Report of the Commission of Inquiry*, p. 85.

25. Karen De Souza, cited in Rodney Commission, *Report of the Commission of Inquiry*, p. 49.

26. Abyssinian Carto, "Abyssinian Carto," in Chung, *A Promise of Revolution*, pp. 49–50.

27. Cited in Rodney Commission, *Report of the Commission of Inquiry*, p. 50.

28. Patricia Rodney, personal communication with author, April 8, 2021.

29. Support groups quickly organized demonstrations against the government.

30. Cited in Rodney Commission, *Report of the Commission of Inquiry*, pp. 50–51.

31. Cited in Rodney Commission, *Report of the Commission of Inquiry*, p. 51.

32. Clive Thomas, "Clive Yolande Thomas," in Chung, *A Promise of Revolution*, p. 100.

33. Boukari-Yabara, *Un historien engagé*, pp. 306–9.

34. Boukari-Yabara, *Un historien engagé*, p. 309.

35. Cited in Rodney Commission, *Report of the Commission of Inquiry*, p. 28.

36. Patricia Rodney, personal communication with author, April 27, 2021.

37. Patricia Rodney, personal communication with author, April 22, 2021.

38. Letter to chairman of the Walter Rodney Commission of Inquiry, in Rodney Commission, *Report of the Commission of Inquiry*, p. 130.

39. See "Gov't, Opposition Trade Words on Inquiry into Rodney's Death," *Jamaica Observer*, August 8, 2016.

40. See the editorial "Donald Rodney," in *Stabroek News* April 16, 2021. As late as 2010, two High Court judges were implicated in attempting to call the appeal of Donald Rodney behind his back, which, if successful, would have resulted in bail being withdrawn, imprisonment for Donald, and Walter Rodney being considered irreversibly guilty in the eyes of the court. However, in 2019 the court of appeal ruled that the High Court had no jurisdiction whatsoever in (Donald) Rodney's appeal.

41. See the article "PNCR Should Not Accept Blame for Rodney's Death" in *Starbroek News*, March 2, 2015, https://www.stabroeknews.com/2015/03/02/news/guyana/pncr-should-not-accept-blame-for-rodneys-death (accessed January 28 2022.)

42. Jesse Benjamin, "A Life of Praxis with Walter Rodney," *Review of African Political Economy*, June 9, 2020, https://roape.net/2020/06/09/a-life-of-praxis-with-walter-rodney-interview-with-jesse-benjamin/.

43. See *Report of the International Commission of Jurists on the Preliminary Assessment of Dr. Walter Rodney's Death on 13th June 1980*, which states on page 7, "Indeed, it was on occasion of the preliminary assessment conducted by this team that for the first time an official recognition of the existence of Gregory Smith was made by former General Normal McLean. Gen. McLean was the GDF's Chief of Staff who denied Smith's existence in June 1980."

Chapter 13: Enemies of the State

1. Clive Thomas, "Clive Yolande Thomas," in *Walter Rodney: A Promise of Revolution*,

Clairmont Chung, ed. (New York: Monthly Review Press), p. 109.

2. Cited in Robert Hill, "Walter Rodney and the Restatement of Pan-Africanism in Theory and Practice," *Ufahamu: A Journal of African Studies* 38: 3 (2015), p. 142.

3. Amzat Boukari-Yabara, *Walter Rodney: Un historien engagé: 1942–1980* (Présence Africaine, 2018), p. 277, my translation.

4. Boukari-Yabara, *Un historien engagé*, p. 278.

5. The speech was published as C. L. R. James, *Walter Rodney and the Question of Power* (London: Black Rose, 1982), https://www.marxists.org/archive/james-clr/works/1981/01/rodney.htm.

6. Cited by Dwayne Wong (Omowale), *The Political and Intellectual Legacy of Walter Rodney* (Wroclaw: CreateSpace Publishing, 2016), pp. 87–88.

7. James, *Walter Rodney and the Question of Power*.

8. Cited in *Guyana: The Terror and the Time* (pamphlet, Victor Jara Collective, 1979), Box 1, Folder 8, Walter Rodney Papers, Archives Research Center, Atlanta University Center.

9. Cited in Walter Rodney Commission of Inquiry, *Report of the Commission of Inquiry on the Circumstances Surrounding the Death in an Explosion of the Late Dr. Walter Rodney*, Volume 1, *Reports and Appendices*, February 2016, pp. 44–45.

10. Rupert Roopnaraine, "Rupert Roopnaraine," in Chung, *A Promise of Revolution*, pp. 112–13.

11. Cited in Rodney Commission, *Report of the Commission of Inquiry*, p. 46.

12. Cited in Rodney Commission, *Report of the Commission of Inquiry*, p. 72.

13. Leo Zeilig, *Voices of Liberation: Frantz Fanon* (Chicago: Haymarket Books, 2016).

14. Roopnaraine, "Rupert Roopnaraine," 111. There is some dispute about claims of "building up arms," and great sensitivity about it. However, it seemed clear to many at the time that armed protection and defense of WPA militants was a perfectly sensible proposition in the context of widespread repression and murder. As one WPA militant, Tacuma Ogunseye, explained, "We felt that the WPA would have to acquire some amount of arms for self-defence purposes and we took steps to deal with that." Cited by Dwayne Wong (Omowale), *The Political and Intellectual Legacy of Walter Rodney* (Wroclaw: CreateSpace Publishing, 2016), p. 82.

15. Patricia Rodney, personal communication with author, May 10, 2021.

16. James, *Walter Rodney and the Question of Power*.

17. Boukari-Yabara, *Un historien engagé*, p. 297.

18. Odida T. Quamina, *Mineworkers of Guyana: The Making of a Working Class* (London and New Jersey: Zed, 1987), p. 107.

19. Quamina, *Mineworkers of Guyana*, p. 107.

20. Quamina, *Mineworkers of Guyana*, p. 108.

21. Quamina, *Mineworkers of Guyana*, p. 109.

22. Horace Campbell, *Rasta and Resistance: From Marcus Garvey to Walter Rodney* (London: Hansib, 1985), p. 9.

23. See, for example, Freddie Kissoon, "Clive Thomas Is a Hero, but He Has to Explain This Incredible Hypocrisy," *Kaieteur News*, June 21, 2017, https://www.kaieteurnewsonline.com/2017/06/21/clive-thomas-is-a-hero-but-he-has-to-ex-

plain-this-incredible-hypocrisy/.

24. James Turner to Ricky Singh, December 10, 1980, Box 1, Folder 8, Walter Rodney Papers.

25. Rodney Walter, *The Russian Revolution: A View from The Third World*, eds. Robin D. G. Kelley and Jesse Benjamin (London and New York: Verso, 2018).

26. Horace Campbell, "Walter Rodney—People's Historian," *Ufahamu: A Journal of African Studies* 10:1–2 (1981), pp. 35–42.

27. Wole Soyinka, "The Man Who Was Absent," Box 1, Folder 11, Walter Rodney Papers.

28. Soyinka, "The Man Who Was Absent."

29. Walter Rodney, *People's Power, No Dictator* (Guyana: Working People's Alliance, 1979), available at https://www.marxists.org/subject/africa/rodney-walter/works/peoplespowernodictator.htm.

Chapter 14: Walter Rodney's Legacy Today

1. Angela Davis, "Foreword," in Walter Rodney, *How Europe Underdeveloped Africa* (London and New York: Verso, 2018 [1972]), p. ix.

2. Davis, "Foreword," p. xi.

3. Davis, "Foreword," p. x.

4. Davis, "Foreword," p. xi.

5. Davis, "Foreword," p. xii.

6. Rodney, *HEUA*, p. 346.

7. Walter Rodney Commission of Inquiry, *Report of the Commission of Inquiry on the Circumstances Surrounding the Death in an Explosion of the Late Dr. Walter Rodney*, Volume 1, *Reports and Appendices*, February 2016, pp. 104–6.

Index

civil rights movement, 54, 55, 60–61, 64, 85; Congo relations, 42; Council on Interracial Books for Children, 300; Grenada invasion, 327; Guyana relations, 3–4, 10, 218–24 passim, 231, 305; Jamaica relations, 65; Nicaragua attacks, 327; Reconstruction, 85; Rodney in, 182–83, 191–92, 198–99, 202–6, 208, 216, 237, 298–301 passim, 364n54, 372n17; Rodney job opportunities in, 101–2, 201, 211, 214–15; Roopernaraine in, 223; slavery, 85; Urban Center for Black Studies, 177–78

University of Dar es Salaam, 36–37, 43–59 passim, 101–27 passim, 166–94 passim, 237; USARF, 5, 104–5, 121, 180, 192–93

University of East Africa, 37, 114

University of Guyana, 15, 195; Ratoon, 224–25; Staff Association, 242

University of Guyana Students' Society (UGSS), 200–201

University of London: SOAS, 15, 19, 23–29, 102, 199, 213; West Indies, 7, 10–16 passim, 23

University of Michigan, 182, 364n54

University of Pennsylvania, 102

University of the West Indies (UWI) (Jamaica), 7, 10–16 passim, 23, 44, 60–69 passim, 78, 91

University of the West Indies (Trinidad), 201

University of Waterloo, 208, 300

University Students African Revolutionary Front (USARF), 5, 104–5, 121, 180, 192–93

Urban Center for Black Studies (Poughkeepsie), 177–78

USSR. *See* Soviet Union

Van Sluytman, Lincoln, 235

Vassar College, 177–78

Wallace, Rob, xi–xii

Wallerstein, Immanuel, 44, 112, 214–15

Walter Rodney Speaks (Rodney), 89

Wamba dia Wamba, Ernest, 210

Wangoola, Pao-Paul, 120

Weekes, George, 313

West, Michael O., 13, 70–71, 73

West African Students' Union (WASU) (London), 20

Western Sudan, 98, 136–37

Westmaas, Nigel, 29, 224, 225, 235

What Is to Be Done (Lenin), 244

white power, 83–91 passim, 95–96, 183–84

wildcat strikes, 8, 9, 227–28, 244, 285, 292, 296–97, 324

Williams, Eric, 87

women's rights, 235, 337

Wong, Dwayne. *See* Omowale

Working People's Alliance (WPA) (Guyana), 216–17, 222–49 passim, 267–71 passim, 285, 305–31 passim, 338; arming of, 323, 376n14; capitulation, 331

World Bank, 280

World War II, 8, 149

The Wretched of the Earth (Fanon), 51, 86, 122, 176, 276, 324

Wright, Marcia, 101–2

Young Socialist League (Jamaica), 15

Young Socialist Movement (Guyana), 310, 323

Zaireanization, 274

ZANU (Zimbabwe African National Union), 113, 301–4 passim, 325

Zanzibar, 39, 42, 281

Zimbabwe, 51, 86, 113, 137–38, 238, 239, 301–9 passim, 325–26

Zulu (people), 143, 164

About the Author

Photo © Ellie Chestnutt

Leo Zeilig is a writer, researcher, and activist. He has written extensively on African politics and history, including books on working-class struggle and the development of revolutionary movements and biographies on some of Africa's most important political thinkers and activists. Leo is an editor of the *Review of African Political Economy*—the radical African-studies journal founded by activists and scholars in 1974—and an Honorary Research Associate at the Society, Work and Development Institute (SWOP) at the University of the Witwatersrand in Johannesburg, South Africa. Leo's critically acclaimed novel *Eddie the Kid* was published by Zero Books in 2013. It was praised in the *Guardian*: "This passionate, sad and well-told book offers a compelling portrait of a flawed young radical." *Eddie the Kid* won the 2014 Creative Work prize at the University of the Western Cape in South Africa. In 2017, Leo's second novel, *An Ounce of Practice*, was published by Hoperoad. Praised in *The Conversation* as "a brilliant work of literary imagination that takes the reader to new realities in an engaging, moving read, hilariously humorous at times." Leo has recently published *The World Turned Upside Down* with the Nigerian publisher Books Farm House & Publishers.